THE

ANTI-SLAVERY CRUSADE

IN AMERICA

THE ANTI-SLAVERY HISTORY
OF THE JOHN BROWN YEAR

ARNO PRESS
&
THE NEW YORK TIMES
NEW YORK   1969

Reprint edition 1969 by Arno Press, Inc.

*

Library of Congress Catalog Card No. 70–82169

*

Reprinted from a copy in the
Harvard College Library

*

Manufactured in the United States of America

THE ANTI-SLAVERY HISTORY
OF THE JOHN BROWN YEAR

THE

ANTI-SLAVERY HISTORY

OF THE

JOHN-BROWN YEAR;

BEING THE

TWENTY–SEVENTH ANNUAL REPORT OF THE AMERICAN
ANTI-SLAVERY SOCIETY.

NEW YORK:

AMERICAN ANTI-SLAVERY SOCIETY,

No. 5, BEEKMAN STREET.

1861.

ANNUAL REPORT

OF THE

American Anti-Slavery Society,

BY THE EXECUTIVE COMMITTEE,

FOR THE

YEAR ENDING MAY 1, 1860.

NEW YORK:

AMERICAN ANTI-SLAVERY SOCIETY,

No. 5, Beekman Street.

1861.

BOSTON:

PRINTED BY PRENTISS AND DELAND,
No. 40, Congress Street.

REPORT FOR 1859-60.

Another year having reached its close, the Executive Committee of the American Anti-Slavery Society, according to their custom, present, with their account of the doings of the Society, a brief sketch of such noteworthy events of the past year as belong to the history of the Anti-Slavery movement.

KANSAS.

Our last Report mentioned the steps which the people of Kansas were then contemplating, to bring themselves regularly before Congress for admission to the Union. These have since been successively taken, as arranged at the last previous session of the Territorial Legislature. On the 6th of June delegates were chosen to meet in Convention, and frame a Constitution. The contest, at this election, was not, as heretofore, between Free-State men and avowed Pro-Slavery men; the Free-State sentiment being now so decisively in the ascendant as to leave no hope for open opposition to it; so parties fell into the same division as in the country at large, and took the same names, — Democrats and Republicans. The latter prevailed, choosing thirty-five of the fifty-two delegates, or more than two-thirds of the whole Convention. The Convention met at Wyandotte, on the 5th of July, and, after finishing its work to the acceptance of the great majority of its constituents, adjourned without day, on the 29th. The Constitution which it framed, is substantially the old Topeka Free-State Constitution. It provides that "there shall be no Slavery in the State, and no involuntary servitude, unless for the punishment of crime ;" that "the right of trial by jury shall be inviolate, and extend to persons of every condition ;"— words evidently intended to include persons claimed as Fugitive Slaves ; — and that "no citizen of the State shall be held to appear before the Supreme Court of the United States on an appeal from the Supreme Court of the State, but when appeals are taken on questions of interstate law, they shall only be through or from District Courts of the United States." The design of this last-mentioned provision, no doubt, is to put the State on the same ground which Wisconsin is understood to occupy, in relation to State Rights, and the independence and supremacy of the Judiciary of the State within its own boundaries. So far, the leaning of the new Constitution is in favor of Freedom. But in another particular that Republican majority of more than two to one, strong enough to do, if it would, whatsoever was right in its own eyes, had either too much prejudice, or too little courage and manliness to deal justly with the weak. It denied to colored men the right of suffrage. The Democratic minority signalized its truth to party instincts by a still baser proposition. One of its members introduced, and the rest, with several Republicans, voted for, a resolution that a Committee be appointed "to inquire into the expediency" of forbidding "negroes and mulattoes" to come into the State, making void all contracts with any who shall come in, subjecting to a fine of from twenty to five hundred dollars any person employing them, or otherwise encouraging them to remain, and appropriating the fines to the colonization of such of those already in, as may be willing to emigrate. Of course we can feel no surprise at such a proposition from such a source ; rather have we to wonder at the gracious state of its propounders, that they were content to ask so little, and that instead of a prohibition of future immigration of colored persons, they did not demand the prompt and forcible expulsion of those already in the State, and especially of such of them as had been at all active in rescuing it from the clutches of Border Ruffianism, and securing it to (*white*) Freedom.

The Constitution was adopted in the Convention by a strict party vote, every Republican present voting for it, and every Democrat voting against it, and refusing to sign it. On the 4th of October, it was submitted to the people, and ratified by

about two-thirds of the popular vote, notwithstanding the strenuous opposition of the "Democracy." The Republicans also
elected their Territorial Delegate to Congress, and two-thirds
or more of the Territorial Legislature. On the 6th of December, the State organization was completed, by the choice of State
Officers and a Representative to Congress. In this election, also,
the Republicans prevailed by decisive majorities. For Governor,
they chose CHARLES ROBINSON, and for Member of Congress,
MARTIN F. CONWAY; the same men who were chosen to those
offices respectively under the Topeka Constitution of 1855.

On the 29th of February, Mr. PARROTT, Kansas Delegate in
Congress, presented to the House of Representatives resolutions
of the Territorial Legislature, asking admission to the Union;
and, soon after, the Committee on Territories, to which they
were referred, reported a bill in accordance with their request.
Mr. SEWARD, on the 21st of February, introduced in the Senate
a bill for the same purpose, and, on the 29th, made it the occasion for a long, carefully-considered and able speech, reviewing
not only the Kansas question, but also the general subject of
Slavery and its relations to the Federal Government; and showing plainly enough, by the tenor and spirit of his remarks, that
he had not forgotten what is to be the great event of this year,
in the political world. The House bill, after an earnest debate,
continued at intervals through several weeks, during which its
enemies labored hard to defeat it, was passed, on the 11th of
April, by 134 yeas to 73 nays. The Senate has not yet come
to a vote on the question; and, controlled as it is, by the party
which has from the first so violently and unscrupulously opposed the cause of Freedom, in Kansas, it seems very doubtful
whether it will suffer the bill to go through at this session.
Evident as it must be to all, that Kansas must come in as a
Free State at last, an opportunity still remains to subject her to
the vexation of another half year's delay, and to disappoint her
of the anticipated satisfaction of taking part in the approaching
presidential election, and casting her vote against the corrupt
and oppressive dynasty which she has such ample reason to
abhor. And it seems almost too much to hope, that they who
have struggled so long and desperately to give the Territory
over to the despotic rule of the Slave-power, should be willing,
in the fresh bitterness of fully-ascertained defeat, to yield grace-

a million dollars worth of Slave-property, which would be taken from the owners by that prohibition. Runaway Slaves were advertised, by their masters, within the most Anti-Slavery county of the Territory (Douglas), and rewards offered for returning them to bondage. In Leavenworth County, not long before the act was passed, a Slave was advertised for sale on execution for debt. Other tokens were given, from time to time, that President BUCHANAN's declaration, "Kansas is, to-day, by virtue of the Constitution, a Slave State as much as Georgia or South Carolina," was no mere "flourish of rhetoric."

In our last year's account of the affairs of Kansas, we spoke of the kidnapping of Dr. DOY and his son, with a number of colored persons; the enslavement of the latter, and the imprisonment of the white men, in Missouri, to await trial on the charge of Slave-stealing. Soon after that account was written, we learned that the young man had been released, no charge being sustained against him. The father was subsequently tried and convicted, — though so manifestly against law and evidence that it is said even the Missouri judge, who presided at the trial, regarded the verdict as illegal and unjust, — and was sentenced to five years' imprisonment in the State prison. Having appealed to the Supreme Court, he was committed to the jail, in St. Joseph, to await the decision upon his appeal. On the night of Saturday, July 23, ten or twelve men went over from Kansas, reached the jail — in the midst of a city of ten thousand inhabitants — about midnight, gained entrance by pretending to have brought a criminal to be confined, and, when within, drew their weapons, threatening the jailor with instant death if he should resist or give an alarm, took out the prisoner and returned safely with him to Kansas. A large reward has been offered for his reärrest, but we do not learn that any attempt has been made to earn it. After spending some time in Kansas, Dr. DOY has come to the East, where he appears in public, and goes about his private business, as occasion calls, with no attempt at concealment, and no apparent fear of molestation.

NEBRASKA.

Last winter, the people of Nebraska, through their Legislature, attempted to exercise the power which, six years ago, it was pretended that the Kansas-Nebraska bill conferred upon them, of "regulating their domestic institutions in their own way." Their "way" was to pass an Act forbidding Slavery in the Territory. But that way did not accord with the views of the Territorial Governor, BLACK, whom the Slave-power, using the Federal Executive as its organ, had placed there to see that the interests of Slavery should receive no detriment. He therefore promptly returned the Act, with his veto, conveyed in a long, argumentative message, in which was announced what we take to be the latest discovery yet made in political science by the devotees of Pro-Slavery Democracy. The Governor admits that, according to the organic act, the people of Nebraska are "perfectly free to regulate their domestic institutions in their own way;" but he denies that the act of their Representatives, in the Legislature, is the act of the people. The members of the Legislature, his sagacity has found out, are not "the people," in contemplation of the organic act; and have no power to act for the people in this matter. There is no pretence that the Legislature has not acted in entire harmony with the wish of the people, having been duly authorized, by fair election, to act in the name and by authority of the people; but — they are not the people, and so cannot do the very work which the people chose them to do. In other words, the people can do a certain act, but cannot do it by the hands of their own chosen agents and instruments. Verily, the wisdom of Pro-Slavery Governors is "past finding out," and very "marvelous in our eyes." When a gang of Missourian invaders, by brute force, without a shadow of right, in defiance of the known wishes of a great majority of the people of Kansas, thrust themselves into the legislative hall and usurped the legislative power of that Territory; and then enacted into the forms of law some of the vilest abominations and blackest atrocities which ever defiled the pages of a statute book, — atrocities abhorred, repudiated, and loudly protested against by five-sixths of the people whom the usurpers falsely pretended to represent, — *these* enactments were upheld by every official minion of Slavery in the land, from the President, in Washington, to his lowest underling, executive or judicial, in the Territory, as the strictly legal expression of the people's will, and as having all the sacredness and binding force of law; and whatsoever questioned their validity, was treason and rebellion. But when a Legislature, fairly and lawfully chosen by the free voice of the people of Nebraska, attempts to carry into effect the known and undenied wishes of the people, in an act demanded also by every consideration of justice, humanity, and enlightened policy, but hostile to the purposes of the Slave-power, the act is void, forsooth, because it is one which only *the people* can do, and the people's agents, chosen by them to do it in the people's name and by the people's authority, are not the people!

Projects for New Slave-States.

Our last Report mentioned the introduction into the Legislature of California, of a bill to divide the State, with the purpose, no doubt, on the part of the friends of the measure, to make a Slave State of the southern portion. Shortly afterward, we learned that the bill had passed both Houses, and wanted but the Governor's signature, to become a law. An attempt, in the lower House, to reconsider it, called out a long and warm discussion of the Slavery question, and was at last defeated by a vote of thirty-one to twenty-seven. Whether the Governor has since signed the bill we are not informed, but suppose he has, as it was expected that he would do so. The New-York *Tribune*, alluding to the subject, says, " As there does not seem to have been any recent popular agitation in the southern part of the State, having this division in view, the passage of this bill is probably a mere expedient of the GWIN-BUCHANAN Pro-Slavery politicians, a part of the same system of Pro-Slavery agitation with the proposed organization of the prospective Territory of Arizona. The projected acquisition of Sonora and Chihuahua, to be organized as Slave-holding Territories, and the recent recognition of Slavery as an institution entitled to the protection of law by the Territorial Legislature of New Mexico, are parts of the same scheme."

2*

The Speaker of the House of Representatives, in New Mexico, last winter, introduced a bill to repeal the barbarous Pro-Slavery enactment of the previous session; but the House, preferring its Slave-code to its Speaker, rejected the bill without a dissenting voice, and requested him to resign his office. He resigned both that and his seat in the House. From this issue of the attempt to right the wrong of the former year, it would seem that "Popular Sovereignty," in New Mexico, means the sovereignty of the Slave-power. A letter, however, published last summer in the Vermont *Watchman*, from an old resident of the Territory, who has spent about twenty years there, intimates that the triumph of Slavery there is not due to pure Popular Sovereignty acting of its own motion; but to influences emanating from the high places of the land. The writer says he "was astonished at the passage of those stringent laws for the protection of property in Slaves," that he has "taken some trouble to learn how it was brought about;" and has "learned, through members of the Legislature who *should know*, that a letter was received from our Delegate in Congress, stating that, unless such laws were passed, his influence at Washington with 'the powers that be' would be at an end; and that all his efforts to secure anything for the protection of the Territory would be powerless. This, being with them a matter of life and death, had a tremendous effect." So we have here, if this witness may be trusted — and the Watchman vouches for him as trustworthy — another instance of the use of virtual bribery by the Federal Government, to promote the interests and extension of Slavery. We can the more easily believe the writer's statement, because of its intrinsic probability. Enough has been overwhelmingly proved against the Government, as now and for years past administered, to raise a strong presumption in favor of every charge of this kind which is brought against it.

Another scheme for adding to the number of Slave States, and thus increasing the weight of Slavery in the Senate, is the revival of an old project for forming a new State out of Northern Mississippi and so much of Tennessee and Kentucky as lies between the Tennessee and Mississippi Rivers. The proposed State would contain, it is said, about seven hundred thousand inhabitants. The scheme has been sanctioned by the Legislature of Tennessee, but we do not learn that those of Mississippi and Kentucky have yet taken action upon it, or whether it finds favor with the people of those States.

The formation of Slave States out of the Indian Territories south of Kansas continues to be agitated, a part of the plan in contemplation being the opening of the region to settlement by white men, but so as to ensure the keeping out of all who would be likely to favor Freedom. A letter from the Indian country, published in the St. Louis *Democrat*, says that "a secret political organization is formed in the South for the purpose of securing all the available territory to the Slave-power. Their efforts are just now directed to this vast and fertile country, known as the Indian Territory. Their plan is to induce the several nations to sectionize their respective domains, retaining a section for every man, woman, and child, and reserving the surplus for sale, with the understanding that no land is to be sold to northern emigrants, and that none but those who are '*sound on the goose*' are to be allowed to settle in the country thus dedicated to Slavery. The secret society of propagandists already have active agents and emissaries among the civilized Indians, zealously laboring to carry out their schemes. I have good reason for believing that the Commissioner of Indian Affairs, the Superintendent, and the Indian Agents — all officers of the General Government — are conniving at, if not actually aiding in, these propagandist schemes. This new secret political organization boasts of being a power — of being strong in numbers, influence, and material means. There is a large fund to be applied to bribery." A letter from a Southerner in Kansas, published in the *Charleston Mercury*, with the remark that it points in the right direction, says, "it is conceded that Kansas will be a Free-soil, Black-Republican State, beyond question. * * * * * * We have about two thousand seven hundred southern men in Kansas still, and they intend emigrating South as soon as Kansas is admitted into the Union. We are connected with a southern organization, and, including all, we have about seventeen thousand men. The next theatre for action *will be the Indian Territory south of Kansas*, including Cherokee, Creek, and Choctaw nations. The South should prepare for this in time, and stand by her territorial rights. They are of the last importance to our colonization."

It is said that JOHN ROSS, head chief of the Cherokees, a large Slave-holder, and nearly white, secretly favors a territorial organization for the Cherokee country, opening it to settlement by the whites; but that the bitter opposition of a portion of the tribe, who fear that the Indians will lose their rights if the whites come in, deters him from advocating it openly. A letter from the Cherokee nation to the Fort Smith *Times,* written on the 30th of last March, represents that there is much excitement in the nation in regard to Slavery, that party-spirit runs high, and that there is even danger of civil war between the Pro-Slavery and Anti-Slavery parties.

The Federal Administration continues to betray its eagerness to "extend the area" over Mexico and Central America; for such, we believe, is the true meaning of its persistent endeavors to obtain power to work its own will in those regions, unchecked by the constitutional authority of Congress. Having failed in its attempt, last year, to wheedle out of Congress a virtual grant of power to make war, at its own pleasure, upon those weak republics, it is now seeking the same end by means of treaties with them; their weakness making it possible to gain their consent, while the strongly Pro-Slavery character of the Senate, with which rests the ratifying power, probably induces a hope that it will be more compliant than the other House. Treaties have accordingly been negotiated with Mexico and Nicaragua, by which rights of transit through their respective territories are granted; and it is provided that, if they are unable to protect the transit-routes, then, at their request, the United States shall employ force to protect them; and farther that "in the exceptional case of unforeseen or imminent danger to the lives and property of citizens of the United States, the forces of said Republic are authorized to act for their protection, *without such consent having been previously obtained.*" As to when this "exceptional case" arises, the President and his subordinate army-officers are, of course, to judge; in other words, they are substantially empowered to make war at their own discretion. To these degrading stipulations, so incompatible with true national independence, a reluctant assent has, indeed, been extorted from feeble Nicaragua and distracted Mexico; but the ratification by the Senate still lingers. The Republican Senators unitedly oppose it, and without them, or at least a part of them, though the majority may be ample for the ordinary purposes of legislation, it cannot reach the two-thirds required to ratify a treaty. The present prospect, therefore, seems to be that this year's attempt will succeed no better than that of last year.

Equally unpromising appears the outlook toward Cuba, on which the Slave-power still keeps its greedy eyes fixed. On the 8th of last December, Mr. SLIDELL gave notice, in the Senate, of a bill making an appropriation to facilitate negotiations for the acquisition of Cuba; but we do not learn that any farther progress has been made there in the matter. The American Ambassador to Spain has lately returned to Washington, having, it is said, negotiated a treaty with the Spanish Government whereby all the questions hitherto in issue between the two nations are adjusted, and the most amicable relations reëstablished, thus removing all pretexts for hostile demonstrations or offensive demands in regard to Cuba. It is stated that the transfer of the island to a new sovereignty was not even proposed in the negotiation; the Spanish Government having previously announced that, after its decided refusals, such a proposition would be regarded as an intentional insult. Were not our zealous and redoubtable champions of "manifest destiny" as wanting in modesty and courtesy as in respect for the rights of others, we might hope that this would be the end, for our time, at least, of schemes to rob Spain of her colony, in order to give strength and permanence to the "domestic system" of robbery, by which colored Americans are plundered of freedom and manhood. But it is too wild a hope for any to indulge who know the characteristics of that species of rapacious animals.

FOREIGN SLAVE-TRADE.

From the tone of the southern press, the language of southern politicians, and such statements of fact as appear from time to time, the inference seems unavoidable that the project of reopening the African Slave-trade is persisted in and continues to gain strength at the South. The Southern Commercial Convention, held last May, in Vicksburg, Miss., voted for it by a large majority, and denounced, as unconstitutional, the law of

Congress declaring it piracy. Just after the Convention adjourned, a portion of its members formed an "African Labor-
Supply Association," having for its object to convince the
South, by publishing facts and arguments, and promoting a
general discussion of the subject, that to obtain a supply of
African labor is necessary, feasible, and right. A correspondence between Messrs. YANCEY and DEBOW, two prominent
friends of the movement, appeared last summer in the Montgomery, (Ala.) *Advertiser*, explaining and vindicating the purposes of the new Association. Mr. YANCEY holds that the
laws against the traffic grew out of an opinion once prevalent
at the South, though wholly baseless, that Slavery is morally
wrong, was founded in kidnapping, and is defensible, if at all,
only because it cannot be got rid of; that they are, therefore,
offensive to the South (in the light of the juster notions now
entertained there), as fixing an undeserved reproach upon her
institutions, and ought to be repealed; that the Federal Government has no right to act on Slavery, but to protect it; and
that each State should be left to decide for itself as to permitting or forbidding the African Slave-trade. He pretty plainly
intimates that all southern men whose views essentially differ
from these, are thoroughly unsound on questions vital to southern rights and interests. Mr. DE BOW, if a little more charita-
ble towards dissenters, is no less firm in the new faith. The
South needs more labor; immigrants from Europe do not go
there; the price of Slaves is getting very high. He does not
wonder, then, that the South turns her eyes "to the fatherland
of our present labor system;" and it is a fair subject of discussion whether that land shall not be made to contribute yet
farther to the system's growth and strength. He proposes to
enlist in the scheme those who hold few or no Slaves, commending it to them as a means of keeping labor from concen-
tration in a few hands; while he hopes to reconcile the large
Slave-holders to it, as a means of strengthening Slavery by
broadening its base, so to speak, increasing the number of
those interested in it; and at the same time as not likely to
reduce the present price of Slaves, though it may prevent its
rising. He is even sanguine enough to expect that "our
northern brethren," who are "very practical and far-seeing,"

will come to favor the measure, for the sake of sharing the enlarged prosperity which it is sure to bring to the country.

The Yazoo (Miss.) *Democrat* says, "the only practical means of perpetuating our present system of labor is by importing Africans," and adds, "if the South believes that her necessities demand more labor, and she has not the courage to procure that labor at any hazard, then let her perish as ignominiously as her cowardice deserves." About the 1st of last June, the Black Oak (S. C.) Agricultural Society adopted resolutions requesting the Legislature of South Carolina, in view of "the great need of negro labor" at the South, and because "the planter is the best missionary to the African," to "take such steps as will induce a change of the unconstitutional and iniquitous law of the United States forbidding the introduction of the negro from Africa into the Southern States." A Washington correspondent of the New-York *Tribune,* writing on the 2d of June, affirms that "whatever the more conservative Democrats of the South may advise to the contrary, there is an interest in that party, bent upon forcing the repeal of all laws against the Slave-trade, as a practical issue, and in a living form." And a Washington letter of a few weeks later date, says, "from information recently received in this city, it appears that some of the southern representatives, while claiming to be opposed to reöpening the African Slave-trade, are pledging themselves to introduce in Congress a bill repealing all the statutes upon the subject; leaving it, as they profess to desire, to the regulation of the several States."

Early in July last, A. H. STEPHENS, of Georgia, on retiring from the seat he has long filled in Congress, made a farewell speech to his constituents, reviewing the history of the Government during his Congressional career, and hinting at the present needs and duties of the South. After glancing at the series of important triumphs of Slavery, from the annexation of Texas to the DRED SCOTT decision, — triumphs, he claimed, "of justice, truth, and right,"— he went on to say that "we must expand our institutions;" or they cannot be maintained. "We can divide Texas into five Slave States, and get Chihuahua, Sonora, &c., if we have the Slave population; but it is as plain as anything that *unless the number of African stock be increased,* we have not the population, and might as well abandon the race

with our brethren of the North in the colonization of the Territories. * * * * * * Slave States cannot be made without
Africans. I am not telling you to do it, but it is a serious
question concerning our political and domestic policy; and
* * * * * * it is useless to wage war about abstract rights,
or to quarrel and accuse each other of unsoundness, unless we
get more Africans. * * * * * * Negro Slavery is but in its
infancy, it is a mere problem of our Government; our fathers
did n't understand it. I grant that all the public men of the
South were once against it; but they did n't understand it. It
is for us to meet questions with the firmness which they did.
The problem is yet unsolved."

In commenting upon this speech, the New-York *Tribune*
truly says of its author, " he is one of the ablest and shrewdest
of southern statesmen, a keen judge and a cautious expositor
of the drift of public opinion and of the ideas that control, or
soon will control, the public mind; " and alluding to his emphatic affirmation of the need of more Slaves, adds, "where
this increase is to be found, Mr. STEPHENS does not explicitly
declare. He does not mean to alarm the public by rashly and
bluntly stating his conclusion; but prefers to leave it to make
its own way into the mind. But it is plain what it is. The
needed additions to the Slave population can be procured only
from one source, the continent of Africa. In this we have
the gist and signification of this important speech. It is as
much in favor of the reöpening of the African Slave-trade as
if it said so in terms, and probably it is a great deal more
effective."

The Mobile *Register*, edited by JOHN FORSYTH, late Minister
to Mexico, in an article relating to this question, on the 12th of
last July, alluded exultingly to the victories which Slavery has
already won, and thus continued; "but one stronghold of its
enemies remains to be carried, *to complete its triumph* and
assure its welfare, — that is the existing prohibition of the
African Slave-trade. * * * * * * We are decidedly of opinion
that both the honor and the interests of these southern States
require that the Federal Statutes against the African Slave-
trade should be repealed, and that the treaty complications of
our Government with other nations, aiming at its prohibition,
should be withdrawn from. * * * * * * If the African Slave-

trade is wrong, and sinful, and infamous, *the same is true* not only of our interstate Slave-trade, but *of Slavery itself.* * * * * * * * If the African Slave-trade is wicked and criminal now, it was so during all the time when our country was stocked with negroes from Africa. If it was sinful and infamous then, to bring Slaves from Africa, it was equally so to purchase and hold them, and the vice and infamy of the tenure have been transmitted to the present time, *pervading the whole institution of Slavery at the South with crime,* and branding every Slave-holder in the land with the mark of guilt and dishonor. Now is it consistent with the self-respect, the dignity, the honor of the southern people, to rest satisfied under the degrading stigma upon their most essential political institution, which these statutes against the Slave-trade imply? Should they continue to tamely acquiesce in those odious laws, and thus stand convicted, on their own tacit confession, of guilt * * * * equivalent to piracy? * * * * * * For our part, as a southern man, persuaded and convinced of the morality of Slavery, and devoted to it as the beneficent source and wholesome foundation of our civilization, we chafe with a scarcely repressible impatience under the degrading reflection which these Slave-trade statutes cast upon our institutions and our people. * * * * * * The reöpening, or continued prohibition of the African Slave-trade is a question which properly belongs to the several Slave-holding States, and should be remitted to their determination, and they should insist on having the exclusive control over it."

The *Register* thinks "the time is not ripe for making this a political and party issue:" that "the mind of the South is *as yet* unprepared for it:" but it means to help prepare the southern mind, and ripen the time for it, by "developing and elucidating the question," in the fashion indicated by the extracts we have given. A few weeks after the publication of this article, the editor of the *Register* was elected to the Legislature of Alabama; being returned at the very head of his ticket. Such was the response of the people of his district, to this avowal of his sentiments.

JOHN J. McRAE, member of Congress from Mississippi, whose election was mentioned in our last Report, as having been boasted of by the *Southern Citizen,* as a popular expression for the revival of the Foreign Slave-trade, wrote a letter, last summer, to the Secretary of the Interior, advocating that measure; announcing his belief that the people of Mississippi are in favor of it, and that the North will not refuse, "should the South unite in so just a demand;" and arguing that nothing would so allay the Slavery agitation and strengthen the bonds of Union as for the North to join in repealing all Federal laws against the traffic. The *Mississippian*, the leading organ of the dominant party in that State, in copying an announcement that several cargoes of Africans had been landed in the South, heads it, "Speed the Pirates," and introduces it thus: "May prosperous gales speed the honest pirates in their noble mission to augment the supply of southern labor, and to obey the injunction to feed the hungry and clothe the naked. The wants of the southern people, and the requirements of commerce, call loudly for more and cheaper negroes; and, thanks to the adventurous Slave-traders, they are coming." The same paper says that the agitation for the repeal of the Slave-trade law is confined to no political party nor class of our citizens, but is fast becoming the popular sentiment of the southern people. "The sooner," it adds, "our northern fellow-citizens are convinced of the fact, and make up their minds to accede to our just demand, the better for the peace and prosperity of our political Union.'' The *Sea-coast* (Miss.) *Democrat*, of December 7, greets as "Good News" the intelligence that "a cargo of Africans is expected the latter part of this month;" wishes "the gentlemen engaged in the enterprise much success in their patriotic and humane undertaking;" and declares that if the Slaves arrive "they will be landed without any attempt at secrecy, the consignees trusting to the sentiment predominant in Mississippi for a triumphant acquittal, in the event of a prosécution." A Democratic Convention, held at Port Gibson, Claiborne County, on the 8th of August last, resolved that the law of Mississippi, forbidding the bringing of Slaves into the State from beyond the limits of the United States, "ought to be expunged from the statutes; as being an endorsement of Federal usurpation, a reflection upon the institution of Slavery, and contrary to sound southern policy;" and that "the Legislature ought to repeal it at its next regular session." The friends of repeal, however, we perceive, are not yet strong enough in the Legislature to carry their point. A bill for that purpose was brought in, last winter, and, on the 26th of January, was indefinitely postponed by 66 ayes to 22 nays. But this by no means proves that so large a majority, or indeed *any* majority, or minority either, regards the traffic as wrong, or opposes it on other ground than present policy. For aught which appears, these ayes may all have come from men holding the opinions of JEFFERSON DAVIS, their United States Senator; who, addressing a Democratic State Convention, on the 6th of last July, declared that his "policy would be to maintain the existing law of Mississippi," but earnestly disclaimed "any coincidence of opinion with those who prate of the inhumanity and sinfulness of the trade. The interest of Mississippi, not of the African," he said, "dictates my conclusion. Her arm is, no doubt, strengthened by the presence of a *due proportion* of the servile caste, but it might be paralyzed by such an influx as would probably follow if the gates of the African Slave-market were thrown open. * * * * * * This conclusion, in relation to Mississippi, is based upon my view of her *present* condition, *not* upon any *general theory*. It is not supposed to be applicable to Texas, to New Mexico, or to any *future acquisitions* to be made south of the Rio Grande."

An instance of that accidental association of utterly incongruous ideas, which makes what is meant for sober earnest look like broad caricature, and provokes a smile in the midst of sadness or stern abhorrence, is seen in a notice, published last fall, in South Carolina, that "the citizens of *Christ Church* parish, near Charleston, have voted to have a grand *Slave-trade barbecue*, at that place, on the 20th of October, at which all the prominent advocates of the reöpening in the State will be invited to attend." Early last summer, as we learn from the Savannah (Geo.) *News*, at a very large meeting of the people of Savannah and its vicinity, held to listen to an address on the reöpening of the African Slave-trade, "Resolutions in favor of the repeal of all laws, State and Federal, against the importation of African Slaves, and recommending the opening of the trade, were adopted without a dissenting voice." A few weeks later, the Savannah *Republican*, which had all along treated the movement for the revival of the trade as of no serious moment, had an article conceding that the measure is gaining favor at the South, and stating, in support of that opinion, that nine-tenths of the delegates in the Democratic Congressional Convention of that District went for the repeal of the laws against the Slave-trade, while every single aspirant for the nomination declared himself for the revival of the trade. Many who are not willing to be counted in favor of the actual revival of the trade, join in demanding the repeal of the laws against it, because they imply a moral condemnation of Slavery. Even the grand jury, who, last spring, indicted, in Savannah, some of the alleged participants in recent violations of those laws, took care to say that they did so unwillingly, and only because compelled by their oaths and the instructions of the Court. They published an emphatic protest against the laws, declaring that, while living under them, they "are freemen but in name," are "under a tyranny as supreme as that of the despotic governments of the Old World;" that "longer to yield to a sickly sentiment of pretended philanthropy and diseased mental aberration of (higher-law) fanatics, the tendency of which is to debase us in the estimation of civilized nations, is weak and unwise;" and that they "unhesitatingly advocate the repeal of all laws, as baneful in their effects, which directly or indirectly condemn the institution of Slavery, and those who have inherited or maintain it."

Nor is it in words alone that the unholy traffic is advocated, and the laws forbidding it are condemned. The proofs are too strong to admit of reasonable doubt, that talk has more than begun to pass over into action. "A Native Southerner," writing from Washington to the New-York *Tribune*, on the 20th of August last, said that in conversation, at a recent meeting of politicians, "Mr. DOUGLAS stated that there was not the shadow of doubt that the Slave-trade had been carried on quite extensively for a long time back, and that there had been more Slaves imported into the southern States, during the last year, than had ever been imported before in any one year, even when the Slave-trade was legal. It was his confident belief, that over fifteen thousand Slaves had been brought into this country during the past year. He had seen, with his own eyes, three hundred of those recently-imported, miserable beings, in a Slave-pen in Vicksburg, Miss., and also large numbers at Memphis, Tenn." The statement derives confirmation from the fact, that though the publication of it was complained of

as a breach of confidence (as we gather from the writer's subsequent apology, pleading ignorance of its confidential character), yet it has not been contradicted. Letters from Washington, in July and August, to the New-York *Herald*, from
"a careful correspondent," so says the editor, "stated that
large cargoes of imported 'savages'" had been lately landed
on the Coast of Florida; that "there are said to exist depots
of 'savages' in over twenty large cities or towns at the South,
in some of which the initiated may find them, at times, to the
number of several hundred;" that a trustworthy informant,
who had visited such depots in Charleston, Memphis, and
Columbus, "had seen altogether, in these three places, about
nine hundred imported blacks," and said "it was notorious,
throughout Georgia and Alabama, six weeks ago, that quite a
fleet of Slavers was expected to land cargoes, within a month
or two, in one of the Florida inlets, not far from Key West;"
that "a gentleman of the most undoubted veracity," a Democratic Senator, had informed the writer of a boast "made to
him by a person interested, whose name is known throughout
the Union, that twelve vessels would discharge their living
freight upon our shores within ninety days from the 1st of
June last;" and had estimated the number of cargoes successfully transported into the interior, within eighteen months, at
between sixty and seventy," by which "more than fifteen
thousand" native Africans must have been added to "the Slave
population of the South." The *Tribune*, having referred to
these statements as "to be received with a good many grains
of allowance," JOHN C. UNDERWOOD, formerly of Virginia,
writes to that journal that "a tour and sojourn of some weeks
in the South has satisfied me that the 'careful correspondent'
of the *Herald*, whose opinions you seem to distrust, is correct
in his conclusions, and deserves the thanks of every friend of
Freedom and humanity for the courage and fidelity of his
disclosures. I have had ample evidences of the fact, that reopening the African Slave-trade is already a thing accomplished,
and the traffic is brisk, and rapidly increasing. In fact, the
most vital question of the day is not the opening of this trade,
but its suppression. The arrival of cargoes of negroes, fresh
from Africa, in our southern ports, is an event of frequent
occurrence. Many of the public journals of that region are

supposed to be in the interest of the traders, and the publishers of others are prevented from announcing such arrivals by well-grounded fears that such action would expose themselves to the vengeance of the brutal and barbarous men engaged in this business." The St. Augustine (Fla.) *Examiner*, of July 21, gives an account of a case in Florida, in which the Federal authorities had notice of a Slaver's being off the coast, but, upon going to the region indicated, were 'told that the vessel (schooner Experiment), had landed her cargo near Jupiter's Inlet, six weeks before, and of course the "birds had flown." "We understand more are expected shortly," adds the *Examiner*, coolly taking it for granted that caution is needless, and censure uncalled for, in speaking of the business. The Pensacola (Fla.) *Observer* confirms, on the authority of Col. BLACKBURN, United States Marshal, a statement sent from Jacksonville, on the 16th of last July, that "a cargo of six hundred Africans has been landed on the Florida coast, near Smyrna;" and says, that "as soon as the landing was effected, the vessel was set on fire and abandoned to the elements." Alluding to a "hope" expressed by the Tallahassee *Floridian*, "that the parties guilty of such a high-handed violation of the law, may be arrested and dealt with to the fullest extent," the *Observer* asks how that "can be expected when the United States Marshal is denied the power and means of doing so? If this official," it continues, "was vested with sufficient power, and provided with ample means (as he applied for to the proper authorities), he would, perhaps, have been able to prevent such violation of the law; but as it is, with his limited power and want of means, it is almost impossible." Whether "the proper authorities" have given occasion for this complaint, we have no means of knowledge; but the probability seems to us decidedly in the affirmative.

The Memphis (Tenn.) *Avalanche* announced, nearly a year ago, that "three of the six native Africans brought here, a few days since, were sold, yesterday, at the mart of Mr. WEST, and brought, respectively, $750, $740, and $515. These negroes are a part of the cargo of the yacht Wanderer, landed some months since." We have heard of no attempt, by the Federal authorities, to bring to justice any of the parties to this publicly-proclaimed violation of the laws, or to restore the vic-

tims of it to the rights of which they have been — if the
statute book speaks truth — piratically deprived. The *Richmond* (Texas) *Reporter*, of the 14th of last May, has this
advertisement.

"FOR SALE. — Four hundred likely AFRICAN NEGROES, lately
landed upon the Coast of Texas. Said negroes will be sold upon the most
reasonable terms. For further information, inquire of C. K. C., Houston,
or L. R. G., Galveston."

Among a company of Slaves which CHARLES REEMELIN, of
Ohio, saw on the railroad cars, in Alabama, a few weeks ago,
"some," he says in a letter to the Cincinnati *Commercial*,
"looked as if just imported from Africa." He adds that "the
conductor frankly admitted that negroes, whom he could not
mistake to be Slaves directly from Africa, did frequently come
on their road; that two hundred such came the week previous,
and that eight hundred more were contracted for."

The Washington correspondent of the New-York *Tribune*
writes, on the 2d of June last, that "the pecuniary success
which attended the speculation of the Wanderer, and the immunity of her owners, and the traffickers in human flesh who
were associated with them, have conspired to encourage other
enterprises of a like character, and more vessels have recently
been procured for, and sent to, the Coast of Africa, than were
ever concerned in this diabolical commerce before." Another
correspondent of the same journal, on the 30th of September,
just after a visit to Savannah, describes an interview with the
notorious LAMAR, owner of the Wanderer, who showed him
one of the Africans of the Wanderer's cargo, as a sample of the
importation; told him "the number already imported is large,
greater numbers are needed, the disposition to import them is
increasing, and the whole civilized world cannot prevent them
from coming." He also declared his late importation to be
"the kindest, gentlest, most affectionate and docile creatures in
the world, and worth quite as much as Virginia niggers;"
which, if true, goes rather strongly against the Slave-traders'
pet theory, that the African race is vastly improved by the
civilizing and Christianizing influences of American Slavery,
and that consequently the African Slave-trade is the grandest
and most beneficent of missionary enterprises.

It must not be supposed that the efforts making to turn a portion of the traffic directly to our own shores, have withdrawn from its other channels, in any perceptible degree, the American capital and enterprise heretofore employed in them. It still continues to be true, according to the testimony which reaches us from various quarters, that, wherever the trade is carried on, it is done mainly under the American flag, and in vessels built and equipped in American ports. The New-York *Herald*, last summer, published an estimate that "from thirty to forty Slavers are fitted out, every year, in New York, Boston, Bristol, R. I., Portland, Me., and other eastern ports; but New York and Boston are the favorite ports, from the fact that the operations of the traders, in preparing and fitting out vessels, can be carried on with less risk of detection. Comparatively a limited number," it adds, "are captured on the Coast of Africa, and those that are so captured are taken by English cruisers, while a few fall into the hands of United States vessels." A New-York correspondent of the Charleston (S. C.) *Mercury*, alluding, on the 15th of August, to a former statement that a dozen or twenty Slavers leave New York annually, says, "facts which have recently come to my knowledge convince me that this is no exaggeration. * * * * * * It is not possible for any one person to know the whole extent of the business, but some general facts cannot be kept secret, and are well known to many. * * * * * I know of two ladies, now attracting adoration at a fashionable watering-place, who invested in a little venture of this kind not long ago, and, as a result, have augmented their banking accounts — one to the extent of $23,000, and the other $16,000. The headquarters of the traffic, in this city, are mainly in South, William, Broad, and Water Streets. Two vessels are now fitting out here for the business." And only a few days ago, the *Herald* claimed to have "information that no less than six vessels have left New York for the African coast within the past fortnight, all of which expect to have negroes for their return cargoes." A writer on board the United States ship Portsmouth, on the African coast, says, — Dec. 20 — "the few months' experience we have had on the coast has thoroughly convinced us that the whole Slave-coast is, we may say, lined with Slavers, who are generally from New York, cleared from the custom-house, bringing all the appliances of the trade with them, and manœuvering about on the coast, under various pretences and disguises of legal traffic, until the favorable moment having arrived, the cargo is shipped, and a few hours finds them out of danger, on their way to the West Indies."

A letter to the New-York *Journal of Commerce*, dated St. Helena, Nov. 30, mentions a vessel — the Tavernier, "French built, but evidently fitted out in New York," — which had just been taken with nearly six hundred Slaves, in a most wretched condition, on board, and names five or six American vessels which had lately escaped the cruisers and left the coast "with full cargoes." One of these was "the bark Rebecca, which *took out some of the emigrants*, of the McDONOUGH estate, *to Monrovia*," under charter from the Colonization Society, and on her return voyage, had "gone from the Congo with nine hundred negroes," — thus doing a double share of "missionary" work; taking out a cargo of ready-made "missionaries," and bringing back one of raw material for the manufacture. A letter from Zanzibar, Sept. 8, states that "an American clipper ship took off twelve hundred negroes from the coast a few days since." In April, of last year, the bark Orion, of New York, was seized in the river Congo, as a suspected Slaver, and sent home for examination; her outfit and internal arrangement being such as to leave scarcely a doubt of her destination, which, moreover, was confessed by her captain, who died on the homeward passage. But, on examination, in June last, she was — *of course*, we might almost say — released for "insufficient evidence;" giving another illustration of what the *Journal of Commerce* said, not long ago, that "the captured Slaver, unless found with his cargo on board, is almost sure to escape in the courts." On the 30th of November, about five months after her discharge in New York, a British cruiser captured her on the African coast, with nearly nine hundred Slaves on board, — the first mate of the former voyage being now captain, — and surrendered her officers to an American cruiser, to be sent home for trial.

The famous Wanderer also figures in the Slave-trade operations of the past year. About the middle of last October, a Captain MARTIN stole her, so it was pretended, and went to sea without papers, intending to go to Africa for Slaves. LAMAR, the owner, pursued a little way in a steamboat, but — probably by preconcert — without success; for the theft had most likely been arranged between owner and thief, as a shrewd way of getting the vessel to sea without the trouble and risk of custom-house preliminaries, and of securing to the owner a pretext for reclaiming her without even the trifling cost of a sham purchase, should she fall into hands unfriendly to the cause of missions. The crew, it seems from subsequent events, knew nothing of her destination till they were out at sea, and most of them went on unwillingly after learning it. On the 22nd of November, when near the Canaries, the captain, taking four men with him in a boat, boarded a French vessel which they had met, to obtain a supply of provisions. The rest of the crew seized the opportunity to escape, set all sail, and steered for Boston, where they arrived on the 24th of December, bringing also with them two Portuguese women, whom the captain had decoyed on board at one of the Azores, and carried off with the intention of exchanging them in Africa for negroes. The crew surrendered the vessel at once to the United States authorities, and legal proceedings were commenced against her as a Slaver. She was also libelled by the crew for their wages, and by persons who furnished her with supplies, for their respective dues. LAMAR, on hearing of her arrival, made a formal demand for her, offering, in support of his claim, the copy of an indictment in the United States Circuit Court for the District of Georgia, against the late master for piratically running away with her. The latest news we have of her is, that she has been restored to LAMAR, on his giving bond in $ 5,940, to abide the decision of the Court in her case. If she is worth, as has been said, more than three times that sum, this looks like a virtual abandonment of the charge of Slave-trading, and retention only of the claim for the seamen's wages and other expenses of the voyage.

The bark Emily is another vessel which, after being once seized as a suspected Slaver, was suffered to slip off to sea without a clearance. She was taken, last fall, on the African coast, and disappeared early in February, from the port of New York, whither she had been sent for trial. She went away, it is said, under the command of Captain TOWNSEND, formerly of the Echo. "Perhaps," significantly remarks the New-York *Tribune*, of February 9, "the United States authorities, who had her in charge until very recently, may know something about her sudden and unannounced departure;" and says, also, it is stated that the United States officers, in New York, knew of Captain TOWNSEND's being on board under an assumed name, when the bark was captured and brought in, and that they "were desirous of preventing his real name being made known to the public." From all which, the public will perhaps draw its own inferences. Other instances of suspected Slavers have come to our knowledge during the year, more than we have space to mention in detail; some on the African coast, others on this side the water, in the ports of New York, New London, Ct., New Bedford, Mass., and Portland, Me.; in some, the suspicion leading to seizure, in others not; but we recall none in which the law has been executed upon either the men or the vessel implicated.

Our last Report mentioned the acquittal of the seamen of the Echo, and the transfer of the case of Captain TOWNSEND from Boston to Key West, for trial. He was tried last May, in the United States District Court, and acquitted, as had been expected. Though every fact necessary to bring the case within the terms and obvious meaning of the law was proved,— it being clearly established that the Echo was an American vessel, and was on a Slave voyage, and that TOWNSEND was on board and in command of her, and was an American citizen; yet the judge ruled that the evidence was insufficient to warrant the going of the case to a jury, and without argument or summing up, directed the jury to return a verdict of "not guilty;"—ostensibly on the ground that, besides all the facts we have enumerated, it was necessary to prove that the vessel was owned and fitted out by an American citizen. To prove this, a certified copy of her register was offered, in which TOWNSEND was named as owner; but the judge, "anxious, apparently," says the New-York *Tribune*, "like all the United States district judges of whom we have ever heard, to put such a construction on the acts for suppressing the Slave-trade as will effectually prevent any convictions under them, held, first, that being a copy, this document could not be admitted in evidence; and, secondly, that if it were admitted, it did not prove TOWNSEND to be the owner." The Charleston *Mercury* thinks "the inducing ground of the verdict" acquitting the seamen of the Echo, was a belief of the jury that "it would be inconsistent, cruel, and hypocritical for members of a community where Slaves are as much articles of commerce as sugar and molasses, to condemn men to death for going to a far country to bring in more of these articles of trade;" and that, if so, every other case will be echo to this; and further prosecution is idle, expensive, and vain.

In the case of Captain CORRIE, of the Wanderer, we have another exhibition of the southern purpose, judicial as well as popular, that the law shall not be enforced. Soon after the United States Judge of the South Carolina District had refused, as stated in our last Report, to give the captain up, to be tried in Georgia, on an indictment for piracy, under the law of 1820, the authorities of the Georgia District demanded him on a new indictment, under the Act of 1818, for the lower offence of aiding to fit out a vessel for the Slave-trade. Though this made a case unquestionably within the jurisdiction of the Georgia District, within which the offence was committed, yet Judge MAGRATH, of the South Carolina District, again declined to surrender the prisoner, alleging that he held him for trial on the higher charge. When at length the case came up in South Carolina, Judge WAYNE of the Circuit Court presiding, assisted by Judge MAGRATH, the grand jury at first refused to find a bill; but afterwards,— remembering, or being reminded, doubtless, that if the prisoner were discharged without trial, there would then be no pretext for refusing the demand of the Georgia Court,— they asked that the bill might be recommitted to them. Judge WAYNE refused the request, Judge MAGRATH dissenting; but the grand jury, after a short retirement, returned and presented CORRIE for violating the Act of 1820. The trial was delayed from time to time, till the latter part of April, in the present year, when, Judge WAYNE being engaged in Washington, it came on before Judge MAGRATH alone. The district attorney, under instructions from Washington, as he said, asked leave to enter a *nolle prosequi*, in order that CORRIE might be transferred to Georgia for trial on the second indictment there; but the judge refused, denying the president's right to interfere for such a purpose. He gave, moreover, a new interpretation to the Act of 1820; holding that it does not, as heretofore has been supposed, declare the buying of Slaves, in Africa, or other foreign land, and bringing them to this or any country for sale, to be piracy; but that it applies solely to the *seizing of free men* on the Coast of Africa, and bringing them away to make Slaves of them. So, if the victims have already been kidnapped, ready to the Slaver's hand, and he only buys of the kidnapper, and transfers his purchase to the place of consumption, the Act of 1820 does not touch his case. Of course the judge knows very well that the cases to which the law, so interpreted, would apply, never happen; that American Slavers understand too well the advantages of a division of labor, to do, in person, the kidnapping as well as the transportation of their prey; and that, consequently, this decision, if accepted as law, practically annuls the Act of Congress which it purports to expound. The slaver must be slow, indeed, of apprehension, who fails to see in this a very broad hint that he is safe enough wherever Judge MAGRATH administers the law. In the United States Court for the District of Alabama, a decision was rendered, a few days ago, which may be regarded as the complement of Judge MAGRATH's. One HORATIO N. GOULD was indicted for having brought some of the Wanderer's cargo, in violation of a section of the Act of 1818, which imposes a penalty of $1,000 upon every person who shall hold, purchase, sell, or otherwise dispose of as a Slave, any negro brought from any foreign kingdom, place, or *country*, contrary to the provisions of that Act. Judge JONES, before whom the case was tried, opened a door of escape for the defendant, and all others similarly charged, by deciding that when a negro, illegally imported, has passed out of the control of the importer and his agents, the laws of the United States no longer apply to him. Having become mingled with the inhabitants of the State, any offence committed upon him must be dealt with by the State tribunals alone.

Some attempts were made in Congress, during the present session, to supply the deficiencies of the existing laws. In the early part of March, Mr. WILSON submitted to the Senate a resolution instructing the Committee on Foreign Relations to inquire and report whether the treaty with Great Britain for the suppression of the African Slave-trade has been executed, and whether any further legislation is necessary for suppressing the traffic. In the latter part of the same month, he introduced a bill for the building of five small steamers, suitable to serve on

3

the African coast, and increasing, from twenty-five dollars to one hundred dollars, the prize-money for the capture of Slavers; also a resolution, authorizing the president to negotiate with other nations for the right of search within two hundred miles of the western Coast of Africa; and an order instructing the Judiciary Committee to report a bill substituting imprisonment for life instead of death, and applying the penalty to persons fitting out Slave-ships, or having interest in them. About the same time, Mr. MORSE, of Maine, offered, in the other House, resolutions to substitute small steamers and fast-sailing brigs and schooners for the larger vessels now kept on the African coast; to adopt some system, with other maritime powers, for ascertaining the nationality of suspected vessels; to sustain officers in the discharge of their duty against the traffic; and recommending negotiations for making the trade a crime against international law. But we do not learn that final action has been taken upon the propositions in either House.

DOMESTIC SLAVE-TRADE.

Statements and incidents illustrative of the character, extent, and flourishing condition of the domestic Slave-trade meet us continually. A few of these, out of what we have gathered up during the year, we here present. While the trade has been fully up to its wonted activity, from all the Slave-producing States, special causes appear to have made it, from some of them, even more so than in former years. For example, among the various ways in which the generally-admitted probability, that Slavery will soon be banished from Missouri, is working to bring about that event, not the least noticeable is the rapid selling off of Slaves from that to more southern States. Many Slave-holders, fearing that emancipation will ere long become the settled policy of the State, and unwilling to risk, by delay, the loss of their human "property," are hastening to exchange it for something less precarious. The St. Louis *Democrat*, of October 18th, says that "forty-five chattels of the 'peculiar institution' passed down Locust Street, yesterday morning, on their way to the 'sunny South.' They were a motley group, composed of men, women, and children, whose ages ranged, apparently, from five to forty years. On the one hand, the sight was suggestive of the 'good time coming' for Missouri; but on the other hand, awakened the liveliest sympathy for the condition of this gang of miserable beings. Nearly every Sabbath morning witnesses the exodus of these parties from our shores." The same paper, of October 27th, mentions the shipment of about one hundred and seventy Slaves on the day before, for a Southern market, and adds; "the frequency of these shipments is beginning to excite much attention and remark among our citizens. Scarcely a day passes but gangs of these unfortunate creatures are seen trailing, in couples, with drivers in front and in the rear, down the principal streets leading to the river. Missouri, undoubtedly, is being rapidly depleted of her young and vigorous Slaves. At present prices, they are entirely too valuable to hold, in this, for them, unhealthy climate, and in such precarious proximity to the Free States. The old and infirm remain to die, or watch the slow but irrepressible exodus of their children, and the gradual fading away of the system of Slavery."

A correspondent of the New-York *Tribune*, writing from St. Louis, relates an incident of the traffic so briskly going on thence. Among the two or three dozen Slaves bought by a Mississippian, who came to Missouri to supply his plantation, was a little girl, about nine years old, as fair as the average of white children. Her mother was a handsome mulatto woman, and her father a member of Congress from that State, but not the owner of her mother. On the steamboat by which she was brought down to St. Louis, one of the passengers was her father. "He conversed with her owner about her, and said he would have bought her were it not for his wife. Here was a child of tender age, torn from her mother, and doomed to a Mississippi plantation, while her father, in the august Senate of the United States, declaims of Liberty. He stands coolly by, while his own child, bearing his own lineaments, is taken forcibly from her mother, and driven off with a gang of Slaves to a distant land, among strangers, never again to know a mother's love or caress, but to be thenceforth the victim of a tyrant's lash or lust. She is the innocent proof of his own faithlessness to solemn vows, and must be removed to a safe distance."

Delaware appears, also, to be passing through the same process as Missouri. A letter to the *Tribune*, from Lewes, in that State, on the 18th of February last, says, "it has been estimated that one man engaged in the trade has exported one hundred negroes from the County of Sussex;" and it is said, that he "sends off two or three every week;" and that "this is but one case out of many. It has been computed that at least six Slaves a week, or three hundred and twelve a year, leave this county," in which the whole number of Slaves, by the census of 1850, was but one thousand five hundred and forty-nine; making the year's exportation, if rightly estimated, over twenty per cent of the whole "stock" in the county. And this, too, in spite of legal restrictions upon the business; for no Slave, the letter states, can be legally sold out of the State without an order or permit from the associate judge of the county. But "the speculators pay from $600 to $1,100, and occasionally as high as $1,500," for each human chattel, and what is the restraint of law, against such temptations, to men whose moral standard is low enough to permit their holding men as property? A letter from the same place, written two months later, says, that "so long as the traders confine themselves to buying and exporting *bona-fide* Slaves" [which they do not always, as facts stated in this very letter show], "very little notice is taken of it, though the law forbids it. There are very few prosecutions against this class of dealers." The writer thinks that if the trade makes bad citizens of buyer and seller, it also "diminishes the fungus of the body politic; and for this reason, there are those who would tolerate it as a means of emancipation of the State;" but he adds "another effect is the diminished number of manumissions. But two or three have been recorded in the county, within the last three years. Formerly, the number was much greater. Most persons will not be so generous as to manumit their Slaves when they command such prices as the present. Years ago, when the prices were low, deeds of manumission were common."

The *Tribune*, of February 4, says "the movement in this staple [Slaves], on the shores of Chesapeake Bay, is exceedingly lively. Within the last two months, reports have reached us of an unusually active traffic going on in Northern and Eastern Virginia, even to such a degree that the unobservant traveller could not fail to remark the unusual number of the 'three-fifths' class in the railroad cars. The same causes which, perhaps, have produced the brisk demand for the rough material on the Coast of Congo, may also have had influence on the better bred and more valuable Virginian article. * * * * * * But a more potent influence than even the love of money has been at work in that region," the alarm created by JOHN BROWN's inroad. "The region more immediately within its influence is becoming fast depopulated of its Slaves."

The Washington correspondent of the *Anti-Slavery Standard*, after speaking, on the 23rd of January last, of a disturbance in one of the Washington boarding-houses, produced by the keeper's selling, to be sent to the far South, three young men, brothers, his Slaves, because he was angry with one of them, adds that in that city "scarce a day passes which does not witness dreadful, heart-rending cases of the sale of a human being from all his associates and family relations to the far South, never to see them again." In the New-York *Tribune*, of April 2, is a copy of a paper which had "been circulating in Washington, for a day or two past," stating that "the wife of SAMUEL MARSHAL, a woman of excellent character," had been sold to a trader, was in the Slave-pen, and would be taken "from her husband and children on Saturday next, unless purchased from the trader for $800 before that time." "Her husband is one of the most upright and trustworthy persons;" she "has been his loyal wife for twenty years, and is the mother of eleven children, seven of whom are living." An appeal is made "to all who have hearts, to aid in restoring a wife to her husband and a mother to her children." And it is in the Capital of the "Model Republic," that a woman must be ransomed from the soul-trader, to prevent her being torn from husband and children; while we are told by politicians that the Slave-trade has been abolished in Washington, by that blessed "Compromise of 1850," which saved our "Glorious Union" from being shivered to atoms.

CHARLES REEMELIN, of Ohio, while making a southern tour, was lately on a train, in Alabama, to which were attached two car-loads of negroes on their inland "middle passage." He says, writing to the Cincinnati *Commercial*, "there were some one hundred and fifty negroes, young and old, men, women, and

3*

children, mothers of large families, some alone, some surrounded by their offspring. They came, the trader said, from Virginia and North Carolina, from which region and Tennessee one hundred thousand are taken South each year; at this time the emigration amounts to three thousand a week. They were destined for the New-Orleans Slave-market, where the trader expected to get $2,000 for every healthy, full-grown negro." A statement is just now going the rounds of the periodical press, that, " during the quarter ending March 31, the number of Slaves that arrived in Texas was about twenty-seven thousand." Many of these, probably, accompanied their immigrating masters; but the greater part, we presume, were taken thither by the traders. A letter written to the New-York *Tribune*, from Fairfax County, Va., on the 29th of August last, shows a specimen of the happy blending of business and religion in the Old Dominion. After describing a camp-meeting, held in that county the week before, it thus concludes : " Immediately after the camp broke up, last Friday, twenty-seven negroes were sold, on the ground, to some southern traders. Among this number, one woman and seven children. One of the men was on his knees, engaged in prayer, when the trader slapped him on the shoulder, and told him he must go with him. He intimated his willingness to go, but assured his former master that if they should meet up in heaven, he would have a settlement with him there. The trader stopped his mouth with his hand, and handcuffed him. The whole party were then put into an omnibus, which was ready for them, and they were conveyed to Alexandria. Such is the way in which the Virginian Methodists 'follow Christ.' "

Among " A Woman's Observations in the South," published in the *Tribune*, of October 22, we find the following. A man who, by many years' Slave-trading, from Virginia to Mississippi and· Louisiana, had made enough money to give him a good standing in society, now thought of marrying. He had for years kept a beautiful mulatto woman, in a richly-furnished house, with servants to wait on her, and her babies rocked in a mahogany cradle; she believing that they were all free, and would inherit their father's wealth. But one dark night they were surprised in their slumbers, gagged, put aboard a steamboat, carried to New Orleans, and sold. " The bride of that man knew all these facts." She called on the writer, who was willing to see her only from " curiosity to see if there was anything womanly about such a person;" and who, naturally enough, " could but wonder" at finding that "she was very beautiful," and "spoke softly — with a woman's voice."

We glean from the southern journals a few of the statements, from time to time appearing in them, to show the market-value of human merchandise. The Richmond (Va.) *Despatch*, in July last, announced, as the prices in Richmond, at that time, "No. 1 men, 20 to 26 years old, from $1,450 to $1,500; best grown-girls, 17 to 20 years old, from $ 1,275 to $ 1,325; girls, from 15 to 17 years old, $ 1,150 to $ 1,250; girls, from 12 to 15 years old, $ 1,000 to $ 1,100; best plough-boys, 17 to 20 years old, $ 1,350 to $ 1,425; boys, from 15 to 17 years old, $ 1,250 to $ 1,375; boys, from 12 to 15 years old, $ 1,100 to $ 1,200." The Atalanta (Ga.) *American*, a few weeks later, records the sale of twenty-eight Slaves, in Henry County, men, women, and children, for an average of $ 796 each. One field-hand, 18 years old, brought $ 1,640; three boys of 14, an aggregate of $ 3,829; two boys of 10, $ 1,708; one of 7, $ 726; a woman of 23, with three boys, of 5 years, 3 years, and 8 months, $1,995; a woman of 23, with a boy of 3 years, and a girl of 18 months, $ 2,305; a girl of 19, $ 1,200; one of 15, $ 1,023; one of 7, $ 778. The Selma (Ala.) *Sentinel* gives the prices of " a lot of negroes " sold in Selma, about the 1st of March; one of whom, a carpenter, 29 years old, brought $ 2,050; another, a blacksmith, of 24, $2,245; a boy of 17, $ 1,570; a boy of 13, $ 1,165; an unsound boy of 11, $ 900; girls of 16, 18, and 19, respectively, $ 1,626, $ 1,380, and $ 1,600; a woman of 27, with a child, $ 1,670; a girl of 11, $ 1,600; and a girl of 13, $ 3,205. In St. Louis, on the 29th of February, a sale of Slaves took place, at which two boys, of 14 and 16, brought $ 2,435; a woman of 20, with a child of 4, $ 1,500; a woman of 23, with two children, 5 and 3, $ 1,750; and so on. Some sales are mentioned, at prices which average somewhat below these; but at one, in West Baton Rouge, La., about the end of February, they went up still higher, the figures standing thus: — " One woman and four children, $ 5,650; one boy, $ 4,400; do. do., $ 3,475; do. do., $ 3,400; do. do., $ 3,305; do. do., $ 3,200." And the Greenville (S. C.) *Enterprise* tells of "a likely fellow, said to be a good joiner and carpenter," his wife and child, formerly Slaves of a widow, in Maryland, by whom they were manumitted, and since then residents of Cumberland County, Pa., where they were "highly esteemed," says the Carlisle *American*, "for their industry, sobriety, and general good behaviour," were secretly and forcibly carried off to Maryland, and thrust into the jail of Frederic County, as "fugitives from service." The principal kidnapper was one MYERS, a citizen of Frederic County, and a sort of professional negro-catcher. He admitted having carried off the family, but claimed to have done it legally. Some days before the abduction, he applied to a Mr. BIDDLE, of Carlisle, who had been a United States Commissioner, for a warrant to seize his victims; but, learning that Mr. BIDDLE had resigned the office, he said he would take them by force, without a hearing. The Ex-Commissioner warned him not to attempt it, but he heeded not the warning. A deputy sheriff, of Cumberland County, soon after decoyed him into Pennsylvania, by stratagem, and arrested him, and he was subsequently tried and convicted as a kidnapper, and is now, we believe, undergoing the penalty of his crime, in the penitentiary, though the authorities of Maryland have made some efforts in his behalf, to arrest the course of justice.

About the 1st of July, as we learn from the Vicksburg (Miss.) *Whig*, one A. R. BURKS was arrested in Vicksburg, charged with kidnapping a woman and her three children, of white and Indian blood. The woman and one child were found in his possession; one child he had sold for $500, the other had disappeared, and he could not or did not account for it. On the examination before the mayor, it was proved that the woman and children were free, "being descendants of a white woman," and that BURKS had told the witness, before whose eyes they were forcibly taken away, that "it was no harm to sell them, as free Africans were being brought in and sold." BURKS was bound over for trial, and the woman and children were set free.

On the 11th of August, a decision of the Probate Court, in Abbeville, Ala., released a young woman and her child, "poor whites," of Georgia, from Slavery, into which the woman had been sold, under circumstances of peculiar atrocity. One JAMES C. WILSON went, about the 1st of March, to the house of a Mrs. HICKS, in Columbus, Ga., where he was taken sick, and for several weeks was nursed by Mrs. HICKS and her daughter. He rewarded their kindness by stealing the daughter away and selling her, as a Slave, to a Rev. JOHN GUILFORD, in Henry County, Ala.; then returning, decoying her brother, a boy of fifteen, from his home, and selling him also into Slavery. After several months, the mother learned where her daughter was, and that she had, in the meantime, become a mother. She interested several lawyers in her cause, and a writ of habeas corpus was procured, by means of which the girl and her child were released.

The Edwardsville (Ill.) *Journal* mentions an attempt made, in the latter part of August, by two men, one of them colored, to consign a white mechanic, one ISAAC DICKSON, to Slavery, on pretence that he was a runaway Slave. He was stopped on the road, bound, and taken to Edwardsville, but there he found witnesses to prove his freedom, and was discharged. A correspondent of the Chicago (Ill.) *Tribune*, writing on the 1st of November, tells of four instances of kidnapping, accomplished or attempted, within a few weeks preceding, near Jonesboro'. The first man seized, on the 12th of September, proved to be a Slave, travelling on business for his master. A second was taken, the next day, and put into Jonesboro' jail, to wait a requisition from a master. Another was the porter of the sleeping car on the Illinois Central Railroad. He would have been thrust into jail, also, had not the conductor interposed, and, revolver in hand, attested his freedom. In the fourth case, the victim was captured near Carbondale, after a chase of about eighteen miles, during which he was several times fired upon. The writer adds, " examples of this species of villany are furnished us almost daily; they are, absolutely, ' too numerous to mention.'"

On the 12th of October, OLIVER ANDERSON, a colored man, living in Chilicothe, Ohio, was forcibly dragged from his home, at night, and carried off to Slavery. The *Scioto Gazette*, in giving an account of the outrage, says, " ANDERSON has been a resident of this city four or five years, and was a quiet, inoffensive, and industrious man. That he was a freeman, there is but little doubt." A committee, appointed at an "indignation meeting," of the citizens of Chilicothe, to inquire into the facts of the case, reported, as the result of their investigations, their belief that he "was taken without law, by persons who had no claim to him, even under the fictions of the southern code." Happily we have later news from him, in the Columbus *Journal*, to the effect that, "one frosty night," last January, he left Kentucky, taking with him two Slaves, one, his brother; that, "they reached the Underground Railroad in good time, were rushed through on the express train," and are now in Canada. "This," adds the *Journal*, "ought to be quite satisfactory to the managers of the Underground Railroad — two hundred per cent on the original investment, and expenses paid by the kidnappers." A little later than the seizure of ANDERSON, an attempt was made to enslave a free colored family, in Louisville, Kentucky. The particulars appeared in the *Democrat*, of that city. A negro and his wife had been emancipated by will, some years before, and had afterwards, with the fruits of their industry and frugality, bought their son and his wife, and set them free. On the 23rd of October, the father suddenly died. A neighbor, named McGRATH, knowing that he had bills of sale of his children, but not aware that he had given them free papers, conspired with a lawyer, CLARY, and another man, to defraud them of freedom. The lawyer forged a bill of sale from the old negro to McGRATH, and, armed with that, the conspirators went to seize their prey; but the production of the free papers baffled their design, and exposed their villany. The lawyer and McGRATH were promptly lodged in jail to await a trial; the result of which we have not seen.

The New-Haven *Palladium*, of December 2, states that one GEORGE W. BISHOP, of New Haven, had just been arrested in Philadelphia, "charged with enticing a free colored man from New York to Alabama, and there selling him." BISHOP went to Alabama, with horses for sale, and employed the colored man to assist in taking care of the horses, but returned without him. Being asked what he had done with the man, he replied, that he had left him in Alabama. "It is rumored," says the *Palladium*, "that BISHOP sold the negro for $1000. Certain it is, that on his return he had more money than he was ever known to have before, and displayed it in a manner to excite considerable comment." Near the end of December, as JAMES LEWES, a free colored boy, living near Harrington, Del., was going, one evening, from his father's house to his employer's, one MORRIS met him in the woods, tied him to a tree, went home, and got his horse and carriage, and took the boy to Maryland, and tried to sell him to a Slave-dealer. The dealer's suspicion that the boy was free, led to inquiries, which brought out the truth; the boy was sent back, and the kidnapper committed to Dover jail. These facts we find in the Milford (Del.) *News.* The same paper mentions the arrest, some time in March last, of a man, who, with five others, had recently stolen a negro, and sold him out of the State. And adds, that "negro-stealing and selling out of the State, contrary to the law, is said to be carried on extensively in Sussex; and one man, residing at Seaford, it is said, has made a large amount of money at the business." A correspondent of the New-York *Tribune*, writing from Lewes, Del., on the 25th of April, corroborates the testimony of the *News*, as to the frequency of kidnapping in Delaware. He says, that, "at the recent session of the Superior Court, in Sussex County, indictments were found against two men for imprisoning a free negro, with intent to kidnap, and against six men for kidnapping, and assisting to kidnap."

On the night of the 2nd of March, four men went to the house of JOHN BROWN, a free colored man, living in Sadsbury, Lancaster County, Pa., pretending they had come to take him before a magistrate, on a charge of having robbed a neighboring store. Confident in his innocence, and recognizing two of the men as well-known neighbors, BROWN went with them, raising no alarm. They took him to a carriage, in the woods near by, put him in, drew pistols, and, with threats, compelling him to silence, drove with him to Baltimore, and lodged him in a Slave-pen, for sale. Upon his protesting that he was free, the Slave-dealer refused to buy or sell him, and soon after a man coming in who knew him, and confirmed his assertion of his freedom, he was released, and sent home. Meanwhile the alarm had somehow been given, and pursuit, though too late to be availing, was made. But two of the kidnappers had been arrested, and subsequently two others, who had escaped to Cincinnati, were followed and taken, and all were committed or bound over for trial; as also were a tavern-keeper, at whose house BROWN was kept concealed, by his captors, through the day after he was seized, and one or two others suspected of participation in the kidnapping.

We have accounts before us of a dozen or more other instances of the perpetration of this crime, within the year. Some of the victims afterward escaped or were rescued, others are no doubt still in bondage. Among the latter is believed to be CHARLES FISHER, of Kansas, two attempts to kidnap whom were mentioned in our last Report. How he was taken the third time, is not known; but, while Dr. DOY was in a Missouri prison, FISHER was brought there, and horribly tortured, till his assent was extorted to a confession, dictated to him, that he had a master somewhere. He was then taken away, and has not since been heard of. A Kansas correspondent of the New-York *Tribune*, who relates these facts, adds that "during the few months of Dr. DOY's incarceration, many such cases came under his notice." One, of which he gives particulars, was that of a free colored man, born in Illinois, and owning eighty acres of land, with some improvements, near Aurora, in that State. He had gone to Kansas to look at the country, with a view to removal thither, and on his return through Missouri, was seized, thrust into the jail, and compelled, like FISHER, by torture with a scourge of sheet-iron jagged with sharp points, to own himself a Slave, and to name, as the place whence he escaped, some part of Virginia, named to him, in which he had never been.

One attempt, of which we have an account in the Cleveland (Ohio) *Leader*, and some of the Canadian journals, was made in Canada, upon a woman, born free in New-York city, stolen thence, and held as a Slave, in Texas, about eleven years. Last summer, she escaped from her mistress, during a visit to Niagara Falls, and had been employed about a month, as a servant, at the Clifton House, when her master, aided by the keeper of the house, made an effort to reënslave her, but happily was defeated by the interference of the colored waiters, who had learned, in some way, what was going on. Another case, related on the 10th of April last, by a Washington correspondent of the Boston *Traveller*, is that of ALEXANDER SCARBOROUGH, a colored seaman, from New Bedford, who left his vessel in Baltimore, and set out to walk to Washington. Near Annapolis he was arrested on charge of being a runaway Slave, and imprisoned to await the demand of a master, till he was in danger of being sold to pay jail-fees; as he probably would have been, but that his condition came to the knowledge of Mr. ELIOT, member of Con-of opposing counsel — a removal of the case to Kent County, notorious for being intensely Pro-Slavery, and for having driven out of its limits — as related in our last Report — Mr. J. L. BOWERS, one of its best citizens, because of his Anti-Slavery sentiments. In April, 1859, by such a verdict as was to be expected from a Kent County jury, MOSES WRIGHT was robbed of his wife and children, and they of the freedom which was theirs, alike by human and divine law. Their counsel took exceptions to the ruling of the court, in order to carry the case up to the Court of Appeals; but we hardly dare to hope for a reversal of the unjust decision of the lower tribunal. "On the side of their oppressors is power, but they" — the helpless victims — we fear, "have no comforter." Still, there may be a possibility that the higher court, holding a more conspicuous position, and having its reputation more at stake, may feel itself so far amenable to public sentiment outside of the Slave-region, as to shrink from ratifying the iniquity of its judicial inferior.

MANUMISSIONS.

We have the satisfaction of knowing that attempts at manumission are not always so unfortunate in their issue as this of Mrs. BULLEN seems likely to be. In spite of all the counteracting influences almost everywhere powerfully at work, a sense of justice, or humane feeling, or natural affection, at times asserts itself with force enough to undo the heavy burden, and let the oppressed go free. And sometimes an unusual concurrence of circumstances brings about an emancipation, not, perhaps, in the strictest sense voluntary, though it may take, at last, the appearance of being such.

The *Times*, of Cincinnati, announced, about a year ago, the arrival of one CAMPBELL, in that city, from Louisiana, for the purpose of emancipating "a young and beautiful mulatto woman," and her infant child, of which he was the father. He bought them for $1,200, in order to set them free. In July last, the Missouri papers stated that Miss BATES, the sister of Hon. EDWARD BATES, of St. Louis, recently emancipated the last of thirty-two Slaves, who formed part of her inheritance, and whom she has gradually set free as they became prepared to take care of themselves in freedom. The Ohio *State Journal*, of August 22, said there were then in Columbus, "twenty-one Slaves, likely-looking men and women, manumitted by the will of their late owner, PLEASANT BURNET, of Mecklenburg County, Virginia," and sent to Ohio, to be settled on good lands selected for them in Hardin County; the will having provided for the purchase of the lands, and for furnishing all necessary tools with which to begin operations. About the middle of October, the Lynchburg (Va.) *Republican* described the departure, for a free State, of thirty-seven Slaves, set free by the will of FRANCIS B. SHACKLEFORD, of Amherst County. Forty-four were freed, but seven of them remained, "preferring servitude in Old Virginia to freedom elsewhere." On one day, in the latter part of January, twenty-eight Slaves were manumitted in the Probate Court of Cincinnati; fourteen by WM. McGINNIS, of Bourbon County, Ky., and fourteen by the will of SAMUEL TOWNSEND, of Madison County, Ala. Early in March, as we learn from the Cincinnati *Enquirer*, "a young female, of almost classic beauty, about eighteen years old, so nearly white that the tinge of African blood in her veins was scarcely perceptible, and perfect enough in form and feature to have served as a model for a Praxiteles or a Powers, was manumitted" in the same Court, "by a well-known New-Orleans merchant."

Nearly a year ago, a case of much interest, which had been pending eighteen or twenty months, came to a happy conclusion in the arrival of a manumitted Slave-girl, at Oberlin, Ohio, in charge of a faithful guardian, to join an already liberated sister; both being provided with means of support and education, by their father's will. We gather the following particulars from an account published in the Cleveland *Leader*, about the middle of last May. In the summer of 1857, JAMES OLDHAM, of Coahoma County, Miss., left home to take his two Slave daughters, about fourteen and ten years old, to Oberlin, there to emancipate and educate them. On the way, the younger child, who had been a household pet, became so reluctant to exchange the indulgence of home for the expected restraints of school, that she was permitted to return. The day after her father, with his elder daughter, reached Oberlin, he was taken fatally ill. He called to his aid a Dr. REA, whose acquaintance he had made, and who attended him till his death, and then accompanied his remains to his Mississippi home. While expecting death, the father was intensely anxious for the freedom of his younger daughter, which he felt it was then by no means easy to secure. By the laws of Mississippi, he could not emancipate her in the State, nor by will free her to be sent out of the State, nor give her in trust to another to free her, nor sell her to be freed. Such are the difficulties in the way of a father's saving his own child from the degradation and horrors of Slavery. But an attempt must be made. Under the counsel of Judge BLISS, of Elyria, whose heart was warmly enlisted in the task, a will was executed, setting forth the father's earnest wish, bequeathing to his daughters their freedom, and $ 4,000 for their support and education, and appointing Dr. REA executor, with power to expend the whole $ 4,000, if needed, in securing freedom for the younger daughter, should the heirs endeavor to prevent it. They did make the attempt, with most disgraceful earnestness, and for a time seemed likely to succeed; and not till after a severe struggle, in which they contested warmly every point, putting the doctor's energy and firmness to full proof; and not till the Supreme Court of the State had, in another case, decided unfavorably to them some important points involved in this, did they consent to a compromise which yielded the freedom of the girl and $ 3,000 of the money.

The Meigs County (Ohio) *Telegraph*, of the 9th of last May, says that a girl, almost pure white, intelligent and beautiful, to whom a Virginian Slave-dealer is both master and father, has been attending school at Pomeroy, in Meigs County, for two or three years past, her father paying her board and tuition. For some months he has tried hard and made large promises to induce her to return to his home; but, though "much attached to him," she refuses to go, fearing the fate of the chattels he trades in. Her mother was sent over to persuade her back, but failed, and on her return was shipped to the South; as it was believed, on the Ohio side, the daughter would have been also, had she crossed the river. On the 5th of May, her father, "with a very hard-looking customer, both well armed with revolvers," came to see her. Her friends, suspecting a design to kidnap her, raised an alarm, and a crowd soon gathered. The Virginians solemnly denied any evil purpose, but suspicion only grew stronger, when the father, declaring that he had emancipated her, produced in proof a pretended deed of manumission, which, on examination, was found to be of no validity. The Virginians, at last becoming fearful for their personal safety, retreated across the river; and, soon after, the father — whether making a virtue of necessity, or really actuated by right feelings — sent his daughter a valid deed of manumission. On the 19th of last July, MARIA GASKINS, a Slave-woman brought from New Orleans by one WILLIAM HOLMES and his wife, on a visit to Plymouth, Mass., was declared free by Judge METCALF, of the Supreme Court of the State, before whom she had been taken by a writ of habeas corpus, issued on petition of N. B. SPOONER, of Plymouth; an emancipation evidently not intended by the master when he took his Slave beyond the reach of the Louisiana Slave-code. Another case of unintended emancipation occurred, a few weeks ago, in Philadelphia. Rev. JOHN MILLER, of Lexington, Rockbridge County, Va., brought a Slave-woman to Philadelphia, as a child's nurse for his wife. The woman soon learned her right to freedom, under Pennsylvania law; and on the evening of February 23, availed herself of it by leaving her master, and seeking service where the hire of the laborer is not kept back by fraud or force. And of yet another instance, about the 1st of March, we have a fragmentary mention, in an extract from the Iowa City *Republican*, from which we gather that one CURTIS, master and father of two Slave-girls brought from some Slave State to Iowa, signed an instrument, partly under legal pressure, and partly, it is to be hoped, as the paper itself affirmed, for "the love, regard, and affection entertained" by him for the children, — emancipating them, and "conferring upon them all the rights, privileges, and responsibilities which would pertain to them if born to him in lawful wedlock."

In this list of manumissions it may be proper to include that of little SALLY MARIA BRIGGS, commonly called "Pink," a nearly white girl, of nine years, bought into freedom for $900, by HENRY WARD BEECHER and his congregation, about two months ago. She was the child of a prominent physician in Maryland, an octoroon Slave. Her mother and five children had been sold separately, and she had been living, in the belief that she was free, with her grandmother, a free woman by self-purchase, residing in Washington City; the Slave-dealers assuring the old woman that Pink should never be taken from her. But that was only a Slave-dealer's promise. Last winter, the child was sold to a trader. A kind young man, determined, if possible, to secure her freedom, after much negotiation and divers discouragements, at last obtained possession of her, under a bond that she, or the price above-named, should be returned within fifteen days. He took her to Brooklyn, and Mr. BEECHER, after his next Sunday morning's discourse, set her before his congregation, and made a simple statement of the facts concerning her. The collection which followed amounted to more than $1000; Pink goes back to her grandmother, a free child; and it is said steps will be taken to secure her education.

FUGITIVE SLAVES.

The newspapers, of all parts of the country, have furnished ample proof that those who choose not to wait for freedom from a master's tardy justice, and do not feel bound to pay a robber for surrendering his plunder, have by no means fallen off in number during the past year. While some attempts to find a better home in higher latitudes have sadly failed, success, so far as we have heard, has been the very general rule. And of the exceptional instances, some have ended in a way to give the Slave-system a severer shock than even a successful flight could give it. For they have shown a spirit in the bondman which scorned life itself, as an alternative for liberty.

One case of this sort was published, last summer, in the Baton Rouge (La.) *Gazette*. At Rodney, Miss., a man having found, on the steam-packet Charmer, a negro who had fled from him, seized him, and tied his hands; the negro, declaring "he would sooner die than go with the man, to be treated as he had been, jumped into the river and was drowned." From the New-York *Tribune* we learn that on the 1st of September, while a vessel laden with turpentine and rosin, from St. Mary's, Ga., was unloading in Brooklyn, the body of a young black man was found in the hold, with a bundle of clothing and a small supply of provisions lying by him. He had evidently hidden himself there, in the hope of escaping to freedom, but the hatches having been battened down, shutting out the air, and the fumes of the turpentine filling the hold, he had died of suffocation. The Vevay (Ind.) *News*, of November 23, describes a chase, on the 13th, after a runaway Slave, from Woodford County, Ky., by a party of white men in Carroll County. After tracking the fugitive a long way, they overtook him on the banks of the Kentucky River, but before they could seize him he ran out upon a log projecting twenty feet into the river, faced them, and placing the muzzle of a pistol at his head, threatened to send a ball through his own brain, if a man attempted to approach him. A brief parley followed, then two of the pursuers, with cocked pistols, advanced, but as they stepped upon the log he fired, and fell, bleeding, into the water. He was dragged out, and when restored to consciousness, expressed deep regret at his failure; but, the *News* says, "he can hardly be expected to recover." A late paper from the South tells us that, about the 1st of April, a runaway negro, at Montgomery, Ala., resisted his pursuers, severely wounded one of them, and could not be taken till he was shot dead. Cases like these, are emphatic answers to the assertion that the Slaves are happy in bondage, and have no wish for freedom. They hint with fearful plainness, also, at the possibility, to say the least, that a day may come when, this same desperate determination animating masses of the enslaved, the cry of "liberty or death" shall rise on the midnight air "like the voice of many waters." Of like ominous import is the account, in a St. Joseph (Mo.) paper, in July last, of a Slave killing his purchaser, near that place, and making his escape; and, in the same month, the discovery alleged by the Clarksburg (Va.) *Register*, to have been made, of a conspiracy among the Slaves of Harrison County, to run off, defending themselves in so doing; to which end, it is said, "they were well supplied with fire-arms." Less terrible to the oppressor, if not less fatal, at last, to his unrighteous system, is the significance of those happily more frequent events, some of which we chronicle below.

In June last, the Detroit (Mich.) *Advertiser* announced that "seventy Fugitive Slaves arrived in Canada, by one train, from the interior of Tennessee. A week before, a company of twelve arrived. Nearly the same time, one of seven, and another of five, safely landed on the free soil of Canada, making ninety-four in all. The Underground Railroad was never before doing so flourishing a business." On the fourth of July, as we learn from one of the agents of the road, "six fugitives from Maryland passed through Philadelphia," and not long after, "one arrived in that city, in a box so short, that he could not lie his length," and "two females escaped, one in a trunk and the other in a dry-goods box." The same agent mentions the arrival of "twenty-eight at one time," and states that "one of Ex-President TYLER's Slaves had gone on his way north, rejoicing." Four Slaves, although handcuffed and chained together, managed, on the night of August 26, to escape from the hotel, in St. Joseph, Mo., where their master was stopping. So says the next day's *Gazette*, of that place. The Rochester (N. Y.) *Express*, of October 25, states that on the 22nd, "not less than fifteen thousand dollars worth of 'property' passed through this city, on the 'Underground,'" in the shape of "a dozen smart, intelligent, young and middle-aged men and women," who were "part of a large shipment from Alexandria, Va., about the time of the Harper's Ferry insurrection." The Troy (N. Y.) *Argus* learns from "official sources," about the same time, "that the Underground Railroad has been doing an unusually large business this year, the train taking, some days, a dozen at a time, and the aggregate of the year is counted by hundreds." It adds, that "one gentleman, who is ranked among the high-toned, conservative Democrats — a sustainer of the Fugitive-Slave Law, the Nebraska Bill, and the Pierce and Buchanan Administrations, on principle — is regularly called on, for his subscription, when funds are needed. His sober and invariable reply is this: — 'Give money to help a Fugitive Slave escape? not a cent! it's illegal and against the Compromises of the Constitution! send him back to Virginia! send him back — *and here's a V to help pay the expenses of returning him back to his master!*'" A correspondent of the *National Anti-Slavery Standard*, writing from Utica, N. Y., on the 23rd of January, says, "three or four weeks since, a 'fugitive from service or labor' appeared in Utica, and called on a United States Deputy Marshal for assistance, in journeying northward, and he actually sent the guilty, ungrateful chattel to a well-known agent of the Underground Railroad." The Syracuse *Standard*, a few days earlier, reported the passage of six fugitives through Syracuse, one of them direct from Harper's Ferry, and they brought news of seven more on the way. An Albany correspondent of the New-York *Tribune* says, on the 2nd of February, "the Underground Railroad, under the energetic management of Superintendent STEPHEN MYERS, is doing a prosperous business. Twenty-six passengers, coming over the main road and its various branches, have passed through here during the past month." The writer continues thus: "It would astonish some portion of the public amazingly, to know the class of people who contribute regularly to the funds of the 'Underground,' — such as staunch Democrats, who swear by Mr. BUCHANAN, the Fugitive-Slave Law, and the Dred Scott dicta — but then, when they hand over their contribution to STEPHEN, they tell him to use it in sending Slaves back to their kind masters, where they are sure they are much better off than in the frozen regions of the North." The *Free-Church Portfolio*, of Newcastle, Pa., said, about the end of February, "We learn, on good authority, that, during the last two or three weeks, there has been doing quite an active business on the Ohio section of the Underground Railroad. Fugitives, stout, athletic fellows, from Eastern Virginia, have been passing, in small companies, almost daily. We believe all, who have passed along lately, have reached their place of destination in safety." The Ravenna (Ohio) *Democrat* says, that on the 22nd of February "a full-freighted car, on the Underground Railroad, passed through, loaded with passengers, from 'Old Tennessee.'"

Besides these, we have many accounts of Slaves escaping singly, or in groups of from two to six. One somewhat remarkable case was related, a few weeks ago, in the New-York *Independent*. A placard, announcing that a woman in Missouri was soon to be sold at auction, to go South, fell under the eye of a man in Kansas, who resolved to rescue her. With a span of horses, a covered carriage, and two or three trusty companions, he hastened to the master's house; went in alone, and found him sitting, and the woman standing near. Pointing a cocked pistol at the master's head, he kept him sitting, while the woman, at his suggestion, took from her mistress's closet a shawl and shoes for herself, and blankets for her two children, and got, with the children, into the wagon. He then retired backward, keeping his pistol in steady aim till he reached the carriage, when he drove rapidly off across the Kansas line. The New-York *Tribune*, of February 13, gives, from a Missouri paper, an account of another case not widely unlike this. Half a dozen Slave-hunters, from Missouri, pursued a fugitive into Kansas. At a tavern, on their journey, some Free-State men met them, bringing the fugitive; introduced him to his master; and, his hat and coat being shabby and ragged, "invited the master to exchange with him, which he cheerfully did, and was then persuaded to lend him money enough to defray his expenses to Canada, and also to furnish him his horse, to lessen the fatigues of the journey." They then parted; "the colored man went North, and the Slave-holder and his friends back to their homes."

A correspondent of the New-York *Herald*, who has lately been journeying through the South, and sending back glowing descriptions of the beauties of Slavery, the happiness of the Slaves, and "the affection existing betwen Slave and master," comes at length, on his homeward way, to Kentucky, and puts the finishing touch to his rose-colored picture, in this style; — "The negroes are getting very scarce in the northern part of the State, owing to the close proximity of the enemy across the Ohio. None but the most faithful of Slaves can be kept by farmers along the border, so well arranged is the Underground-Railroad system, in the southern counties of Ohio and Indiana." Happy as they are, — "the happiest people on the face of the globe," says the *Herald's* delighted correspondent, — it seems, by his own showing, that, only give them a chance to get away, and all their happiness and all their affection can't keep them in that southern paradise. An important testimony to the frequency of escapes, and the seriousness of the loss thence resulting to the Slave-holders, is given in the introduction of a bill in the Maryland Senate, at its late session, to incorporate a Slave-holders' Insurance Company, to insure against loss by the running away of Slaves.

Of the unsuccessful attempts to escape, none became more notorious, or excited more attention, by reason of the issues coming to be involved in it, than that of COLUMBUS JONES, who left Pensacola on the 1st of May, 1859, on board a brig bound for Boston. On the voyage, the mate (who was in command, the captain being in Massachusetts) discovered him, and put him in irons, and endeavored to put in at Key West, and afterward at Norfolk, in order to land him, but was prevented by stress of weather. On the 8th of May, the vessel anchored in Hyannis, Mass., and the mate went ashore and brought off the captain. On their way, they met JONES, who had escaped from the vessel, and had hired a man, passing in a skiff, to take him ashore. By false assurances of safety they persuaded him to go back with them. Learning that a schooner in the harbor was about to sail to Philadelphia, they offered the master, Captain BACON, $500 to go out of his course, and carry the Slave to Norfolk, Va.; whence he could be sent back to Florida. The schooner sailed, the next day, with JONES chained to the capstan. When the facts became known, the captains of the brig and of the schooner, and the mate and the principal owner of the brig, were indicted for kidnapping. The trial took place at Barnstable, beginning on the 15th of November. The defence first offered a special plea, that JONES was a Fugitive Slave; that the defendants arrested him as agents of the owner; and that the statutes, under which they were indicted, were unconstitutional. This plea was overruled, when they pleaded the general issue. After hearing evidence for nearly two days, and arguments of counsel for half another, the jury brought in a verdict of acquittal, on the ground that the offence was not committed within the jurisdiction of Barnstable County. But whether the kidnappers gained anything by the whole transaction is still, perhaps, open to question. Of one of them, the Boston correspondent of the New-York *Tribune* says, "poor BACON has fared very hardly. By going out of his way, to serve the doughface owners of the vessel in which JONES escaped, he forfeited his freight-money, and has lost the expected profits of the voyage; and, I understand, he has not yet received a dollar of the bribe by which he was bought into Slavery's service." It would be nothing strange, if men who would employ another in such a business, *should* be base enough to cheat him out of his wages; and he who would be hired to do it deserves small sympathy if he *is* thus cheated.

In arguing the case, on behalf of the kidnappers, CALEB CUSHING, titularly honorable, took the ground, that a master, by the Constitution, has a right, which State laws cannot impair, to seize his Fugitive Slave in any State, and take him back; any coercion, needful to this end, would be no breach of the peace; no Act of Congress is required to give this power; no process of law is needed to legalize the seizure and return; a Slave, secreting himself upon a ship without the owner's consent, is in their custody, as an involuntary deposit, and so continues, while within the jurisdiction of the United States, until he is returned; a vessel, duly registered in the United States, is a part of its territory, unless within a foreign jurisdiction; the entrance of a vessel into the jurisdiction of a State does not discharge a fugitive on board; the question, whether a person is a Slave in any State depends on the United States laws; any person may recapture and return a Slave, as the owner's agent, and, in doing it, may exercise all rights pertaining to the owner; the agent may be constituted by deed, letter, or other unsealed proof, acts, or implications; subsequent notification, by the owner, suffices to confer an agency; in extradition of fugitives, agency may proceed as in civil proceedings, and the burden of proof, as to jurisdiction, rests on the prosecutor. Now, if all this is law and Constitution rightly construed, what safeguard, for his freedom, does it leave to any man within this "glorious Union?" Who is secure from seizure, without legal process, or even conformity to the succinct formalities of the black statute of 1850, by any scoundrel who may choose to call himself the agent, made by "implication," of some congenial scoundrel, in the South, who, hearing of his act, will give the "subsequent notification" to set all straight? Not CALEB's honorable self, although, no doubt, he may be safe from seizure upon other than strictly legal grounds; his southern masters, judging it expedient to let him, of pure favor, run at large, as being, so, more serviceable than in plantation drudgery. Heaven only knows how much the harder drudgery falls to his share, however.

Another attempt which ended in disaster, was made at Charleston, S. C., on the 22nd of June, by the Slave of one GOODRICH. He hid himself on board the steamship Marion, just before its departure for New York; but unfortunately was

found by the steward, betrayed to the captain, and sent back
to his master, "who," the Charleston *Mercury* is careful to inform us, "had him suitably punished at the work-house." As
he was found in the porter's room, the porter, a young Irishman, named FRANCIS MITCHELL, was suspected of having aided
him, and was consequently handed over to the authorities
of South Carolina. "The prompt action of Captain FOSTER
and his steward," says the *Mercury*, "deserves high commendation." After several months' imprisonment, MITCHELL was
tried, convicted, and sentenced to death; but, through the
"benignant mercy" of South Carolina, he was pardoned by
the governor, whether because his alleged criminal attempt had
failed, or because his long imprisonment was deemed penalty
enough for a humane act which injured nobody but himself, or
because he was, as the *Mercury* tells us, "the sole support of
a widowed mother," or for what special reason, we do not
learn.

About the 1st of July, as the Chicago *Press* informs us, three
Slaves of a Captain FROST, of St. Louis, left him, and went to
Chicago, with intent to settle there. Two men, NOYES and
SMITH, formerly of the city's detective police, tempted by a
reward of $ 2,500, which Captain FROST had offered for his
stray chattels, laid a plot to take them, and with the aid of a
treacherous colored man, named TURNER, and one or two
others, proceeded to execute it. Through their colored accom-
plice they found access to the men, and NOYES pretending to
have bought a farm in the western part of the State, offered
them liberal wages to go and work upon it; and, to deceive
them more effectually, he took them to the agricultural stores,
to select tools and seeds which he bought ostensibly for their
use. This was on the 15th of July, and on that night a second-
class car was chartered on the Illinois Central Railroad, and
the unsuspecting victims were carried off before any but the
conspirators knew of the plot. The next news heard of the
poor fugitives was, that on the 18th they were landed on an
island opposite St. Louis, and that they were cruelly whipped.
The excitement thereupon, in Chicago, was intense. TURNER
had to be locked up in a prison-cell, for a time, to guard him
from the fury of the colored people. Warrants were issued
for the kidnappers, and SMITH, TURNER, and another, were

taken and bound over for trial; SMITH in $ 3,000, and the others in $ 1,000 each, but NOYES escaped with the blood-money. The *Press* says "this affair has justly made a most profound sensation here, more so, perhaps, than any like event for ten years past."

On the night of July 2, an old colored man, named SNOW-DEN, of Steubenville, Ohio, assisted by a colored friend or two, attempted to carry off his own family from Slavery, in West *Liberty*, Va., but was intercepted by a party of the citizens, and after a desperate fight was captured, and, with all his company, committed to jail, in Wheeling, to await trial.

A Slave of Rev. MICHAEL ROBBINS, of Wilmington, N. C., secreted himself on board the schooner Geo. Harris, which left that port for New York, on the 16th of August. He was missed, the vessel was pursued and overtaken, and the man was found. Four colored sailors, WM. TUBBS, WM. WEAVER, JOHN WILLIAMS, and TOM WINISFIELD, were arrested on the charge of helping his escape; an offence punishable with death by the law of North Carolina. They were tried in October, three were acquitted and two discharged. WINISFIELD was found guilty, against the judge's charge, and for that reason a new trial was granted; and TUBBS, though acquitted, was kept in prison, as liable to be indicted again, because, on account of a defect in the first indictment, he could not have been sentenced if he had been convicted. The result of the second trial we have not seen.

About the middle of January, a Dr. BOYD was tried in Washington city, on a charge of negro-stealing, having been arrested in Maryland, driving a peddler's wagon towards Pennsylvania, with a Slave concealed in a box. Though the judge instructed the jury that the offence was only abduction, and not negro-stealing, if the prisoner intended to free the Slave, and though the evidence made it quite clear that such was his intention, yet, against law and evidence, he was convicted of the higher offence, and the judge, whose instruction was thus set at nought, refusing, nevertheless, to grant a new trial, sentenced him to fourteen years in the penitentiary.

CASES UNDER THE FUGITIVE-SLAVE ACT.

The year may be said to have begun with an enforcement of the notorious Act of 1850. About the middle of last May, one JACK-SON, for three years before a resident of Belmont County, Ohio, was decoyed to Zanesville, betrayed into the hands of Deputy Marshal Cox, and taken before a United States Commissioner, who straightway heard the case, that is, the claimant's side of it, with locked doors, and doomed the man to Slavery. By writ of habeas corpus he was then brought before Judge MARSH, of the State Court, and was declared free; but was immediately seized again by Cox and his underlings, and taken to the railroad station, to be sent off by the next train. The colored people made a brave fight for a rescue, but were over-come. Another writ of habeas corpus brought him again be-fore Judge MARSH, who, after argument, in which it was con-tended that the law was unconstitutional, and the certificate invalid, remanded him to the marshal; deciding that the cer-tificate conformed to the law, and that, though "he had no doubt of the unconstitutionality of the law," he must yield to decisions of the Supreme Court of the United States and various circuit courts. Next morning, the man was sent to Slavery. The Zanesville *Courier* closes its relation of these facts, by declaring that they "inspired, in all intelligent and well-disposed people, disgust for an institution which required such disgraceful proceedings to sustain it, and scorn for those who, for a paltry pittance, became its willing creatures." The Baptist Church, in Zanesville, of which Marshal Cox was a member, promptly excommunicated him for his participation in the infamous business; thereby extorting from certain sorely aggrieved Pro-Slavery organ-grinders, the utterance of dismal forebodings of fearful peril to "this free government" and its loyal upholders, should such "relentless and blood-thirsty bigotry" ever come into political power. Very terrible! — that the official agents of "this *free* government," in its work of legalized kidnapping, should be told in a somewhat em-phatic way that serving Mammon, or Moloch for Mammon's sake, is not entirely compatible with serving God.

On the 20th of June, AGNES ROBINSON and her child, MARY,

were arrested in Washington City, and brought before Judge
MERRICK, of the Circuit Court, claimed as Fugitive Slaves by
DAVID WITMER, of Washington County, Maryland. "The
forms of the Fugitive Act," says the Washington *States*, "were
complied with, and Judge MERRICK remanded the woman back
to Hagerstown, Md., where the question of their right to freedom must be determined, the judge having, of course, no power
to decide that point." And pray then, what power had he to
send her back to Maryland? seeing that, by the express terms
of the Constitution, his only power in the premises is, to send
back "persons *held* to service" by the law of the State they
fled from; not persons merely *claimed* as so held. So that
"their right to freedom" is, precisely, the *very* point to be decided *before* they can be constitutionally surrendered. It is a
gross error to suppose, as so many seem to do, that the same
rule of proceeding applies to fugitives "from service," as to
fugitives "from justice." As to the latter, the provision is, that
a person *charged* with crime is to be given up, on demand of
the Executive of the State he fled from; so the truth or falsehood of the charge affects not the obligation to give him up.
But, as to the former, it is not a person *charged* with owing
service who is to be given up, but one actually *held* to service;
and he is to be given up to the person, not who *claims* his service, but to whom it is *due*. That he *owes* it, and owes it *to the
claimant*, are, therefore, just the facts to be proved, in order to
make out an obligation or a right to give him up. Happily,
however, in the case of AGNES ROBINSON and her child, the
judge's error only delayed, instead of defeating justice; for a
Maryland jury finally declared them free, under a deed of
manumission from the woman's former master, the father of the
present claimant.

On the 28th of October, JOHN RICE, a colored man, living in
Morrow County, Ohio, where he had a wife and child, was seized
in Columbus, whither a tool of the Slave-hunters had lured him,
on pretense of employing him in a refreshment saloon; the by-
standers were quieted by being told he was taken for robbery; he
was ironed, locked up in the closet of a railroad car, carried to Cincinnati, and taken immediately before Commissioner NEWHALL.
A writ of habeas corpus, issued by a judge of the Court of Common Pleas in Greene County, and served on the marshal, in the

car, by the sheriff of that county, was treated with open contempt; and a kind-hearted lawyer, who, happening to be on the train, volunteered to act as counsel for the prisoner, was not permitted even to see either him or the warrant on which he was arrested, until they reached the commissioner's office; and then, before the lawyer had time to finish a brief conversation with him, and examine the writ, the examination of the claimant's witnesses began. No cross-examination of them was permitted, though urgently and repeatedly demanded, by the prisoner's counsel, as a right; nor was he allowed to offer testimony to prove his freedom, though he affirmed that it could be established by witnesses in Morrow County, if time were given to produce them. In spite of the earnest remonstrances of his counsel, he was surrendered to the claimant, and, at once hurried across the river; "the whole time of the trial," says the Cincinnati *Gazette*, from which we gather this account, "not occupying more than fifteen minutes." Verily, Commissioner NEWHALL is a model commissioner; not more prompt and eager to earn his $10 fee than faithful to the very inmost spirit and purpose of the Slave-catcher's black statute, in his energetic administration thereof. The Columbus *State Journal* mentions persons who had known RICE as living in Morrow County, for nearly eight years, and as having been married, in the State, six years; whereas, the testimony for the claimant made it less than five years since he ran away from Virginia. The *Journal* thus gives vent to its feeling, at the issue of the case; — " Incidents like this, among us, leave no room for indignation or horror at JOHN BROWN's invasion. If arms can be put into this man's hands, to hew his way to freedom by whatever killing is necessary, there is not a man or woman in the State, that will not justify, both the man that armed him and the man that slew those that enslaved him. See what a narrow line divides us all, Republicans and Democrats, from old JOHN BROWN!"

One year, wanting a few days, from the time when the trial of DANIEL WEBSTER, described in our last Report, was filling Philadelphia with excitement by its progress and happy termination, another case was tried, in that city, reaching a result in painful contrast with that of the former year. On Monday, the 26th of March, a man claimed, under the name of MOSES HOR-

NER, as a fugitive from Virginia, was arrested near Harrisburg, Pa., by two deputy marshals from Philadelphia (one of them bearing the not inappropriate name of SHARKEY), and was brought, the next morning, before Commissioner CADWALLADER, of the latter city. Notice of the arrest reached the Abolitionists of the city, on Monday afternoon, and they hastened to make such preparation for a stout defence as time would allow. Early on Tuesday morning, counsel for the prisoner sought an interview with him, at the marshal's office, but it was not allowed, and the hour appointed for the hearing found them wholly ignorant of the merits of the case. The court began its sitting at ten o'clock; B. H. BREWSTER, notorious as Slave-hunter's counsel in the Webster case, acted the same part in this, and GEO. H. EARLE, RYLAND WARRINER, WM. BULL, and EDWARD HOPPER volunteered for the defence. A delay of two or three hours was obtained, against BREWSTER'S opposition, to enable counsel to confer with the prisoner, and prepare for the trial.

In the afternoon, the trial proceeded. BREWSTER offered, as the foundation of his case, a transcript of a record, in a Virginia county court, to which HOPPER and EARLE objected, on the ground that it contained erasures, and gave the prisoner's name in several different forms. The objection was overruled, and the document received. Witnesses were then called to prove the man's identity. In the cross-examination (which was allowed, CADWALLADER being, evidently, not *quite* so perfect a specimen of the Slave-catching commissioner as NEWHALL), an attempt was made once, or twice, to bring to light defects in the claimant's title, but it was not permitted; the commissioner ruling that the only point to be settled was that of identity; — as if the Constitution had not made it equally important to show that the claim comes from one to whom the service claimed is due. After the claimant's witnesses had testified, the court adjourned to ten o'clock the next morning, to give time for the arrival of witnesses for the defence, who had been sent for, by telegraph, to Harrisburg; but none came. One witness only was examined for the defence; a colored woman, in Philadelphia, who testified that she had seen the prisoner in Pennsylvania some months before the time when he was said to have escaped. The case was then argued ably and at length, for the defence, when the commissioner, declining to hear argument on the other side, surrendered the prey to the spoiler.

By this time a writ of habeas corpus had been obtained from Judge ALLISON, of the State Court, and was now served on the marshal, commanding him to produce the body of MOSES, the next day, at ten o'clock, and show cause why he restrained him of his liberty. After conference with the United States District Attorney, the marshal decided to disobey the writ, and sent the man out of the State early the next morning; making return to the State Court, through his counsel, that he had done so in obedience to a mandate of the United States Circuit Court. At our latest intelligence, the hearing before the court, as to the sufficiency of this return, had not been concluded.

As the marshal's posse were removing the prisoner from the Commissioner's Court to the jail, a small band of colored people, moved by a sudden impulse of generous sympathy, made a gallant effort for a rescue, which required the most vigorous exertion of the numerous band of officers to defeat it. The rescuers were at length overpowered, and several of them arrested and sent to prison. And so ends another chapter in the long history of the country's disgraceful complicity with man-stealing.

The Philadelphia Abolitionists, who displayed, throughout, their wonted vigilance, promptitude, and determined resolution, though saddened, seem not to be discouraged by the result. One of them, writing to the *Anti-Slavery Standard*, says that, "on the whole, though the Slave has been taken back, we do not feel that we have quite lost our case. We have made a good fight, and the enemy has gained a damaging victory. The feeling of the community is in our favor, and our opponents are tired of the contest. The marshal and several of his officers have expressed to our friends their 'hope in God that they might never have another case.' They know our purpose to contest every inch of the ground, and to give them all the trouble in our power. My impression is, that the business of Slave-catching, in Pennsylvania, has about come to an end." The Juvenile Anti-Slavery Society of Philadelphia, an organization which is doing efficient service to our cause, met on the 3rd of April, and passed resolutions appropriate to the late events, condemning the rendition of HORNER as "a fresh evidence of" the city's "subserviency to the Slave-power;" declaring the striking down of the sacred right to freedom to be equally "an outrage upon our sense of justice," whether done "according to the forms of law, or in violation of them;" and expressing "sympathy with the colored men awaiting trial for having obeyed the most generous impulses of our common nature, in a brave attempt to rescue a fellow-creature from a doom worse than death."

The last number of the *National Anti-Slavery Standard*, published the 5th of May inst., says that "two men, ALLEN GRAFF and JOSIAH HAY, alleged to have recently escaped from Frederic County, Md., have been sent from this (New York) city into Slavery, the present week, by Commissioner BETTS, under the provisions of the accursed Fugitive-Slave Law. It was done so secretly that it was not known in time for any serious effort to be made in their behalf. What must be the public sentiment in this great city, where two human beings can be thus consigned to life-long bondage, with less excitement than is caused by sending a common thief to the penitentiary, and where, of all the pulpits existing therein, there are not, probably, three, if even so many, that will have courage to rebuke the outrage!" Courage to *rebuke* it! — would that this lack of courage were all we have to deplore in regard to those pulpits. But how many of them would have the audacity to *defend* the outrage, with the Bible before them, — Golden Rule, denunciations against oppression, "the law made for men-stealers," the doctrine of human brotherhood, the Mosaic Fugitive-Servant Law, and all!

RESCUES AND RESCUE-TRIALS.

On the 27th of April, for the first time since the Fugitive-Slave Act was passed, an attempt was made to execute it in Troy, N. Y.; but not with such success as will be likely, we think, to induce a hasty repetition of the experiment. CHARLES NALLE, the man on whom it was made, was formerly a Slave, in Culpepper County, Va. In October, 1858, he went to Columbia, Pa., where his wife and three children, emancipated in Virginia, not long before, were and still are living. He was pursued, but escaped. Lately he lived, for a time, at Sand

Lake; and, early in April, came thence to Troy, where he was employed as a coachman. "He is said," the Troy *Whig* tells us, "to have been an excellent and faithful servant." Information given to his former master, it is supposed by a reporter for the "Democratic" organ, in Troy, led to his arrest. He "was handcuffed, and literally dragged" before Commissioner BEACH, says a Troy correspondent of the New-York *Tribune;* and, after a private and very brief examination, was given up to the master's agent. But, notwithstanding the quiet and secrecy of the proceeding, word somehow got about, of what was going on; a large and highly-excited crowd gathered about the office; a writ of habeas corpus was obtained from Judge GOULD, of the Supreme Court, and served on the marshal; and an attempt was made to take the prisoner before the judge. But, the instant he stepped into the street, the crowd rushed upon him; and, after a furious struggle, bore prisoner, officers, and all toward the ferry; rescued the captive, and sent him in a skiff across the river. At the other side, immediately on landing, he was arrested by a West-Troy constable, and taken to a justice's office, locked in, and guarded by several officers and the West-Troy postmaster, armed with pistols. The crowd on the Troy side, meanwhile, rushed to the steam ferry-boat, and hundreds crossed over; followed NALLE to the office, and, in spite of a stubborn resistance by the officers, burst open the door, seized the prisoner, and, in a few minutes more, "the fastest horse in West Troy" was conveying him, with two well-armed companions, toward a land of freedom. "This incident," adds the *Tribune's* correspondent, "has developed a more intense Anti-Slavery spirit here, than was ever known before." And the correspondent of the *Times* bears witness that "the rescuers numbered many of our most respectable citizens, — lawyers, editors, public men, and private individuals. The rank and file, though, were black, and African fury is entitled to claim the greatest share in the rescue."

A man, claimed as a Fugitive Slave by one PHILLIPS, of Missouri, was brought, by writ of habeas corpus, in October last, from Union County, Ill., to Ottawa, La Salle County, for a hearing, under the Fugitive-Slave Act, before Chief Justice CATON, at his chambers; Deputy Marshal ALBRIGHT claiming to hold him under a writ issued by the United States Commissioner of the southern district of Illinois. The hearing took place on the 20th, and resulted in the remanding of the prisoner to the marshal; whereupon a crowd, including some of the best and most respectable people of the place, pressed upon the marshal, took the man from his hands, hurried him into a carriage waiting in readiness, and sent him at full speed out of town. At the November term of the United States District Court, in Chicago, eight citizens of Ottawa were indicted for participation in the rescue; and three of them, Dr. Stout, and his brother, and John Hossack, were arrested and lodged in the Chicago jail. Bail was promptly offered, and, though at first declined, was afterwards, at the urgent solicitation of their friends, accepted by two of the prisoners; the other, Dr. Stout, still refusing, and awaiting in prison the time of trial. Three others, the day before the trials began, hearing that warrants were issued for them, sent for an officer to meet them at the railroad station, put themselves into his hands, and were lodged in jail. The trials took place at the February term of the United States District Court, beginning on the 28th, and resulting, after some difficulty in getting juries to agree, in the conviction of Hossack, Dr. Stout, and a Mr. King; with a recommendation " to the mercy of the court." The Government seems, then, to have abandoned the other cases. "The sympathy of the people," says a Chicago correspondent of the New-York *Tribune*, "is entirely with" the rescuers; who, he adds, are "some of the best and purest men in Illinois," and whom "everybody respects as good men." The court wishing to consult Judge McLean, of the Supreme Court, on some points of law involved in the case, the pronouncing of sentence was postponed to the next term.

At the date of our last Report, the trial of the Oberlin rescuers of John Rice was still in progress; Simeon Bushnell had been convicted, and the case of Charles H. Langston was before the court. On the 10th of May last, Langston's case was given to the jury; who, after a half-hour's consultation, pronounced him guilty. On the 11th, Bushnell was sentenced to sixty day's imprisonment, a fine of $600, and costs of prosecution. On the same day, the sheriff of Lorain County arrested Jennings, Mitchell, and Davis, indicted, as mentioned in our last Report, for an attempt to kidnap Rice; and they were bound over for trial. The next day, LANGSTON was called up to receive his sentence, and, to the customary question, whether he had anything to say why sentence should not be pronounced upon him, responded in a noble speech, full of vigorous eloquence, undaunted courage, and a spirit of thorough manliness; blending a genuine modesty with a dignified self-respect, which commanded the respect of all who heard him, not excepting even the judge who was about to deal with him as a convicted criminal. Scarcely, indeed, could there have been upon the bench itself, at that moment, an exception to the feeling which must have been wellnigh, if not altogether, universal in the crowded court room; that the well-marked contrast between the judicial tool of tyranny, and the unblenching " convict," bravely vindicating his just and generous " crime," was anything but favorable to the former. As the speech came to a close, with these emphatic words, — " I will do all I can for any man thus seized and held, though the inevitable penalty, of six months imprisonment and $1,000 fine for each offence, hangs over me : we have a common humanity ; you would do so, your manhood would require it ; and, no matter what the laws might be, you would honor yourself in doing it ; your friends would honor you for doing it ; your children, to all generations, would honor you for doing it ; and every good and honest man would say you had done right ; " — all the efforts of the court and marshal could not prevent its being greeted with loud and prolonged applause. The judge was, or affected to be, favorably influenced by the speech. " You have," said he, " presented considerations, to which I shall attach much weight. * * * * * * I am constrained to say, that the penalty in your case should be comparatively light." It was, " therefore," made twenty days' imprisonment, $100 fine, and the costs of prosecution. The trial of the remaining cases was, on motion of the prosecutor, postponed to a future term ; and the prisoners were consigned to the Cuyahoga County jail.

As the Ohio Supreme Court's refusal of the application for a writ of habeas corpus, before any of the prisoners had been sentenced, was on the ground that the cases were still pending ; and as that left the question open whether the writ would not be granted after sentence, a second application on behalf of BUSHNELL and LANGSTON, was made to Judge SCOTT, of that court, on the 17th of May. He immediately issued it, returnable before the full bench; and the sheriff, of Cuyahoga County, disregarding a written protest from the United States Marshal, against the removal of the men from jail, took them to Columbus, and, in obedience to the writ, brought them before the court on the morning of the 25th; when the case was argued at much length by A. G. RIDDLE and the State's Attorney General, WOLCOTT, in favor of discharging the prisoners; and on the other side, a printed brief, merely stating points and citing authorities, was presented without oral argument. The court took till the 30th to consider its opinion, when the discharge was refused, by three judges against, to two in favor of granting it.

The positions taken by the majority, Chief Justice SWAN and Judges SCOTT and PECK, were, that the Constitution, in the fourth article, second section, guarantees to the owner of an escaped Slave the right of reclamation; that intentionally to interfere for the purpose of rescuing an escaped Slave from the owner, is to violate the Constitution, whether the Acts of 1793 and 1850 are constitutional or not; that the question, in this case, is not whether the Act of 1850 is constitutional, in certain specified particulars, but whether Congress can pass *any* law for the reclamation of Slaves; that Congress has, from the earliest period, vindicated the constitutional right of the Slave-owner against unlawful interference; that such legislation, beginning when many of the framers of the Constitution were in Congress, has been acquiesced in by all departments of government, National and State, and the power of Congress has been recognized by the Supreme Court of the United States, and of every State where the question has been made; that if judges can overrule this unbroken current of decisions, then there is no limit upon judges, at any time, or under any circumstances; and that whatever difference of opinion may exist as to the power of Congress to punish rescues, as provided in the Acts of 1793 and 1850, its enactment of such laws is no such vital blow to constitutional rights or State sovereignty, as to demand of this court the organization of resistance.

Judges BRINKERHOFF and SUTLIFF dissented. The former held that the indictments, under which the prisoners were convicted, were fatally defective in not averring that the rescued man

6

was held to service in Kentucky, "*under the laws thereof;*" that
this defect is an illegality, for without the omitted words no
crime is charged, and, consequently, the judgment of the United
States District Court, on the indictments, is extra-judicial and
void; that on the face of the record, it appears that the person
rescued had been "deprived of his liberty without due process
of law," or any color of process, and therefore the rescue was
no crime, and any judicial procedure treating it as a crime, is
unconstitutional and void; that the Acts of Congress referred
to, and all warrants issued under them, are unconstitutional
and void, because they attempt to confer judicial power upon
commissioners, who are not appointed and paid in the manner
in which the Constitution requires that all judicial functionaries should be; that, therefore, the commissioner's warrant is
a nullity, and to rescue a person held under it is no crime, and
imprisonment to punish such rescue is an illegal restraint of
liberty; that Congress has, under the Constitution, no legislative power on the subject of rendition of fugitives from labor,
as is evident, both from the language of the Constitution and
from the history of its formation, that such rendition belongs
exclusively to the States, and is to be performed by *their* laws
and functionaries; that the question is not settled by the
usurpation of Congress, sanctioned by the Federal Judiciary,
through the medium of lame and contradictory reasonings, unwarranted assumptions, and false history; for the decisions of a
usurping party, in favor of its own assumptions, can settle
nothing; that the State decisions, the same way, have been decisions of acquiescence, rather than of independent inquiry;
that the agreement with himself, of such jurists as HORN-
BLOWER, WALWORTH, and WEBSTER, on this subject, and the
admission of a majority of his brethren that *they* would be
with him if this were a new question, show that it is not settled; that contemporaneous construction speaks with a divided
voice, for though Congress legislated early on the subject, so
did nearly or quite every one of the old States, and State legislation on it continued till the United States Supreme Court, in
the Prigg case, in 1842, assumed for the Federal Government
exclusive control of it; that, moreover, that court, by over-
turning, in the Dred Scott case, all its own previous decisions
as to the power of Congress over the Territories, has invited
us back to the consideration of first principles; and neither it

nor those who rely on its authority, have a right to complain if we accept the invitation; that only through the action of the State governments can the reserved rights and powers of the States be preserved, and the guarantees of individual liberty be vindicated; and that if the Federal Government is conceded to be, in the last resort, the authoritative judge of its own powers, the limitations of the Constitution will soon be obliterated, and that government will become practically omnipotent.

Judge SUTLIFF held that the Fugitive-Slave Act is unconstitutional, both because Congress has no power to legislate on the subject, and because the Act is repugnant to express provisions of the Constitution, in giving commissioners judicial power, in denying a jury-trial, withholding due process of law, and subverting the laws of the States for the protection of the rights of their citizens; that the State and Federal Judiciaries are left by the Constitution independent of each other, and it is the right and duty of the former not to suffer a question to be settled as to any case coming before it, against its own convictions of the rights of the State or its citizens; and that this is the only position to maintain, with due respect toward the Federal Judiciary, the independent State sovereignty contemplated by the framers of the Federal Government.

As soon as the decision was given, Marshal JOHNSON and the District Attorney told the sheriff that the journey made to Columbus, by his prisoners, in obedience to the writ of the State Court, must be regarded as a constructive escape from jail, and six days must be added to their term of imprisonment, in place of the six spent in the journey and at Columbus. But the sheriff, under advice of counsel, took a different view of his duty, and refused to detain them beyond the time first set. LANGSTON was accordingly discharged, two days after, on the 1st of June; his twenty days having then expired.

As the day approached — July 6 — set for the trial of the kidnappers, LOWE, DAVIS, and their Kentucky employers, forebodings of pretty certain conviction weighed heavily upon their minds, and naturally prompted plans to shun the issue. They tried, at first, for a judicial release, by the writ of habeas corpus. By falsely swearing that they were " illegally restrained of their liberty," when in fact they were at large, on bail, they easily enough obtained the writ from Judge MCLEAN; but to make it available, they must get into custody before the trial should begin; and, unfortunately for them, the Lorain sheriff, by a "very remarkable coincidence," had urgent business elsewhere whenever they attempted to give themselves into his keeping. So this plan failed. Negotiation was next employed. The Cleveland *Herald* says, that several weeks before the day of trial, "some of the Federal officials proposed to some outside friends of the rescuers, that the latter should plead *nolo contendere*, receive the mild fine of $20 each, and pay the costs; and the prosecution of the kidnappers should be abandoned. The offer was indignantly spurned." At last, however, only one day before the time of trial, the counsel of the kidnappers, R. H. STANTON, of Kentucky, prevailed on the United States District Attorney, not without much urgency, it is said, to consent that better terms should be proposed; in effect, that if Lorain County would stop where it was, so would the Federal Government. This offer was accordingly made to the Lorain prosecutor; and, on the 6th of July, was accepted. All the pending prosecutions, on both sides, were abandoned; and all the unconvicted prisoners were at once set free.

Differing judgments have been passed upon this result. The Pro-Slavery "Democratic" press treated it as a signal defeat of law and order, a victory of fanaticism and faction. Says the Cleveland *Plaindealer*, edited by the Cleveland postmaster, "the Government has been beaten, at last, with law, justice, and facts, all on its side; and Oberlin, with its rebellious higher-law creed, is triumphant." On the other hand, the great majority of the people in Northern Ohio, and, it would, perhaps, be safe to say, in the North generally, seem to have regarded it as a substantial triumph of justice and freedom over iniquity entrenched behind the forms of law. The Cleveland *Leader* says, with evident satisfaction, "the attempt to enforce the Fugitive-Slave Act on the Western Reserve, by government officials, for political effect, has resulted in a most disastrous defeat of the projectors, and of the whole scheme." And again, "it was the unanimous opinion of the public in general, and of the *Plaindealer* in particular, that it was a triumph; not a mere triumph, but a decided triumph for the rescuers." The Cleveland *Herald* even ventured the assertion, that "this has put an end to nigger-catching in Northern Ohio." The Sandusky *Commercial Register* exclaims, "what greater triumph could Freedom ask? The very hand which has been menacingly raised to crush her out, has been employed to place the laurels of victory upon her brow." A dispatch from Cleveland to the New-York *Tribune*, on the 6th of July, says, "the Government has backed down, and fully discharged the Oberlin rescuers, without trial or any concession on the part of the prisoners. One hundred guns are now firing in honor of the victory." The hundreds who gathered, as fast as the news spread, to congratulate the prisoners on their release, hailed it as a "signal triumph;" and Judge BRAYTON, of Newburgh, in an eloquent speech, at the railroad station, — whither an immense crowd, with martial music and jubilant shouts, escorted them, — regarded the event as cause of congratulation to them, to their friends, and to the nation.

A series of resolutions, adopted by the prisoners themselves, before leaving the jail, shows that, at all events, they did not feel themselves "subdued;" for, in one of them, they declared, that, "after all which has been inflicted on us, in the attempt to enforce the Fugitive-Slave Act, our hatred and opposition to it are more intense than ever. No fine or imprisonment, however enforced, by whatever court, can induce us to yield obedience; we will, hereafter, as we have, heretofore, help the fugitive to escape from those who would enslave him, under whatever authority they may act." And the "nearly three thousand," who came out at Oberlin to greet their return, almost literally emptying the town upon the border of the railroad, and then packing it into the great church; welcoming them, in the words of Professor MONROE, with "unqualified satisfaction and heartfelt joy;" did certainly receive them with a welcome befitting only the return of victors from a well-won field; and, moreover, manifested their conviction that Oberlin was still unconquered, by unanimously "resolving," in full assembly, and requesting the Town Council to enter on the records of the village, "that, in view of all the consequences attendant upon this prosecution, and all the light shed upon the subject, we express our greatly increased abhorrence of the Fugitive-Slave Act; and avow our determination, that no fugitive shall ever be taken from Oberlin, either with or without a warrant, if we have power to prevent it."

There was truth, too, we believe, in the eloquent professor's words of greeting, when he said, " you have come back without the shadow of a stain upon that strict integrity, which it is the duty and privilege of a Christian Anti-Slavery man to cherish. You have made no compromises with Slavery. There has been no bowing of the body, no bending of the knee. Erect, as God made you, you went into prison ; erect, as God made you, you have come out of prison." For, whatever may be thought of the transaction which immediately led to their release, we have heard of nothing connecting them with any questionable feature of it. They were not parties, we are told, to the negotiation of the compromise; nor, so far as appears, were they consulted about it at any stage of its progress.

But if to them, personally, the victor's palm may fairly be awarded, still, whether on the whole the issue of the contest was the signal victory for right and freedom, which so many have believed it, admits of serious question, and is more than doubted among the more radical of Anti-Slavery men. They think that the State of Ohio — whatever may be said of those of its upright citizens persecuted for a just, humane, and Christian act — has failed to do its duty, or maintain its dignity, or assert its rightful sovereignty against the arrogant assumptions of the Slave-power; that a majority of its Supreme Court has either faltered through fear, or betrayed the right through sympathy with the wrong; that the authorities of Lorain County have sadly erred in consenting to a compromise which lets a gang of kidnappers go unpunished, in order to save a company of righteous men from the apprehended consequences of their fidelity to right; and that thus the principle at stake has not been clearly vindicated, nor any ground of firm assurance won, against a repetition of the outrages perpetrated heretofore. They say, that, if the rescuers were guilty of no crime, and deserved no punishment, the State was bound to liberate them, unconditionally, by an act of unbought justice; but, if they had incurred the just penalty of violated law, it had no right to buy exemption for them by compromising the claims of law and justice in the case of other men, criminal or innocent; or, if it were still uncertain, till the trial should reveal it, what was their relation to righteous law, that question ought to have been settled first, before attempting to decide what could only, after that, be intelligently decided. So, too, if the alleged kidnappers had been indicted with good cause, say they, there could be no good cause for releasing them without trial; leaving them, if innocent, under an unjust imputation of guilt; permitting them, if guilty, to escape deserved punishment.

It is not easy to escape the force of this reasoning, as against the Governments, both State and Federal (for both are in like, if not equal, condemnation); or, we might say, against the people at large, whose fault it is, if these Governments are not the exponents and executors of their will. But, in relation to the struggling cause of Freedom, and its few and faithful champions wheresoever found, the result may be pronounced a victory; not a complete one, it is true, or to be regarded with unqualified satisfaction, but still (considering against what formidable odds it has been won, — of wicked statutes, and constitutional provisions, and judicial precedents, and courts eager to frame mischief by a law, and a corrupt, Pro-Slavery administration, and, we fear it must be said, scheming politicians, who, avowing friendliness to freedom, consent to compromise her claims for personal or party ends), an event to rejoice at and be thankful for, as one step forward in the march to final triumph. Even if it should be said, that nothing was won but an exchange of prisoners, better that, than, as too often has happened, the escape of the Slave-hunters unscathed, while the rescuers suffer all which base and tyrannical officials had meditated against them. Moreover, considered as a mere exchange of prisoners, the advantage was with the friends of Freedom; for they gained more than three for one.

Not, however, through the action of courts or government officials, State or Federal, or both, did this contest exert its best influence for the right. It stimulated discussion, roused popular feeling, extended and deepened the abhorrence felt toward Slave-catching and Slave-catchers' black acts, and all the executive and judicial machinery of legalized man-stealing, and called forth many an emphatic utterance of that sentiment, from pulpit, and press, and public meeting, and so helped on the preparation of the public mind for that inevitable death-grapple with the Slave-power, toward which all events are surely drifting us. While the affair was still in progress, large and enthusiastic gatherings were held at Jefferson, Painesville, and

many other places; at which stirring speeches were made, and
strong resolutions were adopted, manifesting a hearty sympathy with the men of Oberlin, and the cause for which they
were suffering. Of these, the largest, and behind none in enthusiasm, was held at Cleveland, on the 24th of May, in answer
to a call signed by five hundred persons, including judges and
lawyers, and distinguished citizens of various professions and
pursuits. The Cleveland papers state that, at the lowest estimate, from ten to twelve thousand persons were present.
Among the speakers were J. R. GIDDINGS, who presided;
Gov. CHASE, Judge TILDEN, Judge SPAULDING, E. WADE, J.
M. ROOT, E. K. CARTTER, and other men of note. Resolutions were adopted, "by a thundering vote," denouncing the
Dred Scott Decision, the Fugitive-Slave Act, the proceedings
of the District Court in the pending rescue-trials, the subserviency of the United States Supreme Court to objects of
party politics, and the Pro-Slavery policy of the Federal Administration; declaring that the Federal Government was not
made the final judge of the extent of its own powers, but
that "each party [Federal and State Government] has an
equal right to judge for itself, as well of infractions as of the
mode and measure of redress;" affirming the indispensable
need of an amendment of the Federal Judiciary system; expressing cordial sympathy with the imprisoned rescuers, and
recommending "that a fund be raised for their relief and in-
demnification."

Mr. GIDDINGS advocated an immediate application, to the
nearest judicial officer, for a writ of habeas corpus on behalf
of all the prisoners; and was ready, if all peaceful means
should fail, to maintain the liberty of the people against the
Fugitive-Slave Act by force. He called on all who would
submit to tyranny to speak out, but none replied. He asked
all to speak who were resolved to resist the enforcement of that
Act, when all other means fail, and was answered with a
"deafening roar from thousands of voices." J. M. ROOT said,
if the courts would not release the prisoners, "we would have
another meeting to talk it over." He thought that "whatever
else might happen, Ohio shall not, in God's name she *shall not*,
be made a hunting-ground for Slave-catchers." Gov. CHASE
spoke of the rescuers as "some of the most respected citizens

of the State, and as wrongfully imprisoned for an act which not one man in ten thousand would say was not right;" pledged himself, as chief executive of the State, that if the State Courts should issue process for the release of any prisoner, it should be executed; declared that the editor of the *Plaindealer* had uttered truth in saying, when the Fugitive-Slave Act was passed, that "it was infernal in its origin;" but he "did not counsel revolutionary measures;" * * * * * "the great remedy is in the people, at the ballot-box."

Just before the governor's arrival, the meeting had adopted, with enthusiasm, a resolution, appointing J. R. GIDDINGS, and two other able lawyers, a committee to carry out the suggestion of Mr. GIDDINGS, as to an immediate application for a writ of habeas corpus. We cannot help believing that if this movement had been promptly made, and some one of the magistrates, then on the ground, had issued the writ, immediately returnable, its service — with the governor at hand to sanction it, and his pledge fresh from his lips, that the process of the State Courts should be enforced, and a *posse* of ten thousand eager volunteers at call, and the sheriff, in whose immediate custody the prisoners were, much more than willing to obey the writ — would have been eminently easy; and, with all due forms of law, the men might have been set free in the presence of the rejoicing multitude, and such a moral victory won, moreover, as would have made the minions of the Slave-power shrink from any attempt to rearrest them, or would have ensured the right another triumph, had the contest been renewed. That would have been a day's work to go home from with honest exultation. That it was not done, there seems, in view of all the circumstances, but too much reason for believing was due to the countervailing influence of Gov. CHASE. That he held back the enthusiasm of the crowd, and did his utmost to prevent decisive action, is the impression sedulously given by one of the more "conservative," — in plainer English phrase, Pro-Slavery, — of his own party organs. The Cincinnati *Commercial* says, "his influence was potent in the preservation of peace. His words were calculated to restore public tranquillity,— not to influence the rage of fanaticism. He gave the people good counsel, of which they stood greatly in need. If there is any portion of the community more conservative than another, that portion should be especially grateful to the governor for his presence in Cleveland." And after his arrival at the meeting, all we hear of the Committee on the habeas corpus is, that "it subsequently met, and, Mr. GIDDINGS dissenting, decided to await the decision of the Supreme Court in the cases of BUSHNELL and LANGSTON." What the decision was, we have already stated. It has been publicly declared on the authority of "an influential member of the Republican party, in Ohio," that the decision was such as it was, through "fear of injuring CHASE's presidential prospects." And though, at the nomination, following soon after, for Chief Justice of the Supreme Court, Judge SWAN was not deemed by his party available enough to be re-nominated; yet, on the other hand, Judge SPAULDING, the choice of the more Anti-Slavery portion of the party, failed to get a single ballot in the nominating Convention, and a *compromise* was made upon Judge GHOLSON, a conservative, who, — the Cincinnati papers say, and he does not deny, — approves Judge SWAN's decision.

The Oberlin rescue-cases came to an end on the 14th of July, with a brilliant ovation to BUSHNELL, on his discharge from prison at the expiration of his sentence. An immense crowd, with banners and a band of music, escorted him from the prison to the cars, and took leave of him with hearty cheers. Many accompanied him to Oberlin, where he was greeted with a hundred guns, by an artillery company from Cleveland, which had preceded him for the purpose, and by the joyful shouts of five thousand people, in whose behalf Professor FAIRCHILD met him with a speech of welcome. Then moved the long procession to the church, where speeches from J. R. GIDDINGS, Judge SPAULDING, and other eloquent orators, singing by a choir of a hundred and fifty voices, music by instrumental bands, and other appropriate expressions of the general exultation, filled the long summer afternoon; and not till 6 o'clock the final words were spoken and the multitude dispersed.

Our last Report made mention of the case of a free colored man, in Washington, awaiting trial, on the charge of harboring his own son, a Slave. He was tried, and convicted on the 28th of March; though all that was proved against him was, that the boy having run off, he knew not whither, he did not give him up on demand of the officer sent for him; nor, at the officer's request, go in search of him, and bring him back. After waiting in prison forty-nine days, without a bed and with poor and scanty food, he was sentenced, on the 16th of May, to pay a fine amounting, with costs, to about $ 200, and to remain in prison till it should be paid. His name is EMANUEL MASON. He was, formerly, a Slave in Maryland; but, some years ago, being crippled with inflammatory rheumatism, and given up by the doctors, as incurable, his mistress sold him to himself, for $ 300, after finding that no one else would give so much for him. Having paid for himself, by instalments, and meanwhile partially recovered his health, his wife being still a Slave, he hired her time by the year, and they kept house in Washington, and reared several children, wholly at their own expense, his wife's mistress *appropriating* them, as they became old enough to be sold or put to service. "Little BEN," a boy of ten years, whom he was convicted of *harboring*, was his youngest child, and, for two or three years, the only one the plunderers of his home had left him. A number of respectable citizens of Washington, who had known MASON for years, in petitioning the judge for a lenient sentence, declared him "to be an industrious, moral, temperate, poor, peaceable, honest, man." And such a man it is, who is robbed of his children, one by one, then of his wife (who had been taken from him about a year before little BEN's escape), and, at last, punished with barbarous severity for not joining the hunt to run down the last youngling of his little flock, and, with his own hands, give him over to the devourers. On the 23d of January last, almost ten months after his conviction, the Washington correspondent of the *Anti-Slavery Standard* writes, that "he lies in jail, a wretched old man; his fine unpaid, and he complains bitterly of the treatment he receives." But, on the 7th of February, the same writer says, "President BUCHANAN has pardoned MANUEL MASON out of jail, and remitted his fine."

JOHN BROWN.

The year just past will long be memorable for the bold attempt of JOHN BROWN and his companions to burst the bolted door of the southern house of bondage, and lead out the captives, by a more effectual way than they had yet known;

an attempt, in which, it is true, the little band of heroes dashed themselves to bloody death; but, at the same time, shook the prison-walls from summit to foundation, and shot wild alarm into every tyrant-heart in all the Slave-land. What were the plans and purposes of the noble old man is not precisely known, and, perhaps, will never be; but, whatever they were, there is reason to believe they had been long maturing, — brooded over silently and secretly, with much earnest thought, and under a solemn sense of religious duty. As early as the fall of 1857, he began to organize his band, chiefly from among the companions of his warfare against the Border Ruffians in Kansas. Nine or ten of these spent the winter of 1857–8 in Iowa, where a Col. FORBES was to have given them military instruction; but, he having fallen out with BROWN, did not join them; and AARON D. STEVENS, one of the company, took his place.

About the middle of April, 1858, they left Iowa, and went to Chatham, Canada, where, on the 8th of May, was held a convention, called by a written circular, which was sent to such persons only as could be trusted. The convention was composed mostly of colored men, a few of whom were from the States, but the greater part residents in Canada; with no white men but the organized band already mentioned. A "Provisional Constitution," which BROWN had previously prepared, was adopted, and the members of the convention took an oath to support it. Its manifest purpose was to insure a perfect organization of all who should join the expedition, whether free men or insurgent Slaves; and to hold them under such strict control as to restrain them from every act of wanton or vindictive violence, all waste or needless destruction of life or property, all indignity or unnecessary severity to prisoners, and all immoral practices; in short, to keep the meditated movement free from every possibly avoidable evil ordinarily incident to the armed uprising of a long-oppressed and degraded people. Beginning with a preamble, which declares Slavery in the United States to be a "most barbarous and unprovoked war, by one portion of the citizens against another, the only conditions of which are perpetual imprisonment and servitude, or absolute extermination," it goes on to deal with Slave-holders and their abettors according to the principles of civilized warfare. But, though it provides for the choice of executive, legislative, and judicial officers of the organization, bearing the same titles as those of the United States, it expressly disclaims any purpose to overthrow any government, state or general, or to dissolve the Union, or to look to anything more than "amendment and repeal." BROWN was unanimously chosen commander-in-chief of the little army, and J. H. KAGI, A. D. STEVENS, ALBERT HAZLETT, JOHN E. COOKE, and others, as subordinate military officers; KAGI was made secretary of war, and RICHARD REALF (who afterwards deserted the enterprise), secretary of state. It was intended to proceed, at once, to action; but, when the convention closed, news came that FORBES had betrayed their design to the government; and this, with intelligence from Kansas, which BROWN regarded as rendering his presence there advisable, caused the expedition to be postponed; and the company soon after disbanded.

In the summer of 1859, BROWN, under the assumed name of SMITH, hired a farm in Maryland, known as the Kennedy farm, on which were three unoccupied houses, about five miles from Harper's Ferry, in Virginia; and thither, from time to time, his followers gathered, and arms and munitions of war were transported, carefully boxed up, and passing as farming tools, and implements to be used in the opening of mines, which it was given out were to be worked somewhere in that region. About two hundred Sharp's rifles and two hundred revolvers had been procured, nearly three years before, and deposited, for a time, at Tabor, Iowa, and afterward in Ashtabula County, Ohio; whence they were taken, first to Chambersburg, Pa., and then to BROWN's hired house, in Maryland. To these were added a thousand or fifteen hundred pikes, manufactured in Connecticut, and a few swords and bayonets. While these preparations were going on, the Government received distinct, though anonymous, warning of the approaching movement. The following letter was received by Secretary FLOYD, not long after its date; but, strangely enough, does not appear to have led to any action or investigation on the part of the Government.

"CINCINNATI, Aug. 20, 1859.

"SIR, — I have lately received information of a movement of so GREAT IMPORTANCE that I feel it to be my duty to impart it to you without delay. I have discovered the existence

7

of a secret association, having for its object THE LIBERA-
TION OF THE SLAVES, AT THE SOUTH, BY A GEN-
ERAL INSURRECTION. The leader of the movement is
OLD JOHN BROWN, late of Kansas. He has been in
Canada, during the winter, drilling the negroes there, and they
are only waiting his word to start for the South, to assist the
Slaves. They have one of the leading men, a white man, in an
armory in Maryland; where it is situated, I have not been able
to learn. As soon as everything is ready, those of their number who are in the Northern States and Canada are to come, in
small companies, to their rendezvous, which is in the mountains
in Virginia. They will pass down through Pennsylvania and
Maryland, and enter Virginia at HARPER'S FERRY. Brown
left the North about three or four weeks ago, and will ARM
THE NEGROES and strike the BLOW in a few weeks, and so
that whatever is done must be done at once. They have a
large quantity of arms at their rendezvous, and probably distri-
buting them already. As I am not fully in their confidence,
this is all the information I can give you. I dare not sign my
name to this, but I trust that you will not disregard the warning on that account."

    REDPATH's Biography of BROWN states, that the night of
October 24 was the time originally set for the descent on
Harper's Ferry; and the chief reason for the change, which was
suddenly made, to an earlier day, was said by one of the company to be, "that they suspected there was a Judas" among
them. "But this decision," REDPATH adds, "however necessary, was unfortunate; for the men from Canada, Kansas, New
England, and the neighboring Free States, who had been told
to be prepared for the event on the 24th of October, and were
ready to do their duty at Harper's Ferry, at that time, were unable to join their captain at this earlier period. Many, who
started to join the liberators, halted half way; for the blow had
already been struck, and their captain made a captive. The
negroes, also, in the neighboring counties, who had promised to
be ready on the 24th of October, were confused by this precipi-
tate attack; and, before they could act in concert, were
watched, overpowered, and deprived of every chance to join
their heroic liberators." What are the grounds for belief in
these statements, we have no means of knowing, nor would
they be likely to be disclosed, as events have turned; but the
extensive preparation of arms and munitions, so far beyond
what his actual followers could use, would certainly seem to

argue BROWN's own expectation of a much larger force when the decisive hour should come; and from all we know of his character, it appears more probable that he had substantial reasons for his expectation, than that he deliberately acted, in a matter of such moment, on vague and groundless hopes. If the time, when the whole truth about this enterprise can be safely revealed, should come while those yet live who can reveal it, amazement at its boldness may possibly, in part, give place to admiration of its sagacity; and agreement may be general with the opinion of a bitterly hostile critic, VALLANDIGHAM, the Pro-Slavery Congressman of Southern Ohio, that "certainly it was one of the best-planned and best-executed conspiracies that ever failed."

But, leaving speculation, we return to known facts. On Sunday evening, October 16, the invaders held their final council, and, after full discussion, decided unanimously for immediate action. This done, BROWN said, " now, gentlemen, let me press this one thing on your minds. You all know how dear life is to you, and how dear your lives are to your families; and in remembering that, consider that the lives of others are as dear to them as yours are to you; do not, therefore, take the life of any one, if you can possibly avoid it; but if it is necessary to take life in order to save your own, then make sure work of it." That night, a little after ten, he entered Harper's Ferry with twenty-one followers (sixteen white and five colored), extinguished the lights of the town, occupied the buildings of the United States Armory, and took prisoners the three watchmen and the watchman of the Potomac bridge. Others, outside of the town, cut the telegraph wires, and, somewhat later, after the train had passed, tore up the railroad track. The men assigned to this part of the work, afterwards escaped. At midnight, the man who came to relieve the watchman on the bridge was hailed by BROWN's sentinels, and, thinking they were robbers, fled and gave an alarm, of which, however, nothing seems to have come. Meanwhile, a detachment under STEVENS was sent to the house of Col. LEWIS WASHINGTON, four miles from the town, where they arrived a little after midnight, made him prisoner, took his carriages and horses, and such arms as they found, and proclaimed liberty to his Slaves, accompanied by whom, they returned to the armory, stopping by the way to take a Mr. ALLSTADT and his son, and free his Slaves, who also went with them. A little after one o'clock, the eastward-going train arrived, and was stopped at the bridge. One man — afterward ascertained to be the colored porter of the railroad station — refusing to stop at command, was shot and mortally wounded. After a detention of nearly two hours, BROWN sent word to the conductor that he might go on with his train; but he did not venture to do so till after daylight.

Soon after the return of STEVENS and his party, with their prisoners and the liberated Slaves, COOKE, C. P. TIDD, LEEMAN, and four Slaves, were ordered across the river, with Colonel WASHINGTON's large wagon, to take TERENCE BURNS, and his brother, and their Slaves; and while COOKE and LEEMAN held the BURNSES prisoners, in their own house, TIDD and the Slaves were to go on to BROWN's house, load in the arms, and bring them down to a school-house, standing about a mile from the ferry, stopping on their way down for the prisoners and their guard. Then COOKE and one of the Slaves was to remain and guard the arms, LEEMAN was to return to the armory with the prisoners, and TIDD, with the other Slaves, was to go back for the rest of the arms.

While this was doing, the work went on in the town. As day dawned, and men began to go out from their houses, all who appeared in the street, and the workmen of the armory, as they approached the buildings, were arrested, and imprisoned in the armory; but with assurances that they would be un-harmed, and that the sole object of their captors was to free the Slaves. By eight o'clock the number of prisoners ex-ceeded sixty. BROWN, with his sons, OLIVER and WATSON, STEVENS, and two others, occupied the armory-grounds; KAGI, LEEMAN (after his return with his prisoners from the Maryland side), and three others, held the lower part of the town and Hall's Rifle Works, on a small island in the Shenandoah; OWEN BROWN, FRANCIS J. MERRIAM, and BARCLAY COPPOC, with COOKE and TIDD, were on the Maryland side, doing duty at the Kennedy farm, the school-house, and between the two; and the other six were standing guard at bridges, street corners, and public buildings. During the whole forenoon the town, with its two or three thousand inhabitants, was held by a force of seventeen men. The hotels were laid under requisition to

little worth and so perilous to hold, that in the end they would
be glad to escape from a life of harassing inquietude, by abolish-
ing a system already, by that time, half disintegrated. How
far such expectations, if really cherished, as there seems reason
to believe that something like them was, were likely to be
realized if the original plan had been carried out, we will not
stop here to consider. Not by such means, the event has shown,
was the bondman's exodus foreordained; or, if by such, the
fulness of the time had not yet come for his passage through
the red sea to the promised land of Freedom. Not to accomplish such a work, but — may we not say, in view of what came
after? — for an achievement nobler far, and mightier in its
beneficent influence on behalf of truth and right and oppressed
humanity, had GOD raised up and qualified and sent forth the
brave old hero-martyr and his handful of generous young en-
thusiasts, not unworthy to follow such a leader. It was not
decreed that they should do what they attempted; at least,
not in the way they undertook it. They were too few to break
for the Slave a path to Freedom through the hostile array of a
Slave-holding nation in arms; but not too few to bear a glorious testimony, before that nation and all nations, that the cause
of impartial Freedom, of justice to the poorest and weakest of
GOD's children, is a cause worth dying for; and can inspire
souls, large enough to comprehend its worth, with courage to
smile at danger, and strength to triumph over death. And the
power of such a testimony who can measure? How far it
shall reach, how long it shall act unexhausted, nay, with still-
growing force, who can estimate? It certainly looks strange,
at first view, that one so well-fitted as JOHN BROWN had often
shown himself, for all the exigencies of guerilla warfare, should
let slip the favorable moment for escape from enemies who, he
could not have doubted, would speedily be gathering around
him in overwhelming numbers. But "there's a Divinity that
shapes our ends." The firm believer in a universal Providence,
which lets not a sparrow fall unnoticed, nor leaves unnumbered
one hair of all our heads, will readily admit, as the easiest solution of the seeming mystery, that the shrewd, sagacious leader,
being but an instrument of One far wiser than himself, had
been predestined to a higher use than even the success of his
military plans could have attained. Nor was he, we may be-

lieve, unconscious of this possibility, which he appears to have taken into account when calculating beforehand the chances of his bold adventure. For, writing from his Virginian prison after sentence of death had been passed upon him, he says, "before I began my work at Harper's Ferry I felt assured that, in the *worst event*, it would certainly PAY;" and expresses his belief that he should have kept to his own plan, if GOD's had not been "infinitely better."

So, by the overruling Providence, he was diverted from his purpose of an early retreat. Through what suggestions to his mind this was effected, may not be wholly known; but one controlling reason was his wish to show the people that his prisoners were safe from insult and abuse while in his power; and thus, if possible, to let them see the character of his movement: — that it was no raid for vengeful or wanton slaughter, but a humane attempt to free the enslaved with only so much violence as wrongful resistance by the oppressors should make unavoidable in self-defence. He had lingered till about noon of Monday, the 17th, when a colonel of militia, with a hundred men, arrived from Charlestown. The colonel formed two companies of the citizens of Harper's Ferry, and sent one of them to occupy the Galt House, in the rear of the arsenal, and to post a strong guard on Shenandoah bridge; while one of his own companies crossed the Potomac in boats, two miles above the ferry, marched down on the Maryland side, and took possession of the Potomac bridge, with orders to let no one pass. "The insurgents," he says, "were at that time "variously estimated" by the citizens, at "from three hundred to five hundred strong." BROWN's sentinels, at the Shenandoah bridge, were first attacked by the Charlestown Guards. WILLIAM THOMPSON was taken prisoner, and another was killed. Next, KAGI, and his four men were driven from the rifle works, and attempted to cross the river. Four reached a rock, in the middle of it, and kept up the fight, two hundred Virginians, by this time, firing on them from both sides of the river, till KAGI fell, "riddled with balls," one of his men was killed, and another mortally wounded. The other then surrendered, and, with his wounded companion, who died twelve hours after, was imprisoned in the town. LEEMAN had just before been sent, it is supposed, by KAGI, with a message to Captain BROWN, and was seen, pursued, overtaken in the river while trying to cross, and basely shot by one of the militia, after he had surrendered. Meanwhile, Captain AVIS, with one of the Harper's Ferry companies, occupied the houses around the armory-buildings, and a sharp skirmish ensued. A Captain TURNER, while raising his rifle to fire, was shot dead by a sentinel at the arsenal-gate. DANGERFIELD NEWBY, a colored man, of BROWN's company; JIM, one of Colonel WASHINGTON's newly liberated Slaves; and a free colored man, who had lived on WASHINGTON's estate, were killed while fighting as bravely as the bravest. Mr. BECKHAM, mayor of the town, venturing, though unarmed, within range of the rifles, was accidentally killed. OLIVER BROWN received a fatal shot, had barely time to retire within the gate, and died without a word. The prisoners in the armory, being in some danger from the firing of their friends outside, wished that, if possible, terms might be made to ensure their safety; and at the request of one of them, Mr. KITZMILLER, STEVENS went out with him, bearing a flag of truce, to attempt negotiation, but was shot down, and taken prisoner. Witnesses at BROWN's trial spoke also of another of his men, probably DAUPHIN THOMPSON, who, at some time during the day, went out on a like errand, under a flag of truce, and was shot, and, it would seem, mortally wounded.

Enraged at the death of Mayor BECKHAM, a number of young Virginians, eager for vengeance, rushed to the hotel where WILLIAM THOMPSON was held a prisoner, unarmed and bound, and would have murdered him, at once, in the public parlor had not a Miss FOUKE, the hotel-keeper's sister, interposed, and with much difficulty prevailed upon them not to shoot him *in the house.* They dragged him roughly to the bridge, and deaf to his appeal, " don't take my life — a prisoner," shot him and threw him from the bridge, and sent a volley of bullets into his body as it lay on the rocks where it lodged. "Before he reached the ground, five or six shots had been fired into his body;" so testified one of the murderers, a son of HUNTER, counsel for the State, in BROWN's trial. Miss FOUKE in a letter, written for publication, a few weeks afterward, clearing herself from suspicion of having acted from humane feeling toward the helpless prisoner, assigns these as the "three powerful reasons" for her interference: — "first, my sister-in-law was lying in the adjoining room very ill, under the influence of a nervous chill, from sheer fright, and if they had carried out their design it would have proved fatal to her, no doubt. In the second place, I considered it a great outrage to kill the man in the house, however much he deserved to die. Thirdly, I am emphatically a law and order woman, and wanted the self-condemned man to live, that he might be disposed of by the law." So she shielded him, "*without touching him*," as she is careful to say, in italics, till assured by one of the murderers that he should not be shot in the house. "That," she adds, "was all that I desired." The letter concludes with "I am happy to assure you that I have a birthright in the 'Old Dominion.'" We can easily believe it. From the murder of THOMPSON, the youthful chivalry of Virginia went back to bring out STEVENS, and, as young HUNTER testified, "serve him in the same way;" but finding him suffering from wounds thought to be fatal, they were at length dissuaded from their purpose. Captain SIMMS, of a militia company from Maryland, who arrived about 5 o'clock, was just in time to prevent the cowardly atrocity; for, as he stated in his testimony at BROWN's trial, he "saw STEVENS, and shamed some young men who were endeavoring to shoot him as he lay in bed, apparently dying."

About the time THOMPSON was murdered, a body of men came in from Martinsburg, and, forming in two divisions, attacked at once the front and rear of the armory-buildings. One party broke the windows of a building in which some of the prisoners were confined, and eighteen of them escaped. BROWN and his scanty remnant, pressed by the overwhelming number of the assailants, retired to the engine-house, firing as they fell back. Fifty men attacked the engine-house, but were repulsed, with a loss of two killed and five or six wounded, including one of the leaders of the assault. WATSON BROWN, we are told, though mortally wounded five or six hours before, rallied his failing strength to join his comrades in repelling this attack. The besieging forces, which had been increasing all the afternoon, and amounted now to fifteen hundred men, were placed under one command; and so disposed as completely to surround the armory-buildings. To oppose them, BROWN had but three

or four unwounded men. Ten or twelve of the rescued Slaves
were still with him, armed with pikes; but none of these
appear to have taken part, at any time, in the fighting; whether
for want of will, or for want of skill with firearms, and of opportunity to use other weapons, we have no certain information.
An offer, from Brown, to release his captives if his men might
cross the bridge unharmed, was rejected; while the coming on
of night stopped the firing on both sides.

Before morning, Colonel Lee arrived, with ninety United
States marines, and two pieces of artillery; and took a post
near the engine-house. In preparation for the final struggle,
the besieged had pierced the door and walls of the engine-house
with loopholes for rifles; and with cool courage awaited the
onset, — four men opposed to four hundred times their number.
As the cannon could not be used without danger to the captive
citizens, the assault was made without its help. First, a flag of
truce was sent to the besieged, with a demand of unconditional
surrender; and a promise of protection from immediate violence, and of a trial by law. Brown answered with his former
proposition, — in substance, that he should be permitted to
march out with his men, and arms, and prisoners, unpursued, to
the second toll-gate, when they would free the prisoners; then
the soldiers might pursue them, and they would escape or fight,
as best they could. He would accept no other terms. These
were refused, and the flag-bearer withdrew. The marines then
advanced in two lines, on each side of the door, and tried to
force it with heavy sledge-hammers; but, failing in this, they
seized a long ladder, and, advancing at a run, burst open the
door at the second blow. They rushed to the breach, led by
Major Russell and Lieutenant Green. Anderson, one of
the besieged, was shot, and fell dead; the other three fired,
killed one marine, and wounded one or two others, when the
firing ceased; and, the next moment, the marines poured in.
Though Brown had laid down his arms, yet Lieutenant Green
struck him to the earth with his sabre, and several times
repeated the blow after he was down; and a soldier twice
thrust a bayonet into his prostrate body. Edwin Coppoc and
Shields Green, a colored man, "only," according to a Virginian writer, " escaped immediate death, by accident; the soldiers
not at once distinguishing them from the captive citizens and

Slaves." The same writer says, "the citizen captives, released
from their long confinement, hurried out to meet their friends,
with every demonstration of joy; while the bloody carcasses
of the dead and dying outlaws were dragged into the lawn
amidst the howlings and execrations of the people." From
the Baltimore *American* we learn that, "when the insurgents
were brought out, some dead, and others wounded, they were
greeted with execrations, and only the precautions that
had been taken saved them from immediate execution. The
crowd, nearly every man of which carried a gun, swayed with
tumultuous excitement; and cries of 'shoot them!' 'shoot
them!' rang from every side." The prisoners were taken to
the guard-house, where STEVENS, also, was brought soon after;
but though three of them were wounded, it was supposed, unto
death, yet they had only the floor or bare benches to lie on.
COPPOC begged, in vain, for a bed, or even a blanket, for WAT-
SON BROWN, who was really dying. "I took off my coat,
and placed it under him," he afterwards wrote to WATSON's
mother, "and held his head in my lap, in which position he
died, without a groan or a struggle." By the next day, as
appears from the newspaper reports, the wounded men had
been provided with "miserable shakedowns, laid on the floor,
and covered with some old bedding."

We have omitted from our narrative certain barbarities,
practiced by the Virginians, after the tide of battle began to
turn in their favor, and panic-fear was giving way to, or taking
the form of, brutal vengeance; the gross indignities offered to
the bodies of their slaughtered enemies, which, as related by
the Pro-Slavery press of the region, seem more like the deeds
of wild Camanches, than like those of men who claim a Christian civilization and boast of an exalted chivalry. But, in the
light of what is told, let the world say which of the contending
parties had the better right to claim the name of chivalrous or
civilized.

While the events, above related, were passing in the town,
COOKE and his four companions, with a number of rescued
Slaves, were on the other side of the Potomac. TIDD had
brought down one load of arms to the school-house, and gone
back for another, when COOKE began to hear the firing at the
ferry; but, although anxious to know the cause, he kept his

post at the school-house, as he had been ordered, till TIDD's
return, about four o'clock in the afternoon, with the second
load. Then, taking one of the negroes, he went down toward
the ferry. On his way he heard, at several points, from persons whom he met, accounts and rumors of what was doing on
the other side; and sent the negro back to tell TIDD what he
had heard. When opposite the ferry he climbed the mountain, for a better view; and saw his friends surrounded, and the
Virginians on High Street, about half a mile from him, firing
down upon them. To draw the hostile fire on himself, he
discharged his rifle; his fire was returned, and several shots
were exchanged, till one cut off a small branch he held by,
causing him a fall and severe bruising. Then he went down
the mountain, saw some persons whom he knew, and made
inquiries of them, as to the position and number of the hostile
troops, and hastened back to the school-house. It was dark
when he arrived there; he found no one, and got no answer to
his repeated calls. Going on towards BROWN's house, he met
his comrades and one of the negroes, and learned that the
other negroes had disappeared while TIDD was gone for the rest
of his party. After a short conference, thinking it useless to
attempt to join their friends across the river, the party proceeded to BROWN's house, got a few necessary articles, went a
short distance into the timber on the mountain-side, and slept
till three o'clock Tuesday morning; when one of them awoke,
and finding that the negro had left them, roused the rest, and
they went to the mountain-top; thence after a few hours, to
the other side of the mountain; and, after dark, crossed the
valley to the range beyond. Making their way northward,
they were, on the 25th, near Chambersburg, Pa.; when COOKE,
having ventured down into a settlement to get provisions, was
betrayed by a villain named LOGAN, in whom, it seems, that in
his extremity, almost starved, and nearly worn out with fatigue,
he confided; and by whom, and one FITZHUGH, he was captured, after a desperate struggle, and given up to the authorities
of Pennsylvania. On the 28th, he was surrendered, on the
requisition of Virginia, and consigned to the Charlestown jail.
On the 22nd, a man was arrested in Carlisle, Pa., supposed,
at first, to be COOKE, and afterwards to be ALBERT HAZLETT,
another of BROWN's officers. Though he denied having been

at Harper's Ferry, and the proof of his identity seems not to have been very clear, he was, on the 5th of November, given up to the authorities of Virginia, as HAZLETT, on the requisition of Governor WISE. TIDD, MERRIAM, OWEN BROWN, and BARCLAY COPPOC made their escape.

A report that COOKE was on the mountain, only three miles off, reached Harper's Ferry on Tuesday morning, the 18th; whereupon the Independent Grays, of Baltimore, set off to find him, but soon returned with the arms and ammunition left by BROWN's men at the school-house; and, each man having appropriated to himself a SHARPE's rifle and a pair of revolvers, they deposited the residue in the arsenal. In the evening, a party of marines, with a few volunteers, went to BROWN's house, where they found a quantity of blankets, clothing, provisions, &c., with a number of pikes, copies of the Chatham Constitution, books, papers, and documents; and, what was, at first, supposed to be especially important, a carpet-bag, belonging to BROWN, filled with letters and papers, which it was expected would "throw much light on the affair," and show connection with it, on the part of prominent men in different parts of the country; but which, upon examination, we believe, were found to contain nothing of particular moment. The same day, as the Baltimore *American* tells us, "perfect order having been restored, the military, with the exception of the United States Marines, who remained in charge of the prisoners, left in various trains for home. The reporter of the New-York *Herald* states, that "as soon as the neighbors around the Kennedy farm learned of BROWN's capture, they rifled the house of its contents. The wearing-apparel, boots, quilts, blankets, &c., were speedily appropriated by the people, some of whom, we were assured, were sadly in want of them. Barrels of flour were rolled out; the cooking-stove, and its appurtenances were removed; loaves of bread were distributed to the hungry; and, in fact, in a short time the house was completely sacked."

The strife with shot and steel was over. It ended on that Tuesday morning, the 18th of October, when the armed array of despotism, with overwhelming strength of numbers, broke the last remnant of the heroic, little, liberating band; and shared it between slaughter and captivity. As the brave old captain lay on the bloody floor, sorely wounded and a prisoner, between his dead and his dying son, a mark for the scoffs and curses of a rabble frenzied with fear and savage vengeance, (and by so much as the former feeling had been abject, when they deemed him strong, by so much was the latter bitter and ferocious, when they saw him helpless), men thought and said that he was utterly defeated. And so, in that strife of shot and steel, he was; but not so in the *essence* of the conflict, of which the strife of shot and steel was only a rude, transient form. From that hour, indeed, began his course of victory; of triumph following triumph, in continuous succession, achieved with tongue, with pen, by manly bearing, by constant revelations of the firm, unconquered soul, the generous heart, and pure, unselfish purpose; by the simplicity of transparent truth and daylight frankness; by quiet gentleness; by steady faith in God, and the almightiness of right; all culminating in that last victory over death, and what was meant for ignominy, which showed the grave as an open gate to life, and turned the intended shame to everlasting honor, "making the gallows glorious like the cross." He extorted admiration and respect, even from his enemies, and filled his friends and the friends of Freedom with an honest pride in him as, for the time, the most conspicuous representative of the bondman's cause; and one whose character, as it came fully out to light, — however he might have erred in judgment, as all men do at times, — would not reflect discredit on the noblest cause. He won from all but utter baseness, and almost from that, a recognition, willing or reluctant, of his deep sincerity; of his having been impelled to action by earnest good-will, and a clear conviction that his cause was just, and his measures, in the existing exigency, right. The candid were convinced, and even the captious were .compelled to own, that his warfare was conducted as humanely as war can be; and with perfect singleness of purpose, to free the Slaves at as little cost of life and property, as that mode of liberation could permit. He made it plain to all, hardly excepting those who *would not* see, that his enterprise proceeded on a principle most sharply defined to his own perception, and apprehended with a most tenacious grasp; that he acted, in strictest logical consistency, with premises which he no more doubted than he did his own existence, and which were, moreover, held in theory as true by the whole nation, though with a most *in*consistent practice; that he regarded himself (and rightly, reasoning from those premises), as acting wholly on the defensive, against a terrible aggression, no whit the less aggressive or the less unjust because so long continued and so long submitted to; and, therefore, no less rightfully to be resisted, in the persons of all who forcibly uphold it, than highway robbery or piracy; while the blood, shed unavoidably in such resistance, would, as in every other case, be on the aggressor's, and not on the resistant's head. And he held his sharp-cut thought, aglow with the flameless heat of his earnest, still, enthusiasm, so long, so steadily, so firmly, on the nation's heart, unconsciously, involuntarily, laid open to it, that it must have burnt in an uneffaceable impression which, though hidden now by policy and fear of consequences, is secretly shaping, we doubt not, the nation's thought; and will, some day, give course and character to the issues of its life. Such victories, the imprisoned, dying hero won. His warlike achievements and attempts served as a background for a more distinct display of moral power; their immediate results had set him prominently before the nation and the world, so that every word and movement could be heard and seen. More dangerous to Slavery, than all his pikes and rifles and revolvers, were the bold, true words he spoke; the noble dignity with which he fronted the world's gaze; the quiet exhibition which he made of a constancy and calmness unshaken and unruffled by failure and its consequences, and of a confidence in right and in its success, at last, which lived on in the midst of outward disaster and seeming defeat, uttering such prophecies, as by the very laws of human nature, always help on their own fulfilment; the watchful fidelity, which turned every opportunity to account for the bearing of his testimony to the truth for which he suffered; his steadfast refusal to sanction, by acceptance of the tendered sacred offices of a Slave-holding religion, the pretension of its ministers to be servants of the Christ he believed in, and of the Father God he worshipped; and, in short, the emphatic attestation of his whole demeanor to the worth and power of Anti-Slavery principle, the strength of its hold on manly hearts, and the deeds and endurance to which it can prompt for the promotion of its triumph.

While the dead and wounded yet lay on the lawn before the engine-house, BROWN was assailed with questions by the by-standers, "which," the Baltimore *American* says, "he answered clearly and freely. He talked calmly to those about him, defending his course, and avowing that he had only done what was right." The modesty of genuine worth speaks out in his characteristic answers to two of the questions put to him. "Are you Captain BROWN, of Kansas?" "I am sometimes called so." ["He never assumed the title of captain," says REDPATH, "even in Kansas, where titles were as common as proper names."] "Are you Osawatomie BROWN?" "I tried to do my duty there." In the words of REDPATH, "this sentence was a key to his whole life. Neither honor nor glory moved him; the voice of duty was the only one he heard." When asked if he expected to kill people, in order to carry his point, he answered, "I did not wish to do so, but you forced us to it." He reminded the questioners that he had the town at his mercy; that he could have burnt it, and murdered the inhabitants, but did not; he had treated the prisoners with courtesy. "His conversation," says the *American*, "bore the impression of the conviction that whatever he had done to free Slaves was right, and that, in the warfare in which he was engaged, he was entitled to be treated with all the respect of a prisoner of war."

Hundreds of men from Richmond, Alexandria, Baltimore, and other places, came into the town on the mid-day train, and among them Governor WISE, who "boiled over" with wrath, as a Virginian writer says, when he learned what a mere handful of men the people had suffered to conquer the town and hold it so long. In the afternoon he visited the prisoners, at the guard-house, and conversed at much length with BROWN, who, according to the writer just quoted, "was frank and communicative, answering all questions without reserve, except such as might implicate his associates, not yet killed or taken." When reminded by the governor, that his end was, probably, near, and he would better think of eternity [HENRY A. WISE talking in that strain to JOHN BROWN!] his answer was, in substance, "you are not likely to be more than fifteen or twenty years behind me in the journey to eternity, a very trifling difference, and I want *you* to be prepared; whether I go in fifteen months or fifteen days or fifteen hours, I am prepared to go; you Slave-holders have a heavy responsibility, and it behooves you to prepare more than it does me." What the governor thought of him after this interview, he told, in a speech to the people of Richmond, after his return. "They are mistaken," said he, "who take him to be a madman. He is a bundle of the best nerves I ever saw, — cut and thrust and bleeding and in bonds. He is a man of clear head, of courage, fortitude, and simple ingenuousness. He is cool, collected, and indomitable; and it is but just to him, to say, that he was humane to his prisoners; and he inspired me with great trust in his integrity, as a man of truth. He is a fanatic, vain and garrulous, but firm and truthful and intelligent. His men, too, who survive, except the free negroes with him, are like him. * * * * * * Colonel WASHINGTON says, 'he was the coolest and firmest man he ever saw, in defying danger and death.'" Whoever is at all familiar with the governor's illimitable displays, with pen and tongue, may be excused for smiling at his coupling "vain and garrulous" with the name of BROWN; but his words of eulogy are, perhaps, worth all the more for this little fibrous fringe still hanging to them, to show how they were torn out of him, in spite of his prejudices, by sheer force of the old man's native nobleness.

The next day, he was visited by Senator MASON, of Virginia, VALLANDIGHAM, member of Congress from Ohio, and other "distinguished gentlemen," who held a long conversation with him, evidently aiming and hoping to draw from him some statement which could be used against their political opponents; but, in this they were signally disappointed. The reporter of the New-York *Herald* states that Colonel LEE offered to keep all visitors from the room, if the wounded men were annoyed or pained by them; "but BROWN said he was not annoyed, but was glad to be able to make himself and his motives clearly understood. He converses freely, fluently, and cheerfully, without the slightest manifestation of fear or uneasiness, evidently weighing well his words, and possessing a good command of language. His manner is courteous and affable, and he appears to make a favorable impression upon his auditory." The reporter of the Baltimore *American* wrote that, "during his conversation no signs of weakness were exhibited. In the midst of enemies, whose homes he had

8*

invaded; wounded and a prisoner; surrounded by a small
army of officials, and a more desperate army of angry men;
with the gallows staring him full in the face, BROWN lay on
the floor; and, in reply to every question, gave answers that
betokened the spirit that animated him. The language of
Governor WISE well expresses his boldness, when he said, 'he
is the gamest man I ever saw.'" From this conversation, as
reported in the New-York *Herald*, we give a few extracts,
confirmatory of statements made in the preceding pages. To
some of MASON'S questions, BROWN replied, "I could easily
have saved myself, had I exercised my own better judgment,
rather than yielded to my feelings. I had the means to make
myself secure without any escape, but I allowed myself to be
surrounded by being too tardy. I should have gone away, but
I had thirty odd prisoners, whose wives and daughters were in
tears for their safety; and I felt for them. Besides, I wanted
to allay the fears of those who believed we came here to burn
and kill. For this reason, I allowed the train to cross the
bridge, and gave them full liberty to pass on. I did it only to
spare the feelings of those passengers and their families, and
to allay the apprehensions that you had got here, in your
vicinity, a band of men, who had no regard for life and property, nor any feelings of humanity." When asked his object in
coming there, he answered, "we came to free the Slaves, and
only that." "How do you justify your acts?" "I think I did
right, and that others will do right who interfere with you, at
any time and at all times. I hold, that the golden rule — 'Do
unto others as you would that others should do unto you' —
applies to all who would help others to gain their liberty." To
a bystander who put, in substance, the same question, some
time after, he replied, "Upon the golden rule. I pity the poor
in bondage, that have none to help them; that is why I am
here: not to gratify any personal animosity, revenge, or vindictive spirit. It is my sympathy with the oppressed and the
wronged, that are as good as you, and as precious in the sight
of God." To another question, he said (telling the reporter
"you may report that"), "I want you to understand, that I
respect the rights of the poorest and weakest of colored people,
oppressed by the Slave-system, just as much as I do those of the
most wealthy and powerful. That is the idea that has moved

me, and that alone. We expected no reward, except the satisfaction of endeavoring to do for those in distress and greatly
oppressed, as we would be done by. The cry of distress of the
oppressed is my reason, and the only thing that prompted me to
come here." "Why did you do it secretly?" "Because I thought
that necessary to success; for no other reason." When asked
if he had seen GERRIT SMITH's letter, which, according to the
New-York *Herald,* of the day before, "speaks of the folly of
attempting to strike the shackles off the Slaves by the force
of moral suasion or legal agitation, and predicts that the next
movement made, in the direction of negro emancipation, would
be an insurrection at the South,"— he said, "I have not seen the
New-York *Herald* for some days past; but I presume, from
your remark about the gist of the letter, that I should concur
with it. I agree with Mr. SMITH, that moral suasion is hopeless. I don't think the people of the Slave States will ever
consider the subject of Slavery in its true light, till some other
argument is resorted to than moral suasion." VALLANDIGHAM
asked, "Did you expect a general rising of the Slaves, in case
of your success?" "No, sir; nor did I wish it. I expected to
gather them up, from time to time, and set them free." "Did
you expect to hold possession here till then?" "Well, probably, I had quite a different idea. I do not know that I ought
to reveal my plans. I am here a prisoner, and wounded,
because I foolishly allowed myself to be so. You overrate
your strength in supposing I could have been taken, if I had
not allowed it. I was too tardy after commencing the open
attack, — in delaying my movements through Monday night,
and up to the time I was attacked by the government troops.
It was all occasioned by my desire to spare the feelings of my
prisoners and their families and the community at large." The
reporter having offered to report anything further he would
like to say, he answered, "I have nothing to say, only, that I
claim to be here in carrying out a measure I believe perfectly
justifiable, and not to act the part of an incendiary or ruffian;
but to aid those suffering great wrong. I wish to say, further-
more, that you had better, — all you people at the South, —
prepare yourselves for a settlement of this question, that must
come up for settlement sooner than you are prepared for it.
The sooner you are prepared, the better. You may dispose of

VALLANDIGHAM, in these words, gives the impression made on him by his contact with the unvanquished captive. " Captain JOHN BROWN is as brave and resolute a man as ever headed an insurrection, and, in a good cause and with a sufficient force, would have been a consummate partisan commander. He has coolness, daring, persistency, the stoic faith and patience, and a firmness of will and purpose unconquerable. He is the farthest possible remove from the ordinary ruffian, fanatic, or madman."

"The result of these visits," says REDPATH, "was one of JOHN BROWN's greatest victories. Never before, in the United States, did a recorded conversation produce so sudden and universal a change of opinion. Before its publication, some who subsequently eulogized JOHN BROWN with fervor and surpassing eloquence, as well as the great body of the press and people who knew not the man, lamented that he should have gone insane; while, after it, from every corner of the land came words of wonder, of praise, and of gratitude, mingling with sincerest prayers for the noble old hero."

On Wednesday evening, October 19, the prisoners were taken from the guard-house, where they had been lying more than thirty hours, without so much attention as the washing off of the blood of their wounds; and were conveyed to Charlestown, escorted by a party of marines. On their way to the railroad, a Virginia paper says, "they were followed by hundreds of excited men, exclaiming, 'lynch them;' but Governor WISE, who was standing on the platform of the cars, said, 'O, it would be cowardly to do so now;' and the crowd fell back, and the prisoners were safely placed on the train." On reaching Charlestown, they were placed in jail, under the charge of Captain AVIS, who had commanded a company in the battle of the 17th. One whom REDPATH quotes as "a trustworthy writer" says of him, "AVIS is a just and humane man. He does all for his prisoners that his duty allows him to. I think he has a sincere respect for BROWN's undaunted fortitude and fearlessness. BROWN has a pleasant room, which is shared by STEVENS; has opportunities for writing and reading, and is permitted to receive such visitors as he desires to see. He states that he welcomes every one, and that he is preaching, with great effect, upon the enormities of Slavery, and with arguments which everybody fails to answer."

Of the general panic which the events at Harper's Ferry spread over Maryland and Virginia as fast as the news was carried; of the apprehensions of meditated insurrection here and there and almost everywhere; of the stories of incendiary fires, and signals seen at night on the mountains, and detected or suspected tokens of a good understanding between the Slaves in the region about Harper's Ferry and the northern invaders; of the fear of "many wealthy Slave-holders, living at a distance from their neighbors," to lodge at their own houses; of the alarming paragraphs appearing, from time to time, in the newspapers of that region; of the prevalent belief that spies and emissaries of BROWN were prowling about, watching for opportunities of rescue or revenge; of rumors of projected inroads by guerilla bands of Abolitionists all along the border of Maryland, Virginia, and Kentucky; of the mustering of police, the multiplying of patrols, the organizing of military companies; of the strict surveillance over travellers and strangers, and the ceaseless annoyances and frequent injuries to which they were subjected; and, in a word, of all the jumble of truth and falsehood, absurdities, exaggerations, extravagances, and enormities to which the pervading terror was continually giving birth, our space is utterly inadequate for even the most summary account. Attempts, indeed, were made to conceal the real state of things, and it was publicly denied, at times, that the Slaves had shown or felt any sympathy with BROWN's movement, or any disposition to avail themselves of the chance it offered them to become free. But the fright was too serious to be hidden; and testimonies to its existence and extent, borne both in unguarded words and still more in the unmistakable language of deeds,— in the multiplication of precautionary measures — were too abundant and emphatic to be successfully gainsaid. We cite a single witness out of many, but one whose position gives weight to his words. Thus speaks Governor WISE to the people of Richmond. "I shall go on arming and supplying ammunition to our frontiers, until every neighborhood where there are Slaves has the means of self-defence. * * * * * * I shall implore the people to organize and take arms in their hands, and practice the use of arms, and I will cause depots to be established for fixed ammunition along our borders, and at every assailable point." Moreover, there is reason to believe that the Slaves of that region did, to some extent either find or make, just then, an opportunity to escape from bondage. A telegraphic despatch from Washington, on the 18th, says, "it appears from intelligence received here, to-day, from various portions of Virginia and Maryland, that a general stampede of Slaves has taken place." RED-PATH speaks of "large numbers of negroes, reported to have left the neighborhood of Hagerstown, Md., and Alexandria, Va.;" and affirms that he has "positive knowledge of sixteen Slaves who succeeded in escaping from Harper's Ferry."

On the 20th, oath was made, in due form, before a magistrate, by Governor WISE and two others, against BROWN and his fellow-prisoners, for murder and other crimes; and, on the 25th, they were brought before a preliminary court of examination, consisting of eight magistrates. They were escorted from the jail by eighty armed men; BROWN and COPPOC manacled together; and both BROWN and STEVENS so weak from their wounds as, according to the reporter of the New-York *Herald*, to be "unable to stand without assistance." Before the examination closed a mattress had to be brought in for STEVENS to lie upon. "Guards were stationed around the court-house, and bayonets glistened on all sides." Emphatic attestations, were this formidable military array and this indecent haste in dragging men from beds of sickness to be tried for their lives, that Virginia trembled before her feeble captives with the weakness incident to her "peculiar system." So, in effect, a Pro-Slavery observer, the *Herald's* reporter, represents, in his despatches on the 25th. He says, "there is an evident intention to hurry the trial through, and execute the prisoners as soon as possible, fearing attempts to rescue them. * * * * * * It is rumored that BROWN is desirous of making a full statement of his motives and intentions through the press, but the court has refused all further access to him by reporters, fearing that he may put forth something calculated to influence the public mind and to have a bad effect on the Slaves. * * * * The reason given for hurrying the trial is that the people of the whole county are kept in a state of excitement, and a large armed force is required to prevent attempts at rescue."

The prosecution was conducted by CHARLES B. HARDING, attorney for Jefferson County, and ANDREW HUNTER, counsel for the State. The court asked if the prisoners had counsel. BROWN replied, "Virginians, I did not ask for any quarter at the time I was taken. I did not ask to have my life spared. The Governor of the State of Virginia tendered me his assurance that I should have a fair trial; but under no circumstances whatever will I be able to attend to my trial. If you seek my blood, you can have it at any moment, without this mockery of a trial. I have had no counsel; I have not been able to advise with any one. I know nothing about the feelings of my fellow-prisoners, and am utterly unable to attend, in any way, to my own defence. My memory do n't serve me; my health is insufficient, although improving. There are mitigating circumstances that I would urge in our favor, if a fair trial is to be allowed us; but if we are to be forced with a mere form — a trial for execution — you might spare yourselves that trouble. I am ready for my fate. I do not ask a trial. I beg for no mockery of a trial — no insult — nothing but that which conscience gives, or cowardice would drive you to practice. I ask again to be excused from the mockery of a trial. I do not even know what the special design of this examination is. I do not know what is to be the benefit of it to the Commonwealth. I have now little further to ask, other than that I may not be foolishly insulted only as cowardly barbarians insult those who fall into their power."

The court then assigned two Pro-Slavery, Virginian lawyers, CHARLES J. FAULKNER and LAWSON BOTTS, as counsel for the prisoners. BOTTS accepted, but FAULKNER declined, because, among other reasons, from what BROWN had said, it was plain he regarded the appearance of counsel as, under the circumstances, a mockery. When asked if he would accept these men as counsel, BROWN answered, "I have sent for counsel who have had no opportunity to see me. I wish for counsel, if I am to have a trial; but, if I am to have nothing but the mockery of a trial, as I said, I do not care anything about counsel. It is unnecessary to trouble any gentleman with that duty." Being told he was to "have a fair trial," and asked again, if he would accept the counsel assigned, he said, "I cannot regard this as an examination, under any circumstances. I would prefer that they should exercise their own pleasure. I feel as if it was a matter of very little account to me. If they

had designed to assist me as counsel, I should have wanted
an opportunity to consult them at my leisure." The other
prisoners, when asked, severally acquiesced in the assignment,
and the examination proceeded; ending, of course, in remanding the prisoners for trial by the circuit court.

In the afternoon, Judge PARKER of the circuit court charged
the grand jury, dwelling with emphasis upon "the enormity of
the guilt" incurred by those "who raise the standard of insurrection among us, and shoot down Virginia citizens defending
Virginia soil against their invasion;" but declaring that the
accused should have a fair and impartial trial, and giving a plain
hint—which we may, therefore, presume he considered necessary
— that no attempt to administer lynch law would be tolerated.
The grand jury retired, and the next day, at noon, Wednesday,
the 26th, returned "a true bill" against each prisoner, for conspiring, with negroes, to produce an insurrection; for treason
against the Commonwealth; and for murder. A Mr. GREEN,
a Virginian, was put in the place of FAULKNER, as counsel for
the prisoners. While the indictment was read, the prisoners
were required to stand, which BROWN could do with difficulty,
and STEVENS only by being held upright by two bailiffs. The
State elected to try BROWN first. He asked for delay on account of the state of his health, and the impaired condition of
his hearing by reason of the wounds on his head; also, because he expected counsel of his own choice to arrive soon.
"A very short delay" was all he asked. Mr. BOTTS, as his
counsel, said two or three days would suffice, and hoped the
court would grant it. The prosecutors opposed delay as
"dangerous, to say nothing of the exceeding pressure upon the
physical resources of the community," occasioned by the circumstances connected with the case; and contended that it was
"a public duty to avoid, as far as possible within the forms of
law, and with reference to the principle of giving the prisoners
a fair trial, the introduction of anything likely to weaken our
position, and give strength to our enemies abroad, whether it
comes from the mouths of the prisoners, or any other source."
What all this means,—unless that northern counsel, if time
should be given them to come, might bring out facts discredit-
able to Virginia and her "institution," which Virginian counsel would take no special pains to elicit,—we do not pretend

9

to understand. No delay was granted, though, while the trial went on, the old man, too weak to walk or sit, lay on his cot, when in the court room, and, in going to and from it, was carried or supported between two men.

Wednesday afternoon was consumed in impaneling a jury, and on Thursday morning the trial began. A despatch was read, from Akron, Ohio, suggesting the plea of insanity, and stating facts, provable by witnesses living there, which would show insanity to be hereditary in BROWN's family; but he promptly and emphatically rejected the plea, declaring that he did not regard himself as insane, nor wish to be defended on any such ground. His counsel then renewed, but without avail, the request for a postponement; asking but a single day, that the counsel sent for might arrive. The day was spent in the respective openings of counsel and the hearing of testimony. "The report of the day's proceedings ended with this announcement: 'Orders have been given to the jailors *to shoot all the prisoners, if an attempt is made for their rescue.'*"

On Friday morning, GEORGE H. HOYT, a young lawyer from Boston, appeared as a volunteer counsel for BROWN, but having had no opportunity to become acquainted with the case, he did not at once take part in the defence. The giving of evidence for the prosecution continued. Mr. HUNTER put in the Chatham Constitution and letters found in BROWN's carpet-bag. The witnesses related particulars of the taking of the armory, and making prisoners of the workmen and others; also of the firing and the killing of citizens; and "all testified to BROWN's anxiety to avoid shedding blood needlessly;" and, that he "was as considerate of the lives and comfort of his prisoners as was consistent with his object." Colonel WASHINGTON stated "that negotiations for the release of the prisoners were opened, before the general firing commenced, on Monday. During the conflict, BROWN frequently gave orders not to fire on unarmed citizens." He said, also, that BROWN often complained of the bad faith of the people in firing on his men when under a flag of truce; "but he heard him make no threat, nor utter any vindictiveness against them."

In the afternoon, among other witnesses, was HENRY HUNTER, who described the murder of THOMPSON, an account of which is given on a preceding page. When the prisoner's counsel sought to bring out this testimony, the prosecutor objected. "The circumstances of the deed might be such as he himself might not at all approve." [*Might* be! — indeed.] "He did not know how that might be, but he desired to avoid any investigation that might be used for out-door effect and influence. Not that it was so designed by the respectable counsel, but he thought such was the object of the prisoner in getting at it. Unless the knowledge of it could be brought home to the prisoner and his after conduct, he could not see its relevancy." But the judge admitted it, as part of the general transaction, the whole of which might be inquired into.

No wonder Mr. HUNTER felt somewhat sensitive about its coming to light; sensitive, both as a citizen of Virginia, — on whose reputation the "out-door influence" of such a narrative must be far from good, — and as father of the chief perpetrator of the cowardly atrocity. In the South, indeed, it might not be deemed a stain on the character of the murderer, or of his native State; if, as REDPATH says, — and we are aware of no reason to doubt his assertion, — "this sworn statement of a cold-blooded murder [hot-blooded, we think, however, in charity, nay, in justice, it should be called], by one of the perpetrators of it, elicited not one word of condemnation from any journal published in the Southern States." But the danger was, that it "would give strength to our enemies abroad;" which it was "a public duty to avoid as far as possible."

The State's testimony being closed, several witnesses for the defence were called, but did not answer. The subpœnas had not been returned, nor was it known whether they had been served. We do not learn that the prisoner's Virginian counsel made any effort, at this point, to secure his rights; and, for aught which appears, the trial would here have closed, without the hearing of a single witness called on his behalf, if the old man had not interposed for himself. Rising from his mattress, he thus addressed the judge, — "May it please the court, I discover that, notwithstanding all the assurances I have received of a fair trial, nothing like a fair trial is to be given me, as it would seem. I gave the names, as soon as I could get at them, of the persons I wished to have called as witnesses, and was assured that they would be subpœnaed. I wrote down a memorandum to that effect, saying where those parties were;

but it appears that they have not been subpœnaed, so far as I can learn: and now I ask, if I am to have anything at all deserving the name and shadow of a fair trial, that this proceeding be deferred until to-morrow morning; for I have no counsel, as I have before stated, in whom I feel that I can rely, but I am in hopes counsel may arrive who will attend to seeing that I get the witnesses who are necessary for my defence. I am myself unable to attend to it. I have given all the attention I possibly could to it, but am unable to see or know about them, and can't even find out their names; and I have nobody to do any errand, for my money was all taken from me when I was hacked and stabbed, and I have not a dime. I had two hundred and fifty or sixty dollars in gold and silver taken from my pocket, and now I have no possible means of getting anybody to go any errands for me, and I have not had all the witnesses subpœnaed. They are not within reach, and are not here. I ask at least until to-morrow morning to have something done, if anything is designed. If not, I am ready for anything that may come up." He then "lay down again, drew his blanket over him, and closed his eyes, and appeared to sink in tranquil slumber."

Mr. HOYT seconded this very moderate request, so manfully urged; stating that other counsel would probably arrive that night. Messrs. GREEN and BOTTS immediately withdrew from the case, saying that after the prisoner's public avowal of want of confidence in them, they could no longer act in his behalf; but hoped the court would allow the night, to the counsel from Boston, for preparation. Messrs. HUNTER and HARDING, of course, strenuously opposed delay. "We have now reached the point of time," said HARDING, "when we are ready to submit the case to the jury upon the evidence and the law;" and he seemed to take it very hardly that when *they* were ready, after putting in all the testimony they desired, and feeling sure that the prejudice of judge and jury was already with them on every question of law, the other party should be so unreasonable as not to be equally ready, before offering a single witness, or having a chance to argue a single legal point. But the court could not fail to see that a refusal, as the case then stood, would be too glaringly indecent; and might even have a worse "out-door effect and influence" than anything which delay might enable the prisoner's expected counsel to do in his defence. So, at six in the evening, the court adjourned till the next morning. But, at even this slight concession to justice and decency, the telegraph announced that "the town is greatly excited; the guard has been increased; the conduct of BROWN is generally regarded as a trick."

From such despatches, it is manifest that the alarmed Virginians did not guess the purpose of the "trick." JOHN BROWN was quite beyond their depth; though doubtless shrewd Lawyer HUNTER, talking about "out-door influence," had some glimmering and imperfect notion of what he would be at. But, while the excited town and strengthened guard showed fear of an attempt at forcible rescue of the prisoners' bodies, the brave old leader had his mind intent upon a rescue of another sort, worth more than many such as that; one which should help the cause of Freedom in all coming years, not only in this land of Slavery, but in all lands to which the fame of their bold deeds should reach; making the memory of it and them an educator of successive generations into hatred of oppression, and unselfish love of right; into nobleness of thought and aim and life. It was the rescue of their movement from all imputation or suspicion of ferocity or vengeful passion or wanton violence or causeless bloodshed, or even of unkindness or discourtesy in act or word; the showing of its perfect singleness of purpose, and the faithfulness with which its one grand object was pursued; in short, the vindication of its character, as strictly a defensive war for liberty, and all the purer from any stain of selfishness, because not for their own, but for the liberty of a despised and outcast race. To this end, he gave these brief directions to his northern counsel, — "those furnished to the Virginians," REDPATH says, "were fuller and more specific." "We gave to numerous prisoners perfect liberty: get all their names. We allowed numerous other prisoners to visit their families, to quiet their fears: get all their names. We allowed the conductor to pass his train over the bridge with all his passengers; I myself crossing the bridge with him, and assuring all the passengers of their perfect safety: get that conductor's name, and the names of the passengers, so far as may be. We treated all our prisoners with the utmost kindness and humanity: get all their names, so far as may be.

Our orders, from the first and throughout, were, that no unarmed person should be injured, under any circumstances whatever: prove that by all the prisoners. We committed no
destruction or waste of property: prove that."

When the court was opened, at ten o'clock, on Saturday,
SAMUEL CHILTON, of Washington, D.C., and HENRY GRISWOLD,
of Cleveland, O., appeared as additional counsel for the prisoner.
They asked for a short delay, if only for a few hours, for preparation; having had no time even to read the indictment,
and the evidence already given. But, as usual, the prosecutor
objected, and the court refused the request.

Witnesses for the defence were then examined. JOHN P.
DANGERFIELD, one of BROWN's prisoners, testified, among
other things, that, "from the treatment of Captain BROWN, he
had no personal fear of him or his men during his confinement.
One of BROWN's sons was wounded while out with a flag of
truce. The prisoner frequently complained, that his men were
shot down while carrying a flag of truce." HUNTER tried
again to stop the giving of this testimony; but the court
decided that it was admissible as going to show the absence
of malice. The witness went on, — "BROWN promised safety
to all descriptions of property, except Slave-property. After
the first attack, BROWN cried out to surrender. Saw BROWN
wounded on the hip by a thrust from a sabre, and several sabre-
cuts on his head. When the latter wounds were given, Captain BROWN appeared to be shielding himself, with his head
down, but making no resistance. The parties outside appeared
to be firing as they pleased." The same witness also stated
that his wife and daughter were permitted to visit him, unmolested, and free verbal communication was allowed with those
outside. "We were treated kindly, but were compelled to
stay where we did n't want to be." Major MILLS, master of
the armory, gave the same testimony as to the shooting of
BROWN's son when under a flag of truce, and BROWN's complaint that the citizens acted barbarously; adding, "he did not
appear to have any malicious feeling. His intentions were to
shoot nobody, unless they were using or carrying arms."
BROWN asked if the witness saw any firing, on his part, not
purely defensive. He answered, "it might be considered in that
light, perhaps; the balls came into the engine-house pretty

thick." SAMUEL SNIDER corroborated DANGERFIELD's testimony, and said the prisoner "honestly endeavored to protect his hostages, and wished to make peace more for their sake than for his own safety."

In the afternoon other witnesses confirmed the statements of these; then the arguing of some legal points, which were decided against the prisoner, consumed the time till nearly dark. Mr. GRISWOLD, therefore, asked the court to adjourn after the opening argument of the prosecution, to enable the counsel for the defence to read the notes of the evidence given before their arrival, and prepare their argument. This, of course, HUNTER stoutly opposed, insisting that the case be brought to a close that night. If the prisoner's counsel were unprepared, it was through his own fault, "in dismissing his faithful, skilful, able, and zealous counsel on yesterday afternoon." The jurors were kept from their families by these delays, and, besides, "there could not be a female in this county, who, whether with good cause or not, was not trembling with anxiety and apprehension." The court consulted with the jurors, "who expressed themselves *very anxious to get home*." However, for a second time, a sense of justice or of decency prevailed; and, after being assured that the argument for the defence would not occupy, on Monday, more than two hours and a half in all, the court, in opposition to HUNTER's " earnest protest," consented to adjourn as requested.

Monday forenoon, the 31st, was occupied with arguments of counsel; GRISWOLD opening, and CHILTON closing, for the defence, and HUNTER closing for the prosecution. For the defence, it was urged that BROWN could not be guilty of treason, for he was not a citizen of Virginia; that the evidence did not sustain the charge of levying war against the State, his purpose being to run off Slaves, and the fighting being incidental to that, which would not constitute levying war, even if murder ensued, as that may not have been contemplated; that the Constitution of the Provisional Government, itself, proved that it was not meant to overthrow the government of Virginia; that, as to the charge of conspiring with Slaves, no one had testified to anything said or done by BROWN, or his men, to induce the Slaves to rebel; that no Slave had been proved to have taken part with them, except one who attempted to drill a port-hole, which was done for self-protection and not rebellion; that the charge of murder implied premeditated malice, but no such malice had been shown; that their firing, or intending to fire, only on armed men refuted the idea of such malice; and that though they were amenable to punishment under the laws of Virginia, it was for other offences than those named in the indictment, and, consequently, under that, they were entitled to acquittal.

The prosecution contended that, inasmuch as, by the Virginia code, all white persons born in any State of the Union, and resident in Virginia, are citizens of the State, BROWN was a citizen, for he had come to Harper's Ferry to reside and hold the place permanently; that his occupation of a farm, in Maryland, was not to fix his domicil there, but "for the hellish purpose" of rallying forces against Virginia; that his acts, if not his declarations, showed that he came there not to carry off Slaves alone; that his Provisional Government was a real thing, and, in holding office under it and exercising its functions, he was guilty of treason; that conspiring with Slaves could be done by acts as well as words, and arming them while holding their masters captive was advising them to rebel; and that the law does not require positive evidence, but only enough to remove all reasonable doubt of guilt.

The jury retired, and the court took a recess for half an hour. After an absence of three-quarters of an hour, the jury returned with a verdict of "guilty" of all the offences charged in the indictment. "BROWN sat up in his bed while the verdict was rendered, then lay down very composedly, without saying a word." The reporter of the New-York *Herald* thus describes the scene. " The crowd filled all the space from the couch inside the bar, around the prisoner, beyond the railing in the body of the court, out through the wide hall and beyond the doors. There stood the anxious but perfectly silent and attentive populace, stretching head and neck to witness the closing scene of old BROWN's trial. It was terrible to look upon such a crowd of human faces, moved and agitated with but one dreadful expectancy — to let the eye rest for a moment upon the only calm and unruffled countenance there, and to think that he, alone, of all present, was the doomed one above whose head hung the sword of fate. But there he stood,

just that man of indomitable will and iron nerve, all collected
and unmoved, even while the verdict, which consigned him to
an ignominious doom, was pronounced upon him." CHILTON
moved an arrest of judgment, for errors in both the indictment and the verdict; the former charging an offence not
appearing on the record of the grand jury, and the latter
being a general verdict on the whole indictment, and not on
each count separately. The motion was ordered to stand over
for argument till the next day.

The facts of this trial, so little honorable to the Virginian
character, are gathered from the statements of Pro-Slavery
reporters, for the Virginians had allowed no others to be present, nor was their vigilance eluded by any other till the day
after the rendition of the verdict, when a correspondent of the
New-York *Tribune* somehow succeeded in establishing himself at Charlestown.

On Wednesday evening, November 2, BROWN was brought
into court to receive sentence. He was now able to walk,
though with difficulty. Seating himself by his counsel, he
remained motionless, while the judge read his decision, overruling the motion in arrest of judgment; and, when asked, in
the usual form, if he had anything to say why sentence should
not be passed upon him, "he rose," the reporter of the *Tribune*
says, "and leaned slightly forward, his hands resting on the
table. He spoke timidly — hesitatingly, indeed — and in a
voice singularly gentle and mild. But his sentences came confused from his mouth, and he seemed to be wholly unprepared
to speak at this time. [As in fact he was. Not expecting to
be called up for sentence till the other prisoners had been tried,
he was taken by surprise.] The types can give you no intimation of the soft and tender tones, yet calm and manly, withal,
that filled the court-room, and, I think, touched the hearts of
many who had come only to rejoice at the heaviest blow their
victim was to suffer." We give his brief and noble speech
entire.

"I have, may it please the court, a few words to say. In
the first place, I deny everything but what I have, all along,
admitted, of a design, on my part, to free Slaves. I intended,
certainly, to have made a clean thing of that matter, as I did,
last winter, when I went into Missouri, and there took Slaves

without the snapping of a gun on either side, moving them through the country, and finally leaving them in Canada. I designed to have done the same thing again, on a larger scale. That was all I intended to do. I never intended murder or treason or the destruction of property or to excite or incite Slaves to rebellion or to make an insurrection. I have another objection, and that is that it is unjust that I should suffer such a penalty. Had I interfered in the manner which I admit, and which I admit has been fairly proved,— for I admire the truthfulness and candor of the greater portion of the witnesses who have testified in this case,— had I so interfered in behalf of the rich, the powerful, the intelligent, the so-called great, or in behalf of any of their friends, either father, mother, brother, sister, wife, or children, or any of that class, and suffered and sacrificed what I have in this interference, it would have been all right, and every man in this court would have deemed it an act worthy of reward rather than punishment.

"This court acknowledges, too, as I suppose, the validity of the law of GOD. I see a book kissed, which I suppose to be the Bible, or at least the New Testament, which teaches me that all things whatsoever I would that men should do to me, I should do even so to them. It teaches me further to remember them that are in bonds as bound with them. I endeavored to act up to that instruction. I say I am yet too young to understand that GOD is any respecter of persons. I believe that to have interfered as I have done, as I have always freely admitted I have done, in behalf of His despised poor, is no wrong, but right. Now, if it is deemed necessary that I should forfeit my life for the furtherance of the ends of justice, and mingle my blood further with the blood of my children and with the blood of millions in this Slave-country, whose rights are disregarded by wicked, cruel, and unjust enactments, I say let it be done.

" Let me say one word further. I feel entirely satisfied with the treatment I have received on my trial. Considering all the circumstances, it has been more generous than I expected. But I feel no consciousness of guilt. I have stated from the first what was my intention, and what was not. I never had any design against the liberty of any person, nor any disposition to commit treason or excite Slaves to rebel or make any general insurrection. I never encouraged any man to do so, but always discouraged any idea of that kind. Let me say, also, in regard to the statements made by some of those who were connected with me. I hear it has been stated, by some of them, that I have induced them to join me, but the contrary is true. I do not say this to injure them, but as regretting their weakness. Not one but joined me of his own accord, and the greater part at their own expense. A number of them I never saw and never had a word of conversation with, till the day they came to me, and that was for the purpose I have stated. Now, I have done."

Sentence of death was then pronounced, fixing December 2, as the day of execution. BROWN's counsel put in a bill of exceptions, to be referred to the Supreme Court of Appeals, at Richmond; which, about two weeks later, unanimously sustained the judgment of the circuit court, without allowing the prisoner's counsel to be heard.

On the 1st and 2nd of November, COPPOC was tried and convicted, HOYT and GRISWOLD acting as his counsel. The next three days were occupied in trying and convicting the colored men, COPELAND and GREEN. They were ably defended by GEORGE SENNOTT, of Boston, "who," it is said, "though a democrat, excited the ire of the Virginians by the strong legal points which he unexpectedly made." The count for treason had to be abandoned on the ground that colored men are not recognized as citizens. On Monday, the 7th, STEVENS was brought in, with "three bullets in his head and two in his breast," and laid on a mattress, to undergo, like the rest, the form of a trial, the result of which had, of course, been predetermined. But before a jury had been completed, a message came from Governor WISE, advising the transfer of STEVENS to the United States Court, and after some discussion among the lawyers, the case was postponed, and that of COOKE was taken up. He was defended by his brother-in-law, Governor WILLARD, of Indiana, two other lawyers from the same State, and BOTTS and GREEN, of Virginia. Much interest was excited by the announcement, during the trial, that a written confession, from the prisoner, would be read; and it was generally hoped that a full revelation of the supposed complicity of distinguished northern citizens with BROWN would be made;

but the reading of the confession utterly disappointed this hope, doubtless, for the very cogent reason that there was nothing of what was looked for, to be revealed. Such facts only were disclosed, as we have mentioned in the preceding narrative. The trial lasted three days, and ended in a verdict of not guilty of treason, but guilty of the remaining counts — for conspiracy with Slaves to rebel, and murder. "Cooke received the verdict without any exhibition of emotion." The four prisoners were brought up on Thursday, to be sentenced; and when the usual preliminary question was asked, Copeland and Green had nothing to say; Coppoc and Cooke replied with substantially the same denials and affirmations which Brown had made, touching the charges against them, and the purpose of their expedition. They were all sentenced to be hung; the colored men in the forenoon, and the white men in the afternoon, of December 16.

The knowledge that most of the prisoners now lay under sentence of death, seemed no way to abate the general excitement and alarm, which were at once attested and kept alive, — not to say augmented, rather, — by rumors of all sorts, coming from all quarters and flying in all directions, some true, more false, chiefly referring to alleged designs to rescue the doomed men by force, and to events which were believed to show that sympathy with them prevailed to a perilous extent among the Slaves of the surrounding country. Barns, stacks, and other property, to a large amount, belonging to several of the jurors in the trials, were destroyed by fire, supposed to have been set by Slaves or "abolition emissaries." Letters and messages, in great numbers, "from intelligent and responsible persons," came, it was said, to Gov. Wise, warning or threatening that bands were organizing in the North and West, to attempt a rescue. One rumor was, that Governor Chase, of Ohio, and another, that Marshal Johnson, of the same State, had warned the Virginian governor of a contemplated movement to that end, by John Brown, Jr., with from six hundred to a thousand men, from Ohio. Another told of five hundred from Wisconsin, to drop in by ones and twos and threes, in time to join "the Ohio thousand" at the proper moment. Ample military preparations were made to meet the apprehended invasion. The town was filled with soldiers, — infantry, cavalry, artillery.

The *Tribune's* reporter wrote, " Cannon are planted in front of
the court-house, the jail, and in positions commanding all the
main streets. The approaches to Charlestown are also strongly
guarded. At Harper's Ferry, there are companies of Virginia
militia and United States troops. At Martinsburg, there are
three or four hundred soldiers. Elsewhere it is the same."
The presence of strangers in Charlestown was thought so
dangerous as to require a proclamation from the mayor, which
accordingly was issued on the 12th of November, commanding
all such as could not give a satisfactory account of themselves,
to leave the town and county; and requesting certain official
personages and distinguished citizens named, "to make it their
special business" to bring such strangers before some magistrate,
"to be dealt with according to law." Mr. HOYT, of the
prisoner's counsel, and Mr. JEWETT, of FRANK LESLIE's paper,
— suspected of being a correspondent of the New-York *Tribune*, — were told by Colonel DAVIS, commander of the military, that they, particularly, were meant in this warning; that,
if they did not leave the place, the mob would certainly be
upon them the next day (Sunday), and he had no force on
which he could rely to protect them. They thought it prudent
to withdraw. It is said, too, that Mr. SENNOTT, who was
collecting BROWN's property, for the benefit of his family, was
admonished that he was one of the strangers whose absence
was desired; and that, for a time, he was debarred from private
communication with his clients; but that his emphatic repre-
sentations induced a second thought, that it was "wisest to
restore him to his just position as counsel." A sculptor, also,
who had come from Boston to obtain a likeness of BROWN, and
measurements of his head, to aid him in making a bust of the
old hero, was deemed, — if not himself a dangerous man, — to
be about a dangerous business; and perhaps that judgment
was, after all, not wide of the mark: for these men who "give
bond in stone and ever-during brass" to guard the memories of
those who have "bled nobly" in defence of injured weakness,
are *not* altogether safe men for the upholders of tyranny to
tolerate in the prosecution of their calling. Anyhow, the Virginian authorities and people appear to have thought so, and
Mr. BRACKETT, after much solicitation, was denied access to
BROWN. The jailor told him, as we learn from the *Tribune's*

ance, that "had you made application to me for the aid which the Constitution and laws of the United States would enable me to afford, this should have been cheerfully and cordially granted;" and farther, that "one measure it is both my right and my duty to adopt, that is, to reënforce the guard already stationed at Harper's Ferry. * * * * * * I have, therefore, as a precautionary measure, directed the secretary of war to order two companies of artillery to proceed immediately from Fortress Monroe to Harper's Ferry."

The copy of the governor's letter which was sent to Ohio, was accompanied by a letter to Governor CHASE, saying, "I submit it to you, in the confidence that you will faithfully coöperate with the authorities of this State in preserving the peace of our coterminous borders. Necessity may compel us to pursue invaders of our jurisdiction into yours; if so, you may be assured that it will be done with no disrespect to the sovereignty of your State." Governor CHASE replied to this insolent menace of invasion, and the pretended "information" sent with it, that he had no intelligence of the "preparations" alluded to, but what the letters themselves convey; and that was not such as "to enable the authorities of the State to interpose with certainty or effect;" that when it should be made to appear that unlawful combinations for the invasion of Virginia are forming in Ohio, the executive will promptly do its duty in breaking them up; that "the people of this State will require from her authorities the punctual fulfilment of every obligation to the other members of the Union; but they cannot consent to the invasion of her territory by armed bodies from other States, even for the purpose of pursuing and arresting fugitives from justice." A civil and gubernatorial way, we take it, of saying, to his brother governor, "You are a good deal more scared than hurt; but if you attempt to execute your threat in this direction, you 'll be likely to be as much hurt as you are scared."

How many of the letters, on the strength of which Governor WISE so ostentatiously falsified his patronymic, were palpable forgeries, like that purporting to come from A. HYATT SMITH, a prominent democrat, of Wisconsin, and instantly detected at a glance, by Senator DOOLITTLE, of that State, when shown to him; how many were the wicked work of thoughtlessly cruel wags, seeking their own sport in aggravating the terror of the hapless Virginians, and goading the governor into that betrayal of weakness which he mistook for a display of strength; how many were seriously designed to inflict the torment which is in all fear, as a just punishment of tyranny which naturally breeds cowardice; how many were honestly intended warnings from northern men of "conservative" proclivities, who, taking counsel of their own fears, excited, perhaps, by the free and careless talk of their neighbors, really believed that they had made some grand discovery nearly concerning the nation's welfare; and how many, of all sorts, the valiant governor *actually did receive*, are probably of those things which no man knoweth, or ever will know. One thing, however, is certain; that if Virginia, from them all, learned anything worth knowing, she had to pay roundly for the knowledge, not only in disquietude of mind, but in current coin. But the wise governor consoled himself, and sought to satisfy the people, with the reflection that even if all his formidable military preparations should prove to have been called out by false alarms, still "they would be useful, to Virginia, in the end, as showing the alacrity with which her volunteers responded to a public call, and the ease and promptness with which she could concentrate them in force to maintain her laws, or to repel the violent invasion of her soil." Very likely, if there were such doubts of that before, as to require an experiment on so large a scale for their removal. But even the Virginians were not all convinced of the governor's wisdom, for we find the Petersburg (Va.) *Intelligencer* saying, "the excess of zeal, or of courage, or of timidity, whichever it is, that is now being played off, is only of a piece with the general conduct of public men of the South, since the Slavery agitation has absorbed all our politics. If Governor WISE makes so much fuss where there is no danger, what would he do if there were real danger?"

Of the events of JOHN BROWN's six weeks of prison-life and the many deeply interesting incidents thereto related, our space permits us to say very little. Mrs. CHILD's beautiful and touching letter to the brave old man; her request to be allowed to visit him in prison, and nurse him while suffering from his wounds; her consequent correspondence — on her part so admirable and effective — with Governor WISE and with Mrs.

MASON; the visits of Judge RUSSELL and his wife, of Boston, and Mrs. SPRING and her son, of Eagleswood, N. J., and the displays which thence resulted of Virginian chivalry, in the shape of rude behavior, coarse insolence, and threats of lynching; the many conversations with southern Slave-holding or Pro-Slavery visitors, in which the martyr-hero "wielded 'the sword of the spirit,'" as he himself expressed it, "on the right hand and on the left;" all these and many things besides we must pass over with little more than a bare allusion, or leave unmentioned altogether. Some notices, however, of his bearing and appearance, and some extracts from his conversations, we copy, chiefly from reports of newspaper correspondents.

Says the reporter of the New-York *Tribune,* "BROWN's cheerfulness never fails him. He converses with all who visit them, in a manner so free from restraint, and with so much unconcern, that none can doubt his real convictions of self-approval. His daring courage has strongly impressed the people, and I have more than once heard public avowals of admiration of his fearlessness, in spite of ominous murmurs of disapprobation from bystanders." And again, "BROWN's conversation is singularly attractive. His manner is magnetic. It attracts every one who approaches him, and while he talks he reigns. The other prisoners venerate him." And yet again, after describing one particular visit from several southern men, the reporter adds, "in all his conversation BROWN showed the utmost gentleness and tranquillity, and a quiet courtesy withal, that contrasted rather strongly with the bearing of some of his visitors."

The reporter of the New-York *Herald* wrote, a day or two after the sentence upon BROWN, to a question about his health, he replied that, except some inflammation in one of his wounds, "he was easy in mind and body, and thought he had done his duty to GOD and man. If it was decreed that he should suffer for it, very well, it was of small consequence to him." Said the same writer, at a later date, "with all who come in a kindly spirit to visit him, BROWN is exceedingly free and open. He esteems such as friends, and seems to view their leave-taking with regret. But such visits are few," for the prison-doors are generally barred against them, by "the jealousy and suspicion with which the people of Charlestown regard all who are likely to feel for and sympathize with the prisoner," while those known to be hostile to abolition movements "enter in flocks." He concludes, "it is almost needless to say that BROWN awaits death with that resignation and tranquillity which disarm the dreaded phantom of all terror."

In Mrs. SPRING's account of her interview with him, four days after he was sentenced, we read that, alluding to the issue of his late attempt, he said "I do not now reproach myself; I did what I could, and I think I cannot now better serve the cause I love so much than to die for it; and in my death I may do more than in my life." To the question — asked for others, not for herself — whether any feeling of revenge had actuated him, he answered, with "a surprised look," and "slowly but firmly," "I am not conscious of having had a feeling of the kind. No, not in all the wrong done to me and my family in Kansas, have I had a feeling of revenge." To her remark, that such a feeling would not sustain him now, he quickly answered, "no, indeed; but I sleep peacefully as an infant, or if I am wakeful, glorious thoughts come to me, entertaining my mind." Presently he added, "the sentence they have pronounced against me did not disturb me in the least; it is not the first time that I have looked death in the face." To the question, how it would be with him in the long days of his imprisonment, he replied, "I cannot say, but I do not believe I shall deny my Lord and Master, Jesus Christ; and I should, if I denied my principles against Slavery." She continues, "he seems to me to be purely unselfish, and in all that he has done, to have never thought of himself, but always of others. In a noble letter to his wife, which I brought away with me, he entreats his 'dear wife and children, every one, never, in all your trials, forget the poor that cry, and him that hath none to help him.'"

As we have already intimated, he would accept no proffer of spiritual aid from Pro-Slavery clergymen, though free to converse with any who called upon him, as several did, at different times. A correspondent of the Baltimore *American* states that when "approached by a Slave-holding Presbyterian minister, who wished to advise him spiritually, he repelled it, saying that he did not worship the same God." Another writer represents him as replying to a Methodist minister, who defended Slavery, "You know nothing about Christianity; you will have to learn the A B C's in the lesson of Christianity, as I find you entirely ignorant of the meaning of the word. I, of course, respect you as a gentleman, but it is as a *heathen* gentleman." Mr. LOWRY, of Erie, Pa., a former neighbor of BROWN's, after visiting him in prison, spoke of him as " a decidedly religious man, though he sternly refuses to be aided in his prayers by the Pro-Slavery divines of Virginia. One of these gentlemen, in conversation with me, said that he had called on BROWN, to pray with him. He said BROWN asked if he was ready to fight, if necessity required it, for the freedom of the Slave. On his answering in the negative, BROWN said that he would thank him to retire from his cell, that his prayers would be an abomination to his GOD. To another clergyman, he said that he would not insult his GOD by bowing down with any one who had the blood of the Slave upon his skirts." From another source, we have a statement that when asked by a Colonel SMITH, who paid him a visit, in company with a son of Governor WISE, " if he desired a clergyman to administer to him the consolations of religion, he answered that he recognized no Slave-holder, lay or clerical, nor any sympathizer with Slavery, as a Christian. He gave the same reason, afterwards, for his refusal to accept the services of some clergymen who called upon him. He said he would as soon be attended to the scaffold by blacklegs or robbers of the worst kind, as by Slave-holding ministers, or ministers sympathizing with Slavery; and that, if he had his choice, he would rather be followed to the scaffold by barefooted, barelegged, ragged negro children, and their old grey-headed Slave-mothers, than by clergymen of this character. He would feel, he said, much prouder of such an escort, and wished he could have it. He told clergymen, who called upon him, that they and all Slave-holders and sympathizers with Slavery had far more need of prayers themselves than he had, and he accordingly advised them to pray for themselves, and exhibit no concern about him. While making these remarks, he requested that he might not be understood as designing to offer any insult." In a letter to an Anti-Slavery minister, in Ohio, he said, " There are no ministers of *Christ* here. These ministers, who profess to be Christian, and hold Slaves or advocate Slavery, I cannot abide them. My knees will not bend in prayer with them while their hands are stained with the blood of souls."

His letters, written while in prison, to his wife and children and the friends who sent him expressions of sympathy, breathe the same spirit of calm, invincible courage, fortitude, and cheerfulness, of deep religious feeling and firm faith and quiet resignation, which his lips and life so well attested. We cannot forbear to make room for a few extracts, necessarily short, but eminently characteristic.

In his reply to Mrs. CHILD, after expressing his gratitude for her "most kind letter and offer to come and take care of" him, and proposing to her "a different course," with reasons full of good sense, and that considerate regard for others rather than himself, which Mrs. SPRING so justly ascribes to him, he concludes, "I am quite cheerful under all my afflicting circumstances and prospects; having, as I humbly trust, 'the peace of God, which passeth all understanding,' to rule in my heart. God Almighty bless and reward you a thousand fold." To a Quaker lady, who wrote from Newport, R. I., warmly approving "the generous and philanthropic motives" which animated him in his "brave efforts in behalf of the poor oppressed," but, of course, dissenting from him as to his method, he replied, "You know that Christ once armed Peter. *I think he put a sword into my hand, and there continued it so long as he saw best, and then kindly took it from me. I mean when I first went to Kansas.* I wish you could know with what cheerfulness I am now wielding the 'Sword of the Spirit,' on the right hand and on the left. I bless GOD that it proves 'mighty to the pulling down of strongholds.'" Alluding to his family, he said, "they have much greater need of sympathy than I, who, through Infinite Grace and the kindness of strangers, am 'joyful in all my tribulations.' * * * * * * *I do not feel conscious of guilt in taking up arms.* * * * * * * These light afflictions, which endure for a moment, shall work out for me *a far more exceeding and eternal weight of glory.* GOD will surely attend to his own cause in the best possible way and time, and he will not forget the work of his own hands."

A "Christian Conservative," of West Newton, Mass., having written him an excellent letter, addressing him as "dear brother," commending his conduct in certain particulars, and adding, "while I cannot approve of all your acts, I stand in awe of your position, since your capture, and dare not oppose you, lest I be found fighting against GOD; for you speak as one having authority, and seem to be strengthened from on high;" he answered, "I do certainly feel that through divine grace I have endeavored to be 'faithful in a very few things,' mingling with even these much of imperfection. I am certainly 'unworthy even to suffer affliction with the people of GOD,' yet in infinite grace HE has THUS honored me. * * * * * * I cannot feel that GOD will suffer even the poorest service we may any of us render him or his cause to be lost or in vain. I do feel, 'dear brother,' that I am wonderfully 'strengthened from on high.' * * * * * * I have *many* opportunities for *faithful plain dealing* with the more powerful, influential, and intelligent classes in this region, which, I trust, are not entirely misimproved."

Rev. H. L. VAILL, of Litchfield, Ct., of whom BROWN was a pupil in his boyhood, wrote to him, in his prison, a letter of Christian friendship, and received a reply which Rev. L. W. BACON, in sending a copy to the press, calls "heroic and sublime;" adding, "has ever such an epistle been written from a condemned cell, since the letter 'to Timotheus,' when Paul 'was brought before Nero the second time?'" In it, he said, "notwithstanding 'my soul is amongst lions,' still I believe that 'GOD in very deed is with me.' * * * * * * I do not feel condemned of Him whose judgment is just, nor of my own conscience. Nor do I feel degraded by my imprisonment, my chain, or prospect of the gallows. * * * * * * The jailor, in whose charge I am, and his family and assistants have all been most kind; and, notwithstanding he was one of the bravest of all who *fought me*, he is *now* being abused for his humanity. * * * * * * I have often passed under the rod of Him whom I call my Father, * * * * * * and yet I have enjoyed much of life, as I was enabled to discover the secret of this somewhat early. It has been in making the prosperity and the happiness of others my own; so that really I have had a great deal of prosperity." To Mr. MUSGRAVE, of Northampton, Mass., he wrote, "*men* cannot imprison or chain or hang the soul. I go joyfully in behalf of millions that 'have no rights' that 'this *great and glorious*,' 'this Christian Republic' is 'bound to respect.'" To a sympathizing letter from Rev. Mr. McFARLAND, of Wooster, Ohio, he replied, "I would be glad to have you or any of my liberty-loving ministerial friends here, to talk and pray with me. I am not a stranger to the way of salvation by CHRIST. From my youth I have studied much on that subject, and at one time hoped to be a minister myself; but GOD had another work for me to do. To me it is given, in behalf of CHRIST, not only to believe on him, but also to *suffer* for his sake. * * * * * * I think I feel as happy as Paul did when he lay in prison. He knew if they killed him it would greatly advance the cause of CHRIST; that was the reason he rejoiced so. On that same ground 'I do rejoice, yea, and will rejoice.' Let them hang me; I forgive them, and may GOD forgive them, for they know not what they do." To Judge TILDEN, of Cleveland, Ohio, he said, "it is a great comfort to *feel assured* that I am permitted to die *for a cause*, not *merely* to pay the debt of nature, as all must. I feel myself to be *most* unworthy of so *great* distinction. * * * * * * I wish I had the time and ability to give you some little idea of what is *daily* passing within my *prison walls ;* and could my friends but witness only a few of those scenes just as they occur, I think they would feel very well reconciled to my being here *just what I am and just as I am.* My *whole* life *before* had not afforded me one-half the opportunity to plead for the right. * * * * * * I have scarce realized that I am in prison or in irons at all." To Rev. Mr. MILLIGAN, of New Alexandria, Pa., he wrote, three days before his death, "I trust, dear brother, that GOD, in infinite grace and mercy, for CHRIST'S sake, 'will neither leave me nor forsake me' till 'I have shewed *his power* to this generation, and *his strength* to every one that is to come.'" To Mr. HOYT, who had been his counsel, he regretted his inability to make other acknowledgment than words, adding, "may GOD and a good conscience be your continual reward. I really do not see what you can do with me any further. I commend my poor family to the kind *remembrance* of all friends, but I well understand that *they are not the only poor in our world.*"

To his wife and children he wrote, on the 8th of November, "I am quite cheerful, having the testimony (in some degree) of a good conscience that I have not lived altogether in vain. I can trust GOD with both the time and the manner of my death, believing, as I now do, that for me, at this time, to seal my testimony (for GOD and humanity) with my blood will do vastly more toward advancing the cause I have earnestly endeavored to promote than all I have done in my life before. I beg of you all, meekly and quietly, to submit to this; not feeling yourselves in the least *degraded* on that account." On the 22nd, to his children, "a calm peace seems to fill my mind by day and by night. Of this, neither the powers of 'earth or hell' can deprive me. Do not, dear children, any of you, grieve for a single moment on my account. As I trust my life has not been thrown away, so I also humbly trust that my death shall not be in vain. GOD can make it to be a thousand times more valuable to His own cause than all the miserable service (at best) that I have rendered it during my life. * * * * * * I feel just as content to die for GOD's Eternal Truth and for suffering humanity, on the scaffold, as in any other way." And on the 24th, "I have had many interesting visits from Pro-Slavery persons, almost daily, and I endeavor to *improve them faithfully, plainly, and kindly*. I do not think I ever enjoyed life better than since my confinement here. For this, I am indebted to *infinite grace* and kind letters from friends from different quarters. I wish I could only know that all my poor family were as composed and as happy as I." And on the 30th, in his letter to his family, "I am waiting the hour of my public murder with great composure of mind and cheerfulness, feeling the strong assurance that in no other possible way could I be used to so much advantage to the cause of good and of humanity, and that nothing that either I or all my family have sacrificed or suffered will be lost. The reflection that a wise and merciful as well as just and holy GOD rules not only the affairs of this world, but of all worlds, is a rock to set our feet upon under all circumstances. I have now no doubt but that our seeming disaster will ultimately result in the most glorious success; so, my dear shattered and broken family, be of good cheer, and believe and trust in GOD with all your heart, and with all your soul; for He doeth all things well. Do not feel ashamed, on my account, nor for one moment despair of the cause or grow weary of well-doing. I bless GOD I never felt stronger confidence in the certain and near approach of a bright morning and a glorious day than I have felt, and do now feel, since my confinement here."

As the day of execution approached the Virginians grew, if possible, more anxious, and their precautionary measures more formidable. The Richmond *Enquirer* sent forth its admonition that "in view of everything surrounding the State and its border, it will be necessary for the people not to flock in crowds to the scenes of the executions. The times when they occur will be the very times when the homesteads on the border will be most threatened with torches. Let those not under arms at the executions, band together as guards of the border." On the 29th of November, Governor WISE proclaimed that the State had taken possession of the Winchester and Potomac Railroad, and would use it entirely for military purposes on the first three days of December; warned the people to remain at home, on patrol duty, on the day of execution, to protect their own property; forbade the approach of women and children to the place of execution; cautioned strangers of danger in coming to or near Charlestown on that day; and announced that, if deemed necessary, martial law would be proclaimed and enforced. General TALIAFERRO, who had now taken command of the military, also issued a proclamation, saying that all strangers, who could not give a satisfactory account of themselves, would be arrested, and all strangers approaching Charlestown would be turned back or arrested. He, too, "emphatically" warned the people to stay at home and protect their property. The telegraph was put under government surveillance, and the military force was increased to nearly three thousand. A large brass cannon, charged with grape-shot, was planted where it could sweep the scaffold, and other cannon were placed so as to command the jail and every approach to it. The stations for the soldiery and sentinels on the field of death were so arranged that no one else could come within hearing of the scaffold; "with the object," says the *Tribune's* reporter, "of keeping the people beyond the reach of BROWN's voice, should he desire to deliver an incendiary speech," so terrible to Slavery were the words of one old man, hedged in with bayonets, his arms pinioned, and a halter about his neck. "'T is conscience that makes cowards of us all," should have been the motto blazoned on the martial ensigns of Virginia's soldiery that day.

On Wednesday night, the 30th of November, Mrs. BROWN

arrived at Harper's Ferry, on her way to Charlestown, accompanied by HECTOR TYNDALE and JAMES M. McKIM and his wife, of Philadelphia. She bore an order from Governor WISE to General TALIAFERRO, for the delivery of her husband's body to her, or her agent, after the execution; and a letter, also, from the governor, assuring her of his "sympathy with her affliction," and of "the exertion of" his "authority and personal influence to assist" her "in gathering up the bones of" her "sons and her husband, in Virginia, 'for decent and tender interment among their kindred.'" Assurances were given by the officers, at Harper's Ferry, that no measures would be taken to prevent her and her friends from proceeding, on the following day, to Charlestown. But it seems the authorities, at Charlestown, thought she was approaching with an escort dangerously strong; for the next morning came a despatch, from head-quarters, saying, "detain Mrs. BROWN, at Harper's Ferry, until further orders, with the lady and two gentlemen, and watch them." Most certainly! By all means, detain and watch them; for who knows with what desperate designs they come? With two men and one woman, all the way from the "Quaker City," who knows but she may "break through the thick array of your thronged legions," O, valiant TALIAFERRO, and bear away, triumphantly, the body of her husband, and those of his companions, too, without waiting for the hangman to do his office on them? As you value the peace and honor of Virginia, and the sacred majesty of her law, do n't let them come to Charlestown. And he did not!

After "several hours" of "triangular correspondence by telegraph between Charlestown, Richmond, and Harper's Ferry," as the *Tribune's* correspondent tells us, "a despatch from General TALIAFERRO" brought intelligence "that he had sent a file of dragoons to escort Mrs. BROWN, but not the others." When she reached the jail, between four and five in the afternoon, Captain AVIS and his wife received her kindly; but Mrs. AVIS, by order of the higher authorities, took her aside, and searched her, lest she should convey to her husband some means of self-destruction. Meanwhile General TALIAFERRO repaired to BROWN's cell, and asked how long he wished the interview with his wife to last. "Not long," he answered, "three or four hours will do." The general thought he could not grant so long a time. "Mrs. Brown must return, to-night, to Harper's Ferry," he said. "Well, carry out your orders," Brown replied, "I ask no favors of the State of Virginia." The general withdrew, and Captain Avis led in Mrs. Brown. They met in "silence more eloquent than any utterance could have been. For some minutes they stood speechless — Mrs. Brown resting her head upon her husband's breast, and clasping his neck with her arms. At length they sat down, and spoke." In the conversation which ensued, he said, in answer to an allusion to their children, "those that are dead to this world are angels in another. How are all those still living? Tell them their father died without a single regret for the course he has pursued — that he is satisfied that he is right in the eyes of God and all just men." He also "requested his wife to make a denial of the statement, which had gained publicity, that he had said, in his interview with Governor Wise, that he had been actuated by feelings of revenge. He had never made such a statement, and such base motives had never been his incentive to action." She remained with him a little more than two hours, conversed of family affairs, took supper with him, received from him his papers, including his will, and part of his effects, and "was led away with the utmost consideration by Captain Avis," and reached Harper's Ferry again, much exhausted, at nine o'clock the same evening. She had wished, before leaving the jail, to speak to the other prisoners; but General Taliaferro had forbidden that, and though Captain Avis expressed a willingness to permit it, at his own risk, she declined, under the circumstances.

"After her departure Brown wrote till midnight; and, at daybreak, resumed his labor with undiminished energy." The contents of a paper, relating to the affairs of his family, which was sent to his wife with his body, "indicated that it must have been written just before he left the jail for the scaffold." At half-past 10, on Friday morning, he was called upon to prepare for death. The sheriff bade him farewell in his cell. Brown thanked him for his kindness, and was then taken to the cells of the other prisoners, except that of Hazlett, whom he had all along refused to recognize. He took leave of them, with a few words to each, exhorting them to "stand up, like men, and not betray their friends." In his parting with Cooke there seems to have been some severity. He charged COOKE with having made a false statement, in saying [in his confession] that he was sent to Harper's Ferry to gain information. "COOKE replied, 'we remember differently,' and dropped his head." STEVENS answered his old captain's greeting with, "Good-bye, captain; I know you are going to a better land." BROWN said, "I know I am."

As he was about leaving the jail, "a black woman, with her little child in her arms, stood near his way. He stopped, for a moment, in his course, stooped over, and, with the tenderness of one whose love is as broad as the brotherhood of man, kissed it affectionately. That mother, says the *Tribune's* correspondent, in relating the incident, "will be proud of that mark of distinction for her offspring, and some day, when over the ashes of JOHN BROWN the temple of Virginian liberty is reared, she may join in the joyful song of praise which, on that soil, will do justice to his memory." The same writer says, "on leaving the jail JOHN BROWN had on his face an expression of calmness and serenity characteristic of the patriot who is about to die with a living consciousness that he is laying down his life for the good of his fellow-creatures. His face was even joyous, and a forgiving smile rested upon his lips. His was the lightest heart, among friends or foes, in the whole of Charlestown, that day, and not a word was spoken that was not an intuitive appreciation of his manly courage. Firmly, and with elastic step, he moved forward. He mounted the wagon, which was to convey him to the scaffold, and took his seat with Captain AVIS, the jailor — whose admiration of his prisoner is of the profoundest nature. Mr. SADLER, the undertaker, rode with them. He, too, was one of BROWN's staunchest friends in his confinement, and pays a noble tribute to his manly qualities. * * * * * * I was very near the old man, and scrutinized him closely. He seemed to take in the whole scene, at a glance, and he straightened himself up proudly, as if to set to the soldiers an example of a soldier's courage. He remarked on the beauty of the country, 'the more beautiful' to him, because he had 'so long been shut from it.' 'You are more cheerful than I am, Captain BROWN,' said Mr. SADLER. 'Yes,' said the captain, 'I ought to be.'"

The wagon was escorted to the scaffold by a company of

cavalry and five companies of infantry, and, including these, more than five hundred soldiers were stationed around the gallows, and nearly three thousand, in all, were upon the ground, while "lines of pickets and patrols," says REDPATH, "encircled the field for fifteen miles." No spectators, except the military, the members of the press, and some half a dozen privileged civilians, were admitted upon the field, and but a small number, estimated at from two to four hundred, were gathered around it; fears of insurrection or invasion having kept the people, generally, at home. By the aid of a glass a few women could be seen standing at the windows of distant houses, but none within reach of the unassisted eye. As the cavalcade entered the field, BROWN noticed the absence of citizens, saying, "they should be allowed to be present, as well as others." On reaching the gallows, he mounted the platform with unfaltering step, and form erect, giving to Mr. HUNTER and Mr. GREEN, as he passed them, standing near, his firm-voiced "good-bye, gentlemen;" and waited silently the making of the last arrangements. When the cap was about to be drawn on, he bade farewell, with evident deep feeling, to those about him, saying to Captain AVIS, "I have no words to thank you for all your kindness to me;" and then stood motionless while the rope was placed around his neck. "I know," says an eye-witness, "that every one within view was greatly impressed with the dignity of his bearing. I have since heard men of the South say that his courageous fortitude and insensibility to fear filled them with amazement." Being asked if he would have a handkerchief to drop as a signal, he declined it, saying, "I am ready at any time; but do not keep me waiting needlessly." His last request of Virginia was not granted. The proceedings were delayed, at least, ten minutes, for the military to perform some useless evolutions, he waiting all the while, in calm composure, with cap and halter on; till the spectators, to whom "each moment seemed an hour," unable to repress their feelings, began to murmur "shame!" At last the idle show was over; the signal given; and, with a wailing creak of hinges, the falling drop proclaimed the martyrdom accomplished.

"An able writer asks," says REDPATH, "was that wailing creak symbolic of the wail of grief that went up, at the moment, from thousands of friends to the cause of emancipation throughout the land?" Nay, rather say it was a wail of pain from the demon of oppression, conscious of a fatal wound from that victorious death.

The martyr's testimony was sealed; the hero's warfare ended. He had fought a good fight with spiritual, if not with carnal weapons; he had finished his course, as grandly as he had begun it bravely and unselfishly; he had kept the faith, the loving faith of Him who came to preach deliverance to the captives; for his crown of righteousness we fear not to trust him to the Lord, the righteous Judge; and even for his earthly fame we wait, with not a shade of doubt, the verdict of posterity.

> " They never fail who nobly die for right;
>   GOD's faithful martyrs cannot suffer loss;
>   Their blazing fagots sow the world with light,
>   And heaven's gate swings upon their bloody cross."

Virginia, too, must bide the judgment of posterity for having deliberately murdered, with the desecrated forms of law, a man whose worth wrung recognition from her governor under circumstances most unfavorable to the perception and confession of it in such a quarter; constraining an acknowledgment of his "integrity and courage and fortitude and simple ingenuousness, his truthfulness, intelligence, and humanity." She has even now, and amidst a Slave-holder's prejudices and misconceptions, a faint, a very faint, foreshadowing of that judgment, as to a single point, in the words of the Frankfort (Ky.) *Yeoman*, arguing in favor of "clemency" toward her captive. "If a European despot," says the *Yeoman*, "can, with the applause of half a universe, restore to their country and friends thousands of exiled enemies, many of them men of great abilities, think of the shame which must rest upon the Commonwealth of Virginia, with a million of freemen, themselves the sovereignty, and a quarter of a million of Slaves held under patriarchal rule, if her security demands and receives the blood of one old, brave, bad man." If the *Yeoman*, even while condemning him as "bad," thinks it so great a shame for Virginia to-kill the "brave old man," how may we expect the deed to be regarded, when, prejudice dispelled, his

11*

character revealed in all its moral.grandeur, he shall be owned,
by an admiring world, as good as he was brave; and the
harshest criticism coupled with his name shall be, "he erred in
judgment in his choice of means to achieve a just and glorious
end?" One hope, however, Virginia may cherish. The charity
of that coming day will doubtless make a due allowance for
the barbarism of her social state in this, and will not judge
her by the standard which would be applied to civilized com-
munities.

We hardly need to say — so well known is the position,
always held by this Society, as to the proper means of carrying on the Anti-Slavery warfare — that, in our tribute to the
memory of the noble hero-martyr, we mean not to imply ap-
proval of his method, or any doubt or question of the well-
proved wisdom of that plan of action which we have been
pursuing from the first. So far from that, we think that one
important lesson, taught by his experience, rightly read, is the
superior force and fitness of moral over physical power, for the
successful prosecution of a work like ours. It therefore has
confirmed us in the choice we made, at the beginning, of
spiritual instead of carnal weapons for the pulling down of the
strongholds of oppression.

A few hours after the execution, the body of JOHN BROWN
was delivered to Messrs. TYNDALE and McKIM, at Harper's
Ferry. Mrs. BROWN had wished to get the remains of OLIVER
and WATSON, also; but the former had been buried, two days
after the final battle, in a large pit, promiscuously with the
other slain of the company; and the latter had been carried
off to Winchester Medical College, for dissection, so that
neither was in a condition to be removed; but she was assured
by Colonel BARBOUR, Superintendent of the United States
Armory, that all the bodies should be disinterred, and re-buried
with becoming propriety. On Saturday, she and her friends,
with her husband's body, arrived in Philadelphia, at a little
after noon, meaning to stay there until Monday morning;
partly to give herself the rest she greatly needed, and partly
to put the body, as soon a possible, into an undertaker's care.
But the mayor of the city, taking on himself what was, to say
the least, a very questionable authority, insisted that it should
go on by the next train to New York. So it went on, accom-

panied by Mr. McKim; while Mrs. Brown remained in Philadelphia to rest. One of the noblest men that city holds, Rev. Wm. H. Furness, referring, through the press, to the mayor's arbitrary course, remarked that he "thought the time was not far distant when the citizens of Philadelphia would be sorry to remember that the remains of John Brown were not suffered to rest, a few hours, in our city; and that, if the feeling of the public had been up to the greatness of the occasion, the whole population of Philadelphia would have been at the depot, with all our authorities, civil, ecclesiastical, and military, at their head. That the mayor," he continued, "transcended his authority in thus casting out the body of one, of whom an officer of the navy and a native of South Carolina remarked that this country had not produced his like for a hundred years, must be manifest to all. Mrs. Brown arrived in New York on Sunday evening, and the next morning continued on her homeward journey, attended by Mr. McKim and Wendell Phillips. "The friends of the Slave, in New York," says the *Anti-Slavery Standard*, "had expected that some opportunity would be afforded, here, for public manifestations of respect for the remains of the martyr; but his own dying wish, the earnest desire of Mrs. Brown that his children and grandchildren might be permitted to look upon his features before decomposition, and other considerations that need not be mentioned, led to the conclusion that it would be best to take them quietly, speedily, and unostentatiously, to the family residence for interment. This course was, on the whole, deemed most in accordance with the simple, undemonstrative grandeur of the old man's character. * * * * * * It was our privilege to look upon the face, and lay our hand upon the brow of the martyred dead. The features wore a calm and placid expression, as if the noble old man had simply laid down to rest for a night."

Of the journey to North Elba, the reception there, and the funeral services, we glean a few particulars from a deeply interesting and pathetic narrative, published in the *Anti-Slavery Standard*, of December 17th, from the pen of J. M. McKim. Passing through Troy, New York, where they had to wait two hours for the northward train; spending a night at Rutland, Vermont; making a short pause at Vergennes, their last point on the railroad; crossing Lake Champlain in a boat which diverged from its course on purpose to land them at the point most convenient for them; spending the second night at Elizabethtown, the county seat of Essex County, where BROWN was well known and had many friends; and thence toiling, through a long day's ride, over a difficult mountain-road, the party reached their destination, after dark, on Wednesday evening. At the places where they stopped, though notice of their coming had not gone before, the news of their arrival brought together large numbers of the people, without distinction of party, including lawyers, judges, and other leading citizens, eager to do honor to the memory of the departed hero, and show respect and sympathy for his bereaved wife. At Vergennes, after their wants had been hospitably supplied at the hotel, carriages were provided to convey the body and its attendants to the lake-shore, and a procession formed quietly and escorted the party about a third of a mile to the bridge over Otter Creek, then falling into a double line, with uncovered heads, allowed them to pass through, and so took silent leave of them. "It was a spontaneous tribute, and an affecting sight." At Elizabethtown the sheriff offered the court-house as a resting-place for the body through the night, and six young men, including several lawyers, volunteered to guard it there till morning. Thither, although a heavy rain was falling, it was followed by a respectable procession, formed at the moment's call; and "soon the house was filled by the leading residents of the town, eager to learn from Messrs. PHILLIPS and McKIM all the particulars of the execution. They found it hard to realize that their old friend and fellow-citizen, the man whom they had known so well, and only known to respect, had actually been put to death. They had not thought that, in the last extremity, Virginia would do the bloody deed. They did not see how Governor WISE could have deliberately consented to the death of such a man."

The unusually bad condition of the road made their arrival at North Elba later than had been expected; and anxious friends, who had been waiting for them all the afternoon, and were now out with lighted lanterns watching for their coming, met them as they approached, and led them to the house without a word. "A burst of love and anguish" marked the meeting of the widow and her children; "but soon all was composed. Emotion was put under constraint — an accustomed task with these people — and all was quiet." After the evening meal Mr. McKim, at Mrs. Brown's request, related to the family and guests, as fully as the time allowed, all which had happened in the sad pilgrimage from which she had just returned; and "Mr. Phillips then took up the theme, and, in the tenderest and most beautiful manner pursued it, till all tears were wiped away. A holy, pensive joy seemed gradually to dispel all grief, and a becoming filial and conjugal pride to reconcile these stricken ones to their destiny."

The funeral took place at one o'clock, the following day, December 8. The country being thinly settled, the house, with crowding, could hold all who came. Besides the strangers who had come with Mrs. Brown, were present Mr. L. G. Bigelow, and Rev. Joshua Young, and two others, of Burlington, Vermont, who "had travelled all night through the storm, and over the dismal mountain, to be present at the burial." The hymn, beginning, "Blow ye the trumpet, blow," which had been a favorite one with Brown, was sung; a short, impressive prayer, by Mr. Young, was followed by addresses, which we need not say were fit and eloquent, from McKim and Phillips; another hymn was sung; neighbors and friends, and last the family, gave the still face their parting look; the procession moved to the grave, beneath the shadow of a rock near by; and when the body was lowered into it, and "a gush of grief, apparently beyond control, burst from the family," those words of Paul to Timothy, so admirably apt to the occasion — "I have fought a good fight; I have finished my course; I have kept the faith; henceforth there is laid up for me a crown of righteousness which the Lord, the righteous Judge, shall give to me; and not to me only, but unto all that love his appearing;" were uttered in the "deep and mellow voice" of Mr. Young; and then he closed the solemn service with the customary form of benediction. "The words seemed to fall like balm on all who heard them. The sobs were hushed, and soon the family, with the rest, retired from the grave, leaving the remains of the loved one to their last repose."

On the 1st of November, the day after BROWN's conviction, the Executive Committee of the American Anti-Slavery Society met in Boston, and adopted a resolution, recommending " to the friends of impartial freedom throughout the Free States, in case of the execution of Captain JOHN BROWN, to observe that tragical event, ON THE DAY OF ITS OCCURRENCE, in such manner as by them may be deemed most appropriate in their various localities — whether by public meetings and addresses, the adoption of resolutions, private conferences, or any other justifiable mode of action — for the furtherance of the Anti-Slavery cause."   Editors of newspapers were requested to copy the notice, or to give its substance in their columns.   In compliance with this request it was widely copied by the press, and found favor in all directions.   And in a multitude of places, scattered over all the North ; in Philadelphia, New York, and Boston, in Providence and Worcester, Albany and Cleveland ; in short, in cities, towns, and villages, far more than we have room to name, the 2nd of December was a day of solemn convocation ; church bells were tolled, minute guns were fired, and emblems of mourning were displayed, appropriate hymns were sung, and prayers were offered, speeches were made, and resolutions were adopted expressing admiration of the martyr, condemnation of the treatment he received from the Virginian people and authorities, and strong abhorrence of the system for whose safety he was doomed to die. In many meetings his last speech was read, and very generally, we believe, collections were made, or provided for by the appointment of committees to make them, in aid of his bereaved family, and those of his slain companions.   We cannot doubt that the occasion, opening, as it did, so largely the hearts of the people to the appeals of truth and justice and humanity, and faithfully used as it was by so many earnest advocates of right and freedom, did much to spread and strengthen Anti-Slavery feeling and conviction, and to advance the Anti-Slavery cause toward its predestined triumph.

JOHN BROWN'S COMPANIONS.

On Thursday evening, December 15, a sentinel, stationed near the Charlestown jail, discovered and defeated an attempt of Cooke and Coppoc to escape. With a saw, made of an old pocket-knife, they had cut through their irons; and with a sort of chisel, made of an old bed-screw, had removed brick after brick from the prison-wall, until the opening was sufficient to let them through into the yard. Then, aided by the timbers of the scaffold on which Brown was hung, they climbed the outer wall, about fifteen feet in height, and would have dropped down on the other side had not the sentinel observed them, and given the alarm. Could they have gained the open street, ten minutes run, it is said, would have taken them to the Shenandoah mountain, and with the advantage of the darkness, and their thorough knowledge of the mountains, their chance for a complete escape would have been by no means desperate. But, being detected before they reached the ground, they gave up the attempt as hopeless and retreated to the yard, where they were reärrested by General Taliaferro and the officer of the day, who hastened to the jail upon the first alarm.

Green and Copeland were executed in the forenoon of the next day, and Cooke and Coppoc in the afternoon. They bore themselves with a firmness, quiet courage, and composure, worthy of the followers of John Brown. "A few minutes before leaving the jail," as the *Baltimore Sun* informs us, "Copeland said, 'If I am dying for Freedom, I could not die for a better cause — *I had rather die than be a Slave!*'" A military officer in charge, on the day of the execution, says, "I had a position near the gallows, and carefully observed all. I can truly say, I never witnessed more firm and unwavering fortitude, more perfect composure, or more beautiful propriety, than were manifested by young Copeland to the very last." Of Cooke and Coppoc, the *Tribune's* correspondent says, "the prisoners ascended the scaffold with a determined firmness that was scarcely surpassed by Captain Brown." And again, "The calm and collected manner of both was very marked. They both exhibited the most unflinching firmness." In a conversation, at the jail, on the morning of the fatal day, "Cooke said to a gentleman who addressed him, that they fully believed Slavery to be a sin, and that it would be abolished in Virginia in less than ten years, and that by the people of Virginia. He was prepared to die in such a cause, and thought he had done nothing to regret, so far as principle was concerned." Just before they left the prison for the scaffold, a friend remarked that it was hard to die. "It is the parting from friends," responded COPPOC, "not the dread of death that moves us." In one respect their conduct differed from their leader's. They consented to receive the offered services of the clergy, and religious exercises were performed, both at the jail and on the scaffold.

COOKE's body was sent to his friends in New York city, where his funeral took place on the morning of the 20th, at a private house, the place of worship of the church to which his relatives belong having been refused for the purpose, except under such restrictions as rendered the use of it impossible. The attendance was large; "not less," the *Tribune* states, "than six hundred or eight hundred, including many ladies, were standing in the rain two hours, along the street before the house; so great was the fascination of his life and death." Rev. Mr. CALDICOTT, of the South Baptist Church, who, aided by two other clergymen, conducted the services, spoke of the departed as "a child of GOD," attested his affectionate disposition, his faithful attachment to his friends, and his love for the Christian religion, adding that "if he made any mistake in life, it was in pity of those over whom wept Christ; he thought he was laboring for the good of Christ's oppressed ones." The body of COPPOC, also, was given to his friends, and "his funeral took place near Hanover, Ohio, on the 18th, and was conducted according to Quaker rites, his friends belonging to that order. There were two thousand persons at the funeral." COPELAND and GREEN were buried on the spot where they were hung, and all efforts of their friends to get their bodies for interment elsewhere proved unavailing. A correspondent of the Cincinnati *Gazette*, who was present at the execution, says, "they were allowed to remain in the ground but a few moments, when they were taken up and conveyed to Winchester for dissection."

According to a correspondent of the Cleveland *Leader*, the relatives of COPELAND, living in Ohio, applied, by telegraph, to Governor WISE, through A. N. BEECHER, Mayor of Oberlin, for the body of their kinsman, and the governor promised that it should be given, by General TALIAFERRO, to any white citizen. But when, at Mayor BEECHER's telegraphed request, a southern gentleman, sojourning in Washington, "strongly Pro-Slavery in sentiment," provided with an order for the body, and a letter from the congressman of the Charlestown district, called upon General TALIAFERRO, and presented his credentials, he was arrested and kept twelve hours, and then permitted to return to Washington. Some, we have heard, were so uncharitable, as, from these facts, to infer a deliberate design to give the medical students time to secure their coveted prize, although a governor's promise must thereby be broken. A Virginian governor's word is sacred, we suppose, unless the keeping of it will accrue to the advantage of that sort of folks who "have no rights," &c., [see Taney, on Dred Scott,] or, possibly, will gratify the feelings of that other sort who will not take Judge TANEY's dictum for law and gospel both. Unwilling to be baffled so, however, the friends of Freedom, in Ohio, resolved to make another effort to obtain the bodies of the colored men; and, for that purpose, Professor JAMES MONROE, of Oberlin College, went to Virginia, but his endeavor, earnest as it was, was unsuccessful.

On Sunday, December 29, the funeral of COPELAND was attended, in the church, at Oberlin, "by full three thousand persons." Professor MONROE gave an account of his mission to Virginia, from which he had just returned. Professor PECK "preached," we are told, "an eloquent funeral sermon," in which "he marked the providence of GOD, which had furnished for the colored race a not less firm, heroic, and Christ-like champion than had the white race in the person of the immortal JOHN BROWN." "How brightly," said he, "do his virtues shine when the circumstances of his last days are carefully considered! Falsely published, by the highest authority of Virginia, as craven and trembling; fearful, doubtless, that the base slander might be believed; uncheered by the friendly assurance of admiring thousands which so greatly sustained other patriots; surrounded by those who never dreamed of nobleness in a negro, why did he not sink? I answer — GOD inspired him with Christian courage to nobly represent a race; and how worthily did he represent them!" The Anti-Slavery citizens of Oberlin have undertaken to erect a monument to COPELAND, and his colored comrades, LEWIS LEARY and SHIELDS GREEN, "those noble representatives of the colored race of the nineteenth century," as they are called in a circular sent out to ask subscriptions for the object. The circular contains two letters written by COPELAND, while in jail, await-ing execution. A correspondent of the *Anti-Slavery Standard*, justly says, they "are, in every way, creditable productions, and proofs that the writer is not unworthy the monument which his friends propose to erect to his memory."

During the first week in January, a Slave of Colonel FRANCIS McCORMICK, in Clarke County, Va., (adjoining Jefferson County, in which Harper's Ferry is,) was tried, convicted, and con-demned to death, on a charge of conspiring with other Slaves, to rebel. The 17th day of February was appointed for his execution. The court "strongly recommended him to the mercy of the executive;" but the Clarke County *Conservator*, from which we learn these facts, says, "we have not the re-motest idea that Governor LETCHER will be so indiscreet as to commute the sentence." Whether the governor has acted thus indiscreetly, or not, we are not informed. But if we may believe the testimony given at the trial, as reported by the *Conservator*, the loyalty of Slaves to masters, in that region, would hardly seem to stand so high as Governor WISE, Judge PARKER, and Attorney HARDING rate it. The Slave in ques-tion, JERRY, it appears, excited the suspicion of a white man, Mr. CHAMBLIN, by the alacrity of his replies to certain ques-tions, asked, "without any particular motive," as to the number of his master's Slaves, and of the colored people thereabouts, &c. So Mr. CHAMBLIN went on to question JERRY further, *with* a motive. What did he think of the affair at Harper's Ferry? JERRY "was glad to hear of it." Why was he not there? "Because I did not know exactly when to go." Would he have gone if he had known? "Yes; and I have four sons who would have followed me. I would be ready to go at any time." And, turning to another negro, JOE, who was at work with him, JERRY said, "would not you go, too?" JOE would, and asked the white man if he was one of BROWN's men. "Yes;" was the white lie in response; and JERRY added, "he is going about to let us know." He then told CHAMBLIN "where he would find other negroes to talk with on the sub-ject, stating that the patrol was out, and would not let them go from one place to another without a pass. He said there had been some burnings since the patrol commenced, and 'we will keep on burning until they are stopped.'" CHAMBLIN went back, some ten days afterward, to have another talk with JOE and JERRY, and heard from them of plots for house-burning, and the like; and then "the conversation turned upon JOHN BROWN, then in jail, under sentence of death, and the possibility of rescuing him, JOE remarking that he had heard that an army was coming on to take him out of jail, 'and if we join them we can take him out;' to which JERRY assented, provided they could stop the patrol, so they could get about." JERRY, as we have said, was doomed to death for his incautious confidence; but JOE was only "ordered to be sold out of the State;" in the belief, no doubt — for Virginia surely would not scatter fire-brands in her neighbors' powder-houses — that exile will drive out of him all memory of JOHN BROWN, and all uneasy thoughts of freedom; and in any other State he will become at once a quiet, faithful, and contented Slave. Of course he will.

The question, which should have the privilege of hanging STEVENS, Virginia or the United States, was settled, finally, in favor of the former. Mr. HARDING would not yield his prior claim, though for awhile it was supposed he had done so; and the prisoner, his counsel, and the public expected that the trial would take place at Staunton, before the United States District Court. At one time, it was said by those who wished to pass for knowing ones, that the case was to be taken to the Federal Court, mainly in order to obtain the testimony of some distinguished northern men, whom a Virginian process could not reach, but who were thought to have important knowledge in relation to the secret history of BROWN's enterprise. But after one House of Congress had appointed an Investigating Committee to look into the whole affair, with power to call up those reluctant witnesses, the reason for the transfer ceased, if it was what had been surmised. Be that, however, as it may, it was announced, some time in January, that a special term of the Circuit Court of Jefferson County would be held, beginning on the 1st of February, for the trial of the two remaining prisoners. Accordingly, upon that day, the court was opened by Judge KENNEY, Judge PARKER being engaged in other duties; the grand jury brought in new indictments against the prisoners, severally, charging the same

offences as the former against STEVENS (which was now abandoned); and, on the following day, the trial of STEVENS
began. He was "in seeming perfect health, and in good
spirits." He was defended with ability and zeal by Mr. SEN-
NOTT, who contested, manfully, every point on which a legal
question could be fairly raised; and, at the close, after a trial
of nearly three days' duration, made a most earnest and pathetic appeal to the jury in his client's behalf; but all, of
course, without avail. The amiable HARDING, in his opening
argument for the prosecution, blandly pronounced the prisoner
"a blood-thirsty villain and wretch, and worse than BROWN;"
the astute HUNTER, in his closing argument, declared that "the
invasion had been a benefit to the South, as it had shown them
the position in which they were placed;" a profitable, perhaps, if rightly used, but hardly, one would think, a pleasant
sight; and then the jury took the case, at four o'clock, of February 4, and after fifteen minutes' absence, returned a verdict
of guilty on all the counts. "The prisoner received the verdict with most perfect indifference, and smiled at the announcement."

The next week was devoted to the trial of HAZLETT, which
ended on Saturday, the 11th, in a conviction of murder in the
first degree. He was defended by Messrs. GREEN and BOTTS.
Like his fellow-prisoner, he heard the verdict with the same unmoved composure which he had exhibited throughout the trial.
On Monday, the 13th, they were brought in for sentence.
"Both prisoners," says the correspondent of the Baltimore *Sun*,
"wore an unconcerned air, and seemed utterly unterrified at
the awful position in which they have placed themselves." The
morning had been occupied in presenting and disposing of
bills of exception in HAZLETT's case, and it was noon before
STEVENS was brought in. To the customary question before
sentence, STEVENS answered by denying the statement of a
witness, that he had proposed to kill the people and burn the
town; expressing satisfaction with the conduct of his counsel;
thanking the officers in charge of him for their kindness, and
the physicians for services rendered while he suffered from his
wounds; and saying, in conclusion, "when I think of my
brothers slaughtered and sisters outraged [meaning, it was
supposed, his *northern* brethren and sisters in Kansas], my con-

science does not reprove me for my actions. I shall meet my fate manfully." HAZLETT denied having ever committed or contemplated murder, or joined with others to commit it; contradicted several · statements of some of the witnesses to his identity, but forgave them all; acknowledged the kind treatment he had received; thanked his counsel; and closed with, "I repeat, I am innocent of murder, but I am prepared to meet my fate." The judge then preached them a sermon on the enormity of their crime; on their youth and genteel appearance, and his pity for them; on their awful situation, and the importance of preparing to meet a higher Judge; on the invitation of a gracious Redeemer, to even the greatest criminals, to repent of their crimes; on the readiness of the ministers of our holy religion, if called upon, to instruct them in the way of eternal life, and to pray with and for them; and concluded by sentencing them to be hung on Friday, the 16th of March: — all which they appear to have taken as quietly as they had all the previous proceedings. The hint about "the ministers of our holy [Slave-holding] religion," they did not see fit to act upon, not wishing for the guidance or the intercession of Slave-holders and the advocates of Slavery.

An ineffectual effort was made to procure a pardon for the prisoners. As it could be granted only on the recommendation of both houses of the Legislature to the governor, Mr. SEN-NOTT repaired to Richmond, and, on the evening of the 8th of March, addressed the Joint Committee to which the application had been referred. "The senate-chamber, lobby and gallery were very much crowded during the delivery of the address, which was listened to throughout with marked attention. Among the auditors was Governor LETCHER, with many of the prominent members of both houses, and a number of prominent citizens." But Virginia had not the courage to be just or merciful or even worldly-wise. The committee unanimously reported that it was inexpedient for the Legislature to interfere with the sentence; and, consequently, on the appointed day, it was duly executed. This issue of their case brought to the prisoners neither terror nor surprise. They had expected it, and they were ready for it. Before his trial had begun, STEVENS wrote to a friend, "My trial comes on to-morrow, and I shall soon know my *destiny*. I have very little hope of anything short of the Better Land." In the same letter he said, "I thank GOD that he gave me a soul that can feel for the oppressed." And the day after his conviction, "I am cheerful and happy, patiently waiting the fate of man — death." HAZLETT also wrote, the day before his death, "I am willing to die in the cause of Liberty. If I had ten thousand lives, I would willingly lay them all down for the same cause. My death will do more good than if I had lived." What wonder that elective affinity drew such men to JOHN BROWN!

Eight companies of soldiers and an immense throng of spectators attended the execution. The Charlestown *Jeffersonian* says, in its account of the event, "the near approach of the day of execution seemed to have but little effect on the prisoners, and for the last few days they were unusually cheerful, STEVENS declaring it was his wish to be free, and therefore desired the day for his execution to arrive." His sister, Mrs. PIERCE, of Norwich, Ct., was often with him during the last eight days of his life; and, on the afternoon before its close, arrived another welcome visitor, a Miss DUNBAR, from Ashtabula County, Ohio, who had just been to Richmond, on a fruitless errand to the governor, to plead for the prisoner's life. A brother of HAZLETT also came, a few days before the execution, and, on the final Friday morning, the prisoners and their friends took breakfast together, in the passage of the prison; and shortly after exchanged their last farewells. About noon the prisoners left the jail, and walked to the scaffold. The *Jeffersonian* says, "HAZLETT was in advance, and ascended the steps with an easy, unconcerned air, followed by STEVENS. Both seemed to survey, with perfect indifference, the large mass of persons in attendance, and neither gave the least·sign of fear." The reporter of the New-York *Tribune* says, "there were no religious exercises at the gallows, as the prisoners persisted in refusing all the kindly offices of the ministry, in their last moments. They had a peculiar religion of their own, which enabled them to meet their fate with cheerfulness and resignation." [One peculiarity of that "peculiar religion" may be inferred from these words of STEVENS, in a letter which he wrote, three days before. "I hope you will always, as you love yourself, as you love woman, as you love man, as you love GOD, work with hands, head, and heart, for the happiness of all mankind."] A little time sufficed for the adjustment of the ropes, and for "an affectionate farewell to the sheriff, jailor, jail-guard," and each other; then, on the hinges of the falling drop, the gate swung open to the "Better Land," as STEVENS loved to call it, and the freedom they desired was won.

The bodies were immediately conveyed to Eagleswood, N. J., where, at the house of MARCUS SPRING, the funeral services took place upon the following Sunday. The house was crowded by the residents of Eagleswood and Perth Amboy. The Rev. HIRAM P. ARMS, of Norwich, Ct., pastor of the church of which the father of young STEVENS is a member, conducted the religious services. A hymn was sung, then Mr. ARMS read passages of Scripture and made some impressive remarks and an appropriate prayer; THEODORE TILTON spoke "with a power which stirred every heart;" extracts were read by Mrs. SPRING, from letters written by STEVENS, while in jail, showing that he considered it an honor to die in the cause of liberty, and that his last days were cheered by the hope of a blessed immortality; OLIVER JOHNSON made a brief address, and the exercises were closed by the singing of another hymn. "The bodies of the dead, followed by nearly all the residents of the place, in solemn procession, were then borne to the Eagleswood cemetery, where they were interred, side by side, near the graves of JAMES G. BIRNEY and ARNOLD BUFFUM."

The day of this last execution, as well as that on which COOKE and his companions died, was, to some extent, observed as the day of JOHN BROWN's death had been, though by no means so extensively. At a meeting, held in Boston, on Friday evening, March 16, some of the prison-letters of STEVENS were read, from which we copy three or four brief extracts. The first we quote was written the day after his four friends were executed. "I expect," he said, referring to his comrades who had died in battle or upon the scaffold, "to follow them, ere long, to that brighter world where we shall again meet; and what joy it will be to meet with those who have suffered and died for the human family." And after speaking of his wounds, he added, "I feel very cheerful and happy. Of course it is rather disagreeable to be confined to so narrow limits, and wear chains, but I forget all about it when thinking how many are suffering so much more than this. At times, my

heart feels like bursting with sorrow for the crimes and suffer-
ings of the human family, and if I could help wash away that
suffering, I would give ten thousand lives, if I had them to
give. Four of the men passed off, yesterday, to the spirit-land,
through the mercy of Virginia. They were cheerful, and met
their fate like men." Ten days later, he wrote, "I am as cheerful and contented as you could expect; ready to meet anything
that comes. It is true that I should like to live yet awhile, for
I have just got old enough to see how to live." It was no
insensibility to the worth and the delight of life, which gave
him power to face death so calmly. The next was written
three days after he received his sentence. "I have not much
hope that the governor will commute my sentence. There are
many very good-feeling people about here, and I have been
treated very kindly by the better classes, generally. I am very
cheerful and happy, and ready to die at a moment's warning,
if needs be, although I should like to live as long as most
anybody. I do not want you to worry, in the least, about me,
for if I go to the other world I shall be better off than I
could be here. * * * * * * Oh! I should like to see you all,
once more, but it will be but a few years, compared with eternity, before we shall meet in the spirit-land, and that meeting
will wash away all sorrow of parting here."

"I think these letters," said the reader of them, "deserve a
place in that most noble collection of JOHN BROWN'S, the
sweetest and purest utterances of our Saxon tongue." It may
not be amiss to add that those which we have seen from
OLIVER and WATSON BROWN are not unworthy of the same
companionship, and show their writers to be genuine scions
of the noble parent-stock. The former, in a letter to his
sister, said, "if only one good action is done in a lifetime, it
is enough to show that life is not altogether a failure." And
to his wife he wrote, "when I look at your picture I am
wholly ashamed of my every meanness, weakness, and folly.
* * * * * * I am more and more determined, every day, to
live a more unselfish life." And WATSON, writing to his wife
from the neighborhood of Harper's Ferry, said, "I would gladly
come home and stay with you always, but for that which
brought me here — a desire to do something for others, and
not to live wholly for my own happiness. Nothing but the

object before me could keep me from you." And in another letter, "I want to see you and the little fellow very much; but I must wait. There was a Slave, near here, whose wife was sold off South, the other day, and was found in THOMAS KENNEDY's orchard, dead, the next morning. Cannot come home so long as such things are done here."

The Charlestown *Jeffersonian* hoped the execution of STEVENS and HAZLETT would be "the final act in the Harper's Ferry tragedy, and that the remaining wretches of BROWN's party would be permitted to wander through the world with the sting of a guilty conscience, and scorned by all honest men, rather than our county shall be made the theatre of another season of excitement." A generous reason for a humane wish! If the *Jeffersonian* could but find a way to *make* such men as BROWN and his associates suffer for deeds like theirs "the sting of a guilty conscience, and the scorn of all honest men," the discovery would be invaluable to tyrants; saving much cost of dungeons, racks, and gibbets, and softening into down the spines of many a thorny pillow. But how to do it, is the stubborn problem offered by such lives and words and deaths as theirs; and by the warm, spontaneous sympathy and admiration which have greeted them from both sides of the ocean, and from men whose praise is honor now, and the pledge of fair and lasting fame hereafter. At all events, Virginia did not choose to wait the solving of that problem, nor share the *Jeffersonian's* satiety of blood. "The remaining wretches" were indicted for conspiring to excite a servile insurrection, and no thanks are due to Virginia's clemency, that they were not seized and tried and put to death. Hearing that BARCLAY COPPOC, who had fled, at first, to Canada, had since returned to his home, in Iowa, and learning or suspecting that MERRIAM and OWEN BROWN were in Ohio, Governor LETCHER sent to the governors of those States his requisitions for the "fugitives from justice." The governor of Iowa found that the requisition sent to him was formally defective, and consequently could not legally comply with it; and when another, mending the defect, arrived, the fugitive was gone beyond his jurisdiction. The governor of Ohio submitted to the attorney general of the State the requisition sent to him; and the attorney, in a carefully prepared opinion, demon-

strated that Virginia had made out no valid claim upon the
men she asked for. "The papers did not show, or even allege,
that they had ever fled from Virginia," but, if from anywhere,
it was from Maryland. So they were not surrendered; whereat
Virginia was becomingly indignant. The governor sent a
message to the Legislature, telling all about the misbehavior
of his northern brothers; the Legislature raised a special joint
committee on the subject; and the committee made a long
report, reviewing the whole matter, and concluding with a
resolution, which declared that the offending governors had
"wilfully and deliberately violated the Federal Compact, disregarding the comity which should exist between sovereign
States, and justly made themselves morally, if not legally,
accessories to the crimes committed by these criminals and
fugitives from justice." A resolution was also offered, in the
House, proposing to demand from every citizen of Ohio or
Iowa, found within the limits of Virginia, bonds and security
for their good behavior while staying in the Commonwealth.
The vote had not been taken on these resolutions, at our last
intelligence, but we may confidently trust that the Legislature
took such action, in due time, as to assert, with proper emphasis, the dignity and sovereign rights of the ancient commonwealth.

The Legislature, early in its session, had appointed a committee to investigate the proofs, which it was then expected or
pretended would be found abundant, that prominent Republicans and Abolitionists and large numbers of the northern
people were concerned in JOHN BROWN's enterprise. But
after taking all the winter, nearly, for the investigation, and
turning inside out the famous "carpet-bag," and sifting all its
contents, we may well believe, with careful scrutiny, the committee was obliged, at last, to own, in its report, that it could
not find the object of its eager search, the *proof* of the alleged
complicity with BROWN. The *fact* was plain enough to their
fear-sharpened vision still, but the *evidence* was wanting.
JOHN BROWN had cheated them, completely, out of that, by
winnowing before they sifted, and leaving but the chaff to feed
their keen and disappointed appetites. In other words, he had
left them the precious papers, after striking out whatever, they
affected to believe, would surely implicate his secret fellow-

plotters, not leaving proof enough of treason and conspiracy to hang a single " Black Republican," or blacker Abolitionist, of them all. There is much evidence, they say, " to show the existence, in a number of the northern States, of a wide-spread conspiracy, not merely against Virginia, but against the peace and security of all the southern States. But the careful erasure of names and dates from many of the papers found in BROWN's possession, renders it difficult to procure legal evidence of the guilt of the parties implicated." "No doubt of it," comments the New-York *Evening Post*, "there is a great deal of evidence in the brains of the Virginians, but none to be got at elsewhere."

THE HUNT FOR TREASON.

The very first motion made at the present session of Congress had relation to the same subject. On the first day of the session, as soon as the Senate was ready to proceed to business, Mr. MASON, of Virginia, submitted a resolution " for the appointment of a committee to inquire into the facts attending the late invasion and seizure of the armory and arsenal, at Harper's Ferry; * * * * * whether any citizens of the United States, not present, were implicated therein, or accessory thereto, by contributions of money, arms, munitions, or otherwise; * * * * * also, to report what legislation, if any, is necessary for the future preservation of the peace of the country; the committee to have power to send for persons and papers." Mr. TRUMBULL, of Illinois, promised it his cordial support, but proposed to make the investigation impartial and thorough, by an amendment to extend it to the seizure of the arsenal, in Missouri, in 1855, for the purpose of forcing Slavery into Kansas. After a spirited debate, running through eight or ten days, in which Republican senators disclaimed, for themselves and the northern people generally, all sympathy with BROWN's incursion, TRUMBULL's amendment was rejected, the resolution was adopted, and the committee constituted, with Mr. MASON for its chairman, and straightway entered upon its work.

It is not finished yet. A multitude of witnesses have been examined, at no small cost of time and money; and all without eliciting those startling revelations which Mr. MASON sought, desired, and really seems somehow to have expected. Instead of that, the evidence is clear and ample against the conclusions which he wished to reach; and as a machine for manufacturing political capital wherewith to help the sham Democracy, the investigation has already proved a signal failure. Nor has it better served the purpose of creating sympathy for the upholders of oppression, in the peril, fear, and tribulation brought upon themselves by their own persistence in wrong-doing; and of making public sentiment more hostile to the principles and promoters of the Anti-Slavery cause. But, on the other hand, it has drawn out some noble testimonies for the right, and sent them over all the land, through the innumerable issues of the daily press, and has, in other ways, done unmeant service to the cause of Freedom. The testimony of Mr. GIDDINGS, for example, was really an Anti-Slavery argument, terse, vigorous, and impressive; that of Judge ARNY set the views and purposes and character of BROWN in a very different light from that in which Virginia wished them to appear, showing him free from vindictive feeling, " truthful and conscientious, and fully convinced that he was to be the instrument, in the hand of GOD, to emancipate the Slaves;" while GEORGE L. STEARNS declared that he "believed JOHN BROWN to be the representative man of this century, as WASHINGTON was of the last;" and JOHN A. ANDREW plainly told the Senatorial inquisitors that "JOHN BROWN and Harper's Ferry were fruit native to the tree which the Slave-power had planted."

One prominent, and we think not unprofitable effect of the investigation, has been the agitation of the question of the Senate's right to take upon itself judicial powers, exceeding even, in some respects, those of the courts of law. For while the courts cannot compel a man to criminate himself, the law of Congress, under which the Senate claims to act, permits no such exemption. Some of the witnesses, called by the committee, testified under protest, and others positively refused to come. Some went beyond the reach of process, and others, or at least one other, openly and successfully defied it. Of the first class were Dr. S. G. HOWE and JOHN A. ANDREW. The former would not take the oath to testify till he had been permitted to enter his protest against the whole proceeding, on the grounds that "the tribunal is secret and inquisitorial; is created for purposes beyond the legitimate scope of legislative inquiry; usurps powers nowhere clearly delegated by the Constitution to Congress, or either branch thereof; is dangerous, as a precedent, and liable to abuse, to the peril of private right and personal liberty; and is unnecessary, inasmuch as for all the purposes of investigation, testimony by deposition, under the jurisdiction and within the limits of the respective States, is fully adequate." Mr. ANDREW closed his testimony with a protest similar in substance. Dr. DOY, suspicious that to obey the call of the committee would put him on the road back to the Missouri jail, from which he had been rescued, wrote to the chairman, and, alluding to the high reward offered, in Missouri, for his recapture, declined to go to Washington until he should " have the assurance, from some responsible authority," that he should not find himself "in the hands of a kidnapping party of government officials, who are willing to sell their honor for a government bribe."

Marshal JOHNSON, of Ohio, left a summons, from the committee, at the house of JOHN BROWN, Jr.. with a letter giving him Senator MASON's assurance that, if he would come on and testify, he would, according to the law of Congress, be afterward exempt from prosecution for any act he might have done, to which his testimony had referred. The marshal added his own "pledge of sacred honor," that, if BROWN would go with him to Washington, he would see him safely returned to his home, after the giving of his testimony. BROWN replied that, after full consideration, he had resolved, for two reasons, not to obey the summons. First, because he had "experienced too much of Slave-holding perfidy to rely on the faith of a State whose honor and magnanimity are represented by the *author of the Fugitive-Slave Bill,* and whose chief revenue is derived from *the sale of her own sons and daughters :*" and which, even if she could not crush him by judicial process, would not protect him from the violence of her mobs. Second, by swearing to tell the whole truth, so far as he knows it, in relation to the subject of investigation, he would bind himself to tell that which would implicate others, "which. *as the Lord liveth, I will not do.*" To the assurance of exemption from prosecution, he replied that he could not purchase that immunity by an act of treachery. To Slavery he owed no obligations; but to those who labored, by word or deed, to aid the Slaves to throw off the yoke, he owed "unswerving fidelity." He concluded with a plain intimation that he should not leave his home to shun the consequences of his disobedience to the summons; thus openly defying the authority of its senders. This was on the 25th of January. From the New-York *Tribune*, of the 30th of March, we learn that "the sergeant-at-arms, who has been in search of JOHN BROWN, Jr., has returned, and informed the committee that he is in Ohio, but refused to be taken. He defies the committee and Congress, and says his friends will not permit him to leave the State." The latest news we have of the affair comes in a despatch from Washington, on April 6, which says that BROWN "will not be pursued by the sergeant-at-arms, as the Senate Investigating Committee are satisfied that the sergeant cannot call out the *posse comitatus*, as can the sheriff or marshal, and therefore may be overpowered."

Some time in January, F. B. SANBORN, of Concord, Mass., was summoned to appear before the committee. He declined, and asked to be examined in Massachusetts, but was told that he must testify at Washington. But having now begun to doubt the Senate's power to summon and examine witnesses, in a matter like that in hand, he resolved to decline obedience to the summons altogether, unless upon compulsion. Learning, a few weeks later, that the Senate had passed an order for his arrest, he sent a petition, which was presented to that body on the 27th of February, giving his reasons for neglecting to appear. These were, the appointment of the committee before the other House was organized, when only executive business was proper to be done; the Senate's want of constitutional power to examine judicially, or at all on compulsion, except where its privileges are concerned; the secrecy of the examination, contrary to the spirit of our laws, and liable to abuse; the needless inconvenience and hardship of being called from remote places, for an indefinite time, in a period of public exasperation, to the long interruption of regular occupations, or even, as in the petitioner's case, the ruin of private business; the risks of insult and assassination which, notwithstanding the protection offered by the committee, persons of his sentiments must incur in a city where members of Congress are attacked for words spoken in debate; and the unconstitutionality of the statute under which the committee acts. The petition concluded with a declaration that his refusal to appear was not in contempt of the Senate, but because he believed his rights, and those of his fellow-citizens, to be imperiled by its action, and that it was his duty to pray it to reverse that action, "and for himself to maintain these rights as GOD shall give him the means."

So matters rested, to outward appearance, until the 3rd of April; when four or five ruffians, headed by one CARLTON, who claimed to be a deputy sergeant-at-arms of the United States Senate, and to have a warrant from that body, or its committee, or some other authority, — he did not clearly make it appear what, at the time, — attempted stealthily to seize Mr. SANBORN, at the door of his own house, between nine and ten o'clock in the evening, in order to carry him, by force, to Washington, before his friends could have time to interfere. Under pretence of delivering him a letter they called him to the door, arrested and manacled him, refusing to let him see their warrant, dragged him to the street, and tried to thrust him into a carriage, standing ready there. His stout resistance, aided by the prompt and vigorous exertions of his heroic sister, who, at the first sound of altercation, had hastened to the door, gave time for the alarm to spread and bring his neighbors thronging round him; among them came his counsel, who at once obtained a writ of habeas corpus from Judge HOAR, of the Supreme Court of Massachusetts, and had it served immediately; the deputy sheriff took Mr. SANBORN into his own keeping, his irons were removed, and the baffled kidnappers hurried from the town. Next day, the sheriff took his prisoner before the Supreme Court, in Boston; and, after argument by United States District Attorney WOODBURY and his assistant, ANDROS, for the ruffian Federal officials, and by J. S. KEYES and J. A. ANDREW, for the prisoner, he was discharged, upon the ground that the sergeant-at-arms cannot delegate his power to a deputy, and therefore CARLTON had no legal authority to make the arrest.

On his return to Concord, in the evening, SANBORN was welcomed at the railroad station with "the heartiest cheers," from a large crowd of "people, of every class and party," who, form-

ing a procession, escorted him to his house, while all the bells
in town were ringing, and a salute of thirteen guns was fired.
At a meeting, held in the town hall, the following evening,
"SANBORN was introduced with his manacles, and was received
with immense applause:" speeches were made by RALPH
WALDO EMERSON, T. W. HIGGINSON, and half a dozen others;
and resolutions were unanimously adopted, denouncing the
conduct of the United States officers as "base, mean, and
cowardly;" affirming the doctrine of the Revolution, "that resistance to tyrants is obedience to GOD," and avowing a determination "to resist all attempts to abridge the rights of any
citizen to all privileges and guaranties of constitutional liberty."
Preliminary steps were also taken for forming an "organization
to guard against future outrages of this sort." On the 6th, the
kidnappers, who had been arrested in Boston, on complaint of
SANBORN, for assault with intent to kidnap, appeared before a
magistrate, in Concord, and were bound over, in two thousand
dollars each, for trial at the June term of the Superior Court, in
Concord. SANBORN was, the day before, bound over to the
same court, on complaint of one of his own friends, for an
assault upon the kidnappers; and thus the State obtained a
hold upon him which it was thought might be of use in case of
a renewal of the attempt to drag him off to Washington. Mr.
SUMNER presented to the Senate, on the 10th of April, a memorial from Mr. SANBORN, setting forth the facts of the recent outrage perpetrated upon him, and asking for redress. When it
came up for action by the Senate, Mr. MASON, "for the purpose
of determining what the precedent of the Senate shall be in
a like case," moved that it and the former petition from Mr.
SANBORN be both rejected; arguing that "the memorialist is in
contempt of the authority of the Senate, and by a very proper
analogy to proceedings in a court of law," in like cases, should
not be allowed to come before the tribunal except to purge
himself of the contempt. This proposal to condemn without a
hearing, Mr. SUMNER answered with a courteous but somewhat
sharp rebuke, which the Virginian's tart rejoinder showed to
have touched the quick. The chair decided MASON's motion
out of order, and the memorials were both referred to the Judiciary Committee. We do not learn that a report has yet been
made upon them.

Another " contumacious witness," who denied the Senate's right to give judicial power to its committees, was Mr. THAD-DEUS HYATT, of New York. At first, expecting courtesy to be met with courtesy, he voluntarily put himself within the committee's reach, by going to Washington at their call, although their summons was informal, and, by consequence, of no binding force. There he remained, an invalid, for two or three weeks, during which time a notice from the clerk of the committee told him that his presence, at their room, on the 17th of February, was " deemed desirable." He answered with a request for " an extension of time within such range as not to embarrass the action of the committee;" and, in reply, received a peremptory demand for his appearance on the 20th. Rejoining at some length, and with much eloquence and force, alike of thought and language, he reminded the committee that he was in their power " by courtesy," and was " entitled to an equal amount of courtesy from them;" told them that " power, to be respected, must first deserve respect, and every abuse or indecent exhibition of it tends to insubordination;" that resistance to tyranny is reverence for law; that they are the worst conspirators who sap the foundation of government under guise of its functions; that he meant the committee no disrespect, had come to the seat of their power to look the question in the face, if wrong he would recede, but if they and the Senate were wrong, they ought to recede; if they would not, but would persist in trampling on the plain provisions of the Constitution, the hour had come for action, and in order to get an authoritative exposition of the fundamental law, an issue must be made by some one, and he proposed to do it; that, as the committee was not a judicial tribunal in law, and he was not before it, charged with any crime, or as a witness in any criminal case known to the law, he was not in their power by any constitutional right of theirs; and, finally, that in the present state of his health, he could not ask for less than ten days for preparation to meet the requirements of his position. MASON curtly answered, that the committee would meet that day, the 20th, at 11 o'clock, and probably be in session until 12; and " if you do not appear before adjournment, I shall ask for process to compel your appearance." The next day HYATT replied, that as the committee would not

Messrs. SUMNER, HALE, and SIMMONS, who contended that
the Senate was usurping powers which did not belong to it,
and was committing a dangerous invasion of the liberty of the
citizen, and from Messrs. FESSENDEN, DOOLITTLE, CRITTEN-
DEN, and DAVIS, in reply — the resolutions moved by MASON
were adopted, by 44 to 10, committing Mr. HYATT to the
common jail, in Washington, "to be kept in close custody
until he shall signify his willingness to answer the questions
propounded to him" by the committee. He was then conducted to the jail, and, though in feeble health, was, for a time,
debarred the visits of his friends, and, as the Washington correspondent of the Boston *Traveller* states, "such privileges as
are allowed to the worst of criminals were refused to him."
This rigor was, however, soon relaxed; for a letter to the
Traveller, four days after his commitment, speaks of " his
numerous visitors," among whom "are senators and members
of the House." His room, at first, "was bare of all furniture ;"
but he was permitted, at his own expense, to furnish it with
some conveniences, a bed, a table, a few chairs, &c. "Government has supplied him nothing." The same letter says, that
"Mr. HYATT appears not at all downcast by his imprisonment.
He declares his determination to maintain the position he has
assumed, because he believes it would be wrong to accede to
the demands of the Senate. Whenever the Senate will recede
from the compulsory process, he will answer any questions they
may ask, but he denies their right to coërce witnesses, and,
while he has nothing to conceal, he means to test the power of
the Senate. He can suffer as long as they can inflict punishment. He has sent for his library and his maps, has made
arrangements for furnishing his room comfortably, and will
make himself as contented as possible with a view to a stay of
years."

The outrage upon Mr. HYATT, and in him upon the rights
of all his fellow-citizens, has called out, in many quarters, fit
expressions of indignant reprobation of its authors and abettors, and commendations, warm as just, of the noble conduct
of its victim; and both the more emphatic, that his manly
bearing in the controversy, so courteous while so firm, so
frank and fearless, yet respectful, has been in honorable contrast with the plantation-overseer manner of the man of "a

little brief authority," who is, in vain, endeavoring to subdue him. But we are sorry to perceive, in other quarters, not only where it was to have been expected, but also where we had a right to hope for better things, a disposition to treat slightingly his brave fidelity to principle; and to represent him as courting martyrdom, and that upon a mere punctilio. The *Anti-Slavery Standard* truly says, "his treatment at the hands of the Republican party, as represented by its press, has been neither honorable nor wise. Either the magnitude of the principle for which he suffers is not perceived, or it is worked out of sight, lest a manly stand might damage some possible presidential candidate." Because he will not answer on compulsion, but will respond to a civil request which concedes his right to speak or to be silent, even the New-York *Tribune* talks of the difference between "tweedledum and tweedledee;" as if the difference deemed so trivial were not precisely that between the maintenance of Freedom and submission to despotic power; the very difference, in fact, on which turns every struggle for the rights of man. The *Tribune* thinks that, on the question of the Senate's right to coërce testimony, "abstractly, Mr. HYATT is right, and the Senate decidedly wrong." Now, when the attempt is making to stereotype "decided wrong" into a precedent, and one which gives such power as this to a mere fraction of a legislature, is just the time for resolute resistance; and he who has the will and power to meet the issue with such quiet courage, tranquil resolution, and serene fortitude as Mr. HYATT shows, deserves the gratitude and sympathy and hearty moral support of every friend of Freedom. No hope that, in the *Tribune's* words, "the dubious precedent may prove useful in some other case," can justify the setting of it up, or acquiescence in it on the part of those who plainly see that, in the present case, it works injustice.

The eager zeal of the committee to get testimony from the North, wherever there was room for even a suspicion that it could be found, set men, at length, to asking why they did not turn to the South, where such a mass of it was said to be, and summon Governor WISE, with all his carpet-bag of JOHN BROWN's papers. Sometimes the rumor was that he was to be summoned, and then again that he was not to be. The Republican minority of the committee, it is said, wish to have him

called, but the majority keep holding back; till some there are
so little reverent of senatorial dignity as to hint that they are
afraid to call him, lest if he should decline to come, their precedent, in HYATT's case, would force them to commit him, too, to
jail, to keep the recusant New Yorker company.   When Mr.
SUMNER, a few days ago, called the attention of the Senate to
the committee's negligence in this behalf, the only satisfaction
Mr. MASON deigned to give him was, that "the senator from
Massachusetts did not know what the committee had done."
That may be true; but one thing Mr. SUMNER knew they had
not done; they had not put the Virginian ex-governor into
Washington jail, nor even sent a gang of ruffian deputies to
kidnap him, and so the inference was plain that either he had
not been called to testify, or with unwonted meekness, they
could take "contempt" from him and not resent it.   The truth
is, probably, that the mover of the investigation is already tired
and sick of it; disappointed in his hope to turn it to political
account, or to the interest of Slavery in any way; and, conscious that his arbitrary method of procedure is recoiling on
himself, and on the cause he wishes to promote; creating sympathy with those he injures and oppresses, and deepening, in a
widening circle of determined hearts, the resolution to resist
both this and every other movement of the Slave-power.

OPINIONS FROM OVER SEA.

It could not be that such a blow as JOHN BROWN and his
comrades struck, and such a sequel to it as their after lives and
public deaths have given, should fail to rouse attention, and call
forth remark in other lands than this.   If, as we often hear it
said, the judgments of a foreign country, in some sort, fore-
shadow those of future times, Pro-Slavery students of the
prophecies would find some profitable, if not pleasant, reading in
the comments of the European press upon the Harper's Ferry
inroad and its consequences.   We copy a few extracts.

The London *Morning Star* speaks thus of BROWN.   "We
have to do, to-day, with a stern, single-minded, God-fearing,
Puritan-souled man, who has died for an idea, and that a disinterested and generous one.   The world is full enough of those

who, in supine ease, shrink from the discharge of tame duties, and if unselfish heroism gleams on the world from a scaffold, it should not want acknowledgment. * * * * * Brown was a man moulded in hardships and the Bible. He feared God, but evidently, from his youth upwards, feared nobody else. * * * * He was no 'stump orator.' He acted; and stood by his acting. * * * * * * His obvious truthfulness, which no vanity amplified nor any fear abridged, was conspicuous. He neither braved his sentence nor shrunk from it. His conduct was utterly free from effect-making. His speech was always that of a modest, determined, shrewd, sensible, well-possessed man. Mrs. Brown, herself, seems an equally remarkable woman, and is described as being 'courageous without insensibility, tender without weakness;' and her bearing, in the last interview, was worthy of a Roman wife. * * * * * * It is singular that this man should be spoken of as a fanatic. He was no more a fanatic than a tradesman or an artist, who discharges his duties in a right line, is a fanatic. He was no more a fanatic than George Stephenson or James Watt or any of the men whom Dr. Smiles discourses of in his ' Self-Help.' * * * * * * The tone in which he declined any religious ceremony at his death has a majestic mournfulness in it. [The *Star* then quotes his words about preferring to be attended to the gallows by a Slave-mother and her children rather than by Slave-holding ministers, and adds:] This intense reliance on humanity the late Leigh Hunt would have recorded as one of the heroic utterances of the 'Religion of the Heart.' Brown's end became his life. He knew that his life was forfeited, and he made no words about it. Under the circumstances, it was impossible that it should be spared. Mr. Horace Greeley says he ' uniformly took this view of the matter, and discountenanced all appeals in his behalf for pardon or commutation, as well as everything savoring of *menace.*' This last word proves that Brown was strong and wise, as well as brave, and we believe that when the irritation of the South has subsided, it will be seen that he was a worthy foe; and if wrong-headed, at least right-hearted. Upon Brown's act, for which he suffered, this is not the time to pass judgment; but it is not good to keep silence when an honest man dies for an unselfish idea. There is something in this spectacle which will ever stir the pulses of men. Many who here glance, unheedingly, at palace and tower, will descry, with interest, that distant Virginian scaffold which, to-day, becomes one of the historic sights of the world."

The Manchester *Examiner and Times* talks thus: "Old BROWN has died the death of murderers, but no man ever died in a nobler cause, or died more nobly. It is a huge misfortune for any State when its laws condemn men to death for crimes which one half of its own citizens, and the bulk of mankind generally, will extol as virtues. If the United States can afford to hang such men, they are a fortunate people. It would be a glorious thing if the whole race of planters and Wall-street speculators could be made to possess a tithe of the virtues of old BROWN. He is hanged mainly because, bating a few errors, he preferred the service of God to the service of the Devil; and it cannot but go ill with any country where that preference is made, by law, a hanging matter. This is the real evil to be abated, and not the likelihood of more Harper's Ferry insurrections. A nation may outlive an occasional riot, but it cannot outlive determinate, wholesale treason against the first principles of natural equity. * * * * * * His death cannot fail to deepen and embitter the hostility which divides the northern from the southern States, and to advance, by peaceful or by violent means, the cause of the Abolitionists. * * * * * * Will the long-continued conspiracy against human rights be satisfied with a less inexorable expiation than the rupture of the Federal tie? The act for which BROWN has been hanged is, of course, legally, a crime. It is an offence against the State. If the laws of the United States had been in harmony with justice, there would have been no room for the commission of such a crime. We do not wish to blink the fact that BROWN sought to effect his end by violent measures. But viewing his conduct in the very worst light, we find nothing to prevent us from placing him, side by side, with those patriots, of all ages, who have loved liberty, not wisely, but too well. He aimed at a righteous object, he was inspired by the loftiest sentiments, he risked his life for the welfare of the oppressed of another race than his own, he has expiated his chivalrous daring by a death at the hands of the executioner, and he has borne his fate with the lofty spirit of a martyr."

The Liverpool *Mercury* declares Slavery to be "a chronic

provocation to the worst of anarchies. The Virginian authorities," it continues, "have, themselves, taken excellent care that no one shall fancy there is anything conservative in the cause which they so furiously defend. The frenzied rage and terror which seem to have taken possession of the entire State from the day of the Harper's Ferry outbreak, reveal the conscious weakness and rottenness of the 'peculiar domestic institution.' The so-called Abolitionist invasion of Virginia has had the effect of disclosing the frightful insecurity of a social condition based on Slavery; and it has brought out the character of a Slave-owning community in a light at once odious and ridiculous. In no point of view does it appear calculated to increase either the numerical or the moral force of the South and its adherents."

In the London *News* appeared a letter from VICTOR HUGO, the illustrious refugee from tyranny, in France, written the very day of JOHN BROWN's execution. It is not an easy letter to extract from, for, having begun to quote, one feels almost compelled to keep on to the end without a break. But this, the limits of our space forbid, and a few fragments must suffice. Thus he begins. "When one thinks of the United States of America, a majestic figure rises to the mind — WASHINGTON. Now, in that country of WASHINGTON, see what is going on at this hour." Alluding then to BROWN's attempt, he says, "if insurrection be ever a sacred duty, it is against Slavery." And, after a concise and rapid sketch of BROWN's invasion, capture, trial, condemnation, he continues, "I affirm, on my honor, that all this took place, not in Turkey, but in America. Such things are not done with impunity, in the face of the civilized world. The universal conscience of mankind is an ever-watchful eye. Let the judges of Charlestown and HUNTER and PARKER and the Slave-holding jurors and the whole population of Virginia ponder it well: they are seen. They are not alone in the world. At this moment the gaze of Europe is fixed on America. * * * The more one loves, admires, reveres the Republic, the more heart-sick one feels at such a catastrophe. No matter how intense may be the indignation of the generous northern States, the southern States associate them with the disgrace of this murder. All of us, whosoever we may be — for whom the democratic cause is a common country — feel ourselves in a manner compromised and hurt. * * * * * * When we reflect

on what BROWN, the liberator, the champion of Christ, has
striven to effect, and when we remember that he is about to die,
slaughtered by the American Republic, the crime assumes the
proportions of the nation which commits it; and when we say
to ourselves that the nation is a glory of the human race; that
she is the queen of an entire world; and that she bears on her
brow an immense light of freedom; we affirm that JOHN
BROWN will not die, for we recoil, horror-struck, from the idea
of so great a crime committed by so great a people. In a political light, the murder of BROWN would be an irreparable fault.
It would penetrate the Union with a secret fissure, which
would, in the end, tear it asunder. In a moral light, it seems to
me that even the idea of justice and injustice would be obscured
on the day which should witness the assassination of Emancipation by Liberty. * * * * * I implore the illustrious American
Republic to throw down the threatening scaffold, and not to
suffer that beneath its eyes, and I add with a shudder, almost
by its fault, the first fratricide be outdone. For — yes, let
America know it, and ponder it well — there is something more
terrible than Cain slaying Abel, — it is Washington slaying
Spartacus."

In a letter, on the 28th of December, to the people of Hayti,
HUGO says, "I have been sadly deceived in that fraternity of
races, the Southern States of the American Union. In killing
BROWN, they have committed a crime which will take its place
among the calamities of history. The rupture of the Union will
fatally follow the assassination of BROWN. As to JOHN BROWN,
he was an apostle and a hero. The gibbet has only increased
his glory, and made him a martyr."

L'Univers, of Paris, the organ of what may be called the
ultra conservative Catholics of France, had, on November 25,
an article about JOHN BROWN, which speaks of "the barbarity
with which the people of Virginia have condemned a political
prisoner, after having deprived him of the privilege of a free
defence;" briefly relates the facts preceding the trial, up to the
taking of BROWN, severely wounded, and "incapable of holding himself erect;" then adds: "In every civilized country, his
recovery would have been awaited before proceeding with his
trial. But the Virginians were too much terrified to yield their
prisoner the slightest respite. The usual slowness of judicial

14

forms in the United States is well known.   But, in this case,
the most righteous delays were refused JOHN BROWN. * * * *
In Virginia, owners find their interest in transforming their
plantations into manufactories of black children for the southern
markets.   It was to preserve the profits of this immoral repro-
duction of the African race, that the citizens of Virginia armed
themselves against JOHN BROWN."

Even from Russia comes a voice of sympathy with Freedom's
martyr, and reprobation of his adversaries.   The *Northern Bee*,
a Russian journal, reputed to be edited "by a section of the
imperial police," calls VICTOR HUGO's letter, quoted from
above, a "tribute paid to the memory of a defender of a sacred
cause;" and, referring to a reply to HUGO, by General HEN-
NINGSEN, the "fillibuster," says, "Truly, he is a fit advocate of
such a cause.   The juxtaposition of these two names has a high
moral and philosophical signification.   When one of the greatest contemporaneous poets raises his voice in defence of human
liberty, there starts up as his adversary a man who, in spite of
every right and of every duty, invaded the territory of a people
incapable of resistance — an adventurer who, in this age of
civilization, recognizes only one principle — the right of the
strongest."

In the New-York *Tribune*, of the 20th of January, is a statement that "strong sympathy is manifested in the American and
English circles of Florence for the fate of JOHN BROWN, and
for the cause in which he died.   Mrs. H. B. STOWE is at
present sojourning there, and the feeling of the TROLLOPES, the
BROWNINGS, and other prominent *literati*, is as fervent on the
subject of American Slavery as her own.   HIRAM POWERS, the
sculptor, is enthusiastic on the theme of the 'hero-victim,' as he
terms JOHN BROWN, and so expresses himself to everybody."
A letter from Rome, to the Boston *Transcript*, written December 20, says that "we Americans talk of little else than Harper's
Ferry and sublime old JOHN BROWN.   At this distance from
home, there seems to be but one opinion, among our countrymen, on the policy of executing him, and I think the facts will
bear me out in saying that the northern men do not so earnestly
pray for his pardon as the southern deplore his execution.   All
hear in it the knell of Slavery in America; and profound as is
the respect, admiration, and love for this noble old man in the

breast of all men, not Slave-holders or cotton-blinded Northerners, yet I think the feeling is almost universal that, so plainly is the hand of God displayed in this event, to pray for, or attempt his deliverance would seem almost an irreverent interference with the course of Providence! Men are marvellously impressed by it! Men of sober judgment, not given to superstition or sentimentalism, bow solemnly before it, and say it is the hand of God."

The only expression which we have seen, from Europe, of sentiments opposed to those above recited, is from the London *Times*, a journal which has more than once, of late, betrayed Pro-Slavery sympathies. An article in its issue of December 28, inspired by the then recent "Union meetings" in some of our large cities, and mistaking them for signs of the prevailing feeling of the country, speaks of the speedy dying out of the enthusiasm for JOHN BROWN's memory, and the "revulsion of feeling in favor of the South;" commends, particularly, the "patriotic and becoming tone" of the Boston meeting of December 8, and, with the most refreshing simplicity, talks of the "great effect" which Mr. EVERETT's speech "will no doubt produce in all parts of the Republic." Such of the Boston folk as have been favored with a chance to read the article, have doubtless felt a proper gratitude for the information they received, not elsewhere to be had, that "they themselves seem not a little ashamed of their proceedings" at the Tremont Temple, on the 2nd of December, at which, they now first learn, "the speeches were the reverse" of "patriotic and becoming;" although, such is the sad perversity of human nature, we should not be surprised if some of those who joined in the proceedings should suggest that "even" ought to be inserted before "a little," in the sentence just now quoted from the *Times*.

In Hayti, BROWN's exploit and fate produced a great sensation. The press, the public authorities, and the people at large vied with one another in manifestations of grateful respect to his memory. On the 20th of January, a "grand solemn service," in commemoration of his death, was performed at the Cathedral, in Port-au-Prince, at which President GEFFRARD, with his family, was present. "During the day the flags were all kept at half-mast, and the houses hung with black. The church was draped in mourning, and in the middle of the nave was erected a cenotaph, covered with crape, and illuminated with lighted wax-tapers. The upper part was covered with white drapery, on which were depicted a pen, a sword, and a Bible, with the inscription, in letters of gold, 'A JOHN BROWN, MARTYR DE LA CAUSE DES NOIRS.' Many black-satin flags waved over it. At each of its four corners, the purest and sweetest incense burned. The services were celebrated with unusual religious pomp. Abbé MOUSSA, an African, officiated at the High Mass. Eulogies upon JOHN BROWN were pronounced from the pulpit. In the afternoon, a grand procession was made to the end of the city, to a place known as the 'Martyr's Cross,' where further religious ceremonies took place. The principal citizens of Port-au-Prince decided to wear mourning badges for three days."

On the 23rd, a similar display was made at Cape Haytien. "The flags in the harbor were at half-mast, and the bells mournfully tolled." A letter from that city says the day was set apart for "humiliation and prayer, in memory of the greatest cosmopolite that has been in existence the last century—JOHN BROWN. Unborn generations will drop tears of sorrow for this lover of God and mankind. I could not get into the church for the great throng, but the English Consul told me the oration was truly affecting. Tears were seen to drop from the eyes of many while the orator pointed out the virtues of the heroic man." At Aux Cayes, the 26th was observed in like manner. From six o'clock in the morning until noon, the flag-staffs on the harbor and in the city were hung in black. Early in the morning, the military officers and public functionaries, with a multitude of the people, moved in procession from the quarters of the commandant of the district to the church, where they were received by a detachment of the National Guard; the church was soon crowded, mass was performed, addresses were made by several citizens, and the commandant, the magistrates and citizens, and the school-children, threw flowers upon the cenotaph erected in the middle of the church.

At Jacmel, Gonaives, and other places, "the martyrdom" was commemorated, also, "with all possible pomp and solemnity." All over the island, collections were made and subscriptions started in behalf of the widow of JOHN BROWN. In Aux Cayes, for the promotion of this object, a "Central Benevolent Association" was formed, with the commandant of the district for its president, and the head of the Communal Council for one of its vice-presidents. *Le Progres*, a journal newly established in Port-au-Prince, in its urgent appeal on this behalf, says, "not a town, not a village, not even a little hamlet, but should feel it a duty to coöperate actively in this great national work, in proportion to its means. Shame and ignominy should be the portion of that Haytian who will not take his part in this contribution. Hasten, then, every one, to the subscription offices opened in every town, to honor the memory of JOHN BROWN and glorify our race."

The *Revue de Commerce* declares "the death of JOHN BROWN to be a crime against humanity, a bloody defiance of civilization and God. * * * * * We Haytians," it adds, "do not wish to return evil for evil, and we hope that the blood of this glorious martyr will not rise up against his executioners. We pray God to open their eyes and soften their hearts, and, while waiting the happy day of the regeneration of our enslaved brethren, let us raise in our hearts our altar to JOHN BROWN, the immortal benefactor of our race, the holy victim of our cause, and let us adopt, as our sister and friend, his worthy and unfortunate widow. * * * * * * Henceforth, greater than other philanthropists, superior to WILBERFORCE, his sacred name will be pronounced with a holy respect, worthy of one who has given his life for the regeneration of the oppressed of mankind." Says the *Feuille de Commerce*, "the cause of the abolition of Slavery has just counted another martyr. This fact, however indifferent it may be to others, cannot be so to us, descendants as we are of the persecuted race of Africa. This event must weigh upon our hearts as a public calamity. * * * * * But shall we, therefore, say that the hour of emancipation for our unhappy brethren has not yet come? However it may be, the blood of JOHN BROWN guarantees that it is at hand. Reässure yourselves, ye Slaves, nothing is lost; Liberty is immortal. BROWN and his companions have sown this Slave-land with their glorious blood, and doubt not that therefrom avengers will arise." The press of Port-au-Prince published, also, an address to the "Philanthropists of America," which says, in offering "the sincere thanks of the citizens of Hayti" to the citizens of Albany, for the hundred minute-guns they fired on

the day of Brown's execution, "the cannon you fired to commemorate the death of John Brown has reëchoed in the
hearts of Haytians and of the strangers of our land, and reverberates through our fields and cities. Your energetic protest
against an act of barbarity does you the greatest honor."

Barbarism Rampant.

The fright which John Brown gave the whole Slave-region,
exacerbated suddenly, to an acute, inflammatory type, the
chronic malady of lawless barbarism, so long notoriously prevailing there.   In every stranger, especially if known to be
from the North, was seen a possible, if not a certain enemy;
and even southern birth, or, in the case of northern origin, long,
quiet residence at the South, in the pursuit of lawful business,
was not always a sure guarantee against suspicion and its terrible consequences.   The lightest word implying doubt of the
consummate excellence of the "peculiar" system, the slightest
act which could be construed into a leaning toward the doctrine
of equal human rights, gave ground sufficient for the charge
of Abolitionism, and the prompt execution of Judge Lynch's
code.   Nay, even silence was suspicious, for it might be but a
cover of some deep design.   Innocent book-peddlers, who cared
no more for Slavery or Anti-Slavery than for the politics of
Patagonia; harmless venders of patent and unpatented "Yankee notions," without which scarce the outward show of civilized
life could be kept up among the "patriarchs;" school-teachers,
thinking only of their spelling-books and grammars and the
quarter's bills; "drummers" of northern mercantile establishments, untainted with an "ism;" mechanics, who had never
voted· any but the Democratic ticket; clergymen, well known
in northern parishes as stanch assertors of a Bible warrant for
Slave-holding; and many others, no more dangerous than these,
were at once transformed, by excited imaginations, into Abolition emissaries, and hunted down with all the keen vindictiveness of fear.   The mob was legislator, prosecutor, jury, judge,
and executioner.   Arrests and summary examinations before
self-constituted tribunals, followed by speedy execution of the
seldom-failing doom, — brutal abuse, imprisonment, banishment,

or death, — became so frequent that hardly could the daily press find room to chronicle the cases. Sometimes, by way of rare variety, the sovereign mob would condescend to leave a victim to the regular enforcement of some tyrannical statute by the established courts. But where no statute could be found to meet the case, that is, where no unlawful act could be alleged, — no act which even the despotic legislation of a Slave State had forbidden, — the edict of a "Vigilance Committee," or vote of a tumultuous assembly was law enough; and the absurdest tale of malice, or the most unreasonable suspicion of blind terror, was sufficient evidence. The constitutional guarantee, to "the citizens of each State," of "all the privileges and immunities of citizens in the several States," was worth less than the spoiled parchment it was written on. The virtual constitution of the Slave-land seemed, almost, to be summed up in these words of the Atlanta (Ga.) *Confederacy*: "We regard every man in our midst an enemy to the institutions of the South, who does not boldly declare that he believes African Slavery to be a social, moral, and political blessing. Any person holding other than these sentiments, whether born at the South or North, is unsound, and should be requested to leave the country." And "requested" in a manner so persuasive, we may add, that compliance might be counted on with a very near approach to certainty.

Of the multitude of instances of violence and outrage, with or without the forms of law, which have been published, including hanging, scourging, tar-and-feathering, shaving the head, robbing, imprisonment, and so downward, in the scale of severity, to mere expulsion from the South with only threats of personal abuse, our space permits but a brief notice of a very few.

On the evening of October 28, a mob in Newport, Ky., forcibly entered the printing-office of WILLIAM S. BAILEY, publisher of *The Free South*, threw a large quantity of type into disorder, broke one of his presses, and carried off the "forms" on which he was printing one side of the paper. His wife and daughters "begged, without avail, that their property might be spared." The next day the mob returned, battered the door down with a heavy plank, entered and carried off the press and all the printing materials which they could remove, and threw them into the Ohio River, leaving the house "a perfect wreck," and causing

Mr. BAILEY a loss of about three thousand dollars. When, afterwards, about the middle of February, the grand jury found true bills against a number of those who were engaged in the riot, the State's attorney, hearing of it, went before them and argued that where a nuisance existed, which could not be reached by legal process, the people had a right to abate it. The jury, somewhat doubtful as to the soundness of this exposition of the law, asked the opinion of Judge MOOR upon the question, and he confirmed the attorney's statement; whereupon they quashed the indictment.

The Kingstree (S. C.) *Star* says that a public meeting was held at Boggy Swamp, in Williamsburg District, S. C., on the 22nd of November, " to take preliminary steps " for sending off two northern men, W. J. DODD and R. A. P. HAMILTON, private teachers in respectable families in that district. " Nothing definite is known of their Abolition or insurrectionary sentiments," adds the *Star*, " but being from the North, and, therefore, necessarily imbued with doctrines hostile to our institutions, their presence in this section has been obnoxious, and, at any rate, very suspicious." The meeting resolved that it had great respect for the persons in whose employ they were, but the longer continuance of the teachers there was so dangerous as to justify coërcive measures for their removal; and sent a committee of twelve to tell them " they will have till Saturday, the 26th, to leave the district," and, if they should not go by that time, " measures of a coërcive character will be adopted, to put them off by force." Their employers opposed the action of the meeting, as reflecting upon them. A later meeting decided to let them remain till their respective terms of engagement should expire, on the 1st and 15th of December.

Dr. DANIEL BREED, an Orthodox Friend, " who has lived in peace and respectability, in Washington, for the last seven years, and has had high office under successive administrations; " a man " habitually courteous in his manners and temperate in the expression of his opinions," says the editor of the *Anti-Slavery Standard*, who knows him well, was arrested on the 22nd of November, charged with " using language," in a private conversation with a Dr. VAN CAMP, " calculated to excite Slaves to insurrection; " and only escaped imprisonment by giving bond in two thousand dollars to keep the peace for a year.

True, the alleged insurrectionary language was not used in the hearing of Slaves, or even of more than two or three white persons; but Mr. Justice DOGB — DOWN, we mean, who tried the case, nevertheless required the bond, on the ground that, "*if* he had uttered his sentiments before Slaves, or a white audience, it *would* have endangered the peace of the community. Yet the "sentiments," the *Standard* says, "were precisely those held and habitually expressed by a majority of the people of the Free States." Justice DOWN ought certainly to be indicted for kindling a fire in his office-stove, for *if* he had kindled it in a powder-magazine it *would* have blown somebody up. "In the court-room," says the Washington correspondent of the New-York *Evening Post*, "a gang of ruffians was gathered, and threats were openly and loudly made to take the life of Dr. BREED on the spot. One man cried out, in open court: 'Let's hang him up when he goes out!' and no man reprimanded the scoundrel for his offence. The *Star* very candidly admits that if the police had not been present in strong numbers, Dr. BREED would have been in danger."

The Savannah (Ga.) *Republican*, of December 3, states that, on the night of the 1st, SEWALL H. FISK, a shoe-dealer in Savannah, and a native of Massachusetts, was called out of his store, where he slept, and, before he could make noise or resistance, was gagged, placed in a carriage, and driven a little way out the city, then his hair was trimmed close to his head, tar and cotton were applied to his naked body, till not a spot of his skin was visible, and he was left to find his way back as best he could. The alleged cause of the outrage was, "his known Abolition proclivities," which, it was said, "he has taken some trouble to make known to" the Slaves; and a most absurd story that he had "enticed negroes into his cellar, at night, and read to them all sorts of Abolition documents," the previous Sunday night having been "devoted especially to the history of the trial of JOHN BROWN, and a general exhortation upon the institution of Slavery and the advantages of Freedom." The *Republican* thinks that if what is publicly alleged of his sentiments and conduct towards the Slaves is true, he most probably merited all which he received; but it disapproves such proceedings by persons "who work in a mask, and keep their names a secret from the community;" adding that they "can only be justified by considerations of public security; and when this is at stake, no citizen need be ashamed for it to be known that he is willing to come to the rescue." The Savannah *News* says that FISK denied the charges against him, and adds that "it is but justice to say he visited his native State, a few years ago, where, in a public meeting, he defended the institution of Slavery, and brought upon himself the censure of his relations, as well as the animadversion of the papers in Holliston, where he made his speech."

A despatch from Washington to the New-York press, on the 8th of December, says that "thirty-two gentlemen, agents of New-York and Boston houses, arrived here, to-day, from the South, and report the feeling of indignation so great against Northerners, that they were compelled to return and abandon their business. These gentlemen have been known, for years, as traders in the South. They also report that Northerners, of long residence in the South, have been disfigured, and driven from their homes. Eleven business men, who were on their way South, returned, last night, after having reached a station in Virginia, being turned back by a Vigilance Committee." And the New-York *Independent*, two or three weeks later, states that "six salesmen and agents of a large and well-known business house in this city," which had shown "great zeal in getting up the recent Union meeting, were summarily forced to leave the South, and recently returned to their employers." About the middle of December, a book-agent was arrested in Alabama, while soliciting subscribers for "Fleetwood's Life of Christ," published at the North. The case was noticed in the Methodist Conference, then in session, and the members advocated the expulsion of the agent, as needful to the safety of southern institutions. They said in substance, in a paper adopted for insertion in the newspapers of that region : "We have examined this man's case. We find no evidence of his tampering with Slaves; but as he is from the North, and engaged in selling a book published in the North, we have a right to suspect him as being an Abolitionist, and we therefore recommend, in order to guard ourselves against possible danger, that he be immediately conducted, by the military, out of this county into the next adjoining." We can but marvel at the moderation of the reverend censors, in dealing thus with such nefarious deeds.

Trying to sell the "Life of Christ" in the midst of Slave-hold-ers!—and they talk of only "*possible* danger"!—and content themselves with merely sending the offender to "the adjoining county"! Of course, the military promptly did their bidding. But military movements require music. In the neighborhood, was a teacher of vocal and instrumental music, who had lived nine years in Georgia and Alabama, and had never spoken against Slavery, but always in favor of it, although he owned no Slaves. On him the soldiers called, to head their march and play the flute. He declined, and ventured to assign a reason. He thought the agent had done nothing worthy of expulsion. In the evening, he received a written warning to leave the State immediately, under penalty of tar-and-feathers. His wife, a southern woman, fearing the danger of delay, advised his going before daylight; and he knew the people well enough to think her counsel wise. So, at three o'clock in the morning, he mounted his horse, and rode northward, taking only what his saddle-bags could hold; abandoning a thriving business, and leaving wife and children to be sent for when he should have found a northern home to bring them into.

The venerable DANIEL WORTH, a preacher of the Wesleyan Methodist Church; a man of noble presence and sterling quali-ties of mind and heart, and of most respectable social standing; a native of North Carolina, where he was once a magistrate; for many years a resident in Indiana, of whose Legislature he has been a member; had, for about two years before December last, been preaching in his native State; and although some-times threatened, on account of his fidelity to the principles of the gospel he proclaimed, had not been seriously hindered in his work till after the event at Harper's Ferry. The only rea-son for this long forbearance, we are told by a Pro-Slavery correspondent of the New-York *Herald*, who relates his recent persecution, was "the good feeling for the respectable family who bear his name." On the 23rd of December, he was arrested by the sheriff of Guilford County, on a charge of circulating Helper's Crisis, and of preaching in a way "to make Slaves and free negroes dissatisfied with their condition." "We learn," the Raleigh *Standard* says, "that the excitement in Greensborough [the county seat] was very great, and that the officers of the law experienced difficulty in protecting WORTH from the indignation of the people." The examining court required him to give bail in $5,000 for appearance at the spring term of the Superior Court, and in $5,000 more to "keep the peace"— that is, to hold his peace—until that time. The first requirement was complied with, but not the second; so he was committed to prison. While there, he was again arrested, and bound over in $5,000 to appear at the spring term of the court in Randolph County. Between these two arrests, five other citizens of Guilford County, some of them "leading and influential men," were arrested and bound over, on the charge of circulating Helper's book. Several arrests were made in Randolph County, also, on the same charge. Mr. WORTH was put into a cell "wholly unsuitable for any person to live in," with no bedding but "a dirty pallet," and was kept there through the winter; the sheriffs of several neighboring counties "hanging around" to arrest him, if he should come out on bail, and put him into close confinement again. A letter from Guilford County, dated January 13, says that "his keepers observe the strictest vigilance, not allowing even his wife to speak a word to him without witnesses being present; nor do they suffer him to write a word to any person, only what passes under their inspection. They made an attempt, during his trial, to deprive him of the means of writing at all; but finally concluded to let him have two or three sheets of paper at a time, by his giving an account, to the sheriff, what disposition he made of it. One object seems to be to cut off all correspondence with friends, and, indeed, all the friends of Liberty here must suffer likewise."

He was tried the 30th of March, and so eager were his persecutors for the foregone conclusion,—his conviction,—that they could not stop to sleep till it was reached. Impanelling a jury, hearing testimony, arguments of counsel, and judge's charge, filled up the time from morning until midnight; and at four o'clock, on Saturday morning, the expected verdict, "guilty," was brought in. The judge did his part to secure that verdict, by a charge in which, among other lucid expositions of the law, he laid down the doctrine, that, to sustain the allegation of seeking to excite the Slaves and free colored people to discontent, it was not necessary to prove "that the book had been read by or recited to a free negro or Slave, or that any such knew anything of any part of its contents." Perhaps he thought the very air would be infected with " dissatisfaction," by such a poisonous compilation of statistics; or, judging the black people by the white, and seeing that it could excite the latter to alarming discontent without their knowing a syllable of what was in it, he naturally concluded it would have the same effect upon the former. The penalty for the offence of which the prisoner was now convicted, was public whipping or imprisonment, or both, at the discretion of the court; and the court graciously left out the whipping, and fixed the imprisonment at twelve months, the shortest period which the law allows. This certainly was no dangerous extreme of mercy, seeing that other trials and convictions were impending over the old man's head, with chance of sentences ascending in the scale of severity, till all the statute's hoarded wrath should be exhausted. But still it was displeasing to the people. A correspondent of the New-York *Tribune* writes, on April 7, "I hear very many expressions of discontent that WORTH was not publicly whipped, as well as incarcerated, as he might have been — or, according to the popular view, *ought* to have been — under the statute. But the hope that some less lenient judge, in another county, may impose this more degrading penalty, sustains them in their disappointment." The same letter says that "the other trials of Mr. WORTH· are to begin in about three weeks. They can hardly fail to result in his conviction, and lawyers think he will with great difficulty, if at all, escape the punishment of whipping." And if he does not, he will not forget that neither did his Master, who came to earth some centuries ago, " to preach deliverance to the captives," escape the Roman scourge, and a yet sterner fate. Nor do we think, from all we have yet seen, that, come what may, he will desert his Master's cause. He tells us, from his dreary prison-cell, soon after his arrest, and while expecting to endure the utmost rigor of the unjust law, "I seemed to hear my Saviour's voice asking, 'Art thou ready to suffer for my sake? Canst thou enter into dungeons for thy Saviour's love, and suffer shame for my sake?' When I came to the point, and could say, 'Yes, Lord, I am willing to suffer thy righteous will in all things,' he poured his love into my soul so boundlessly that I shouted aloud for joy. And let me say, that I fully believe if I am sentenced to confinement or other punishment, God will glorify his name by my suffering for him

15

laws of the State; that false reports against them had inflamed the public mind; and that they had sought, in vain, the fullest investigation, offering every facility for it. The governor "received the bearers of the petition courteously," but advised them, for the sake of peace, to leave the State, saying that he could not engage to protect them there, but promising them security in going, and protection to their property. Finding no other alternative, therefore, but to go quietly or be thrust out by force, the mob being master and the government a sham, they chose the former; left their homes, school, mill and shops and farms, and passed over to Ohio; hoping still, however, that before long the excitement would subside, so that they could return in peace; and "not indulging even in unkind words about those who have made them homeless." "Friends were around," it is said, "who would have resisted even unto death; but the colonists believed that they should carry on their labor in love and in peace, and they preferred exile, with the silent preaching their absence would furnish, to the shedding of blood."

In Bracken, Lewis, and Mason Counties were other fields of Anti-Slavery labor, in which FEE and his fellow-missionaries had built up little churches of believers in the gospel which they teach. After the banishment of the Bereans, some of the exiles ventured to seek temporary homes in one or other of these counties, of which the first named is the native place of FEE, and of J. G. HANSON, owner of the Berea saw-mill. But the Slave-holders were at once on the alert. A meeting held in Mason County, January 21, passed resolutions denouncing FEE and his associates, and approving the action of the citizens of Madison, demanding to be *let alone* with their "domestic institutions;" and appointing a committee to wait on Rev. J. S. DAVIS, one of FEE's co-workers and an exile from Berea, who had come to Lewis County, and order him to leave the State within seven days, threatening, in case of non-compliance, "to resort to means alike painful to" themselves, "and hazardous to him." The citizens of Bracken and Mason Counties met at Brooksville, in the former, on the 23rd, and unanimously resolved that FEE and HANSON, then within the county, "preparing to make it their home," were "enemies to the State;" commanded them and several of their friends to leave the State by the fourth day of February; threatened forcible expulsion if they failed to obey; and appointed a committee of fifty to execute the order on the persons named, "or any others of like character."

The mob committee, on the 25th, gave notice of the meeting's mandate to FEE and HANSON and five others. One of them, J. B. MALLET, had been, for nearly three years, teacher of an academy in Bracken County, and had acquired for it "the reputation of being one of the best schools in the country." Another had been a teacher, but was now too feeble in health for that employment. Another was a poor, industrious laborer, "noted for his quiet, peaceable character." Of HANSON, it is said, "he had never been charged with any crime unless it was his honesty." Unless! Why! is not that enough to make him a fit object of Pro-Slavery persecution? For what is it but rank *lese-majesty* to Slavery? — or constant *scandalum magnatum* to the livers upon unpaid toil? How dare a man be honest, in the midst of those who steal, from helpless poverty, the bread they eat, the whisky they drink, the clothes they wear, and the very ropes with which they hang incendiary Abolitionists! FEE and his friends made some attempts at argument and remonstrance, but all, of course, in vain. It was admitted that they had done no unlawful act; indeed, one of the mobocrats told FEE he was "smart enough to keep out of the hands of the law, and this was the only way to get him out." One neighboring Slave-holder, intelligent and high in social standing, owned that the neighborhood thus broken up, was "the best one he had seen in all Kentucky." But then, so much the worse, for so much greater would its Anti-Slavery influence be. Before deciding whether to obey the mob or not, the ostracized took legal counsel as to what was best to do. They were advised that they could lawfully meet force with force, but that to do so would not be expedient, in the circumstances. Concurring in this view, they yielded to the lawless pressure, and withdrew to Cincinnati several days within the limit which had been allowed them.

Early in March, HANSON went back to his mill, supposing, probably, that the excitement had had time to cool, and that he might resume his lawful business, unmolested. But no sooner was his coming known, than the committee met again, and ordered him to leave. On the 13th, he sent a protest to one of the newspapers of the county. On the 26th, eighteen or twenty of the committee, armed with shot-guns and pistols, went to Berea, but HANSON had withdrawn. They searched the houses of Republicans living thereabout, and were so abusive in their acts and language to a sick man and his daughter, into whose house they broke, that the incensed Republicans gave them battle and drove them off. Next day they returned, with a hundred and fifty men or more, searched every house and possible hiding-place for miles around, but found no enemy. They then dismantled HANSON's saw-mill, and denounced all those engaged in the fight, and gave their families notice to leave the State by Tuesday following. The facts related in this paragraph we gather from a letter written by CASSIUS M. CLAY, a few days after their occurrence.

The banishment of the "Radical Abolitionists," as FEE and his associates were called, was not enough for the Pro-Slavery zealots. CASSIUS M. CLAY and the Republicans of Kentucky, as it appears from Mr. CLAY's account, as well as from other testimony, were hardly less the objects of their real or pretended fear, and their unquestionably genuine hostility. "After the overthrow of WILLIAM S. BAILEY's press, and the general terror in the Slave States," says Mr. CLAY, "the Democracy thought it a good time to make a clean sweep of all the liberal element here, including me and others in this county. The first vote, at the public meeting, included the 'Republicans' by name. Upon a reconsideration, Republicans were struck out, but in the manifesto we were denounced as 'guilty of crime,' which ought to be, but is not, punishable by law." The attempt was made to identify him and his fellow-partisans, in the public mind, with the proscribed Radicals; and to put them, all together, under the same ban of proscription. For "what was the use, it was said, to drive out FEE and his companions, while CLAY was left to agitate the country." Whether because of CLAY's personal influence and powerful family-connections, or because the Republicans were stronger, in numbers and means of resistance, than the Radicals, or whether because the former showed less willingness than the latter to yield the present exercise of their rights for the sake of avoiding bloodshed, or for whatever reason, the "clean sweep" meditated was not made.

CLAY met the menaces of the mob-party with resolute, and even defiant words. "When I feel," said he, "that I am right, I shall not be driven from my constitutional privilege of avowal, whenever it may suit my good pleasure, although the Lynch-law Committee may not be able to sleep with 'doors unbolted.'" And again: "I shall in no way whatever, recognize or submit to any revolutionary committee. You may be strong enough to overpower me; you cannot drive me from the duty which I owe to myself, to my friends, and to my country." In speeches made at Frankfort and at Richmond, in January and March, in a printed appeal to the citizens of Madison County, on the 31st of March, and through the columns of the county press, at different times, he explained and defended his position; avowing his desire for peace, but letting it be clearly understood that he and his political associates would fight, if need were, to maintain their rights. "The Republican Party may not be large enough," he said, "to meet the wide vision of the Madison Lynchers, but it is large enough to stand by all its convictions, and defend all its rights, whenever, with speech, the pen, or the *sword*, it is attacked by despots."

But, however bold his words, or resolute his purpose, in relation to his own and to his party's rights, and however much we have seen in his career which claims respect and admiration, we are constrained to say, with deep regret, that in his bearing toward those noble men whom he calls "Radicals," he has shown neither justice, manly courage, magnanimity, nor wisdom. He dares not, or at least he does not — and why not, if he dares — demand for them what he demands, and justly, for himself and for his fellow-partisans. For these, he claims the right to hold and freely utter Anti-Slavery sentiments, to organize and speak and write and print and vote for the distinctly-avowed purpose of arraying both the people and the government against Slavery. For these he holds it as a duty to maintain the right, there in Kentucky, where it is assailed; maintain it, even though blood should flow in the struggle. But when the Lynch Committee declare open war upon that right, in FEE and HANSON, he hastens to proclaim himself a neutral. Indeed, by his own showing, he is hardly that, for he proposes to the Slave-holders a way in which they may secure his help in putting down the "Radicals." In a letter, written five days after the Bereans had been warned to leave the State, he tells us, "I have never said that FEE, or any other man, or set of men, ought to be expelled from the State. I have always said that if the Radicals, FEE, or any other man, or set of men, *violated the laws, I would aid in bringing them to punishment ;* and that if there was no law to punish our holding and avowing radical views in a Commonwealth holding Slaves, the Slave-holders had the political power; — let them pass a law to meet the case." This, in a later letter, he affirms, "the Legislature could constitutionally do." Should it be done, he would, of course, be pledged to aid in punishing, what then would be a violation of the law, the holding and avowal of radical views. True, he is opposed to lynch-law process. He is "the sworn eternal enemy of mobs," but will not interfere to protect, from the mob's violence, men whose opinions differ from his own. "I am no Don Quixote," says he, in his Frankfort speech, of January 10th, "to fight the battles of every man who may venture to express an opinion on the subject of Slavery. * * * * * * Wherever a man, planting himself on the broad constitutional ground of our fathers of 1776, follows me, I will stand by and defend him, to the best of my ability, and give him such protection as I can, when the laws of the country refuse to give him what the Constitution guarantees to him as his right." But "I could not stand by FEE and his associates." Why not? "The Constitution guarantees to" them, as much as to the Republicans, the right to hold and speak and act upon their own convictions. Moreover — though that makes no difference as to their right — they also claim to stand "on the broad, constitutional ground of our fathers of 1776," honestly differing from Mr. CLAY as to what is that ground, and honestly believing that he and the Republicans do not stand upon it. "That Mr. FEE was honest," Mr. CLAY, in terms, asserts, and "that he was pure in purpose, actuated by the highest love of Christian charity;" "as pure a man," he says again, "as I ever knew." And between such a man and his assailants, who were trampling down his rights by lawless violence, Mr. CLAY tells us, in his speech, that "my position was one of strict neutrality." So, too, in his appeal to the citizens of Madison County, he says that, when the attempt was making to drive HANSON from the State, after he went back to Berea, in March, "I told" one of the committee "that I should and their friends were banished, as they would be if he were driven out; and their "right" was no less precious than his own. He asks, in the concluding paragraph of the same letter, "Is this my cause only, or that of the American people? Shall I stand or fall alone?" Most pertinent inquiries, and suggestive of important truth and obvious duty. This is *not* Mr. CLAY's cause only, it *is* "that of the American people," and the human race. The right which he is vindicating for himself, the right of free thought and free speech, is the guardian of all other rights, not of one people only, but of man. And it is all men's duty to assert it, not for themselves alone, but for all other men, and most especially for those in whom it is most urgently assailed. No faithful vindicator of it should be left to "stand or fall alone." But just as pertinent these questions would have been, suggesting the same truth and the same duty, if pressed by FEE and HANSON upon CLAY himself.

What would he say, if, to his just appeal, some noted champion of Freedom should reply, "Though I believe that you are honest, Mr. CLAY, and actuated by the noblest motives, yet I do not agree with you in your interpretation of the Constitution; it is not the ground on which I stand, and I am no Don Quixote, to fight the battles of every man who ventures to express an opinion about Slavery?" Would he not answer, with warmth, perhaps, and certainly with truth, "The question now at issue is not whether I am right or wrong in my opinions, but whether I have not a right to hold and speak them, howsoever they are thought, or even *are*, erroneous?" Yet this is just the truth he overlooks, when speaking of the Radical Abolitionists. "They hold," he says, "that there can be no law for Slavery; but I believe that Slavery is a creature of law, and I respect the Constitution and the Laws. I do not believe the 'radical' doctrine right, and therefore will not jeopard my life on any such false issue." Nobody asks him to do that. The issue he is asked to meet is not the truth or falsehood of the "radical" doctrine, but whether freedom of opinion and expression is a right, to be asserted on behalf of all. When putting it so justly to the American people, that it is their cause for which he is in peril, he knew, of course, that many, if not most of them, were quite as wide in sentiment from him, upon the Slavery question, as he from those he styles "the Radicals." Yet he believes, and rightly, that the people ought to "stand by" him in this emergency; stand by him, not as a Republican, but as a man, having a right to think and speak his thoughts. In failing to acknowledge that the same truth holds in favor of "the Radicals," he fails to recognize, or to respect, the principle on which alone the rights of any man can be successfully asserted, the equal sacredness of the rights of every man; and thus he leaves the gates of his own fortress open to the enemy.

We think, too, that he does the "Radicals" injustice, by his treatment of their doctrine of "no law for Slavery." He calls it "revolutionary," representing it as a denial of "the potency of the Constitution and the Laws," as setting up an opposite and independent government, and as inevitably leading "to physical conflict." Yet he must know, at least he ought to know, that the doctrine which they hold leads to no such result. It involves no general denial of the power of law and constitution; sets up no government opposed thereto; tends to no conflict, save of moral power, with those who frame and execute the laws. For it is simply this, that man cannot annul the law of God; that, therefore, Slavery being an immorality, no law to authorize it can bind the conscience; that wicked statutes should be disobeyed, and their unrighteous penalties be meekly borne, if rulers are unjust enough to execute them. Now which is the more likely to bring on "physical conflict" with "the existing government"? — the "Radicals," by carrying out this doctrine faithfully; or Mr. CLAY, resolving to defend, even "to the death," against the mob, against the Lynch Committee, against the Governor, with his Minié rifles and his cannon, what *he* regards as his rights, according to *his* understanding of the Laws and Constitution?

When Mr. CLAY confronts the foes of Freedom, and meets their insolent demands with firm refusal, their ruffian menaces with bold defiance, their noise and bluster with unquailing courage, we cannot choose but honor and admire him. We heartily rejoice that he was able to maintain his ground against the lawless violence which sought to crush him. But when he tries to separate his cause, as the defender of free speech, from that of champions yet worthier than himself; leaves them to be borne down by numbers and driven into exile, while he publicly avows his own neutrality between them and their persecutors;

and even countenances legislation to suppress in them the right he deems so sacred in himself; we cannot let our admiration of his gallant bearing in defence of his own rights, keep back the emphatic reprehension which he merits for his treatment of their no less sacred rights; his untruth to the *principle* on which both his and theirs are based.

Another exhibition of Kentuckian barbarism is mentioned in the New-York *Independent*, about the middle of January. It says: "We learn that Rev. GEO. CANDEE, Rev. WM. KENDRICK, and ROBERT JONES, missionaries of the American Missionary Association, in Jackson County, Ky. (JONES, a colporter), were recently, near Laurel, where they were preaching, waited upon by a committee of five, and requested to leave. They were engaged to preach the next morning, but were prevented by a mob, which took them a half mile and interrogated them, then took them five miles further and left them, after shaving their hair and beards, and putting tar on their heads and faces."

JAMES POWER, a young Irishman, who had been at work, for several months, as a stone-cutter, on the State-House at Columbia, S. C., gave offence to the sovereign mob of that metropolis, by the remark that Slavery " caused a white laborer, at the South, to be looked upon as an inferior and degraded man." The Vigilance Committee hearing of the seditious utterance, ordered the police to arrest him. On or about the tenth of December, he was seized, while trying to escape; put into a cell and kept three days, denied the use of pen and ink, and all communication with his friends outside. Then he was taken before the mayor, the treasonous words were proved, and he was sent back to prison; kept there six days, with but two scanty meals a day; then taken out and dragged about the streets and State-House yard, through the mud and puddles, to the amusement of some thousands of delighted spectators, including several members of the Legislature; marched three miles out of the city, stripped and whipped thirty-nine lashes, laid on with terrible severity; covered to the waist with tar and feathers; and, without being allowed to put on his shirt or coat, thrust into the negro-car on the railroad, and sent to Charleston. At every station, the engineer blew a prolonged whistle, and gathered a mob to insult the sufferer afresh. A citizen of Charleston, on the train, gave him, at one of the stations, a cup of coffee and a biscuit; but was surrounded by the rabble, and threatened with vengeance if he should repeat the kindness. When he reached Charleston, POWER was put in prison and detained about a week; and, while there, was supplied with soap and water to wash off the tar, and oil to soften his sores. A mob repeatedly threatened to break into the jail, to take him out and subject him to further abuse. On Saturday, the 24th, he was transferred from prison to the steamboat for New York, and reached that city on the 26th, still suffering from the effects of his ill treatment. The New-York *Independent*, from which we glean these facts, — related, in its columns, from POWER's own lips, — concludes, by way of comment on the case, "this man informed us that, in common with the great mass of Irishmen, in this country, he had always voted with the Democratic party."

Another Irishman, JAMES CRANGALE, was arrested by a Vigilance Committee, in Augusta, Ga., on the 28th of December, charged with being an Abolitionist. He had been living in Savannah for about two years, most of the time as deputy-clerk of one of the courts there, busy with the duties of his office and with preparation for admission to the bar, and never even expressing an opinion about Slavery. His real offence was, trying to collect a debt due to him from a wealthy firm of dry-goods merchants, GRAY & TURLEY, doing business in Savannah and Augusta. He had obtained a judgment in a Justice's Court, which, on appeal, had been affirmed by the Superior Court, although three lawyers, in succession, had thrown up his case, after delaying it for months, and he was forced, at last, to act as his own counsel. Then, as he could find no officer in Savannah who would execute the judgment, and could not induce the solicitor-general to bring the misconduct of the officers before the grand jury, he went up to Augusta, hoping to be more successful there. But there a brother of a partner in the firm indebted to him denounced him as an Abolitionist, and set the Vigilance Committee on him. On the evening of his arrival he was warned to leave the town immediately. He refused, denied the charge of Abolitionism, and told the business which had brought him thither. That night, about two o'clock, three constables and about twenty of the Vigilance Committee broke into his room at the hotel, arrested him, and, after taking from him his overcoat and valise, hurried him off to jail. He was compelled to give up his keys, being told that his refusal would be taken as evidence of guilt, and would be followed by a speedy judgment. During the day the mayor made an affidavit against him, affirming that his errand was believed to be to stir up an insurrection among the Slaves, which he was doing; and that he had asserted the Slaves' right to rise against their masters, and the right of the northern people to arm them. When told of this, in the evening, and that he would be tried next day, he sent, at the suggestion of his informant, and engaged, as counsel, Col. Cumming, one of the most respectable and influential lawyers in the place.

On his way to court, next morning, he was arrested by the State's authority, upon the mayor's accusation; having been held till then without the shadow of a legal process. He was arraigned before Justices Olin and Piquet; five witnesses were heard against him, but none of them knew anything about him, and all their evidence was only hearsay. It came out, in the cross-examination, that Andrew Gray, a brother of the Gray in the indebted firm, had pointed out the prisoner to one witness, as an Abolitionist; and that another witness had proposed the hanging of the prisoner without a trial. This admission passed without rebuke from the court, but the testimony touching Andrew Gray was ruled out, "on the ground that the trade of Augusta with the North would be injured should it become known that such was their method of dealing with creditors." The prisoner's counsel then addressed the court, denouncing vigilance committees as self-made tribunals, at once witnesses and judges, having no higher aim than to plunder northern men of property, by a charge of Abolitionism, and divide the spoils among themselves. He justified the statute which makes death the penalty for inciting Slaves to insurrection, but condemned the persecution of the innocent. As not a particle of proof appeared against the prisoner, the court could do no other than acquit him; but yet condemned him to pay the costs of prosecution, as well as of the preceding illegal arrest and imprisonment. His valise and coat were given back to him; but a pocket-book, containing nearly a hundred dollars, which he had left in the coat-pocket, was nowhere to be found.

When he told the court of his loss, Justice OLIN answered with abusive and profane language, said he had acquitted him simply for want of evidence, called him a fool, and compelled him to open his valise, saying that, if anything was in it to convict him, "enough of the boys were present to string him up." Happily, it had not been tampered with, while out of his possession, and so contained nothing to imperil him. The loss of his pocket-book leaving him unable to pay the costs of the injustice and abuse which he had suffered, he was committed anew to prison till they should be paid. After staying there thirty-three hours, he sent to Col. CUMMING, asking for an interview. ALFRED CUMMING, the colonel's son, went to the jail and paid the fees demanded, and Mr. CRANGALE was released; and, following Justice OLIN's counsel, "to be off the moment he was out of jail," he reached New York the seventh of January. And so his account with Messrs. GRAY & TURLEY was balanced.

The Charleston (S. C.) *Mercury*, of December 17, states that "a man supposed to be an Abolitionist, and calling himself JAMES W. RIVERS, was taken up on the 13th, by the Vigilance Committee, tarred and feathered, and the right side of his head shaven." On the 19th, the steamer Huntsville, from Savannah, reached New York, with several passengers who had been driven from different parts of the South. Two, exiled from South Carolina, had their heads shaven on one side. Not far from the same time, as we learn from the Wytheville (Va.) *Telegraph*, a northern man, "supposed to be an agent of some Abolition Aid-Society or Underground Railroad," was arrested by a mob in Pulaski County, Va., and — "one of the most influential and worthy citizens of the county acting as judge, jury, and executioner" — was hung by the neck till life was nearly extinct, then taken down, and when sufficiently restored was hung again; and, "after having undergone this process five times, once each for old BROWN, COPPOC, COOKE, STEVENS, and HAZLETT," was sent off, with a warning "that if ever caught in Virginia again, he would have to take the sixth and fatal leap."

While the brig B. G. Chaloner, of East Machias, Me., with Captain A. V. KINNEY, mate, and four seamen, was taking in a load of lumber at Statilla Mills, on the Statilla River, in Georgia, in December, a Mr. MORRISSEY, a wealthy planter, living in that region, who had some time before become acquainted with and much attached to Mr. PATTERSON, the mate, sent him and the captain and the captain's wife a pressing invitation to come and take a Christmas dinner with his family. On the morning of the 25th they took the crew to row them to Mr. MORRISSEY'S landing-place, about fifteen miles distant, and thence went, five miles further, to his plantation, leaving the men at the house of an acquaintance of the captain's, to await their return. Soon after they had gone, a gang of six armed ruffians, headed by one DAVID BROWN, went to the house where the sailors were stopping, pretending to have been sent to take them to jail. The sailors, thinking that they came with legal authority, quietly went with them, and were taken to the woods, tied to a tree, and a negro was made to give three of them fifty lashes each, and the fourth, a tall, strong man, a hundred; then sent them, in a boat, back to the vessel. The next day, as the captain, with his wife and mate, was returning to the boat, BROWN and his gang intercepted them, and, with guns leveled at their heads, compelled the men to take off their coats; then forced a negro to give them each fifty lashes, which being done, they ordered him to give them "four more for tally;" and when the captain's wife piteously interceded for them, she was roughly told to "stop her d——d crying," or they would treat her in the same way. They were then conducted to the boat, shoved off, and left to row against the tide, back to their vessel. A correspondent of the Belfast (Me.) *Age*, who writes from Georgia an account of these facts, says that "the only reason given for the outrage was, that the captain and his men were 'damned Northerners.'"

The *Carolina Bulletin*, of Charlotte, N. C., states that, on the 26th of January, Mr. FRANKLIN DAVIS, a grand juror in the County Court, sitting there, was expelled from the grand jury, on motion of Solicitor D. B. REA, for expressing sentiments opposed to Slavery, and was immediately bound over in $1,000 for his appearance at the next sitting of the Superior Court. The *Bulletin* takes "great pleasure in commending Mr. REA for the prompt and faithful manner in which he has discharged his duty." At Chappel's Depot, S. C., a man named JAMES C. BUNGINGS was arrested on Sunday night, the 5th of February, by a Vigilance Committee, who, on examination, pretended to have found upon him "any quantity of papers," showing him to be one of BROWN's associates, commissioned to go into all the South, and corrupt the minds of the negroes and induce them to escape to the North. The next morning he was hung upon a tree, in front of the railroad station, in the presence of about fifty persons, and, after hanging three hours, his body was cut down and given to the medical students for dissection. On the 12th of February, says the *Virginia Senti-nel*, of the 14th, one NUCKOLS, living in Amherst County, Va., "was taken to a pond and ducked, for having used seditious language." He afterwards procured a warrant for the arrest of the offenders, "but, instead of its being executed, the magistrate who issued it narrowly escaped a ducking himself." On the 10th, a ruffian, named EDMUNDSON, a large and powerful man, who helps to represent Virginia in Congress, exhibited the quality of southern chivalry by assaulting, with a stick, at unawares, Mr. HICKMAN of Pennsylvania, a man of slender frame, and withal consumptive, as he was walking from the Capitol. The provocation was some words, more just than complimentary, about Virginia, in a speech of HICKMAN's, a short time before. As soon as the Virginian bully struck a safe, because an unexpected blow, bystanders interposed, and led the men away in different directions. Among the tokens of the estimation in which the act of cowardly ruffianism was held by the southern compatriots of its author, were the presentations to him, shortly after, of "beautiful" and "elegant" silver-headed and palmetto canes, from Virginian and South Carolinian admirers of his prowess.

In the Quincy (Ill.) *Whig*, of February 28, is an account, given from the victim's mouth, of the barbarities committed, the preceding night, upon FREDERIC SCHALLER, a respectable and intelligent citizen of La Grange, Missouri, in which State he has resided for the past twelve years. He states that he has always been a Democrat, and has never meddled with Slaves or Slavery. On Sunday, the 26th, while in a neighboring town, he was accosted by three men, who told him he was suspected of having aided the escape of a Slave of a Mr. HARRIS, in La Grange, and must go back with them. Confident in his innocence and his ability to prove it, and asking only for a fair and speedy trial, he went with them. They took him to the La

Grange House, where he was held a prisoner. His request to be tried on Monday was refused, and on Monday night an armed gang of twenty-five or thirty took him out, together with his brother and a man named MATTIS, and two other men whom they had seized; released those two, and ordered them to leave the State, tied the hands of the rest, carried them in a hack, three miles from the town, then took them into the woods, and hung SCHALLER on a tree till he was senseless. When he came to again, two men were whipping him with cowhides; his hands were tied to the tree above his head, and he was entirely naked; the night was very cold, and soon his back was crusted with frozen blood. When untied, he fell to the ground, too weak to stand. In putting on his clothes he found that his money ($128 in gold) and his watch were gone. He crawled, as well as he could, to the house of his father-in-law, and was placed under a physician's care. His brother, who had been released, told him the ruffians must have abused him for more than an hour. MATTIS, he said, "is still in La Grange, sick, from a similar treatment."

These may serve as examples of the atrocities of which, for months past, almost every issue of the periodical press has brought us mention of fresh instances. Nor have they been confined to the period since the taking of Harper's Ferry, though much more frequent, since then, than before. Our last Report gave an account of some riotous demonstrations, near the close of our preceding year, against a Conference of the Methodist Church North, which met in Fannin County, Texas; and of the resolution of the Conference to submit the question to the people of their several stations and circuits, whether they should give up the field, or still remain and preach. It seems that their people thought the mob too strong to be resisted; for we learned, a few weeks later, that "the difficulties have been temporarily settled" by the Northern Methodists "agreeing, for a time, to abstain from preaching" in that region. It is also stated that "The Texas Advocate, the organ of the Methodist Church South, fully and warmly endorses the proceedings of the mob, and urges the thorough and immediate eradication of the Methodist Church North, in Texas, with whatever force may be necessary."

The Methodists, however, were not the only troublers of the

16*

peace of Texan Slave-holders. SOLOMON McKINNEY, a Camp-bellite preacher, went, in April of last year, from Iowa to Dallas County, Texas, and spent the summer there, preaching at different places in the county. He is a native of Kentucky, but now a resident of Iowa, and has lived in Indiana, where he was known as a good Democrat, holding Slavery to be sanctioned by the Bible. At the request of a Slave-holder, with whom he boarded, in Dallas County, he preached a sermon on the rela-tive duties of master and Slave, in which he condemned the cruel treatment Slaves sometimes receive. This proved him not a proper man to be at large among the meek and gentle dwellers in that land. They therefore held a meeting in the town of Dallas, on the 12th and 13th of August, and resolved that they were law-abiding and law-loving citizens, looking to the law to protect them in their rights, but determined to resort to other means against offenders whom the law cannot reach; that they protested against the dangerous sentiments which McKINNEY had been preaching to their Slaves; and "warned him to seek a field where the sentiments of the people are more congenial to his own, and not again attempt to preach in this community." Soon after, he arranged to leave the State, in company with another preacher of the same denomination, WILLIAM BLUNT, an old acquaintance, who had been a short time in the neighborhood, and, through his introduction, had preached there once or twice. They had engaged a man to take them on their journey, on the 23rd; but some cause hin-dered him from going till the 25th. On the morning of that day, while they were at a friend's house, six miles from Dallas, waiting for their carrier, four men called on them, as a commit-tee of a meeting held in Dallas, the day before, and told them they must go by Saturday, the 27th, or be helped away. One of the men fired his revolver at McKINNEY, coming out to ask their errand, and he answered with a rifle-shot; but neither took effect, and the man rode back to Dallas, and mustered a party for pursuit, while the other three delivered the message of the meeting. Half an hour afterward, BLUNT and McKIN-NEY set off upon their journey, and had gone about nine miles, when they were overtaken by nine well-mounted men, armed with double-barreled guns, by whom they were taken back to Dallas. There they were put in prison, by the sheriff, who took from BLUNT his money, about sixteen dollars. At three or four o'clock next morning, eight armed men entered the jail, tied them, and took them a little way out of town, pulled off their coats, and gave them eighty lashes each, with a rawhide, then bade them go, and never be seen in the country again. BLUNT was so weak before that he could walk but a few rods without resting, being an old man and in feeble health, and, after the infliction, had to be lifted into the carriage. When he expressed a wish to get his property in Dallas, especially his money, before going, the ruffians insisted that he should go at once, threatening to riddle him with balls, and striking him in the breast with the muzzles of their pistols. "Their shirts were cut into ribbons by the rawhide, and their backs were one mass of clotted blood and gore, and bruised and mangled flesh." BLUNT, in a memorial to the Legislature of Wisconsin, of which State he has been a citizen for twenty-four years, related, under oath, most of the particulars above recited, and further stated that, "for more than thirty years, he had uniformly supported the Democratic ticket, both in the State and Nation, and sustained the views of that party, upon the issues between the North and South to the best of his abilities; and that he has never believed it to be his duty to preach against Slavery, and consequently he has carefully abstained, and did, while in Texas, carefully abstain, from so doing." To which the Madison (Wis.) *State Journal* adds that "he was particularly 'gifted' in the Biblical argument in favor of Slavery." It was said, in the debate upon his memorial, that the abuse which he had received had ruined his health beyond hope of recovery.

A despatch from New Orleans, on the 13th of September, says that "the planters residing in the parish of Lafayette, in this State, having been seriously annoyed by outside persons tampering with their Slaves, formed a Vigilance Committee, a few days since, and expelled a large number of obnoxious persons from the parish, after administering to them a severe punishment." As there are laws enough in Louisiana to punish "tampering with Slaves," when proved by proper evidence, the strong presumption from the interference of a mob, self-styled a Vigilance Committee, is, of course, that these "obnoxious persons" were as innocent of the alleged offence as those whose cases we have been relating.

CENSORSHIP OF THE MAILS AND PRESS.

Another way in which the lawless spirit of the Slave-land showed itself, was in the violation of the mails — to which even high official authority lent its countenance — and in the furious warfare waged against the issues of the northern press. Most of the northern journals which had obtained some circulation at the South, by regular subscription or otherwise, were proscribed as incendiary publications; postmasters refused to deliver them to their subscribers, and petty magistrates burned them in public places, with the appropriate formalities, under statutes framed to give to vandalism the color of law; while, in some instances, men who ventured to subscribe for and receive them, were indicted for the crime of circulating papers calculated " to incite Slaves to rebel."

A postmaster in Doddridge County, Va., having written to Governor WISE, asking what he should do with the New-York *Tribune*, and certain other papers of like character, coming to his office, the governor referred the question to the State's Attorney-general. He answered, on the 26th of November, citing the statute of Virginia, which requires that "if a postmaster knows that any book or writing, advising or inciting negroes to rebel, or inculcating resistance to the right of property of masters in their Slaves, has been received at his office in the mail, he shall give notice thereof to some justice, who shall inquire into the circumstances, and have such book or writing burned in his presence ; if it appear to him that the person to whom it was directed subscribed therefor, knowing its character, or agreed to receive it for circulation to aid the purposes of Abolitionists, the justice shall commit such person to jail; and if any postmaster or deputy-postmaster violate this section, he shall be fined not exceeding two hundred dollars." This law he declared to be constitutional, and binding upon every postmaster in the Commonwealth, and not in conflict with the Federal authority in the establishment of post-offices and post-roads. When the mail matter reaches the point of its reception, the Federal power ceases; the State alone is to determine whether her citizens shall receive it; and any law of Congress impairing this reserved right of the State, is unconstitutional, and cannot exempt a postmaster from the penalty of the State law. "It is eminently important," he concludes, "that the provisions of the law in question should be rigidly adhered to by all the postmasters in the State, and that the justices to whose notice the matter may be brought should firmly execute the law, whenever a proper case presents itself for their decision."

Soon after this opinion was made public, a postmaster in Fairfax County wrote to the Postmaster-general, asking for instruction touching the matter it refers to, and whether the Virginian statute is in conflict with the Act of Congress, which imposes heavy penalties for the unlawful detention of mail-matter from the person to whom it is directed. Mr. HOLT replied, on the 5th of December, stating that it had been fully decided by Attorney-general CUSHING, in a perfectly analogous case, that the State law "was not inconsistent with the Act of Congress, and that postmasters, as good citizens, were bound to yield obedience to such State laws." "The judgment thus pronounced," said Mr. HOLT, "has been cheerfully acquiesced in by this department, and is now recognized as one of the guides of its administration. You must determine whether the newspapers, &c., received by you for distribution, are of the character described by the statute, and if you believe they are, you are empowered and required, by your duty to the State of which you are a citizen, to dispose of them in strict conformity to the provisions of the law referred to." When, some weeks later, the proprietor of the Dayton (O.) *Religious Telescope* sent a complaint, through his Representative in Congress, to the Postmaster-general, that a certain postmaster, in Virginia, was refusing to deliver the *Telescope* to the subscribers for whom he received it, Mr. HOLT directed his Assistant to inform his recusant subordinate that he had misconstrued the statute of Virginia; that if one number of a paper contains incendiary matter, it does not follow thence that every number is to be condemned; but that each number must be judged upon its own merits. A rule, this, which would cut out plenty of work for the postmasters; as well as clothe them with somewhat ample, not to say formidable powers! For it would require them to examine every paper, book, and pamphlet coming to their respective offices — and why not every letter, for "book

or writing" is the language of the statute, and sedition and rebellion may lurk in manuscript as well as in print — else might
some treason slip through undetected. And this is the decree
not of Kaisar or of Czar, but of an under servant of the people
of a free Republic!

The postmaster at Lynchburg, Va., wrote to HORACE GREE-
LEY, on the 2nd of December, "I shall not, in future, deliver
from this office the copies of the *Tribune* which come here, because I believe them to be of that incendiary character which
are forbidden circulation alike by the laws of the land, and a
proper regard for the safety of society." From Occoquan, in
the same State, JOHN C. UNDERWOOD wrote, on the 21st, "ten
or twelve copies of the *Tribune* are taken at this office, and the
postmaster refuses to deliver them to the subscribers! The
Attorney-general of this State has pronounced them incendiary!" The Occoquan postmaster wrote, on the 26th, to the
editor of the Poughkeepsie (N. Y.) *Eagle*, "You will discontinue your paper directed to J. YELVERTON; the magistrates
have burned it, and say they will continue to do the same if
sent." The Springfield (Mass.) *Republican*, the Albany *Evening
Journal*, and the New-York *Independent* are among the journals
which received similar notices from southern post-offices. Even
such eminently "conservative" publications as *Harper's Weekly*,
and *Frank Leslie's Illustrated Paper*, were put under the same
ban. Judge SAUNDERS, of North Carolina, as we learn from
the *North Carolinian*, "put a stop to the sale of" *Harper's
Magazine*, and *Weekly*, in Raleigh. The Columbus (S. C.)
Guardian uttered its protest against the circulation of them,
and of Leslie's paper, in the South. Indeed, so far was the proscription carried that we believe the Springfield *Republican*
exaggerated little, if at all, in saying, "nearly all northern papers
are now excluded from the South, except the *New - York
Herald* and the *New - York Observer*, the one the organ of Pro-
Slavery diabolism and the other of Pro-Slavery piety."

Not far from the first of January, JOHN H. GARGAS and
THOMAS CRUX were arrested in Fairfax County, Va., charged
with circulating incendiary documents, Helper's book particularly. GARGAS is a postmaster, and his crime was handing to a
neighbor one of Helper's books, which came by mail, without
knowing what it was. He was tried by five justices, and dis-

charged; probably because he had sinned in ignorance. Mr. CRUX, who was bound over for trial, in $2,500, conscious, doubtless, that he could not put in the same plea, thought it prudent to leave the State, forfeiting his bond. Near the same time, the Montgomery (Ala.) *Mail* proposed that southern "booksellers who find that, without knowing it, they have bought books containing Abolition sentiments, should destroy such books and refuse to pay for them, on the ground that the law cannot compel them to pay for books the circulation of which is against law." Conclusive reasoning, we think, to men whose honesty consists in doing just what the law compels! A later issue of the *Mail*, on the 17th of February, invites "all persons in Montgomery who possess copies of the sermons of the notorious English Abolitionist, SPURGEON, to send them to the jail-yard, to be burned on next Friday," and adds that "a subscription is on foot to buy of our booksellers all copies of said sermons now in their stores, to be burned on the same occasion." And on the 28th, it thus announces the result of its invitation. "Last Saturday, we devoted to the flames a large number of SPURGEON's Sermons, and the pile was graced at the top with a copy of 'Graves's Great Iron Wheel,' which a Baptist friend presented for the purpose. We trust that the works of the greasy cockney vociferator may receive the same treatment throughout the South. And if the pharisaical author should ever show himself in these parts, we trust that a stout cord may speedily find its way round his eloquent throat." Within a few weeks after this, "a large number of copies of the 'Impending Crisis' were publicly burned at Greenville, S. C., and a young man named HAROLD WYLLYS was sentenced to a year's imprisonment for putting them in circulation." A letter to the New-York *Tribune*, dated March 15, from Harford County, Md., says that "this course of proscription has been carried out by a few demagogues in this county. The sheriff, being a Democrat, summoned a Democratic grand jury, whose first act was to summon before them the postmasters, to inform them if any incendiary or inflammatory documents came to their offices, and who took them." Finding too many to indict them all, they singled out "one T. B. HULL, who had procured some friends to join him in a club" to take the *Tribune*, and presented him as "guilty of a crime which, in Maryland, is punishable with not

less than ten years' imprisonment in the penitentiary." They
also found a bill against one S. B. WALTON, for having and
lending to his neighbors a copy of the 'Impending Crisis;' and
against a poor, educated black man, who has taken the *Tribune*
for the last six years; also against one DAVID TUCKER, a worthy
and highly respected citizen, who had presented, to some members of his Sunday-school class, a year's subscription to the
Methodist *Sunday-school Advocate*, in one number of which
were found some of JOHN WESLEY's sayings against "the sum
of all villanies." A correspondent of the *Tribune* writes from
Lewes, Del., on the 21st of April, that "the grand jury of Kent
County, Md., have had the postmasters before them, made inquiries relative to newspapers taken at the different offices, and
directed the postmasters to retain and not deliver the New-
York *Tribune* and Delaware *Republican*. There appears to be
a goodly number of subscribers to the obnoxious journals, and
they are, without an exception that I know of, persons of respectability, intelligent and law-abiding. Several are Slave-
owners. The postmasters, as far as heard from, retain the
papers. If they would only read them, it would be some conso-
lation." This war upon the northern press has brought within
the reach of northern admiration some precious gems of southern post-official literature, from which one might be tempted to
infer that dictionaries, spelling-books, and grammars are included in the southern *Index Expurgatorius* of incendiary publications. We copy, as a specimen, the following elegant epistle
from a Virginian postmaster, to the editor of the *Western
Christian Advocate*.

WAYNE C. H. Va. Feb. 28, 1860.

To the Editor of the Western Chreston Advocate.

Sir you will Please Discontinue sending your paper to this office as it has
bin found to contain incindary matter, and burnt.   Yours &c.

Just *what* the offending paper burnt, whether the mail-bag or
the unfortunate postmaster's fingers, his Spartan brevity permits
us not to know; perhaps his Spartan hardihood forbade his
telling. But that it "burnt," must be accepted, we suppose, as
proof indubitable that it contained "incindary matter," and,
consequently, was a dangerous thing among the combustible
contents of the mail. Entirely reasonable, therefore, was the
polite request "please discontinue sending." it.

COMMERCIAL PROSCRIPTION.

But not against the northern press alone has the war been waged. The merchants of the northern cities have been threatened with the loss of southern trade unless they would abjure all sympathy with Freedom, and range themselves with the open allies of the Slave-power. Editors or correspondents of southern journals, or fellows claiming to be such, and other incarnations of essential impudence, thrust themselves upon the notice of northern merchants, demanding explanations of their views of Slavery, and avowals of their political opinions and associations, on pain of publication in some "black list" of "Abolition houses," if they answered manfully or not at all; while places in the "white list" of "Conservative" or "Constitutional houses" could be had for pledges of subserviency to southern despotism,—— and an adequate consideration. Offices, for the systematic carrying on of this business of levying black mail, and bribing or bullying northern merchants into tame servility, were opened, under the fair-seeming name of "Southern Mercantile and Business Agency;" with open proclamation of "the purpose"— we copy from the circular of one of them — "of attempting to give a right direction to southern trade, by withdrawing it from our northern enemies, and placing it in the hands of our friends; which we propose to do by furnishing southern merchants and business men with such reliable information regarding northern mercantile houses, as will enable them to trade exclusively with those who are friendly to the South and her institutions." The circular we quote from is dated at Richmond, Va., January 1, 1860, and signed by WM. P. GILMAN & Co. After telling the mercantile public that "our books will contain the names of every northern house ascertained to be worthy of southern confidence; and these names, with the business and locality annexed, will be corrected annually, and published in a book or directory, prepared for the express purpose, and circulated throughout the whole southern country;" and, with divers other important considerations, commending the enterprise to liberal patronage, it concludes with the particularly interesting information that, "to defray the expenses necessarily incurred in establishing our Agency, and in carrying out its design, we shall charge each house, whose name or card appears in our Directory, a sum not less than FIFTY DOLLARS, to be paid at the time of subscribing." The Atlanta (Ga.) *Southern Confederacy* published its "white and black lists," denouncing all who were included in the latter, as "steeped and saturated in Sewardism, Brownism, Greeleyism, Helperism, and incendiarism," and insolently adding, "if they are not, let them deny it under oath before the world, and say who they supported for president in 1856." Not satisfied with urgently exhorting the merchants of Georgia to buy their goods of those alone whose names were in the "white list," it threatened with exposure such as should presume to disregard the exhortation, telling them that "*public sentiment*, as well as their duty as good and loyal citizens of a Slave-holding community, will prompt them" to compliance. The Charleston *Mercury* is another of the southern journals which engaged in this absurd attempt to abrogate the laws of trade, and compel the sale of principles with wares. It denounced, and threatened to expose by name, the Charleston merchants who maintained business relations with a New-York house, of which the partners attend HENRY WARD BEECHER's church.

From the New-York *Tribune*, of February 15, we learn that the editor of the *Confederacy* was then in New-York city, "making a round of calls upon tradesmen, receiving sometimes money, sometimes goods, and always the evidence of the most despicable subserviency, on condition that he will certify to that fact; and that among all these tradesmen not one had kicked him into the nastiest part of the gutter near their premises." Nay, there were even found, among the merchants of that city, some so forgetful of their self-respect, that, when the impudent blood-sucker had put their names into his black list, instead of taking it as an honorable attestation of their manliness, they were actually at the pains to repel, through the daily press, the imputation of "sympathy with any of the forms of fanaticism mentioned;" while others hastened to present him, personally, "the best evidence" [signed, doubtless, by the officers of solvent banks] "that they were never tainted with any Anti-Slavery *isms*," but were "deserving of the continued patronage and support of their former patrons at the South." But these exhibitions of servility seem not to have produced the happiest consequences to their authors. The *Tribune*, of the 21st of February, says that "the merchants who thought to get an advantage by succumbing to the process of explaining their politics, and getting themselves put into white lists, in sundry one-horse newspapers, at the South, are getting the just deserts of their contemptible meanness. A whole crowd of ragged, sponging fellows have arisen, in the shape of correspondents of southern journals, editors, attachés, drummers for advertisements and subscriptions, who surround them like buzzards hovering about a wounded buffalo on the prairie. It is next to impossible to distinguish the real vagabonds from their counterfeit. To make sure work, therefore, each poor, pitiful, mean-spirited, craven, humiliated wretch of a merchant, who has allowed himself to be entangled in the toils of these land-sharks, has no other escape but to buy off from every fellow who besets him."

The great "Union meeting," held in New-York city, on the 19th of December, to reässure the South, alarmed by northern manifestations of admiration for JOHN BROWN, appears to have been, at the same time, a device to help this work of commercial proscription; refusal to subscribe the call for it being regarded as conclusive proof of infidelity to southern interests, while signing it was to be a way to southern favor. To facilitate the working of this device, of the 176 pages of the handsome pamphlet, in which the proceedings of the meeting were published, eighty-four were "beautifully filled," the *Tribune* says, "in clear type and broad margins, with the names of the signers to the call, all carefully, distinctly, and, what is more, *alphabetically* arranged; at a total expense, for meeting and pamphlet, of $10,000. So that hunting to ascertain who is sound on the golden goose of trade in this city, becomes a job easily performed."

While one set of the lordlings of the Slave-land, finding their own advantage in playing go-between to southern arrogance and northern baseness, were willing to discriminate in their proscription, another set, more fierce and not so politic, were for entire non-intercourse with the infected region, fearing alike to trust the true men and the traitors there. Out of the many avowals of the feelings and the purposes of this class, with which the southern press abounded, we give a specimen or two, by which to judge the rest. A meeting held in Westmoreland County, Va., on the 28th of November, resolved to "adopt a strict non-intercourse in trade and commerce with the citizens and merchants of all the non-slaveholding States; neither to sell them any article of the growth or manufacture of our State, nor buy nor consume any article of the growth or manufacture of their States; to cease to travel among them or visit them, except on the most urgent and unavoidable business; to employ no laborers or mechanics from the North; and to arrest and send out of the State, in the most summary manner, all itinerant venders of northern books, newspapers, periodicals, or any other article of northern growth or manufacture; and all persons who are suspected of Anti-Slavery opinions or sympathies, or who cannot give a precise and true account of themselves, as engaged in lawful business, we will treat as vagrants and incendiaries." Some time during the winter the Alabama House of Representatives passed a resolution, declaring it the duty and interest of Alabama, and all other Slave-holding States, to cease commercial intercourse with the northern States; and recommending the people "to hold meetings in every county and neighborhood, and resolve to buy no article of merchandise or manufacture obtained in the northern States, or procured through any northern firm or agency."

On the 19th of December, a resolution was introduced in the House of Delegates of Virginia, "that the Committee of Schools and Colleges inquire into the expediency of reporting a bill prohibiting school commissioners, throughout the Commonwealth, from subscribing to any teacher, male or female, who hails from the north of Mason's and Dixon's line, unless they shall have resided in the State of Virginia for at least ten successive years previous." Another resolution, introduced in the same body, aimed at discouraging insurance, by Virginians, in northern offices. About the same time, two hundred Virginian students started off, in a body, from the medical schools of Philadelphia, indignant at the determined energy with which the mayor and police had crushed a riotous attempt, in which they largely shared, to prevent GEORGE W. CURTIS from delivering an Anti-Slavery lecture in that city, on the evening of the 15th of December. They went to Richmond, where they met a jubilant reception, and were welcomed with a speech from Governor WISE. But the city which they left seemed no way inconsolable at their departure, regarding it as a happy deliverance rather than a calamity. The Philadelphia *Sunday Despatch* declared that they had left the city for the city's good, had relieved the police of a constant source of solicitude, and would now inflict upon the suffering South their riot, drunkenness, and folly. The relief appears, however, to have been but temporary and partial; for a correspondent of the New-York *Tribune* writes from Philadelphia, on the first of January, "it is a solemn fact that the indignant Virginia doctors are back again — the very fellows who went off in such a rage only ten days ago! — not all of them yet; but they are sneaking back in squads of two, three, and half a dozen at a time, careful to avoid fuss, and seeking to excuse their childish folly by saying they only wanted a holiday frolic."

The embryo physicians of Virginia were not the only falterers in this patriotic purpose of abandoning the luckless North to poverty and starvation, by withdrawing southern patronage. Older and sterner hearts had some relentings, too. We learn from the New-York *Commercial*, that, in the latter part of December, a single number of the Richmond *Enquirer*, but a few days after it had strongly recommended strict non-intercourse between Virginia and the North, contained "ten editorial laudatory notices of books, every one of which is published at New York or Boston, with any number of advertisements of goods for sale, of purely northern manufacture, and some headed with northern and eastern titles." In fact, we gather from the statements of the press that the non-intercourse attempt has so far proved a signal failure. The natural laws of trade have been too strong, as yet, for the champions of proscription. The *Tribune's* correspondent writes from Philadelphia, on the 30th of January, "I have talked with fifty men who make for and sell the bulk of their wares to the South, and they neither feel nor fear a diminution of their sales. Southern dealers, in this market, neither write nor talk non-intercourse Our people are satisfied that they will continue to buy as usual, wherever they can be best suited. Everything we have to sell is going off without interruption from this cause, and twenty locomotives, for southern railroads, have just been ordered from New Jersey." The New-York *Evening Post*, a few weeks later,

17*

says, "some of our merchants are absolutely oppressed with the extent of the orders they receive from the South. We spoke with one of them, this morning, who said that the house in which he was concerned had twice the amount of southern trade, this winter, that it had last season. What is quite as worthy of note is that those who come on from the South to purchase, buy, as they did last year, where they can buy to the best advantage, and ask no questions as to the politics of the seller." A writer in the Alexandria (Va.) *Gazette* asks, in the early part of March, "what has been the actual result of all the resolutions lately passed, not only in this city, but in nearly every town and county in the Commonwealth? I was in New York and Philadelphia, last week, and had some opportunities of knowing, and am firmly of the opinion that more goods, of all kinds, have been sold in both places, to southern markets, than was ever before the case. Southern merchants and southern people, despite of everything done and said, will buy where they think they can get the best assortment, and purchase at the cheapest rates."

BARBARITY TO SLAVES.

The illustrations of the barbarism of the Slave-land, contained in the foregoing pages which relate the treatment white men have received when in occasional and brief contact with it, may give some notion of what black men must be liable to suffer from its continual pressure; held, all their lives long, helpless, hopeless, in its grasp; and rated so low in the scale of being, that their suffering or enjoyment is esteemed of small account, compared to the security, the ease, the pleasure, or the gain of those belonging to the higher caste. Men of ordinary intelligence, not utterly awry with prejudice, will hardly be persuaded to believe that they who treat white freemen, their own caste, as we have seen the people of the Slave States do, are likely to be very careful of the comfort of black Slaves, whom they look down upon as creatures of a lower order, "having no rights which they are bound to respect." That they will often practice cruelty without scruple or compunction, upon their human chattels, to quicken indolence, extort submission to the behests of brutal appetite, repress the manly instincts which pride of caste calls insolent, or punish insubordination or slackness to obey, subdue rebellious aspirations or gratify vindictive feeling, is obviously the logical sequence of the premises before us. This inference is amply verified, moreover, by plenty of authentic testimony as to the actual treatment of the Slaves. Indeed, a candid man would be convinced of this, by seeing on what sort of evidence Pro-Slavery advocates rely, to prove the opposite. For instance, the Detroit *Free Press*, of May 16, 1859, to show the falsehood of the stories which it represents as told by Abolitionists, "of cruelty to Slaves at the South, and the impossibility of procuring redress for or punishment of such cruelty," quotes from the *North-Carolina Journal*, of the week before, an "item of fact" which, it says, "puts to flight a regiment of such stories." It is, that at the session of the Superior Court of North Carolina, held at Newbern, the preceding Thursday, in a suit for damages against two men for brutally abusing the plaintiff's Slave, the jury awarded the plaintiff five hundred dollars damages. Now Abolitionists affirm, not quite "the impossibility," but the exceeding difficulty of punishing the frequent crime of cruelty to Slaves. We would not venture to assert that it was *never* punished, under southern law; for though, of all the many cases of the crime, whereof we have heard, we do not now remember one of punishment, it yet seems hard to doubt that some such must have been. But, had we said such punishment is impossible at the South, the "fact" adduced by the *Free Press* would not disprove our word. For, first, it proves that the Slave, in that case, was "brutally abused;" and, second, it shows not even an attempt to "procure redress" for *him*, or to *punish* his abusers; but only a recovery of damages by an "owner," for injury to his property. That one man, of the favored caste, can make another pay for damage done to his goods and chattels, does not *begin* to prove that one of the inferior caste can get redress for wrongs which he endures from his superiors in position; or that their crimes, committed upon him, are practically punishable, whatever laws, enacted for the world abroad to read, may seem to say. If, in the case just cited, the abuse had been the master's act, what chance would the Slave have had to procure redress? *He* could not sue for damages, or enter a complaint for the offence

stitution of barbarian justice, for the calm authority of regulated right which civilized society administers.

We add some exhibitions of this Slave-State barbarism, engaged in its more frequent and familiar work of making black men victims either of blind, utterly wrong-doing vengeance, or of a lawless administration of the penalties of civilized justice, often with a fierce and terrible aggravation of its severity. A correspondent of the Galveston (Tex.) *News*, writes from Grand Cane, May 2, 1859, that, on the 24th of April, a Mr. ROPER, newly come from Alabama to that region, was murdered by his Slave, as they were returning from a journey, alone together. The negro had been brought away from his wife, in Alabama; and, knowing that his master's family wished to return thither, he thought that if his master, who was unwilling to return, was put out of the way, the family would go back, and he could rejoin his wife. But, on his reaching home without his master, suspicion was excited; and some circumstantial evidence being found against him, he confessed the crime; and, on the 30th of April, was burned alive on the spot where it was committed. A letter, on the 20th of July, from Marshall, Saline County, Missouri, to the St. Louis *Democrat*, states that, some time before, a negro killed one HINTON, in that county, for which crime he was convicted, and sentenced to be hung. While on his way to prison he was taken from the sheriff by a mob, who then went to the jail and took out two other negroes, one imprisoned for an attempt to kill a white man, the other for an outrage on a young white woman. Proceeding to the outskirts of the town, they chained the murderer to a stake, piled dry wood around him, and set it on fire. His frantic shrieks and appeals for mercy and for death were to no purpose. Flesh and bones alike were burned into a powder. The other negroes were then hung.

The Independent Monitor says, that on the night of July 23, a Slave, belonging to a citizen of Tarrant, Hopkins County, Texas, attempted to commit an outrage on a Mrs. MORREL, of that place, and failing, through her resolute resistance, he choked and beat her till he thought her dead. He was arrested and imprisoned. On the 27th, the citizens broke into the jail and took him out, conveyed him to the suburbs of the town and hung him. A correspondent of the Ravenna (O.) *Democrat*, writing on the 15th of August, copies from a letter just received from Nashville, Tennessee, what the letter-writer calls "a little incident, of many in the history of Slavery." He says that near his room, a day or two before, a master took offence at some slight misdemeanor of one of his Slaves, for which he had him scourged, with nine cowhide lashes bound together, until the poor man's back was completely lacerated; then pepper was sprinkled on it and the lash again applied; and lastly, two gallons of water were forced down him, soon after which he died. "The people here," he adds, "are very indignant, but, after all, it will be passed over and forgotten. The master is very wealthy, and the victim is only a black man and a Slave!" A. D. RICHARDSON writes from Cincinnati (O.) to the New-York *Tribune*, that, on the 18th of August last, he saw a negro hung by a mob, in Springfield, Missouri, for an outrage on the person of a lady living near that city. In McLean County, Kentucky, sometime last fall, a Slave, sold by his master to another man, objected to the transfer, when he was put in charge of a Mr. CULVER, to be taken to the county seat for safe keeping. He resisted, drew a knife, and killed Mr. CULVER. He was arrested, but a mob immediately gathered, took him by force from the officers, and hung him on a tree. Some time in the former half of March, as we learn from the Montgomery (Ala.) *Mail*, one ALFRED JONES was murdered by two of his Slaves, to avenge a whipping he had given one of them, a few days before. They afterward confessed the crime, and the *Mail* says, "we understand they will be burned to death on Friday, the 16th inst." The Vicksburg (Miss.) *Sun*, of Saturday, March 31, says that a negro man belonging to Mr. WOODFOLK, on Deer Creek, was recently burned at the stake for the murder of a negro woman. All the negroes on that and the adjoining plantations witnessed the burning. "His fate was decreed by a council of *highly respectable gentlemen*."

FREE COLORED PEOPLE.

Our last Report, it will be remembered, mentioned that a Convention for the Eastern Shore of Maryland, a year ago last fall, had called a State Convention, to devise some plan for the regulation of the negro population; and had suggested that the

State should give the free colored people their choice, to leave the State or be enslaved. The Convention met at Baltimore, on the 8th of June last, and sat two days. Its results were so unlike what had been purposed and expected by its callers, and probably by a majority of its members before they met, that the New-York *Tribune* compared it, not inaptly, to the prophet Balaam, who came to curse, and was constrained, against his will, to bless. In the words of the *National Era*, it "unanimously adopted . resolutions condemning, as impolitic and impracticable, the object which called it together." Instead of recommending, as suggested by the Eastern-Shore Convention, at whose call it met, the exile or enslavement of the free colored people, it declared that such a measure would be seriously injurious to the State, as well as oppressive to the blacks. Some frank admissions, too, well worth remembering, as to the general character of the free blacks, and what it is which makes their presence dangerous to Slavery, were made by the extreme Pro-Slavery members. The same men also bore encouraging testimony to the extent of Anti-Slavery feeling in the State. The more fanatical among them did not yield without a struggle — though, overborne by the pressure of outside public sentiment, they had to yield at last — the purpose for which they had come together. But both the nature of the propositions finally adopted, and the reasons urged in their support, show plainly that it was outside constraint, more than its own humanity or conscience, which held back the Convention from the wicked cruelty and folly purposed by its callers.

Col. JACOBS, who had figured largely in the Eastern-Shore Convention, was little less conspicuous in this; being in both the leading champion of the harshest policy against the colored people, while, like so many others of his class, he claimed to be preëminently their friend. Dissenting from the majority of the committee for preparing business, he made a separate report, proposing resolutions which declare "the free negro population positively injurious to the best interests of the State;" asking the Legislature, "at its next session, to terminate free-negroism, in Maryland, at an early day, and on the most advantageous terms to our white population;" suggesting a law allowing free negroes to enslave themselves, and requiring that if they neither do this nor leave the State, "they and their posterity be sold as

Slaves for life," but permitting "discrimination in the case of meritorious and aged free negroes;" and recommending such provision, as to price and mode of payment, "as to enable citizens of limited means to become the owners of such" new-made "Slaves;" also, that "one or more Slaves, belonging to any one person, be exempt from execution." To give weight to his arguments in favor of these resolutions, Col. JACOBS announced himself as a member of the Methodist Church, of twenty-six years standing, and affirmed that if one gentleman on that floor, or within the limits of Maryland, could claim to be the negroes' friend, he had a right to that appellation. Alluding to a passage in the *Christian Advocate and Journal*, in which occurs the phrase "their colored brethren," he proved his boasted friendship by scornfully exclaiming, "does the editor mean that all free negroes are our brethren? We think the Methodists of Maryland will hardly submit to this degradation."

Another colonel, SOTHORON, of St. Mary's County, was for a law to prevent emancipation, and for the gradual abolition of "free-negroism;" and proposed a resolution appointing a committee to memorialize the Legislature for laws to attain "these desirable objects." Mr. MARCUS DUVAL, of Prince George's County, tenderly conscientious and considerate of the rights and interests of "sister States," presented resolutions eulogistic of the condition of the Slaves, and pronouncing the free negroes of the State a nuisance, but declaring that "it would not be equitable and just to drive them into any of our sister States;" and therefore recommending — so as to do nothing which is not equitable and just! — the choice of men to the Legislature who will enact a law for selling, to the highest bidder, every free negro forty-five years old and under, and dividing the price between the State and the county where the sale is made. "A majority of the speakers," says the *National Era*, "showed strong sympathy with these ultra resolutions of Messrs. JACOBS, SOTHORON, and DUVAL. But the men of sense and sagacity, who can 'discern the signs of the times,' though not differing abstractly from them, saw the folly of attempting to force them upon the people of Maryland." So the resolutions, "cold and heartless, but discreet," reported by the majority of the committee, were adopted;"— "bad enough," the *Era* says, "but not so bad as they might have been." They "reject the idea of extirpating or selling the free negroes, not because such measures are wrong, or revolting to the moral sense of honest men and Christians, but because it would be 'inexpedient, and uncalled for by any public exigency which could justify it.'" They treat the increase of free negroes as an evil, and recommend such legislation "as will either prohibit emancipation altogether, or compel the prompt removal from the State of those emancipated."

The preamble to the resolutions, while it speaks of "the existence of so large a number of free blacks in the midst of a Slaveholding State," as being "of itself an evil, and the greater that a portion of them are idle, vicious, and unproductive," admits that "this is not the case with the majority of them, and their removal would be a far greater evil than all the people of Maryland ever suffered from them. * * * * It is unquestionable that quite a large portion of our soil could not be tilled without their aid. * * * * * * Their removal would deduct nearly fifty per cent from the household and agricultural labor furnished by people of this color, and indispensable to the people of the State; would produce great discomfort and inconvenience to the great body of householders; would break up the business and destroy the property of large numbers of land-owners and land-renters; would be harsh and oppressive to those people themselves; would violate public sentiment; and would probably lead to other evils. Such a measure could not receive the legislative sanction, and would not be tolerated by the great body of the people of Maryland, even with that sanction." As the census of 1850 showed the free blacks to be then about forty-five per cent of all the "people of this color" in Maryland, and it is, therefore, probable that they do not exceed "nearly fifty per cent" now, we have here the testimony of a convention of Slave-holders, unfriendly to them in spirit and purpose, that, for labor, they are worth at least as much as Slaves, in proportion to their numbers; and thus the falsehood is refuted, that emancipation would be fatal to the industrial interests of the Slave States.

In the debate, Judge MASON, who agreed in views with Col. SOTHORON, and held that the removal of the free negroes would not be oppressive, said that "if things went on as at present, the State would glide into a free condition within the next

quarter of a century. The gentleman from Calvert surely did
not know what a feeling of Anti-Slavery existed in the State.
Let him take the stump for Anti-Slavery, and he would have
thousands flocking to his standard. It was not the vagabond
who made Slavery sit uncomfortably on the Slave, *but the
thrifty, who are seen by the Slaves, make the dissatisfaction.*"
The judge certainly spoke sound common sense in that remark,
and, in connection with it, his anxiety to get the free negroes
out of the State, for the security of Slavery, is a somewhat
emphatic testimony in favor of their general character. Mr.
Dorsey, of Harford County, thought "the proposition to make
Slaves of the free was monstrous, and worse than the African
Slave-trade." Mr. Johnson said "it was impossible to keep
Slaves in the northern counties of the State. The negroes
would not do forced labor while Pennsylvania was within ten
miles of them. The people of those counties could not keep
negro property, and would not, while a negro is worth fourteen
hundred dollars in New Orleans. He opposed the return of
free negroes to Slavery as impracticable; for, while he did not
think such a thing monstrous, he could not get the people of
the State to think as he did. * * * * * * The negro, in his
opinion, never arrived at the age of discretion, and he should,
by proper laws, be kept in surveillance. The principle should
be well enunciated, but the action should be temperate." Mr.
Sollers, of Calvert County, "was satisfied that no free negro
in the State would willingly go into Slavery, and then what a
social and political shock would the withdrawal of 90,000 laborers produce. * * * * * * It would offend public sentiment.
This was a Slave-holders' Convention, by whatever name it
might be called; and the adoption of such a proposition would
shock the moral and Christian sense, and damn forever those
who adopted it." Senator James A. Pearce urged, against
the policy of the ultraists, that, if they should drive out the
80,000 free negroes, their place would be supplied with "80,000
Germans and Irish, to be added to the Free-soil interest even
now threatening to manifest itself;" and, further, that such an
act would not only revolt the moral sense of Maryland and the
North, but would arouse the opposition of the small farmers,
who, unable to buy Slaves, employ free blacks to till their land;
and of the citizens of Baltimore and other towns, who look to

the same class for domestic servants. These would be forced into the Free-soil ranks, and would demand emancipation, and it would be "vain to resist a demand enforced by the real and fancied material welfare of the whole body of the people who are not Slave-holders." Such was the reasoning which proved efficacious to secure, at last, the unanimous adoption of the more moderate policy. The Richmond (Va.) *Argus* saw, in this result, an evil omen to the patriarchal system, so far, at least, as the Maryland Slave-holders are concerned. "It is easy to see," says the *Argus*, "that the tendency of their policy will be to wipe out Slavery from among them, at a comparatively early day. We shall soon cease to regard Maryland as a Slave State, practically. Politically, she has been dead to the South for a long time past."

But notwithstanding the prevalence of comparatively moderate counsels in the Slave-holders' Convention, an attempt was made at the session of the Legislature, last winter, to procure an act for the enslavement or expulsion of the free blacks. Petitions for such an act were presented, and the measure found support enough to alarm the colored people, and call out from them a memorial in opposition to it, in which they say that the "enactment of laws such as are now proposed, would infallibly lead to an agitation which could do no possible good to any interest or portion of the State. Already a wide-spread alarm has been excited in the minds not only of the colored people, but of a large portion of the white population." The better portion of the press, likewise, opposed it; the Baltimore *Patriot* denouncing it "with scorn and indignation," and the Baltimore *American* warning its abettors that "they will arouse a feeling of indignation throughout the State, which, at present, they seem not to realize. The very interest which is designed to be protected will sustain the severest injury." Finally, bills were passed, which, like the action of the convention, tempered iniquity with prudence, aiming to oppress the weak discreetly. One act prohibits further manumissions unless with removal from the State; and permits free negroes to renounce their freedom. Another appoints a board of commissioners to control the free blacks in eleven counties named; those, probably, in which they are thought most dangerous to Slavery; requires the free blacks to provide homes for themselves, and, if unable to support themselves, that they shall be hired out, and all their children shall be hired out till of age. The act is, however, to be submitted to the people at the next presidential election. Meanwhile the colored people are given to understand that the oppressive legislation, already in existence against them, is not to slumber unused on the statute book. JOHN SCOTT, a free colored man of Cecil County, about twenty years of age, was sold at public sale, on Monday, January 2, as a Slave for life, in default of payment of a fine and costs of suit and of several months' imprisonment, imposed upon him by the Circuit Court, at the preceding April term, for going out of the State and returning thereto "contrary to law."

In North Carolina an act has been passed, compelling the free colored people to choose between Slavery and exile. The Detroit (Mich.) *Free Press* states that twenty-nine negroes crossed the river from Detroit to Canada, about the end of March, being "the first instalment of the northern emigration from North Carolina," in consequence of the late enactment. In Georgia, the Legislature, at its last session, enacted that free negroes, wandering about or leading an idle, immoral, or profligate life, may be indicted as vagrants, and, on conviction, shall be sold into Slavery for any given time, in the discretion of a judge of the Superior Court, not exceeding two years for the first offence; but upon conviction of a second offence they must be sold into perpetual Slavery. A bill to enslave or banish the free negroes, passed both houses of the Florida Legislature, at its last session, but failed to become a law for want of the governor's signature. Attempts are making to procure, in Alabama, the same kind of legislation; and although we have not heard, as yet, of their success, there is little reason to doubt that, if it has not been already, it will, ere long, be achieved. The Montgomery *Mail*, about the first of last November, said, "we are daily receiving encouragement, personally and by letter, in our attempts to direct public attention, and especially that of our Legislature, to the necessity of removing the free negro population of Alabama from its borders. The sentiment is universal, that the 1st of January, 1862, must find no single free negro within the limits of Alabama; their anomalous condition is an eye-sore to the Slaves and an annoyance to the white population." On the 7th of December, the House of

Representatives of Mississippi, by 75 to 5, passed a bill which provides that the free negroes of that State shall leave it on or before the 1st of July, 1860, or shall be sold into Slavery, with a right of choice of masters, at a price assessed by three disinterested Slave-holders, the proceeds to go into the treasury of the county in which the provisions of the bill may require to be executed. The bill was subsequently defeated in the Senate.

In the *Mississippian,* of June 24, is a summary of a decision which has just been given by the High Court of Errors and Appeals, as to the right of a free negro, of another State, to take property by will, in Mississippi. FRANCIS HALL, of Harrison County, gave certain articles of personal property, by will, to a free colored woman, whom he had brought from Louisiana, and who had lived in his house. This property, it seems, his other heirs wished to steal from her in a safe way; so they applied to the judicial tribunals of the State for help in doing it, and were successful. The High Court of Appeals decided that, by the laws of Mississippi, "free negroes are denied political equality or association with the white race; alien free negroes [i. e., all who were not born in the State,] are prohibited from coming into the State, and, on ten days' notice, if they do not leave it, may be taken by the board of county police and be sold to Slavery for life; it is the policy of the State to interdict all intercourse, commerce, or comity with this race, and to enforce the strictest doctrines of the ancient law applicable to *alien enemies* against them, except as to life or limb or personal protection; in the absence of laws confirming such rights, the African can neither take nor hold property in this State, by deed or devise, by descent or purchase, except those free persons of color who may reside here by permission; the free negro, even after manumission here, is only in the position of an alien friend, or enemy permitted here. Free negroes, who are here in violation of our laws and policy, are to be regarded as alien enemies, or strangers prohibited, incapable of acquiring or maintaining rights of property in the State, which will be recognized by its courts; consequently a bequest to a free woman of color, an inhabitant or resident or citizen of another State, not permitted to reside here by our laws, is void in this State."

18*

On the 1st of September, went into effect the acts of Louisiana, passed the spring before, by one of which all free persons of color, arriving in port from abroad, must immediately be lodged in jail, and remain there until the departure of the boat or vessel on which they came;" and by another, any free person of color [not a native of the State, though he may have been no matter how long an inhabitant of it], failing to leave the State on five days' notice, shall be imprisoned, at hard labor, in the penitentiary, not less than three nor more than twelve months, and afterward shall have ten days to leave the State; and, if he returns, shall be imprisoned five years, at hard labor, in the penitentiary. Another act, taking effect at the same time, provides that any free colored person, over twenty-one years old, residing in the State, may choose a master and become a Slave for life, and shall not be sold for debts contracted by the master before his enslavement. The *New-Orleans Crescent*, of September 1, says "there is high excitement among that branch of the free colored population who cannot boast of Louisiana birth, and trepidation among many of them who can." No wonder. The *Crescent* also states that "two bright and intelligent free colored men, who do a good business (both steamboat cooks, one making one hundred dollars and the other seventy-five dollars per month), formally filed their petitions in the First District Court, to become the Slaves for life of a well-known gentleman of this city, he having consented to accept them. * * * * * From what we hear at present, a great many free negroes, not born in this State, will pick out their masters and become Slaves sooner than leave the population and the climate which pleases them so well." Such is the careless tone in which the *Crescent* speaks of the atrocious wickedness and cruelty of forcing men guilty of no wrong, not even likely to become a public charge, but amply able to provide for their own wants, into a choice between enslavement and expulsion from their business and their homes, and from a land they love so well that exile from it is to them more bitter even than Slavery. Well may the New-York *Tribune* say, " compared to this, the Mortara outrage, which so shocked the civilized world, sinks into insignificance. And yet so debased have the moral sense and the political instincts of the American people become by the long-continued domination of the Slave-holding aristocracy, that crimes which will ring forever through history, and stains that will never be effaced from our national fame, are regarded with complacency by a large part of our population; and by the rest, with few exceptions, are passed over with apathy, or at most with a smile or a sneer."

Early in the last session of the Legislature of Tennessee, a bill passed the first reading, which imposes a fine of $500 on the president of any railroad, and $250 on the conductor, who shall permit a free negro to travel on such road, unless under the control and care of a free white citizen of Tennessee, who vouches for the character of said free negro in a penal bond of $1,000! A bill was also introduced, to banish or enslave the free negroes, but we find no mention of its passage. Its introduction led to much discussion, and called out some emphatic words of condemnation from high quarters. The Nashville *Gazette* attests that it was "declared unconstitutional by eminent lawyers." One lawyer, no less eminent than Judge CATRON, of the United States Supreme Court, published a letter in the Nashville *Union*, in which he says that the free colored people "all have a vested right to freedom by the judgments and decrees of courts. Under our Constitution of 1796, the free colored men voted at the polls. That the old Constitution extended to them, and protected their rights to a certain extent, is free from doubt. * * * * * * The bill proposes to commit an outrage, to perpetrate an oppression and cruelty, and it is idle to mince words to soften the fact. * * * * * * This people who were born free and lived as free persons, * * * * * will preach rebellion everywhere that they may be driven to by this unjust law, whether it be amongst us here in Tennessee or south of us on the cotton and sugar plantations, or in the Abolition meetings in the Free States. Nor will the women be the least effective in preaching a crusade, when begging money in the North, to relieve their children, left behind in this State, in bondage. We are told it is a popular measure. Where is it popular? In what nook or corner of the State are the principles of humanity so deplorably deficient that a majority of the whole inhabitants would commit an outrage not committed in a Christian country of which history gives any account? * * * * Numbers of the people sought to be enslaved or driven out are members of our various churches, and in full communion. That

these great bodies of Christian men and women will quietly
stand by and see their humble co-workers sold on the block to
the negro-trader is not to be expected; nor will any set of men
be supported, morally or politically, who are the authors of such
a law. Nor is this half the truth. Take all the Free States,
and how will the matter stand? * * * * * * What northern
man, that has manhood in him, will not exclaim, 'I abhor such
a law!' It cannot be otherwise than odious to the North.
* * * * * * I put it to any fair-minded man to say whether
this law, if it is passed, will not go far to *crush out* our friends
in the North, and yet more strongly mark the *black* sectional
line between the Free and the Slave States?" On the other
hand, the Hon. M. CARUTHERS, in an elaborate opinion, published in the Nashville papers, reaches the conclusion "that the
act of emancipating a Slave only confers upon him the capacity
of acting as a freeman, subject, as the same capacity in a white
man is, to all curtailments of his liberty that may not be forbidden by some specific guaranty of the Constitution; that he is
not a freeman in the sense of the declaration of rights, and
therefore may be exiled." But the Nashville *Banner* says that
" since the subject has been generally discussed, the proposition
has been rapidly losing strength. The action of the Senate of
Mississippi, in defeating the bill, has not been without its influence. We trust the Senate of Tennessee will do itself the
honor to stand side by side with that body on this question."

    In the Legislature of Kentucky a bill of the same character
was proposed, but the Judiciary Committee of the Senate, to
whom it was referred, reported that any attempt to remove the
negroes who were free when the present Constitution was
adopted would be an interference with vested rights, and clearly
unconstitutional. The Constitution itself provides for the removal of all who may hereafter become free. The law of
Arkansas, to drive out or enslave the free colored people of
that State, the enactment of which was mentioned in our last
Report, went into effect on the 1st of January last. The Cincinnati *Gazette*, of January 4, says that "as the time of proba-
tion has now expired, while some individuals have preferred
servitude, the great body of the free colored people of Arkansas
are on their way northward. We learn that the upward-bound
boats are crowded with them, and that Seymour, Indiana, on

the line of the Ohio and Mississippi railroad, affords a temporary home for many others. A party of forty, mostly women and children [whose husbands and fathers, being Slaves, were left behind], arrived in this city last evening." The colored people of the city gave them a formal reception, and assured them, through the chairman of a committee which met them at the railroad, that they were welcome to Ohio, and that by sobriety, industry, and exemplary habits they would win friends and a good livelihood. "They report that hundreds of the free colored men of Arkansas have left for Kansas, and hundreds more are about to follow." A letter to the Boston *Journal*, last fall, from Fort Smith, Arkansas, says that "the greater part of the free negroes" in that place "are industrious and frugal, and some have acquired considerable property. In a few instances they were emancipated, but they have generally purchased their own freedom. One woman, while paying her master ten dollars a month for her time, in five years earned enough besides to buy herself, for $1,000, and shortly after bought her husband (who was old and in poor health) for $500; since which time they have been doing well pecuniarily, though they do belong to the poor creatures who 'cannot take care of themselves.'" And such are the persons whom Arkansas deliberately robs of their hard-earned freedom or their homes! If picking pockets is not far more honest, and highway robbery far more honorable, than this compound of loathsome meanness and atrocious wickedness, then we have yet to learn the rudiments of decency and morals.

On the 7th of March, the Senate of Missouri passed a bill, which had already passed the House, providing that no Slave shall be emancipated unless the master gives a bond to remove him from the State within ninety days; that all free colored persons over eighteen years of age, who shall be living in the State after the first Monday in September, 1860, shall be enslaved; all under eighteen, shall be bound out until twenty-one, then have a year to leave the State, or, after that, to be sold into Slavery; and all shall be enslaved who come into the State, after September, 1861, and stay in it twenty-four hours. The governor refused his assent on the ground that the bill was unconstitutional, in that it proposed to "deprive persons of liberty without due process of law;" and that it would produce a strong reaction against Slavery; as well as for other reasons. An attempt to pass it over his veto failed for want of a sufficiently large majority, though in the House it was sustained by 53 to 30. Four negroes were fined and committed to jail in St. Louis, in January last, for being in the State without a license, and only escaped the additional infliction of ten lashes upon each, by the casting vote of the president of the Board of County Commissioners.

Nor is this shameful persecution of the free colored people confined to the Slave States. Last winter, in Detroit, a colored preacher was fined fifty dollars and imprisoned ninety days, the penalty awarded by the law of Michigan for "negro preaching;" and the Detroit *Free Press* says the authorities are determined to prosecute every violation of this law. It is also said that certain "Democrats," in Indiana, threaten to enforce the "black law" of that State upon the well-known ANTHONY BURNS, if he accepts a call, which he has received, to the pastorate of a colored Baptist Church in Indianapolis. The Chicago *Congregational Herald* tells us that at Carrollton, Greene County, Illinois, one GEORGE BOWLIN was lately sold at auction, for sixteen months, in payment of a fine of sixty-three dollars, imposed upon him for being in the State in violation of the law against the immigration of negroes. The *Herald* says, "here is a law which would disgrace a country of barbarians. And yet we see nothing even in our Republican papers indicating that the party intend to do anything against that law. We observe nowhere any discussion looking towards its repeal. The *Herald* has, in various ways, for months, endeavored to arouse public sentiment against the inhuman statute, but we find little or no response, where we had a right to look for it, in the Republican papers." In Pennsylvania have been found some men at once so foolish and so base as to petition the Legislature of the State, at its last session, for measures to prevent the immigration of colored people; and they declare that if the Legislature has not power to prevent such immigration, "we would prefer a Slave code." In Minnesota, resolutions having the same purpose were brought into the Legislature, on the 9th of January, but were voted down by the Republicans.

The New-York *Tribune*, a few weeks ago, told of an instance

of oppression at once mean and cruel, occurring in the District
over which the nation, by its Congress, has the power "to exercise exclusive legislation in all cases whatsoever." About the
first of last December, two colored citizens of Philadelphia, who
had been serving on a government vessel, in the expedition to
Paraguay, were landed at the Navy Yard, in Washington, and
honorably discharged. On going to the railroad station, to take
cars for Philadelphia, they found that, by a regulation of the
road, no colored person could obtain a ticket, till he had filed a
bond to indemnify the railroad company against loss in case of
his being claimed as a Slave. Knowing nobody in Washington, they could, of course, procure no sureties for such a bond,
and therefore had to give up going home, till they could find
some other way to go. Meanwhile they found employment in
the city in which the government had set them down. There
they had been two months or more, as servants in a hotel, when
they were arrested under a city ordinance of which they had,
before, no means of knowing, whereby all persons of their color
are required, on coming into Washington, to have their names
registered and pay fifty dollars, or else be subject to a fine of
ten dollars for every five days of their stay. The government,
which brought and left them there when they would gladly
have been somewhere else, had told them nothing of this; they
had no fifty dollars to pay for the registration of their names;
and we may easily guess what would have been their fate, had
not their case come, fortunately, to the knowledge of two kind-
hearted northern congressmen, who boarded at the hotel where
they had been employed. Mr. POTTER, of Wisconsin, and Mr.
COVODE, of Pennsylvania, applied, on their behalf, to the mayor
of the city, who admitted that their case was hard, and suggested, as the only way to save them from the heavy penalties they
had unwittingly incurred, that Messrs. POTTER and COVODE
should claim exemption for them from the ordinance, as
servants of those gentlemen. The hint was acted on. The
gentlemen went back to the hotel, engaged the young men as
their servants, and sent notes to the mayor claiming them as
such, whereupon they were discharged. To such devices it is
needful to resort, to save free citizens of this republic from
certain robbery and more than probable enslavement, in the
nation's capital. "This oppressive railroad regulation, and

December, from F. W. CHESSON, of London, states that soon
after Miss REMOND's repulse, an American gentleman, anxious
to save his country from disgrace, as well as to be of service to
persons who had claims upon his sympathy and assistance,
called at the Embassy to get a passport for a lady and gentleman of color wishing to travel on the continent. He assured
the secretary that they were American citizens, but the vigilant
official was not satisfied with that. He must know, also, their
complexion. Of course, when that was known, the passport
was refused. The applicant then asked the secretary to
write to the French Consul General, requesting him to grant
the passport. The secretary promised to consider this suggestion, but never acted on it; so, at last, the gentleman
himself applied to the French Consul, "who, when the circumstances were explained, most cheerfully granted a passport, and
said, moreover, that he had written or should write to his own
government, asking for power to deal with this special class of
cases. Thus, from French Imperialism the colored man obtains
those rights which are insultingly denied to him by Republican
America." So stands the American government before the
world, to-day. Fifty-four years ago, it had a minister plenipo-
tentiary at the British Court — elected president a few years
later — who gave a passport to a *Slave*, describing him as "a
citizen of the United States." The "citizen" was • ESSEX
WHITE, a Slave of RANDOLPH, of Roanoke; the minister was
JAMES MONROE. Whether he acted "under instructions from
his government," of which one THOMAS JEFFERSON was then
the head, is not particularly mentioned. But what instructions
would have been given, if it had been thought needful to give
any, can hardly be considered doubtful; for TANEY, from the
seat — "a world too wide for his shrunk" soul — then filled by
MARSHALL, had not yet taught that in our country's political
vocabulary "all men" means only "white men." This is a pro-
gressive age.

The politicians, exercised by the perplexing problem which
arises from the nation's prejudice against the race it wrongs,
and its unwillingness to do the simple right, are seeking a solution in some plan for the removal, not of the wrong, unchristian,
anti-democratic feeling; but of its hapless victims. Last winter,

19

Mr. DOOLITTLE, of Wisconsin, offered in the Senate a preamble and resolution which, after alluding with most philosophic coolness to the disabilities of free colored persons at the North, and the outrageous wrongs they suffer or are threatened with at the South, proposes that the Committee on Foreign Relations inquire into the expediency of acquiring, by treaty, in Yucatan, Central or South America, the rights of settlement and citizenship for the benefit of such persons of color of African descent as may voluntarily desire to emigrate from the United States, and form themselves into colonies, under the laws of the States to which they emigrate; the United States to have free trade with them, and, in return, to secure the necessary engagements to maintain them in the enjoyment of the rights acquired by such treaty. Mr. BLAIR, of Missouri, brought a similar proposition before the House. The Chicago *Tribune* says, "two undeniable facts establish the wisdom and feasibility of the scheme — the prime necessity of getting rid of the major portion, if not the whole, of our Slave population, and the adaptedness of Central and South America, in soil and climate, to the colored race, and these races only."

We do not clearly see this "prime necessity," and we suspect that the Slave-holders will be found as dull of vision as ourselves. Mr. DOOLITTLE's proposition, and his argument in favor of it, as "the only wise and practical solution of the Slave question," were received, by senators from the Slave States, with the haughtiest disdain. Mr. HAMMOND, of South Carolina, said that "gentlemen on the other side need not trouble themselves with the solution of the Slavery question, for it was already solved. Slavery was always to stand as it now stood, and was to advance with the destinies of the South. It was a matter of indifference what people north thought of the subject." Mr. MASON, of Virginia, "could not conceive a greater curse to the white man or to the free negro than to send the latter to the tropics." Till the Slave-holders are willing to emancipate their Slaves, this scheme of "getting rid of the major portion" of that "population" can hardly be called "feasible;" and when they are, the Slaves will choose to stay at home and enjoy their freedom, instead of "voluntarily emigrating" to unknown regions; while with the masters it would seem more likely that "the prime necessity" will be to keep them where they are, as free, hired laborers. Witness the recent testimony of Maryland, one of the States most likely, among all the Slave States, to be able to dispense with the paid labor of emancipated Slaves. Yet she has just been showing us, in spite of herself, as it were, that she is conscious of her pressing need of her free colored laborers. Can the Gulf States more readily dispense with theirs, when Slavery shall have been abolished there? As to that portion of the colored people who are already free, we think no candid and intelligent observer will deny that they are very nearly of one heart and mind, against all schemes which aim to lure or drive them from their native land, no matter under what pretence of kind regard for them, or "prime necessity," on the part of those who have wronged them, to "get rid of them." Moreover, we believe that they are making stronger, every day, their hold upon this country, by their improvement, intellectual and moral, as well as in regard to their material well-being, wherever anything approaching a fair chance is given them. They have already shown, to the conviction of many a former doubter, that, with fair play, they can take care of themselves, and of the slanders which have been so freely spread against them by ignorance and prejudice. And an approach to a fair chance has been achieved for them in a large portion of the northern States, partly by what themselves have done, and partly by the persistent labors of the Abolitionists, to a degree which, though it comes far short of what is to be desired, yet gives abundant encouragement to future efforts. In a debate in the Senate, a few weeks ago, Mr. WILSON, of Massachusetts, declared that the free negroes in that State "were, in intelligence and character, but little behind the white people. He believed the free negroes of the North and South had made marked progress in a few years." And we are not aware that his statement has been controverted, either in or out of the Senate. The New-York *Tribune* said with truth, almost a year ago, "whatever diversity of opinion may be entertained as to the influence the Anti-Slavery movement has exerted on the condition of the black men of the South, it will hardly be denied, by any persons acquainted with the facts, that it has been productive of very positive improvement in that of the black men of the North."

Among the particulars of this improvement, the *Tribune*

spoke of the admission of colored children to equal rights in
the free schools in most parts of New England, and of the
manifestly good results thereof, especially in Massachusetts;
quoting, with reference to the abolition of caste-schools in
Boston, the testimony of the *Boston Courier*, "certainly a competent authority on this side of the question." The *Courier*
says, "We contemplate it with unmingled satisfaction. We
rejoice that colored men are not set apart in our churches from
their white brethren, and that the children of the two races sit
side by side on the same benches." And again: "The anxiety
of the colored people to have their children educated shows
that they were entirely worthy of the boon bestowed upon
them, of having their children educated at the same schools
with the whites." ["The boon bestowed upon them," we may
say in passing, was but the bare acknowledgment of their
right.] The *Tribune* also gave the testimony of JOHN F.
EMERSON, "for quarter of a century the Principal of the High
School of New Bedford, and standing in the very foremost rank
of his profession." He says, "My pupils are from all classes of
the community. Many of them from families of the very highest respectability. I have had no instance of any difficulty
arising from the admission of colored children. I have noticed
no difference in the aptitude to learn between them and the
whites." "This testimony," the *Tribune* added, "is capable of
ample confirmation from other sources." It further said, alluding to the pamphlets which the colored people of Rhode Island
had addressed to the Legislature of that State, "they are temperate, well-reasoned, and unanswerable." And of "those who
are struggling for their rights" in this behalf, it said, "they
have showed so much discretion and good sense, as well as
spirit, in their way of laying their wrongs before the Legislature, that they deserve success. Their documents, though
calculated for the meridian of Rhode Island, will do for this
State, or any other, where the same mischiefs exist."

On the 1st and 2nd of last August, the colored people of
New England held a Convention at the Meionaon, in Boston,
partly to celebrate the anniversary of West-India Emancipation, partly to deliberate on matters touching their own welfare.
The Boston *Journal* says, "The business of the Convention was
conducted with promptitude and in a manner creditable to

those who participated in it. Many of the speakers showed a degree of intelligence and of oratorical ability which would have reflected credit upon any gathering. The impression made upon the white men who were lookers on was favorable to the theory that the African race in the United States, if placed under circumstances more favorable than it now enjoys, or perhaps, owing to the prejudice against color, can hope to enjoy in this country, is capable of creditably sustaining the duties and responsibilities which ordinarily devolve upon those who manage the affairs of government." In other words, the hindrance to the colored people's elevation here is the white people's prejudice, and not a want of natural capacity in themselves. The white man's fault, and not their own intrinsic weakness, now depresses them; if these "white lookers on" have judged aright. To grant so much, and then to doubt the ultimate success of their praiseworthy efforts at self-elevation in their native country, is to impeach the white man's capabilities in the most important point, and, at least, to question the legitimacy of his social standing. For he who cannot so far overcome his own unrighteous prejudice as to give to other men their due, whether of opportunity to use their faculties, or of a just reward for their exertions, is surely wanting in the best ability, and is far enough from meriting that social grade which white men generally claim. The colored man's success, here, among us of the race which has oppressed him, is needful to the white man's lasting reputation, not to say to his best moral training; and we should be ashamed to say that any man must go away from us, before he can become what God and nature fitted him to be. Our greater strength should give him stronger help, instead of crushing down his weakness; our ampler means of culture should better his advantages; the progress we have made beyond him in science, art, and civilization, should render plainer to his eye and smoother to his feet the road by which he follows us. Even if he should never overtake us, it should be ours to say that he gets on the faster because he travels where we go before him. But who has any warrant for saying that he will not overtake us?

Congress.

The Slave question has engrossed the attention of Congress more largely at its present, than at any former session. No matter what the subject nominally in hand, whether the choice of speaker, the homestead bill, the tariff, the organization of territories, or whatsoever else, Slavery was sure to be the real matter in debate. Its character, its claims, its probable destiny, its bearings, moral and political, social and economical, and the policy to be adopted in regard to it, supplied the staple, wholly or in part, of almost every speech in either House, and wholly that of all the most important. In the Senate, the Slave-holders and their allies, having an indisputable ascendency, could organize for business promptly, and in such manner as would best subserve the interests of Slavery. In accordance with the sense of fairness of our modern chivalry, the chairmanship of every important committee was given to the South. Even Douglas was displaced from the chair of the Committee on Territories, because his heresy of "Popular Sovereignty" may hinder the enactment of a Federal Slave-code for the Territories. But in the other House the state of parties would not let things move so quietly and smoothly. For nearly two months a "conflict," truly "irrepressible," prevented the election of a speaker, and kept the House unorganized; while the extreme Pro-Slavery members spent the greater part of the time in furiously denouncing Helper's "Impending Crisis," and everybody who had aided or approved the circulation of it; in vilifying "Black Republicans" and Abolitionists; and in threatening to dissolve the Union as soon as they should cease to rule it. Indeed the alarm was sounded in advance, by the Pro-Slavery press. Just before the opening of the session, *The Constitution*, President Buchanan's organ in Washington, announced its "firm belief that in the impending crisis, a Black Republican victory in the organization of the House would shake the pillars of the Union;" and asked if it "would not be justly regarded as a declaration of war against the South, and an invitation to servile insurrection."

The Republicans, though outnumbering any other party, yet had not a majority of the whole House, and consequently could not choose a speaker without help. But neither could the other parties, subdivided as they were, unite on an opposing candidate in strength sufficient to elect him. Anti-Lecompton Democrats could not be brought to vote with the Administration Democrats, nor South Americans and North Americans to coalesce. Some of the first and last named were disposed to make the Republican their second choice, seeing the plain impossibility of choosing one of their own sort; but for a long time they were held back, by the clamor of the Pro-Slavery ultraists, from doing so in numbers large enough to be effective. It chanced that the first nominee of the Republicans, JOHN SHERMAN, of Ohio, had suffered his name to be affixed, some time before, with those of sixty or seventy fellow-congressmen of the same party, to a circular recommending the general circulation of a compend of HELPER's book. His adversaries seized upon this fact, and made it an occasion for assailing him and his supporters, with the bitterest virulence, and striving with their utmost energy to keep from his support such of the more liberal of the Democrats and Americans as were inclined that way.

On the first day of the session, December 5, after a single ballot, which resulted in no choice, Mr. CLARK, of Missouri, moved a resolution that the sentiments and doctrines of the Impending Crisis "are incendiary, and hostile to the domestic peace and tranquillity of the country, and that no member of this' House who recommended or indorsed it, or the compend, is fit to be speaker of this House." He was permitted to proceed with a speech, although Mr. STEVENS, of Pennsylvania, urged that only two things were in order till a speaker should be chosen; — a motion to proceed to ballot, and a motion to adjourn. The speech, with frequent interruptions, occupied the rest of that, and a portion of the next day's sitting, exhibiting at once the rude and overbearing insolence of a practiced Slave-driver, and the effrontery in falsehood of a reckless pettifogger pleading a cause he knows the truth would ruin. In it were embodied the circular, and a list of those who signed it, recommending the circulation of the compend; and on the work thus recommended was charged the counselling of murder, treason, and other kindred enormities. Mr. CLARK concluded by declaring that "the Union could not exist, if the recommendations in the circular which he had read were carried out."

Mr. GILMER, of North Carolina, offered as a substitute for CLARK's resolution, substantially the old Whig and Democratic declarations against all attempts at a renewal of Slavery agitation. Mr. BURNET, of Kentucky, advocated CLARK's resolution, by adopting which, he said, " they should set their seal of condemnation on the men who would instigate treason, murder, arson, and servile insurrection. He represented a people loyal to the Union, but ready to go out of it if this warfare was to be made on their institutions, homes, and families. He wished to see how many northern gentlemen would say, by their votes, they have no part or lot in the sentiments of HELPER's book." Mr. MILLSON, of Virginia, thought that, " in view of recent occurrences [alluding to JOHN BROWN's enterprise], southern members should have remained silent in their seats," and " had a good right to expect that gentlemen from other parts of the country should have come to meet them with extended hands, and given them the assurance that these events were not types of northern sentiment and intent. * * * * * * Those who entertained such sentiments as are advanced by HELPER were not only unfit to be speaker, but were unfit to live." Mr. LAMAR, of Mississippi, had seen Mr. SEWARD's "eyes light up with the fires of hell, as he uttered," in the Senate, " a hope that he might live to see the day when there was not a Slave's footprint on this continent." He declared it " the unanimous sentiment of the South that the existence of the Republican party is a standing menace to her peace and security, and a standing insult to her character;" and said, " the South are determined that the institution of Slavery shall be maintained as an existing fact in this Confederacy." Mr. REAGAN, of Texas, complained of northern sympathy with JOHN BROWN, and the " wide-spread fanatical spirit of hostility to the South," evinced in the demonstrations at the North when BROWN was executed. " Whenever the time should come," he said, " that this sentiment should be able to control the Government, the failure of our experiment of self-government would be demonstrated. It would then become necessary to adopt some form of government under which men could be reached who disregard compacts and compromises." Whether that is to be an absolute

monarchy, with a Slave-holder on the throne, or a despotic
oligarchy, a new Venetian Council-of-Ten, of the choice spirits
of Slavedom, the time has probably not yet come to tell. Or
rather, perhaps, it does not concern the people to know. All
they need be told is that "self-government" is no longer for
them. Mr. GARNETT, of Virginia, would rather the House
should remain unorganized until March 4, 1861, than the plu-
rality rule [which would ensure the choice of a Republican]
should be adopted; and his declaration to this effect was loudly
cheered by the Pro-Slavery Democracy. He would "hold up
to the gaze of an indignant country the spectacle of a sectional
party attempting to put into that chair one who indorses the
HELPER book." Mr. PUGH, of Alabama, "would like to perpetuate discord in the House, and thought it would be quite as
well for his constituents that the House should never organize,
and the government come to a dead lock."

Mr. GARTRELL, of Georgia, said "the scenes enacted here
were but a part of the 'irrepressible conflict,' and if that conflict
was to come, perhaps it were better that the House should
never organize. * * * * * Let the North treat them as equals,
and cease to aggress upon the rights of his people, or they
would sever the Union into as many pieces as there are stars in
the national banner. * * * * * * If the principals of the Republican party be carried into effect, the people of the South
will be compelled to disrupt every tie which binds us to the
Union, peaceably if we can, forcibly if we must. * * * * * *
Just as soon as the Republican party should succeed in electing
a sectional president, in his judgment the time would have
come for the South to take prompt, decisive action. * * * * *
But if the North would stay the hand of aggression, respect the
rights of his people, let them alone, *quit agitation of the
question* of Slavery, cease to circulate incendiary documents
and promote insurrection and murder, he believed they might
get on in peace and harmony, in the future as in the past, and
he would say of the Union, *esto perpetua.* Unless the North
consented to these things, upon her own head be the consequences." Alluding to something which had been said about
modifying the Fugitive-Slave Law, he declared that "if it were
materially modified they would consider it good cause to disrupt every tie that binds them to the Union." When asked if

he "was opposed to such a modification of the law as would
not impair its efficiency, and would, at the same time, protect
the rights of free men," he answered that "he did not believe
that was practicable, and was against touching it at all." A
frank admission that the efficiency of the Slave-catcher's statute
is incompatible with protection to freemen's rights! — and a
distinct enough implicit avowal that these rights must be sacrificed to success in Slave-catching.

Mr. LEAKE, of Virginia, replying to a Republican member,
asked "if he believed that any man who would recommend
murder and insurrection was fit for speaker? The South regarded the indorsement of HELPER's book as an insult which
southern members would avenge as they saw fit. * * * * * *
The idea that Virginia would fight for her rights inside of the
Union was absurd. There was a peaceful and constitutional
remedy; Virginia had the right to withdraw from the Union,
and would do so whenever the occasion should require. She
would not fight in the Union, but would fight, if need be, out
of the Union." And in a later speech, denying that he had
said the election of Mr. SHERMAN would be a just cause for
dissolving the Union, he added that "he did think it would be
the initiatory step, and if it were followed by the election of
Mr. SEWARD to the presidency, it would be a *casus belli.*" Mr.
WRIGHT, of Tennessee, "warned the Republicans that if they
elected their president and sought to carry out their doctrines,
they would have one of two alternatives — either war in the
Union, or war out of it. * * * * * * He hoped his people
would never submit to the lordly dictation of a party of
traitors." Mr. SMITH, of Virginia, denounced the doctrines of
the Helper book as "insurrectionary, and hostile to the peace of
the country," and said "the member from Ohio [Mr. BING-
HAM] indorses the book, and for this he deserves the detestation and scorn of every man who forms part of the American
Union." Mr. HINDMAN, of Arkansas, said that "if the Republicans had put in nomination one who had not recommended
the circulation of a book counselling rapine, insurrection, and
bloodshed, there would have been no prolonged opposition to
his election. The Republican party sprung out of festering
prejudices and malignity, by which it is kept alive." Mr.
BARKSDALE, of Mississippi, "rather than his State and section

should be dishonored by the election of Mr. SHERMAN, would repeat the declaration of Mr. PUGH, of Alabama, 'Let discord reign here forever.'" Mr. CLOPTON, of Alabama, said "there was little if any disagreement in his district, that the South should secede in the event of the election of a Republican president. In that event, the Union cannot and ought not to be maintained. The people would not submit to that party."

And in this tone the debate went on for more than eight weeks, the Slave-holding extremists seeming to vie with each other in vehement denunciation, bitter invective, arrogance of language and bearing, threats, and bluster. They paraded extracts from HELPER's volume, culled from it by the Pro-Slavery Democratic press with special aim to choose the passages they deemed the most inflammatory; and, forcing on them, thus disjointed from their connection, a meaning never found in them by any honest and unbiassed reader, used them to prove that SHERMAN and his supporters were in sympathy with treason, insurrection, and servile war; although, as we see it stated in the New-York *Tribune*, the quoted passages were not in the compend, which the men whom they denounced had recommended. The Republicans took comparatively little part in the debate, their policy being rather to press for a speedy organization; but of what they did say — though some spirited rejoinders were made to the insolence of the Slave-drivers — far too much consisted of tame and almost deprecatory explanations of their relation to the Helper book, and disclaimers of any intent, on the part of their party and of the North, "to interfere with Slavery where it exists," or with the "rights" guaranteed to Slave-holders, under the Constitution. Mr. CORWIN was careful to assure the Slave-holders that they "were entitled to a good law relative to fugitives," and that such, he believed, was the feeling of the people of Ohio. "Mr. FILLMORE, so much approved now at the South, had been denounced as an Abolitionist before he was elected vice president, and held opinions identical with Mr. SEWARD's; and any northern man, fit to be elected, would administer the government as fairly as he had." [A significant hint; considering what was the most conspicuous and memorable act of that "fair" administration.] "He thought there was no occasion to quarrel." Oh no! — of course not. Only let us Republicans take our turn

of his book to Mr. CLARK, of Missouri, who began the onset.
For it had proved a most effective gratuitous advertisement of
the book, and did far more to promote the sale and circulation
of it, than had been done by all the publisher's advertising in
the newspapers, and all the recommendations of Republicans,
joined to their subscription of money, to insure the publication
and distribution of a cheap edition. Says the *Anti-Slavery
Standard*, of December 17, "the public curiosity has been
stimulated to such an extent that orders for it are pouring in
upon the publisher faster than he can supply them. It will find
its way, during the present winter, into thousands of families
which, but for the madness of the South, would not have seen
it for years, if ever; and it is so full of striking facts and con-
vincing arguments that it cannot fail to do its work wherever it
is read." The New-York *Tribune*, of January 11, states that
"the Congressional denunciations of Helper's book are producing the most astonishing effect in promoting its circulation.
We have reason to believe that the number of copies ordered
already exceeds 100,000. The work goes everywhere, through
all sorts of channels, to the North, East, South, and West. Old
fogy Union-saving merchants, in the southern trade, stand
aghast at the sly requests slipped in all over the South, in the
shape of notes and postscripts to orders for goods, for 'that
Helper book, that is making such a fuss in Congress.' Innocent
bales, bags, boxes, and barrels, bound South, have each a copy
of Helper tucked furtively away in the hidden centre of their
contents. In this way the work is penetrating the whole South,
in a manner that no hunter for incendiary pamphlets would
suppose, or can possibly arrest. For the extraordinary impetus
thus given to the sale of this highly valuable and interesting
work, we renewedly tender our heartfelt acknowledgments to
the 'Gulf Squadron' of members of the Federal House of
Representatives, at Washington." And, a few weeks later, the
Christian Intelligencer, no over-friendly witness, says, "we are
reliably informed that Mr. HELPER's copyright realizes him
about $500 a week, and one week's receipts amounted to $525.
This is doing a handsome business, and the more noticeable
from the fact that it is all done by opponents." Thus, by the
very bitterness of their enmity, were the Slave-holders made
unconsciously to help the cause they hate, and the men they
wish to crush for advocating it.

The persistency with which HELPER's haters made themselves his helpers, so long delayed the choosing of a speaker that the president grew tired of waiting for them, and sent in his message more than a month before the House was organized. He alluded briefly to "the recent sad and bloody occurrence at Harper's Ferry," but added the comfortable assurance that he did not "entertain the apprehension that these events are symptoms of an incurable disease in the public mind, which may break out in still more dangerous outrages, and terminate, at last, in an open war by the North to abolish Slavery in the South." He implored his "countrymen, North and South, to cultivate the ancient feeling of mutual forbearance and good will towards each other, and try to allay the demon-spirit of sectional hatred and strife now alive in the land." He "cordially congratulated" Congress "upon the final settlement, by the Supreme Court of the United States, of the question of Slavery in the Territories," and the establishment of "the right of every citizen to take his property, of any kind, *including Slaves*, into the common Territories, and to have it *protected there under the Federal Constitution*" — a right which "neither Congress nor a Territorial Legislature, nor any human power has any authority to impair." He pronounced "these principles," which the Court has sanctioned, "manifestly just in themselves, and well calculated to promote harmony among the States;" and declared that "had it been decided that either Congress or the Territorial Legislature possess the power to annul or impair the right of property in Slaves, the evil would be intolerable," for it would have made "*the sacred rights of property* depend on the result of each successive election;" whereas now, "the status of a Territory, during the intermediate period from its first settlement until it shall become a State, having been *irrevocably* fixed by the *final* decision of the Supreme Court, emigrants from the North and the South, the East and the West, will meet in the Territories on a common platform, having brought with them that species of property best adapted, in their own opinion, to promote their welfare." "It is a striking proof," he said, "of the *sense of justice* which is inherent in our people, that the property in Slaves has never been disturbed, to my knowledge, in any of the Territories," not "even throughout the late troubles in Kansas." Such a declaration is certainly "a striking proof" of the moral bedlam in his own brains. The London *Examiner* well says that "in Swift's keenest satire is nothing approaching the American president's congratulations on the subject of Slavery. To talk of the sense of justice scrupulously respecting the right of one man to the body of another by virtue of difference of color, is either the language of the broadest irony, or of the boldest contradiction of ideas."

But the president went on to make the jumble still more complete, by his condemnation of the African Slave-trade and the attempt to reopen it. "All lawful means at my command," he said, "have been employed, and shall continue to be employed, to execute the laws against the African Slave-trade." And, referring to the bringing in of the Wanderer's cargo of Slaves, he added, "those engaged in this unlawful enterprise have been rigorously prosecuted; but not with as much success as their crimes have deserved." As if it were any more a crime to bring African Slaves to Savannah, than to take Georgian Slaves to Kansas. "To reopen the Slave-trade," he said, "would give it an impulse and extension which it has never had, even in its palmiest days. The numerous victims required to supply it would convert the whole Slave-coast into a perfect pandemonium, for which this country would be held responsible in the eyes both of God and man." Then, to crown all, he recommended, in another part of the message, the payment of the impudent claim of those Cuban pirates, RUIZ and MONTEZ, for the negroes of the Amistad — notoriously victims of that very African Slave-trade which he professed so deeply to abhor — brought from Africa to Cuba in well-known violation of Spanish laws and treaties, and afterward delivered from bondage partly by their own shrewdness and valor, and partly by the tardy, not to say reluctant, justice of the Federal Courts. The president's recommendation to pay this infamous demand, was seconded by the Senate's Committee on Foreign Relations; but called out a scathing exposure of the true character of the claim, from Senator DIXON, of Connecticut. He showed that Slaves are not "merchandise," in the meaning of the treaty under which the claim was made; and that, even if they were, the negroes of the Amistad were not legally Slaves, having been brought to Cuba contrary to law; and, consequently, the claimants never were their legal owners. He contended that the decision of the Supreme Court, which declared the negroes free, is binding on the claimants, both because they were parties to the proceeding, and because the decree of an Admiralty Court, as to title, "is conclusive everywhere and upon everybody;" and he rebuked with just severity the president's pretence of zeal against the foreign Slave-trade, while urging payment of a claim well known to have grown out of it.

The Harper's-Ferry affair was made the occasion or the pretext for proposing, in the Senate, new legislative safeguards for Slavery. On the 16th of January, Mr. BIGLER, of Pennsylvania, introduced a bill to empower the president to use the army and navy, and to call out the militia of the neighboring States, against invasions of one State or Territory from another; and to punish with death those who engage in such invasion; and with heavy fines and long imprisonment all who aid or abet it, by concealment, by providing means or money, by enlisting, or procuring others to enlist in it, by fitting out or procuring to be fitted out, vessels, or accepting commissions for it. On the same day, Mr. DOUGLAS, of Illinois, brought in a resolution instructing the Judiciary Committee to report a bill " for the protection of States and Territories against invasion by inhabitants of any other State or Territory, and for the suppression of conspiracies and combinations in any State or Territory with intent to invade or assail the government, inhabitants, property, or institutions of any other." On the 23rd, he made a long speech in support of it, in which he said that "to place the whole military power of the government at the disposal of the president, with proper restrictions, to suppress such invasion, is not sufficient. It is not only necessary to use the military power when the actual case occurs, but to authorize the judicial department to suppress all conspiracies and combinations in the several States, with the intent to molest or disturb its government, citizens, property, or institutions. He would carry this principle out, and make a law to punish conspiracies to carry territorial elections, whether they were under the garb of Emigrant-Aid Societies from New England or Blue Lodges in Missouri. * * * * It was his firm and deliberate conviction that the Harper's-Ferry crime was the natural and logical and inevitable result of the teachings of the Republican party, as explained and enforced

20*

in their platform, their partisan presses, their pamphlets and books, and the speeches of their leaders in and out of Congress. * * * * * * Give us such a law as the Constitution contemplates and authorizes, and I will show the Senator from New York that there is a Constitutional mode of repressing even the 'irrepressible conflict.'" Mr. FESSENDEN, of Maine, "was inclined to agree with" Mr. DOUGLAS "on the Constitutional right to make such laws to suppress invasion," but repelled his charge against the Republicans, and added, referring to the threats of disunion if a Republican president should be elected, that while Mr. DOUGLAS "was devising means to repress the invasion of one State by another, he might have suggested a provision for the threatened contingency." Mr. DOUGLAS answered, that "he had introduced his resolution because occasion called for it. It was not necessary to put in a clause for the contingency referred to, as it was an event not within probabilities."

Some men there were who seem to have thought that there was no propriety in letting the events of the preceding months be used entirely in the interests of Slavery, and a slight effort was accordingly made to offset MASON's investigation, the resolution of DOUGLAS, and the like, with movements in behalf of northern rights invaded and trodden down at the South. On the 20th of February, Mr. LOVEJOY introduced and asked for a vote upon a resolution that a committee of five, with power to send for persons and papers, be appointed to inquire into the alleged ill treatment, in some States, of citizens of other States going into them on lawful business, and unaccused of crime; and whether any further legislation is necessary to give effect to that provision of the Constitution which guarantees to the citizens of each State all privileges and immunities of citizens in the several States. Objection being made, it was laid over, under the rule, to come up at a future day. On the 27th, Mr. CONKLING asked, but also failed to obtain, consent to offer a resolution "instructing the Committee on the Judiciary to inquire whether any, and if so, what legislation is necessary to secure the liberty of speech or person in the District of Columbia; and whether any, and if so, what practical legislation is necessary to secure the rights of free persons in said District." A few days later, Mr. HICKMAN "reported a resolution instructing the Committee on the Judiciary to inquire and report what legislation, if any, is necessary to give protection to citizens from one State going into another, to engage in private and lawful business, and that they report by bill or otherwise." After some conversation among members, "Mr. McQUEEN, of South Carolina, desired to offer an amendment, and the subject was passed over."

Both Houses spent a great part of the session in discussions growing out of the new assumptions of the Slave-power touching Slavery in the Territories. In the Senate, on the 10th of January, Mr. PUGH, of Ohio, moved a resolution looking to the repeal of so much of the Acts organizing Utah and New Mexico, as subjects their territorial legislation to disapproval by Congress. Mr. BROWN, of Mississippi, brought in resolutions, on the 18th of January, affirming the right of citizens of all the States to take their property, so recognized by the Constitution, into any Territory, and the duty of the Legislature, whether Federal or Territorial, to enact laws for the protection of such property; and instructing the Committee on Territories to insert, in bills for organizing Territories, a clause requiring such protection. Subsequently, in accordance with the spirit of his resolutions, he gave notice of an Act to punish offences against Slave-property in Kansas. On the 30th of January, his resolutions coming up, Mr. WILKINSON, of Minnesota, moved as an amendment, "that the Territories are the common property of the people of the United States; that Congress has power to pass all necessary laws for the Territories; that it is the duty of Congress so to legislate as to protect the interests of Free Labor in them, and that the Committee on Territories be instructed to insert a clause in the bills organizing Territories prohibiting Slavery therein." On February 2, Mr. DAVIS, of Mississippi, introduced a series of resolutions asserting more at large the claims of Slavery in the Territories, but not demanding for it legislative protection till experience should have shown it to be needed. These, slightly modified and approved by a caucus of the Democratic members of the Senate, on the 25th, were understood to constitute the platform of the southern wing of the Democracy, for the approaching presidential canvass. They affirm that, in adopting the Federal Constitution, the States acted severally as independent sovereignties, delegating a portion of their powers to the Federal Government for increased security against dangers domestic and foreign, and any intermeddling by one or more States, or a combination of their citizens, with the domestic institutions of the others, to disturb or subvert them, violates the Constitution, insults the States interfered with, and serves to weaken and destroy the Union; that negro Slavery is an important part of the domestic institutions of fifteen States, is recognized by the Constitution as an important element in the apportionment of powers among the States, and no change of opinion in regard to it among the non-slaveholding States can justify attacks thereon to overthrow it, and such attacks are violations of the pledge of mutual protection given by the States respectively; that the Union rests on the equality of rights and privileges among its members, and it is especially the duty of the Senate, representing the States in their sovereign capacity, to resist attempts to give advantages, in the Territories, to citizens of one State which are not assured to those of every other; that neither Congress nor a Territorial Legislature can annul or impair the constitutional right of any citizen of the United States to take Slave-property into the Territories and hold it there while the territorial condition remains; that if experience should prove the judiciary and executive authority unable to protect this right, and the Territorial Legislature should fail to provide the needed remedies, it will be the duty of Congress to supply such deficiency; that the inhabitants of a Territory, when they rightfully form a Constitution to be admitted as a State, may for the first time decide whether Slavery shall be maintained or prohibited in it, and if Congress admit them they shall be received with or without Slavery, as their Constitution may prescribe; and that the provision of the Constitution for the rendition of fugitives from service, "without which the Union could not have been formed," and the laws of 1793 and 1850, enacted for its execution, should be faithfully observed by all who enjoy the benefits of the Union, and all acts of individuals or States to defeat the purpose of that provision and those laws, are hostile, revolutionary, and subversive of the Constitution.

The propositions in these several sets of resolutions were discussed, at intervals, through many days, the apostles and confessors of the new faith taking ample opportunity to set forth and defend its dogmas with great force of assertion if not of argument, and a liberal use of the favorite menace of disunion. Mr. BROWN affirmed that Slaves are property under the Constitution, and may as rightfully be taken to the common territory, and held there, as any other property; that consequently the owner is entitled to the same protection for this property as for any other; that the Territorial Legislature should protect him, and this failing, Congress ought to do it; that the courts could not furnish protection to Slavery without statutory laws; that without further legislation there would never be another Slave Territory or State; and, as Free States were pressing for admission, it would not be long before the Free States would have the two-thirds sufficient to change the Constitution, and could crush out Slavery under constitutional forms; that Slavery was a great social, moral, and political blessing to both Slave and master, and the negro increased more rapidly, and in every aspect was more prosperous in Slavery than in Freedom, hence Slavery was his normal condition; and that Kansas had violated the Constitution in her unfriendly legislation, and had passed a Personal-Liberty Bill more odious than that of Massachusetts. He claimed that the climate, soil, and productions of Kansas fitted it for Slavery. One-fifth of the Slave States were in the same latitude. He had no objection to the resolutions of the Democratic Caucus, except to their proposal to wait for experience in regard to necessary legislation; for which he thought Congress ought not to wait. He never had yielded the point, that Congress was bound to protect Slave-property everywhere. This, the greatest monied interest of the country, had never been protected anywhere. Thousands of Slaves were carried to Canada by the Underground Railroad, yet no notice was taken of it. If he had his way, the sun should not go down before he would file a notice with the British Minister, that unless Canada yielded up the stolen negroes, this Government would use all legal means to force her to do so, and, these failing, would declare war.

Mr. GREEN, of Missouri, regretted the introduction of Mr. PUGH's resolution. The modern development of popular sovereignty, as invoked for the prohibition of Slavery in the Territories, called for resistance and correction. It was common to say "Freedom is national and Slavery sectional." The reverse

cessful at the North, but Slave labor was the true system for the South. One State had no right to arraign another on a moral question. Slavery was confined to the sovereign States by the Constitution. Matters of religion must be kept separate from political matters. The Constitution must be the highest law of political men. He was not prepared to decide in advance what contingency would justify the dissolution of the Union. It was too momentous a question to be hastily determined. He would have no words uttered by southern men which could be interpreted as a menace at the North. At the same time, if all our warnings were disregarded, he was in favor of independence."

Mr. CHESNUT, of South Carolina, favored Mr. DAVIS's resolutions, because they denied two heresies, the sovereign power of the Federal Government over Slavery, and of the people of the Territories over Slavery in the Territories. The first led straight to despotism, the second relieved the Federal Government of its manifest duties. The country was preparing for a grand, and he hoped, a final struggle. Those who assert the equality of all races of men, disregard the lessons of experience, and abandon themselves to fanaticism. The object of the Republicans was the emancipation of the Slaves. The abolition of Slavery would be disastrous to the great northern interests of navigation, commerce, and manufactures. Slavery had stood the severest tests, and was steadily progressing to accomplish its ends. It was not a moral wrong, but had its authority in the Bible. It could be abolished only by the extermination of the black race and the desolation of the country. The Federal Government was a compact between the States, and the States were, as to their institutions, as separate and independent as England and France. The theory of the "irrepressible conflict" between the northern and southern systems of labor was fanatical and superficial. The two systems assisted each other.

Mr. HAMMOND, of the same State, said the South would not consent to be restricted as to her expansion, and contended that all the States had an equal right in the Territories. Mr. CLINGMAN, of North Carolina, complained that "the Abolition feeling had so spread that it controlled nearly all the secular and religious press of the North." He "claimed it as settled that the negro is benefitted by Slavery. * * * * * The South had no more fear of a rising of her negroes than of a rising of horses. * * * * * * The election of a Black-Republican president would furnish sufficient cause for a dissolution of the Union. * * * * * Two things had made the South disunionists; — the small vote Mr. FILLMORE had received, and the manner in which the raid of JOHN BROWN was received at the North. * * * * * * Southern men would not secede from the Capital; this was the last place of all they would ever give up. If the Union was to be dissolved in blood, he hoped the first fruits would be reaped here."

Mr. MASON opposed the Homestead Bill on the ground that it was designed to people Free Territories by Emigrant-Aid Societies, and to give the Republicans possession of the Government : and its end would be to operate on Slavery in the States. Mr. WIGFALL, of Texas, speaking on the same bill, said, "If this Government could give lands to the landless, why not niggers to the niggerless? It might reopen the African Slave-trade on missionary grounds, and bring negroes here to be converted. * * * * As the trustee of the southern States, it had no right to vote away their lands. * * * * * * He owed allegiance to the State of Texas, and whenever she declared the Federal Government no longer her agent, then it would be his duty to return to his State, and if he should be captured fighting under the flag of the 'lone star,' under the law of nations he could not be treated as a traitor. * * * * He thought nothing better could occur than a dissolution of the Union. New England would then beg the South to come back. The people of the North do n't believe we are in earnest. * * * * I believe, upon my conscience, that no Black Republican can ever be inaugurated president of the United States. And you call out your armies to force us, and if we do n't go into Boston — into winter quarters — before you get into Texas, then I am mistaken." After boasting of the military experience of several southern senators, including himself, while "only one man" of those from the North "had ever seen the flashing of a gun," he added, "But, in war, the military-chest is the question. Where will you get your money, if the Union is dissolved? your manufactories will be broken up, for where are you going to sell your goods? Your only market is the South : you cannot sell to us, and you have no carrying trade except for us. Cotton is king, — and we can ship our own cotton. You can't tax your people: they will be starving, and have no money. But we have our cotton, and Europe is obliged to have it. It would travel under the 'union-jack,' and that is a pretty safe flag. If we stop the supply of cotton for one week, England would be starving."

Mr. Toombs denounced the Republicans as "attempting to deprive the people of the Slave-holding States of their equal enjoyment of, and equal rights in the common Territories of the United States, as expounded by the Supreme Court; and of seeking to get the control of the Federal Government, with the intent to enable it to accomplish this result by the overthrow of the Federal Judiciary;" declared, that "large numbers of them were daily committing offences against the peace and property of the southern States, which, by the laws of nations, would be sufficient causes of war among independent States;" and that "nine States had actually violated the Constitution in that section which requires the return of persons held to service or labor;" and, in particular, assailed Wisconsin for her refusal to submit to the decision of the Federal courts in relation to the Fugitive-Slave Act. "If a Republican should be elected, he would implore his State never, for an instant, to allow that party to hold the reins of government. * * * * Let us defend our rights, or else pull down the pillars of this glorious temple, and mingle all in one universal ruin."

Messrs. Hale, of New Hampshire, and Doolittle, of Wisconsin, replying, vindicated the action of Wisconsin and the Republicans; citing against the Georgian senator his own State's Supreme Court, which, as late as 1854, had claimed to be "coequal and coördinate with the Supreme Court of the United States, and not inferior and subordinate" thereto; that the latter, having no jurisdiction over the former, "could not, therefore, give it an order, or make for it a precedent." To this they added the authority of the Supreme Courts of Pennsylvania and Virginia; and that of Jefferson, Jackson, and other distinguished men, against the assumption of exclusive power, on the part of the Federal Judiciary, to construe the Constitution; and showed that almost every president had recognized the right of Congress to keep Slavery out of the

Territories; and that, till within a few years, no one had questioned the constitutionality of such exclusion.

In the other House the Slave-holders were no less emphatic than in the Senate, in affirming the sacredness of property in human flesh, the excellence of their "peculiar institution," its right to unlimited extension throughout the Territories, and their determination to dissolve the Union rather than be ruled by "Black Republicans." Mr. GARTRELL, of Georgia, "claimed that Congress has no power over Slavery in the States, the Territories, or the District of Columbia; that justice to the master, and humanity to the Slave, imperiously require the expansion and perpetuation of the system; that the people of the South had a right to go, with their Slaves, into all the Territories of the United States; and, when there, to be as fully protected in the enjoyment of their rights as the northern man is protected with his personal property; that *none* of the Territories now acquired, or hereafter to be acquired, shall be devoted exclusively to free labor; that the Constitution placed Slaves on an equality with other chattel property, and if the Courts should refuse to protect it in the Territories, it would be the duty of Congress to do so by adequate legislation." Mr. QUARLES, of Tennessee, "believed that Tennessee has a right to carry Slaves into the common Territories, and a right to claim every arm of government to protect it." Mr. HARDEMAN, of Georgia, "was in favor of a Slave code for the Territories, and intended to demand every southern right."

And substantially to the same effect spoke most of the southern members. Mr. REAGAN, of Texas, went still further, and denied that a Territory, even when forming a constitution for admission as a State, could rightfully prohibit Slavery. It has the power, under the Federal Constitution, to do so, he admitted; but to exercise that power would destroy private property, and therefore would violate natural justice. He conceded, however, that a State already existing, with an Anti-Slavery Constitution, has a right to exclude Slavery. "A man has a natural right to retain his property where he lives, but not to carry it into a sovereignty where it is not recognized as property." Whence we infer that Mr. REAGAN's natural rights are somewhat artificial and conventional, — very much of the

State's making, instead of being, like JEFFERSON's, the gift of the Creator.

Mr. ANDERSON, of Missouri, said, "Unless a revolution in public sentiment takes place in the North within the next twelve months, which he did not anticipate, a man from that section would not be permitted to travel in the South, unless he could bring evidence of conservative feeling and friendliness. The South would never submit to the enforcement of the Republican party's principles, which, if reduced to practice, would disrupt all the ties which bind the Union together." Mr. CURRY, of Alabama, "denied that Slavery was anywhere the creature of local or municipal law. No law was found on the statute-book of any southern State, authorizing the introduction of Slavery; and, if positive precept were necessary, the tenure by which they held their Slaves was uncertain and illegal. If Slavery required positive law for its introduction, it could not get into a Territory at all; and thus the South was practically and forever excluded from the occupancy of a common Territory. * * * * Congress could neither abolish nor establish Slavery in a Territory. It had only the affirmative power of protection. * * * * The South held that non-intervention was a pledge that Government would abstain from hostile acts toward Slavery, or doubtful legislation in that regard. * * * * To keep Slavery circumscribed would inevitably result in rendering emancipation certain, or Slave-labor unprofitable, and the extinction of the white race probable. Hence, with the South, the struggle for expansion was a struggle for life. * * * Should you succeed, as you threaten, in cooping us up and surrounding us by Wilmot provisos, or by your homestead bills, in filling up the common Territories with northern and foreign squatters, inimical to Slavery, the time will come when the southern people, gathering up their households together, sword in hand, *will force an outlet for it at the cannon's mouth.*" Mr. SINGLETON, of Mississippi, said, "the South have made up their minds to sustain Slavery. We do n't intend to be prescribed by present limits; and it will not be in the power of the North to coerce the three millions of freemen at the South, with arms in their hands, and prevent their going into the surrounding Territories. Gentlemen must remember that a gallant son of the South, JEFFERSON DAVIS, led our forces into Mexico, and, thank God, he still lives, perhaps to lead a southern army."

Mr. ASHMORE, of South Carolina, warned gentlemen of the Republican side, that they must speedily pause in their career, or expect to see this Confederacy rent asunder as if by the bolt from heaven. The indorsement of the Helper book, the John-Brown invasion, and the emissaries detected in the South, and properly punished, had done more to weaken the bonds of the Union, in the last twelve months, than all else within his memory. * * * * If northern hostility went a step further, all the powers of earth could not keep this Union together. They had heard vain-glorious boasting about coercing the South, and putting eighteen millions of the North against eight millions of the South; but the North had no eighteen millions, while the South had a population of twelve millions. In a crusade of this kind, the North proper would stand alone. The great Northwest, bound to the South, as with hooks of steel, by the great river of the West, would desert her; while the Pacific States, upon the principle of self-preservation, would take care of themselves. The South would stand fire, united and invincible, while the northern States, even granting the eighteen millions, would be divided among themselves. The South had faithful allies there, true to the Constitution and the Union, and they would be no idle spectators. The North would be left, when the hour of coercion arrives, with even less population than the South. The South could sustain more men in the field than the North. Her four millions of Slaves alone would enable her to support an army of half a million. They could raise a yearly revenue, on imports, of forty million dollars; or, if their ports were blockaded by the navy of the North, they could raise nearly as large a sum by taxation. Would the millions at the North, thrown out of employment by secession, rush to the battle-field for employment? Would their strikers for higher wages turn upon their best customers, and butcher the men from whom they derive their subsistence? Where was the population to support the taxation which the South could lay, with impunity, upon her unresisting Slaves? The miscalled free laborers of the North — really slaves to capital — would not submit to taxation. The people of the North were worse than mad to agitate Slavery further; and doubly mad to talk about coercing the people of the South. There would be a confederacy in the North; one in the South; another in the Northwest — the ally of the South; and still another on the far Pacific, destined to be the mightiest and grandest of all. Or, if this should not happen, they could see in the present state of Mexico what is to be the sad and ruined future of our now happy and prosperous country. Whose fault was it? The North had ever been, and was now, the aggressor. * * * * If the sentiments contained in the Helper book, and the programme marked out by Mr. SEWARD, were found to indicate truly the sentiment of the North, nineteen-twentieths of his constituents were in favor of disunion, without an hour of unnecessary delay; and if this course of insult and aggression was pursued, though he claimed to be a Constitution and Union-loving man, he would return to his constituents, himself to sound the alarm, and kindle, with his own hands, the beacon-fires on hill-tops, and maintain the rights of the South with flaming dagger and blazing torch.

Mr. JENKINS, of Virginia, more frank than many of his fellows, betrayed what is really, we doubt not, one of the greatest fears of the Slave-holders. After saying that, under a Republican administration, the Fugitive-Slave Law could not be enforced, and that, consequently, "Slavery would be practically abolished in the border States," he added, "Another misfortune would be the dispensation of patronage throughout the South, by a Republican president, in such a way as to build up and strengthen Republicanism. It was a great mistake to suppose that southern men would not be found to take an office under a Republican president. So the germ of a Republican party would spring up in the very bosom of the South. Then they would find the whole moral weight, not only of this Government, but of the civilized world, thrown into the scale against the institution of Slavery. A southern gentleman would be received at a foreign court very much as would a polygamous patriarch of Utah."

Mr. VANCE, of North Carolina, was at once pious and logical. He "justified southern Slavery, as the best condition for the master and Slave. He did not believe God would otherwise direct, that what is best should not also be right."

Mr. ETHERIDGE, (American) of Tennessee, was almost the

only southern member who spoke decidedly against the extension and protection of Slavery in the Territories, and he took no very high moral ground for his opposition : "He would never give a vote to put Slavery in the Territories, while the Nebraska-Kansas Bill, according to the construction put upon it at the time of its passage, remains in force; for it gives the right to the people, while in a territorial condition, to regulate Slavery in their own way." HENRY WINTER DAVIS, of Maryland, (American) also opposed the extensionists. But nearly all the members of that party, from the South, were as explicitly, if not as vehemently, "in favor of protecting Slave-property in the Territories," as their Democratic compatriots from the same section.

On the Republican side, some strong and effective speeches were made, full of a manly spirit; responding, in a proper tone, to the haughty insolence of the Slave-drivers, and taking as high ground against Slavery as allegiance to the Constitution, with the received interpretation, would permit. But too many were tame and halting, if not worse; evincing a sad want of either moral courage or clear moral perception. Among the best were those of Messrs. SEDGWICK, of New York, and LOVEJOY, of Illinois.

Mr. SEDGWICK denounced Slavery as "from first to last a violation of that Higher Law 'whose seat is the bosom of God, and whose voice is the harmony of the universe.' No law or constitutional guarantees, however solemn," he said, "could bind the conscience of any citizen of any nation under heaven to the support of such a system of outrage and violence. Its most able advocate [Mr. CURRY] the other day admitted that there was no law in the Slave States for the support of the institution. It was a usurpation resting entirely upon force, and by and by some Spartacus would rise among them, to test the question of superior force." Of the Fugitive-Slave Bill of 1850, he said, "Great ingenuity was exercised in making it as bad and villanous as possible; and certainly any man who would give it a cheerful acquiescence might be relied on to do anything mean, even to selling his own mother into the rice-swamps. * * * * I believe it was intended that such a law should produce counter legislation in the Free States, — that personal-liberty bills would be passed, as they have been, though not half as stringent as they ought to be, to discharge the duty which every independent State owes to each of its citizens, however humble: I mean protection to their personal liberty." He did what we believe was never done before on the floor of Congress, not only made respectful mention of the Abolitionists, as a body, but paid their pioneer a tribute of commendation as warm and hearty as any "Garrisonian" could ask; calling him "gentle, loving, peaceful, just, inflexible;" holding up before the house the first number of the *Liberator*, and reading from it — "I am in earnest! I will not equivocate; I will not excuse; I will not retreat a single inch; and I will be heard;" then adding, "That is from the first number of the *Liberator*, published in 1831, by WILLIAM LLOYD GARRISON. It has sometimes seemed to me that that man was sent from Heaven, in answer to the poet's prayer, and to meet the time's necessity: —

> 'We need, methinks, the prophet-heroes still, —
> Saints true of life, and martyrs strong of will, —
> To tread the land even now, as Xavier trod
>   The streets of Goa, barefoot, with his bell,
> Proclaiming freedom in the name of God,
> And startling tyrants with the fear of hell.'"

Mr. SEDGWICK, however, in one respect misapprehended, and consequently misstated the views of the Abolitionists. He represented them as holding "extreme" notions touching the Pro-Slavery character of the Constitution, instead of simply accepting, as they do, the common interpretation of it, as given from the first by judges, presidents, governors, and legislators, and the great body of the people. "He contended that the Republican party was not, and never had been, aggressive; that Slavery had always been, not justly, but leniently and generously treated; that having changed the whole policy of the country, the Republican party was forced into being, not only to restore the Government to its original policy, but to prevent the universal prevalence of Slavery, and the revival of the horrors of the African Slave-trade; and to protect the *habeas corpus*, trial by jury, the freedom of the press and of speech, and all the other safeguards of Freedom. If it could be betrayed into the folly of surrendering its principles, it would only give place to another, stronger, more radical, more virtuous, and more successful party."

Mr. LOVEJOY's bold and earnest utterance of truths unpala-
table to the Slave-power, and his energetic manner and fearless
bearing, roused such a furious storm among the chivalry that,
for a time, he could not proceed; but, resolutely maintaining
his ground through all the clamor and confusion, he finally
succeeded, says a correspondent of the *Anti-Slavery Standard*,
who was present, "in delivering, 'to the bitter end,' one of the
most scathing and denunciatory speeches against Slavery ever
prepared." But it was in the midst of frequent exhibitions of
a courtesy and a decorum as "peculiar" as the favorite "institution" of the exhibiters. "At one time," says the writer just
quoted, "twenty Slave-holders surrounded the speaker, one man
flourishing his cane and many of the others their fists, Mr.
LOVEJOY meanwhile standing as erect as a statue, and refusing
to budge one inch from his position. At every convenient
point, and especially when he uttered a severe sentence, he was
interrupted with such exclamations as the following: "You
d—d nigger-thief," "You liar," "You are inferior to the meanest
negro," "You are a scoundrel." "Liar and scoundrel" was also
the elegant and logical rejoinder of Mr. REUBEN DAVIS, of
Mississippi, to the statement of Mr. VAN WYCK, of New York,
in the course of a temperate and moderate Free-Soil speech,
that Slaves are sometimes burned to death at the South. Mr.
ALLEY, of Massachusetts, responded to the southern threats of
disunion, and warnings of consequent ruin to the North, by declaring that "the average of his constituents were superior,
socially and intellectually, to southern members of Congress on
that floor; that he had made a large fortune in business, and
experience convinced him that the North lost money by its
southern trade; and he did not, therefore, consider that, pecuniarily or intellectually considered, disunion would impoverish
the North."

Mr. CONKLING, of New York, made an able, legal, and constitutional argument against the assumption, in the president's
message, that the question of Slavery in the Territories has
been "irrevocably" settled by the Supreme Court. He contended "that the judgments of the Supreme Court are binding
only upon inferior courts and parties litigant, and so long as
the Court adheres to its decision upon any constitutional question, acts of Congress repugnant thereto will be inoperative *so*

far only as they depend upon the courts for their execution; and that its decisions are not obligatory upon Congress in any sense, but, like other arguments, are addressed to the discretion of that body. And, whenever a decision is, in the opinion of Congress, subversive of the rights and liberties of the people, or is otherwise hurtfully erroneous, it is not only the right, but the solemn duty of Congress, persistently to disregard it." In support of these conclusions, besides urging forcible reasons, he cited "high authority," legal and political; "the civil authorities and tribunals of no less than five States of the Union — New York, Virginia, Pennsylvania, Wisconsin, and Georgia;" Presidents JEFFERSON, JACKSON, and VAN BUREN; Senator (now President) BUCHANAN, and other distinguished personages. In conclusion he said, "a reorganization and reinvigoration of the Court, with just regard to commercial and political considerations, is one of the auspicious promises of Republican ascendency. It is high time that appropriate weight should be given in the Court, and elsewhere, to all portions of the country, not excepting those in which a vast preponderance of its wealth, its business, its intellect, and its numbers reside. With this reform accomplished, the vampire of Slavery, now flitting among the shadows of a sheltering tribunal, will spread its wings once more over that hospitable domain where its ministrations are considered essential to the full development of 'the highest type of white civilization.'"

Mr. STANTON, of Ohio, affirmed that "the Republican party holds to the doctrine of the natural equality of man; not meaning equality of strength, intelligence, social position, or political rights; but that every man has certain inherent, inalienable rights, for all of which he is entitled to protection, as the right to live, the right to enjoy his own earnings, the right of locomotion. * * * * I hold," he said, "that this system [Slavery], which is termed the bright type of Christian civilization, is at war with the very first principle upon which the social organization hangs. * * * * * * If, as the gentleman from Alabama asserts, Slavery is by far the preferable form of civilization, it ought to be established in all the Territories. If, on the other hand, it is a bad system, and opposed to the doctrines of humanity and the principles of our government, then it ought to be prevented from going into them. For these reasons, it is the duty of Congress to inquire into the inherent character of Slavery. * * * * The threat to resist forcibly the inauguration of a Republican president, simply means treason against the United States. Whether the threat to secede and organize a separate confederacy constitutes treason or not, may become a matter of controversy, but either is equally fatal to the existing government and institutions of the country." Mr. HICKMAN, of Pennsylvania, replying to the charge of northern sectionalism, "proved the accuser guilty." He said that "sectionalism has become the parent of all our afflictions; not the sectionalism of the North, but of the South; the determination of the South to extend, rather than to reduce, the limits of Slavery. This arrays the different parts of the country in hostility. * * * * * * The North will endeavor to preserve the Federal Compact in its integrity, and they were fast forming the determination of preventing others from infracting it. He spoke of the humiliating concessions to the South in the compromise of 1850, including the Fugitive-Slave Law, which compels men to leave their fields and shops to run after the fleeing negro, while the North are denied equality in the Union. * * * * * * The South want and strive for unlimited Slavery extension and the subjugation of the North. They would fire this temple; but the North was able to save both it and them."

On the 26th of March, Mr. BLAKE, of Ohio — from the district which includes Oberlin — stirred up no little excitement by offering a resolution, that "whereas the holding of persons as property, contrary to natural justice and the principles of our political system, is a reproach to our country throughout the civilized world, and a hindrance to the progress of Republican Liberty among the nations of the earth, the Committee on the Judiciary be instructed to inquire into the expediency of reporting a bill giving freedom to every human being, and interdicting Slavery wherever Congress has the constitutional power to legislate on the subject." "For a few minutes," says the New-York *Tribune's* correspondent, "the noise and confusion were great." A Republican from Pennsylvania hastened to object to the resolution, but was just too late to prevent the taking of the yeas and nays on adopting it, when it was rejected by 109 to 60. "Fifty Republicans dodged the vote," others voted against the resolution, and for those who voted to adopt it, the

Tribune's special correspondent apologized on the ground that it was "a mere resolution of inquiry," taking care, also, to state that Mr. BLAKE offered it "without any consultation among his political friends," and adding that "these barren generalities only provoke unnecessary embarrassment, without the least service." In a colloquy among the members, however, just after the vote was taken, Mr. KILGORE, of Indiana, one of the Republicans who refused to vote, is reported as saying that, "with the permission of the committee [on the District of Columbia, of which he is a member], he would, at an early day, report a bill for the gradual emancipation of the Slaves in the District;" that he was for striking at Slavery, by Congressional action, wherever he has constitutional power so to do; and that his object was to surround Slavery that it might die." At a later day, Mr. SHERMAN, of Ohio, replying to condemnatory remarks by a southern member, upon BLAKE's resolution, stated, "to show the difference," that, "not fifteen minutes before it was offered, a resolution offered by a gentleman from South Carolina, to provide for the emancipation of the white laborers of the North, was received by a unanimous vote, and referred to the Committee on Ways and Means." But Mr. SHERMAN was careful to say that he was "opposed to interference with Slavery in the District of Columbia," and had so "stated to his constituents over and over again." On the other hand, Mr. BINGHAM, of Ohio, "advocated the exclusion of Slavery from all places where the United-States Government has jurisdiction, as the best method of allaying sectional strife;" and Mr. ELLIOT, of Massachusetts, said "it would be the happiest day of his life, when, at the proper time, and under proper surroundings, and at a proper request of the citizens of the District of Columbia, he could aid them to strike off the shackles of the Slaves here."

The Fugitive-Slave Bill also claimed a share of the attention of the House. Mr. MAYNARD, of Tennessee, brought in a resolution, about the middle of February, with a view to make it more effectual in its operation. Mr. DUELL, of New York, gave notice, a little later, of a bill to amend it so as to give the right of trial by jury to the alleged fugitive. And later still, Mr. BLAKE introduced a bill to repeal it, which was referred to the Judiciary Committee. ·While a motion was before the House to appropriate $40,000 for the suppression of the African Slave-trade, Mr. Jones, of Georgia, offered a proviso, "that no part of the amount be paid for the support and education of the Africans captured in the Echo, and that the sum be applied for the faithful execution of the law providing for the rendition of Fugitive Slaves." In the Senate, on the 20th of March, Mr. Sumner presented the memorial of Samuel May, a distinguished and venerable merchant of Boston, and four hundred others, citizens of Boston, praying for the repeal of the Fugitive-Slave Law of 1850, the abolition of Slavery in the District of Columbia, the prohibition of the inter-state Slave-trade, and the passage of a resolution pledging Congress against the admission of any new Slave State into the Union, or the acquisition of any Slave territory, or the employment of Slaves by any agent, contractor, officer, or department of the Federal Government. He moved a reference to the Judiciary Committee; but, on motion of Mr. Davis, of Mississippi, it was laid on the table, by 30 to 17. On the 18th of April, upon motion of Mr. Mason, of Virginia, the same disposition was made of numerous petitions of the same character, from different parts of New England, presented by Mr. Sumner, and by Mr. Collamer, of Vermont.

On the 12th of April, a bill to grant $25,000, for five years, to the public schools of the District of Columbia, having been taken up, Mr. Clark, of New Hampshire, moved to amend, so that a portion should go to educate the colored population. Mr. Brown, of Mississippi, was very graciously "willing the free negroes, in the District, should be educated in their own schools, and to authorize them to tax themselves for the purpose." [That is, those who, we are told, are so stupid and worthless that "they can't take care of themselves," may pay the expense of their own education; while the "superior race," in the District, shall be educated at the nation's expense.] Mr. Mason opposed the amendment. "He thought it wise policy, on the part of the southern States, to withhold education from the Slaves. Negroes, bond or free, form no part of our political society." Mr. Iverson, of Georgia, replying to a remark of Mr. Wilson, that "the North was not unwilling to let black men learn to read the Bible," showed his ignorance, or his audacity in falsehood, by saying "it was not true that the Slaves were not allowed to learn to read." Mr. Wilson rejoined, "I am sorry the senator does not understand the laws of his own State. I have the laws of the southern States in my room, proving what I say." The amendment was of course defeated.

ACTION OF STATES.

In the action, legislative, judicial, and other, of the several States, the Slave question has claimed its wonted share, during the past year. In June last, the Judiciary Committee of the New-Hampshire House of Representatives — responding to petitions numerously signed, and ably advocated by PARKER PILLSBURY, A. T. FOSS, and others, at a public hearing given to the petitioners — reported a Personal-Liberty Bill which declared that no person, in this State, shall be considered or treated as property; and that whoever shall arrest, imprison, or carry out of the State, any person, on the ground that he or she owes service or labor, as a Slave, or shall attempt the same, or aid and abet in such attempt, shall be imprisoned not over five years for the first offence, and for life for the second. It was ordered to a second reading by 134 to 101, but when the vote was taken on its final passage, Friday, June 24, it was indefinitely postponed, by 277 to 17. The Claremont (N. H.) *Advocate* says "the whole proceeding is unworthy of the high-toned, outspoken position the Republican party has ever maintained in relation to the continued encroachments of the Slave-power," and thinks "the effect will be to shake the confidence of the people in the integrity" of the party. A New-Hampshire correspondent of the *Anti-Slavery Standard*, however, tries to put the best face possible upon the matter; saying that though some of the politicians showed "timidity and spinal weakness" in the discussion, "still I think a large majority of the members were in favor of the principle of the bill. We have a statute against abduction and kidnapping, which, with the *habeas corpus*, under the administration of our courts, was probably deemed sufficient for the protection of personal liberty here, and there was not, perhaps, occasion for passing the bill, except for its moral effect. Should emergency arise, the courts of this State would undoubtedly stand with Wisconsin against the Fugitive-Slave Act; and I think that, in due time, the people of

New Hampshire will place upon the statute-book a stringent
Personal-Liberty Bill." In the evening the House adopted a
series of resolutions, condemning Slavery, the Dred-Scott Decision, and the proposal to revive the African Slave-trade, and
inviting men of all parties to join in opposing Slavery-extension
and "restoring the Government to its original purity."

At a special session of the Legislature of Massachusetts, called
to act upon a revision of the Statutes of that Commonwealth,
and held through several months of the past year, a vote was
obtained on the recommendation, and in great measure, it is
believed, through the influence of Governor BANKS, to accept
and set up, in front of the State House, a statue of DANIEL
WEBSTER, which some of his wealthy friends and admirers had
offered to the State for that purpose. And though it was tendered and accepted on the express condition that its erection
there should cost the State nothing, the Legislature volunteered
an appropriation of $3,000 for the expenses of "inaugurating"
it; a ceremony which took place on the 17th of September, with
EDWARD EVERETT for orator, and an imposing array of digni-
taries, civic, military, literary, ecclesiastical, to give due "pomp
and circumstance" to the occasion; but, unfortunately for the
anticipated grandeur of the display, with such perversity of the
elements that it was thought needful to repeat the oratorical
part of the performance, on a more favorable day. Thus by
legislative act it was declared that, before all her worthiest
sons, the man whom Massachusetts delights to honor is this
conspicuous traitor to the principles she professes to hold
sacred; this man, who, prostituting noble powers to basest uses,
exhorted her to "conquer her prejudices" against kidnapping,
and discharge "with alacrity," and as "an affair of high morals
and high principles," the "disagreeable duty" of human blood-
hound for the southern Slave-hunter. What was the real
motive of an act so dishonorable to the Legislature and the
State, we will not attempt to say. That it was not a sincere
conviction that the intended honor was worthily bestowed,
seems to us fairly inferable from the fact that the very same
body, on the recommendation of the same governor, a few days
after, by way, no doubt, of allaying the strong dissatisfaction
which their former act produced, offset it by a vote permitting
the erection of a statue to HORACE MANN, in the State-house

yard, with the very distinct understanding that it was to be placed there, if at all, as the representative of ideas and principles exactly opposite to those with which the name of WEBSTER was associated in the later portion of his life. Petitions for the removal of the WEBSTER statue were circulated and signed, it is said, among the very crowd assembled to hear the repetition of Mr. EVERETT's inaugural oration. They were also signed at other times, in different parts of the State, and would have been in much larger numbers, doubtless, than they were, had not the public feeling been so largely absorbed by the events connected with JOHN BROWN's enterprise. The petitions were presented at last winter's regular session of the Legislature, but, instead of what they asked for, the petitioners had "leave to withdraw."

Last fall, at a special session, in passing upon the revision of the statutes, the Legislature, by a very large majority, struck out the word "white" from the section providing that "every able-bodied white male citizen shall be enrolled in the militia." Governor BANKS thereupon vetoed the whole code, affirming that the proposed amendment is unconstitutional, and fortifying himself with the opinions, procured for the purpose, of the State's Attorney-General and Supreme Court. They take the ground that the power, granted to Congress, to organize the militia, "includes that of determining what classes of persons shall be so organized; and this has been determined by an Act of Congress" which contains the word "white;" that, therefore, "the General Government having authority to determine who shall and who may not compose the militia, and having so determined, the State Government has no legal authority to prescribe a different enrollment." The weight of this authority, added to the fear of losing all the labor of the session, defeated the amendment, by changing votes enough to secure a majority against it; but a goodly number of its friends were still unconvinced, affirming that the governor and his legal advisers had argued from false premises; that the obvious and dictionary meaning of "organize" does *not* include "determining who shall be organized;" that, according to the express testimony of RUFUS KING, one of the committee which framed the constitutional provision bearing on the question, "by organizing the militia was meant proportioning the officers and men;" that

the Constitution nowhere recognizes color as a ground of difference of rights, and in reality the Act of Congress, and not the
proposed amendment to the State law, is unconstitutional, and
has, moreover, been disregarded by no less than twenty States,
of which two, Texas and South Carolina, leave out the word
"white," and the latter admits aliens, Indians, free negroes, and
mulattoes into the militia, by a law of 1794. At the regular
winter session the subject was again called up, and, against a
strenuous opposition, a bill to strike out the offensive word was
passed by more than two-thirds in the Senate, and by 105 to 97
in the House; but was again vetoed by Governor BANKS, on
the same ground as before.

In answer to petitions bearing nearly 14,000 signatures, an
effort was made, but without success, to obtain the passage of a
law, substantially like that proposed the year before, against
Slave-hunting in the Commonwealth. The strong Republican
majority in the Legislature could not furnish a majority in
favor of declaring Bunker Hill and Lexington and Concord
sacred from the contaminating tread of "legalized" kidnappers.
Whether the nearness of a presidential election, with the
brightening hopes of a Republican success therein, had any
influence on the vote, we will not undertake to say.

Our last Report mentioned the taking of the first step, by
the Legislature of Connecticut, toward giving colored men the
right of suffrage in that State. On the 8th of June last the
question came up in the Senate whether the second step should
be taken, and was answered in the negative by 16 to 5. The
House responded the same way, by 173 to 49. A shameful
retrograde, from the slight forward movement of the previous
year.

Governor MORGAN, of New York, in his message to the
Legislature, last winter, did "not feel at liberty to disregard the
subject which, for so many years, has agitated the country." He
condemned, as "incompatible with perfect amity between different sections," not Slavery itself, but "the novel doctrine that
Slavery is no evil, but a positive good, to be commended,
diffused, perpetuated; and which logically requires the conver-
sion of our Territories into new Slave-marts, and the acquisition
of additional provinces to increase the power of this social evil."
New York had "never claimed the right to interfere, directly

or indirectly, with Slavery in the other States;" and "she disavows all sympathy with those misguided men who have sought, unlawfully, to interfere" with it there. "Bloodshed, incited" by the recent attempt "to liberate and arm the Slaves" of Virginia, "rests, in the eyes of human law, on the heads of those whose violation of laws provoked it. We may admit that their aims were unselfish and philanthropic, but must never forget that social order can only exist through a general recognition of the sanctity of law." [Considering that a governor speaks, and to a legislature, and these the Governor and Legislature of the "Empire State," conscious of course, too, that the nation hears, this guarded and qualified disapproval of "the offenders" alluded to, looks much as if he felt, in his secret soul, that they were not, after all, so very great offenders "in the eyes of" a law infinitely above "human law."] But "when it is proposed to establish Slavery in the Territories, New York will claim the right" to speak "through her representatives in Congress," and her "electors recognize the authority of Congress to prohibit" such establishment.

Petitions for a "Personal-Liberty Bill" were sent, in large numbers, to the Legislature, and were referred to a select committee which, early in February, reported a bill, with an able argument in favor of its passage. It provided "that every person who shall come or be brought into, or be in the State shall be free, and whoever captures or holds a person as a Fugitive Slave, in the State, shall be imprisoned in the State penitentiary, and be fined $1,000, to go to the party aggrieved." It was advocated, with great force, by Messrs. POWELL, MAXSON, BARNETT, and others, whose speeches the *Anti-Slavery Standard* pronounced to have been "seldom excelled, in bold and eloquent annunciation of Anti-Slavery principles, in any legislative assembly in the country," and to be "worth all the labor the friends of the bill have expended in bringing it forward thus far." The bill, however, was defeated, but one result of the effort for its passage was the circulation of more than one hundred thousand copies of valuable Anti-Slavery documents, chiefly the speeches just referred to. About the middle of February the Assembly, by 70 to 36, and a few weeks later the Senate, by 26 to 9, passed the resolution, which had already passed a former Legislature, to so amend the Constitution as to allow colored men to vote without a property-qualification. The amendment now goes to the people, and, if ratified by them, becomes part of the Constitution.

Last January, the Lemmon case was argued before the Court of Appeals; CHARLES O'CONNOR, on behalf of the Slave-holder, contending that Slavery is not morally wrong, there being no law of nature, or of God, against Slave-holding; that property in man rests on the same basis with every other species of property; and that no State of this Union can pass laws to extinguish Slavery within its limits, while a single Slave-holding State remains in the Union. "If Slavery," said he, "is a sin, then it is a sin of the greatest magnitude — of the most enormous and flagitious character that was ever presented to the human mind. The man who does not skrink back from it with horror is utterly unworthy of the name of man. It is no trivial offence, that may be tolerated with limitations and qualifications, that we can excuse ourselves for supporting because we have made some kind of a bargain to support it. If this system is sinful and unjust, its existence under our system of law, supported by our jurisprudence, sustained by the fundamental law of the land, is a public and crying reproach against the whole nation. An honest European gentleman ought no more to associate with one of these Slave-holders, than your honors with a highwayman or pickpocket, merely because in the village of his residence there was a bad police or no law to bring him to justice. But what think you of the inhabitants of the Free States, who know it is wicked, yet live under a Constitution by which they agree to support it, and, if any one of its unhappy victims should escape and fly hither for shelter, would seize and return him, or permit his master to come here and carry him back to bondage? We have no excuse. An enlightened European, if he has a sense of honor, of justice, if he has due self-respect, will turn his back on the wilfully-offending northern man, as the vilest of the vile." All the doctrines of the Abolitionists, he affirmed, are irrefutable, — JOHN BROWN deserves to rank with KOSCIUSKO and LAFAYETTE; nay higher, if Slavery is unjust. If " the phrases concerning human equality, found in the Declaration of Independence, were intended to include negroes," then " the first sentence in the Constitution, that it was made 'to establish justice,' is a piece of hypocrisy and falsehood, and the American name is covered with the undying stigma inwrought with the perpetuation of injustice." The decision was reserved till the March term, and was not given till April. Judges DENIO, WRIGHT, WELLS, BACON, and DAVIES concurred in affirming the judgment of the Court below, by which LEMMON's Slaves were declared to be free when brought by their master into New York. Judge DENIO held that the provision of the Constitution for the rendition of Fugitive Slaves strongly implies "the general principle to be that the escape of a Slave into a State which had abolished Slavery would, of itself, transform him into a free man; and *a fortiori*, he would be free if the master brought him into a Free State. The Constitution set aside this general principle in the case of the fugitive only, it still governs other cases. This was reasonable, as the owner was free to determine whether he would voluntarily permit his Slave to go within a jurisdiction which did not allow him to be held in bondage. The provision that citizens of each State shall be entitled to all privileges and immunities of citizens in the several States, does not mean that a citizen may carry with him, into every State whither he may go, the institutions of that in which he was born, but only that in any State he shall have the same rights as the citizens of that State. If our courts are obliged to respect the title which the laws of a Slave State confer, a Slave-holder may retain his Slaves here during his pleasure, and though he could not, perhaps, sell them to a citizen of New York, he might to any other citizen of a Slave State who had come here, equally bringing with him the immunities of his own State, for these immunities are not limited to time, or by the purpose for which they are desired. The doctrine of international comity cannot sustain the claim here made, for it depends on the presumed assent of the legislative authority of the State where it is asserted, and an express denial by that authority is decisive against the claim. The clause of the Constitution empowering Congress to regulate commerce among the States does not apply to this case. The statute of New York, under which the Slaves were discharged, is not in any just sense a regulation of commerce, and so does not conflict with that provision. Conceding that to facilitate commerce, Congress has power to provide for such a case as this, it has not exercised that power; and the unexer-

case that careful examination which is due to its importance, and therefore was not prepared to determine whether the Act of 1841 is, or is not, in conflict with any express provision of the Constitution." But *without* "that careful examination" he was ready to pronounce it "a gross violation of those principles of justice and comity which should, at all times, pervade our inter-state legislation, as well as wholly inconsistent with the general spirit of our national compact." So, while he could not "give such reasons as would justify" him "in holding the law to be void," he was "equally unprepared to concur" with the majority of the Court. That is, he *would* not say it was valid, though he *dared* not say it was void. And such men wear judicial ermine, in the *free* State of New York; and are not ashamed to show themselves, after such talk as this, among men of decent reputation! As if the Constitution were not wicked enough, in all conscience, here they must eke out its defective iniquity with "rules of comity and justice!" — Heaven save us! — that they may thrust innocent men into bondage without even the poor excuse that the Constitution, bad as it is, compels the outrage! But, happily, their power was not equal to their will for this base work; and, so far as the highest judicial authority of New York can settle the question, it is now decided that the "Empire State" is not yet a highway for the inter-state Slave-trade. We have yet to see, however, what will be the decision of the Federal Supreme Court upon that question. There seems to be but too much reason for the opinion of the New-York *Tribune*, that O'Connor's argument "shadows forth the ground which that Court intends to occupy as the next step in advance," and that "we are on the eve of a decision which will make it law, that property in man stands on precisely the same basis as any other property; that there is no law of nature against Slavery, and that there *can* be no law of any one of the Free States competent to its abolition within the limits of such State, while a single Slave State remains in the Union."

Governor PACKER, of Pennsylvania, in his message to the Legislature, last January, showed himself somewhat over-zealous in his loyalty to the sovereign Slave-power. Alluding to the Harper's-Ferry affair, he said, "it is a source of satisfaction to know that Virginia had the means and determination to punish offenders with promptness and justice; that the military

force of the United States was immediately available to aid in
putting down the outbreak; that the Slave population were
contented with their condition," [how he knows that, we could
ask, probably, more easily than he could tell] "and unwilling to
unite with disorderly white men in acts of treason and murder;
and that the great masses of the people have no sympathy with
any attack upon the institutions of any of the States." He
congratulated the Pennsylvanians that none of them "participated in this unlawful proceeding," and that such of the "guilty
perpetrators" as were arrested in Pennsylvania, "were promptly
surrendered [with indecorous haste, and without the forms usual
in such cases, he might have added,] "to the justice of the
offended and injured State." After pronouncing it "a high
offence against the peace of our Commonwealth, for disorderly
persons, within our jurisdiction, to combine together for the
purpose of stirring up insurrection in any of the States, or to
induce the Slaves in the southern States to abscond from their
masters;" he made a needless display of his officious servility
by telling the Legislature that, in his judgment, "it would be
proper to consider whether additional legislation may not be
necessary to insure the prompt punishment of such offenders
against our peace and security." A "judgment" in which the
Legislature does not appear to have been unwise enough to
concur, for we have heard of no attempt made to legislate in
accordance with it. "In determining our relative duties toward
our sister States," he continued, "the morality of servitude"
[*Slavery* is an ugly *word*, even to governors who are willing to
uphold the *thing*] "is not an open question, for we are bound
by the legal and moral obligation of the compact of the Union
to respect the institutions which the laws of the several States
recognize, and in no other way can we faithfully fulfil our obligations as members of this Confederacy." In other words, "the
compact of the Union" permits us to have no conscience against
man-stealing and all its attendant and consequent enormities.
"The morality" of turning our brothers into brutes, of plunder-
ing labor, abrogating marriage, annihilating the family, and
stifling human souls by millions, "is not an open question" to
any faithful "member of this Confederacy." No wonder the
governor winced a little in making that statement; and chose
another word, rather than that which exactly represents the

thing he meant. But "mincing the matter" do n't mend the matter, Governor PACKER. Your Slave-holding, Slave-hunting Union is none the better for your betrayal of a sort of half-consciousness of how vile and abominable it is. A vain attempt was made, as in the year before, to procure the enactment of a Personal-Liberty Bill. Petitions for such an Act were sent in, but we have heard of no action taken upon them. On the other hand, JOHN H. WHEELER — whose Slaves (JANE JOHNSON and her children) became free, a few years ago, by his bringing them into the State, and PASSMORE WILLIAMSON's helping them to a knowledge and enjoyment of the legal rights thereby conferred upon them — was equally unsuccessful in an application to the Legislature for a grant of $5,000, as indemnity for the loss of his unintentionally-emancipated chattels.

In Ohio, three measures were pressed, by the friends of Freedom, upon the Legislature, in which the Republicans had a decided majority; but all three failed. They were, a bill against Slave-hunting; an amendment of the *habeas corpus* Act, for the purpose of protecting citizens of Ohio against the petty tyranny practised under the Fugitive-Slave Bill; and an Act to forbid the use of the jails of the State as Fugitive-Slave pens. But while these *Republican* legislators could find no time to enact justice, humanity, and a decent self-respect into law, they could turn aside from the proper business of their office to do a little Union-saving homage to the Slave-power, by inviting the Legislatures of Kentucky and Tennessee to visit them, receiving their Slave-holding guests with very distinguished consideration, entertaining them with lavish hospitality, and appropriating $5,000 of the earnings of their "mud-sill" constituents to pay the expenses of the visit. We may as well add here, that in the midst of the banquet came a despatch, by telegraph, from Governor MORGAN, of New York, in behalf of the Legislature of that State, inviting the southern Legislatures to extend their visit to Albany. "The despatch was enthusiastically received."

Since the decision of the Ohio Supreme Court, in the Oberlin rescue-cases, an election has been held to fill the place of Chief-Justice SWAN, whose term had expired. Judge SWAN was a candidate for re-nomination, but the ill odor of his name, on account of his falsehood to Freedom in that decision, insured his defeat; while the "conservative" feelings of one portion, and the timidity of another, of the dominant (Republican) party induced the choice of a man in his place — Judge GHOL-SON — whom nobody knew to be any better than himself on the Fugitive-Slave-Law question; and whom everybody claiming to be interested in that question seems to have purposely avoided questioning as to his views upon it, lest an answer should be given which would endanger a division and defeat of the party. Well! it is something done, if a point has been reached where politicians, though they dare not put forward for so important an office an open and avowed upholder of the unconstitutionality of the Slave-catcher's statute, are at least afraid to nominate one who openly declares it constitutional.

On the 14th of last July, the Court of Common Pleas, in Cuyahoga County, in a case growing out of a refusal of the judges of election to receive the vote of a man having about one-fourth negro blood, decided that the statute of the preceding year, forbidding "persons in whole or in part of African blood" to vote, is unconstitutional, and that "all persons having more than half white blood are legally white." It was held that as the former Constitution of Ohio expressly so declared, and as the present Constitution uses the phrase "white persons," without defining it, the old definition is to be regarded as still in force. The Supreme Court of the State — Judge GHOLSON, the new Chief Justice, delivering its opinion — unanimously decided the same way, last February, in a case of like character, appealed from Butler County.

Our last Report announced the decision of the United-States Supreme Court, then just given, adverse to that of the Supreme Court of Wisconsin, in the Booth case. When the mandate was sent to the latter, requiring it to reverse its decision so as to conform it to that of the Federal Court, Judge DIXON, the new Chief Justice then recently appointed by the governor, to fill a vacancy till the time of the next election, was in favor of obeying; not because he regarded the Fugitive-Slave Bill constitutional, but because he felt bound to yield to the judgment of the Federal Court. Of the other two judges, Judge COLE dissented, denying the appellate jurisdiction of the Federal Court in the case; and Judge PAINE declined to give an opinion, because he had been BOOTH's counsel, in an earlier stage of the proceedings. So the motion to reverse, not having a majority of the court in its favor, failed; as it would have done by having a majority against it, had Judge PAINE given his opinion. Thereupon, instructions were sent from Washington to the United-States District Attorney, in Wisconsin, to have BOOTH rearrested, without heeding the decision of the State Court. Accordingly, on the 1st of March he was arrested, and imprisoned in the Milwaukee Custom-House, where, it is said, he is treated with much harshness, denied intercourse with his family and friends, and permitted very scanty and insufficient opportunity of conferring with his counsel. An application to the State's Supreme Court, for a writ of *habeas corpus*, failed by a tie vote, DIXON for refusing and COLE for granting it, and PAINE declining, for the reason already mentioned, to give his voice either way. The writ was obtained, however, from one of the inferior courts, but when it was served upon the United-States Marshal, he refused to obey it, and BOOTH is still confined. Meanwhile, as we learn from the Milwaukee *Free Democrat*, he has brought suits against the United-States District Judge and the Marshal, for false imprisonment, claiming $5,000 damages; and for the penalty of $1,200, given, by a State law, of two years ago, to any person arrested under the Fugitive-Slave Act, after having been discharged on *habeas corpus*. "In these actions," says a Milwaukee correspondent of the New-York *Tribune*, "he must recover, as under the decision of the State Court the commitment affords no justification to the officer committing him." The captain of a militia company, in Milwaukee, having declared that he would not obey the orders of the State Executive, in case of a collision with the Federal Court, the governor disbanded the company.

On the 3rd of April the election was held for a Chief Justice of the State's Supreme Court. The regular Republican candidate, A. S. SLOAN, avowed himself in favor of sustaining the position of the State Court, against the Fugitive-Slave Act, but Judge DIXON — already holding the office temporarily, by the governor's appointment, and known to be for submission to the Federal Court, although personally dissenting from its judgment — was set up by a portion of the party, as an "independent candidate." The Democrats made no nomination, but, joining

23

their whole strength with that of the disaffected Republicans, gave the election to Dixon, by two or three hundred majority, in a poll of 115,000 votes. This, however, still leaves two of the three judges in favor of the State Court's adhering to its own decision.

In Maryland, the governor's message, sent to the Legislature last January, referred to the events at Harper's Ferry as a reason for thoroughly reörganizing the State militia. It recommended, also, further legislation in regard to the free colored population; and asked for an appropriation to pay the cost of carrying the case of MYERS, convicted of kidnapping, in Pennsylvania, to the United-States Supreme Court, in order to test the validity of the law under which he was convicted.* The Senate adopted resolutions requesting the representatives of the State to take steps for calling on the Government to negotiate with Great Britain for the restoration of the Slave property of American citizens, which may be found in her provinces. Of the action of the Legislature, touching the free colored people, we have already spoken. An attempt to enlist Maryland in the scheme of holding a Southern Convention, to devise measures for protecting the Slave interest against "northern aggression," met with no success.

The Governor of Virginia recommended, in his message to the Legislature, last winter, the appointment of "two most experienced statesmen, to visit the Legislatures of those States which have passed laws to obstruct the execution of the Fugitive-Slave Law, and *insist, in the name of Virginia*, upon their unconditional repeal." So far as we know, no such embassy has been sent. About the middle of January, Mr. MEMMINGER, Commissioner from South Carolina, arrived in Richmond, to invite the coöperation of Virginia in the holding of a Southern Convention, and was received with marked respect by the Legislature. He presented the purposes of his mission in a long and elaborate speech, after which the subject was referred

---

* Since the account of this case, on page 37, was in print, we have learned from the Frederick (Md.) *Examiner*, that shortly after his conviction "MYERS was released from imprisonment, *by arrangement*, upon his own recognizance, which is equivalent to acquittal," and that his victims "have been sold as Slaves, under a decree of the Orphan's Court" of Frederick County; and thus "the difficulty arising from a conflict of laws and jurisdiction between the courts of Maryland and Pennsylvania is *happily* settled." Very happily! especially for the poor, kidnapped colored family.

to a Joint Committee of the two Houses. Two reports were made, a minority of the committee favoring the proposed Convention, that of the majority declaring it inexpedient, and thinking "that efficient coöperation will be more safely obtained by such direct legislative action of the several States as may be necessary and proper, than through the agency of an assemblage which can exercise no legislative powers except to debate and advise." After full consideration, the report of the majority was adopted, whereupon the Richmond *Whig* exultingly exclaimed, "Virginia still occupies her ancient proud position of perfect independence and unsuspected loyalty to the Constitution and the Union; and there let her stand, beside an overwhelming majority of her southern sisters, allowing South Carolina, Alabama, and Mississippi to go out of the Union in a blaze of glory, if they choose. But they will not choose, and there will be an end to the whole matter."

We mentioned, two years ago, the fining of JOHN UNDERWOOD, by the County Court of Prince-William County, for having denied the rightfulness of Slave-holding. The case, it seems, was appealed to the Circuit Court; and a letter from Mr. UNDERWOOD to a friend in New York, in the latter part of May last, states that the decision of the County Court was reversed. With this we learned another fact, which shows the existence of some Anti-Slavery sentiment even in Eastern Virginia. A majority of the voters of Occoquan, Mr. UNDERWOOD's native town, voted for him to represent their district in the Legislature.

In December last, the Legislature of South Carolina unanimously adopted a preamble reciting her affirmation, by the Ordinance of 1852, of her right to secede from the Confederacy whenever she thinks the occasion will justify that act; and resolutions that, in her "deliberate judgment, the Slave-holding States should immediately meet together and concert measures for united action;" that the governor should tell them so, and ask them to appoint deputies to such a meeting; that he should send a special committee to Virginia, to invite her coöperation "in measures of defence;" and that $100,000 be appropriated "for military preparation for any emergency."

The message of the Governor of Florida to the Legislature, last December, denounced "the party dominant throughout the

North" as destitute of fraternal feeling toward the South, and "responsible for JOHN BROWN's scheme of villany and folly;" intimated that such attempts are likely to be repeated, "no one can say how often, while the Union continues;" and expressed a belief that the voice of Florida "should be heard in 'tones not loud but deep,' in favor of an eternal separation from those whose wickedness and fanaticism forbid us longer to live with them in peace and safety;" and a "hope that most of the southern States will not consent to see the General Government pass into hands avowedly hostile to the South." The Legislature adopted resolutions affirming that "the election of a president, committed to interference with Slavery in the States," would warrant the withdrawal of the State from the Union.

A Joint Select Committee of the Legislature of Alabama reported resolutions, a few weeks ago, the final action on which we have not yet seen, asserting the right of any State to secede; that the assaults on Slavery may constrain her to a reluctant but early exercise of that right; that having declared she would not submit to the rule of a northern sectional party, and voted money for military contingencies, she pledges herself to participate, cordially, in all efforts to advance the common interest; and authorizing the governor to appoint deputies to a Southern Convention whenever it may be called." The Governor of Mississippi recommended, last fall, in his message, the passage of a law providing for a State Convention to take part in forming a Southern Confederacy, if a Republican president is elected; and the laying of a tax of twenty-five per cent on all northern manufactures imported into the State; neither of which recommendations, so far as we are informed, has yet been acted on. *The Vicksburg Whig*, said to be the ablest paper in the State, denounced the message as "revolutionary — the very essence of treason;" for which the *Vicksburg Sun*, in turn, denounced the *Whig* as abusing the governor for "hurling his anathemas at the Abolition fanatics of the North." A correspondent of the New-York *Tribune*, writing from Vicksburg, says "*The Whig* speaks the sentiment of the great body of the people of Mississippi." In Louisiana, at the recent session of the Legislature, a bill for transporting to Massachusetts all negroes convicted of capital crimes, passed its first reading, and was referred to the Committee on Federal Relations. If it should become a law, capital crimes would, no doubt, multiply rapidly in Louisiana. .

South Carolina's invitation of the Slave-holding States to a Southern Convention, going to the Governor of Texas, drew from him a long special message to the Legislature, condemning, in the most explicit terms, the project of secession, and somewhat plainly hinting that South Carolina shows a cheap courage in plotting disunion, seeing that several Slave States lie between her and the North, to receive the shock of war before it can reach her. Last December, the Legislature of Missouri, by 82 to 22, refused to charter a Board of Trustees for the building of a University at Jefferson City, because it was to be under the patronage and control of the Methodist Episcopal Church, and would, therefore, the opponents of the charter contended, promote a "Free-Soil sentiment" in Missouri. Two years ago an application for the same purpose was rejected by 92 to 16, so that a little progress seems to have been made. The Legislature of Kentucky has unanimously passed a resolution calling on the General Government to obtain from Great Britain a treaty stipulation for the surrender of fugitives from Slavery, as she now surrenders fugitives from justice. A bill has been introduced to repeal the law of 1833, which forbade the importation of Slaves into Kentucky, for purposes of traffic. It meets much opposition. The Southern-Convention scheme seems to have found no favor in Kentucky. The same appears to be true of Missouri, Tennessee, and North Carolina, at least, if not of others besides the States already mentioned as refusing to give it countenance.

The people of Nebraska, at their recent territorial election, responded to Governor BLACK's veto of the bill forbidding Slavery in that Territory, by giving a strong majority against Slavery extension. More than three-fifths of the members chosen to the Convention for framing a State Constitution are in favor of making of the Territory a Free State.

It may be worthy of mention, as a sign of hopeful import, that during the past year Republican State Conventions have been held in no less than five Slave-holding States — Delaware, Maryland, Virginia, Kentucky, and Missouri, — for the purpose of organizing resistance, if not to Slavery where it is, at least to its further spread. In Kentucky, moreover, the Republicans of Campbell and Kenton Counties have organized under the name of "The Free-State Party of Kentucky," for the purpose, among other things, of promoting emancipation in that State. Among the resolutions, also, of the Republican State Convention, in Missouri, on the 10th of last March, was one "recognizing the irrepressible character of the conflict between Free and Slave labor," in that State, and avowing the purpose "to maintain in that conflict, the cause of Free labor."

The Church.

The relation of the ecclesiastical bodies in this country, to the Slave system, is mainly the same as heretofore. Whatever exceptional facts may be scattered here and there, the year just gone has witnessed no such change of attitude or policy on the part of the churches generally, as can relieve them from the long-recorded charge of efficient partnership in the nation's sin. If a few small churches, or some branches of the larger, have spoken of it, and signified a purpose to act toward it, as befits their Christian name and profession, the vast majority still hold their false position; and even of the few which have seemed to take a better, some, if not most, have, in great measure, neutralized their right words by neglecting to follow them up with corresponding action.

In the Methodist Episcopal Church the struggle still goes on between those who wish to banish Slavery utterly from their communion, and those who persist in letting it remain therein, though all the while protesting, most of them, that they are by no means Pro-Slavery. *The Northern Independent* stoutly combats the assertions of a portion of its northern brethren, "that there is little or no Slave-holding in the South-Western Border Conferences;" and cites, from the organs of the Church, admissions and affirmations which confirm its own statements. "The [Missouri] *Central Christian Advocate*," it says, "not only dares not deny, but actually concedes, that our ministers and missionaries, in that region, admit Slave-holders into the Church." It also quotes a correspondent of the *Advocate*, who, writing, in July last, from South-Western Missouri, hopes there is "patriotism enough at the North to check rampant Abolition-ism," and says, " I have good reason to believe that *many* Slave-holders with whom I am acquainted, members of our Church and of other churches, are good Christians." A correspondent of the *Independent* itself, writing from Missouri, on the 28th of June, says that "members of the Methodist Episcopal Church here are engaged in the Slave traffic. Not a word is ever said, in or out of the pulpit, against Slavery, nor dare they." The *Independent* adds, in some comments on the letter, " our rule against the traffic in Slaves is well known to be a dead letter. It does no good; it is of no use to forbid the traffic in stolen goods, so long as we do not forbid, but encourage stealing itself."

In the course of a debate in the New-York Conference, a few days ago, on the question of so amending the rule on Slavery as to forbid both Slave-holding and Slave-trading, Rev. Mr. PECK said, "in 1844 the Church stood about right on this subject. Since then, the North had gone to one extreme, and the South were driven to the other." [The North *had gone ;* the South *were driven.*] " Let us leave this question to God. If we go more strongly against Slavery we throw a gloom on the whole Southern Church." Rev. Mr. POYSON, coming from a "border experience of twenty years," said, " from the information he was constantly receiving from the border Church, that it was as much as the Church could do to exist under the present rule of discipline. Make the rule stronger, and another division in the great Methodist Church, of this land, was inevitable. [Voices — That's so!]" Rev. Mr. WHEATLEY said that "the peninsula between Delaware and Chesapeake Bays was inhabited by hundreds of Slave-holders, who bought, sold, and flogged, men, women, and children, and yet were in full communion with the Methodist Church." He was willing that they should secede, and if they would not, that they should be made to go. [Loud *amens.*] Rev. Mr. KETTELL contended that "Slavery, as it now exists, is not a sin," and " affirmed, most emphatically, that, under God's providence, Slavery in America had been the only thing which had elevated the negro race. Mr. WESLEY must have been blinded by prejudice, or he never would have said that 'American Slavery was the vilest system under the sun.' The wealth flowing to us from the southern cotton-crop alone kept alive our institutions and so-called elevation." Rev. Dr OSBORN thought "the sin of our position with regard to Slavery could n't be so very awful, or else God would show it by withholding some of the blessings which he now showered upon us." [The Rev. Dr. ought to be invited to preach from the text, "Because sentence against an evil work is not executed speedily, therefore the heart of the sons of men is fully set in them to do evil."] Rev. Mr. GORSE "would like to have his brothers tell him whether Slavery was not recognized by the apostles. Had not the Slavery discussion produced a monomania in the minds of such men as WENDELL PHILLIPS, GARRISON, and others?"

The Kentucky Annual Conference, which met a few weeks ago, declared unanimously against making the general rule on the subject of Slavery more stringent; being careful, however, to say that "although citizens of Kentucky, we are not the advocates of Slavery. We believe it to be morally wrong, and relatively mischievous in all its tendencies. We consider it an evil, even in its most tolerable aspects." But "the question of remedy" they leave "to the developments of the future, and the righteous workings of an overruling Providence;" only premising that "the remedy must be gradual."

Last summer, the friends of the movement against Slavery in the Methodist Church prepared and sent to the British Wesleyan Conference, and to Wesleyan bodies in other countries, an "Appeal to all members of the great Methodist family, affiliating with the Methodist Episcopal Church, throughout the world." Its purpose was to induce the sending of delegates or memorials from all these bodies to the General Conference, in this country, this spring, "to cast the weight of their influence into the scale of humanity and justice in the approaching contest." In this Appeal they say that, in the Methodist Episcopal Church North, "we have thousands of Slave-holders; trustees, stewards, leaders, and local preachers, and even travelling preachers have become Slave-holders, in several instances, and are such still, with but little disapprobation, as a general thing, on the part of the Conferences to which they belong. And a portion of the ministry, especially in the Slave States, are strongly opposed to any ecclesiastical action that will exclude Slave-holders from the Church, or even condemn the practice of

Slave-holding." That the Appeal is signed by only 241 of the 14,000 ministers (travelling and local) in the Methodist Church North, is a fact not so full of promise as could be desired, for the success of the effort which it aims to help. Nor is it a favorable indication that Mr. HOSMER, editor of the *Northern Independent*, was defeated in the election for delegate from Western New-York to the General Conference; and the same "conservative" was chosen, who, nearly four years ago, was appointed to displace him as editor of the local organ of his Annual Conference. Against this, however, may be set the failure of Rev. ABEL STEVENS, the eminently "conservative" editor of the grand organ of American Methodism, the New-York *Christian Advocate and Journal*, to be chosen delegate from his — the Providence — Annual Conference, which gave him but 15 votes, against 91 for his successful competitor.

Last fall, an article in *Harper's Weekly*, which the New-York *Tribune* says "may be regarded as a sort of manifesto of the Opposition," urged, among other reasons for not pressing the proposed amendments of the Discipline, that, besides the masters of the 30,000 Slaves, estimated to be held by members of the Methodist Church North, large bodies of "conservative laymen," in all the large cities and some of the rural districts, will join in a new secession rather than submit to the suggested changes; and that the bulk of the contributors for the payment of ministers' salaries and other church-expenses, and of the interest on church-debts for which most of the Methodist meeting-houses are mortgaged, are so strongly opposed to the new rule that, if it is adopted, they will contribute no further toward the interest on the debt, but will let the church-buildings be sold under foreclosure of the mortgages. Thus, if these statements are true, the General Conference is, in effect, called on to choose whether it will have meeting-houses in which to preach a corrupt religion, or a pure religion and no meeting-houses wherein to preach it. The threatened secession on the border appears to have begun, already, in Virginia. On Sunday, the 5th of February last, "two large and influential churches in Accomac County," against the earnest opposition of the pastor and presiding elder, "seceded from the Philadelphia Conference, and joined the Virginia Conference of the Methodist Episcopal Church South."

A slight exhibition of the spirit of the Methodist Church South is given in a letter from JAMES C. WILSON, one of its ministers in Texas, to its organ in that State, the *Texas Advocate*. *Zion's Herald* having asked if men in Texas, who disapprove Slavery, may not form an association and hold meetings from which they exclude Slave-holders, WILSON answers, "No, forever no! Texas is a Slave-holding State, every inch of her wide domain is Slave soil, and, by the blessing of God, shall be." Slavery, he calls "that gracious and benevolent system which elevates the heathen cannibal and his children into the civilized, intelligent, contented, and happy domestics who surround us; * * * * nay more, into humble, simple, faithful, and most joyous worshippers of the true and everlasting God. Bless God for such a system!" he fervently and piously exclaims. But he does *not* say why it is necessary, after these "heathen cannibals" have become civilized, intelligent, humble, pious, faithful, and all that, it should still be necessary to *keep* them Slaves. He continues, "the people of Texas are Pro-Slavery, through and through; we don't apologize for negro Slavery — we glory in it; and no society can or shall exist within our wide-extended border which disqualifies or stigmatizes the Slave-holder." Addressing the editor, he says, "neither you nor any other man has said, or is likely to say, in print, one-half as much as the Methodist Church and the people at large, in Texas, feel on the subject."

The General Assembly of the Old-School Presbyterian Church met, about the first of last June, at Indianapolis. Its action, so far as it bore on the Slave question, confirmed the testimony we have given, heretofore, against it. *The Free-Church Portfolio*, whose editor formerly belonged to the Old-School body, and is thoroughly acquainted with its condition, classes its members as "Anti-Slavery men, who honestly believe the testimony of 1818, that Slavery is a sin, and ought to be put out of the communion of the Church; Pro-Slavery men, who pretend to believe that Slavery is right, and a Bible institution, a blessing to the master and a still greater blessing to the Slave; and Hunkers, who have not one particle of heart or of conscience in regard to the wrongs of the Slave, but who are eaten up with the spirit of Church extension and aggrandizement." This last class "is headed by Dr. RICE, of Chicago, who proved himself, at the last General Assembly, the Autocrat of the Presbyterian Church. He has made war upon the Anti-Slavery party, and completely crushed it for the time being." The main contest at that meeting of the Assembly appears to have been for the control of the North-Western Seminary, an institution planned by "the Anti-Slavery party," to be established at Chicago, under the care of the Synods of the North-West instead of the General Assembly; with "Drs. M'MASTER and THOMAS, two men as finished scholars, and as well fitted for their posts, as the Church could produce," for Professors; and with the purpose of inculcating the doctrines of the testimony of 1818 upon theological students who are to be the future pastors of the churches. But Dr. RICE managed to get the contemplated Seminary out of the hands of the Synods, and under the care of the General Assembly, and to have himself elected to the most important chair in the Theological Faculty; while "Dr. THOMAS's name was not even mentioned, and Dr. M'MASTER received scarcely what the politicians call a complimentary vote." *The Portfolio* adds that "before the vote was taken, Dr. M'MASTER delivered a speech, in which he showed up the design of the Slave-power in subjugating the Church by this movement. It justifies all we have said, and more, as to the 'impudent domination' of the Slave-power in the affairs of the Old-School Church." As one of the "straws" which "show which way the wind blows," we may mention that, not long before the sitting of the Assembly, the Secretary of its Board of Domestic Missions refused to commission, as a missionary to California, a young minister educated at Princeton; telling him that "the funds were very low;"—a falsehood, for $25,000 were then lying unused in the treasury—but saying to others, who asked the reason of his refusal, that something in the young man's character was so bad he could not mention it. This "something," Dr. VANDYKE, of Brooklyn, N. Y., told the Assembly that he had found, on investigation, to be that the applicant was an Abolitionist.

The New-School General Assembly met at Wilmington, Del., on the 19th of May. From the *Free-Church Portfolio* we learn that "at the suggestion of certain New-School brethren, who desired the Free Presbyterians to unite with them, the Free Synod sent an overture to the Assembly, proposing terms

of union." But, through the fearfulness or indifference of the
committee into whose hands it went, it "was smothered to
death, and never saw the light. The Assembly knew nothing
of it." The reason for suppressing it, the *Portfolio* says, as
given in a private remark of a member of the Assembly, who
had seen it, was that "from the premises of 1818, it travels on
to the conclusion that Slave-holders should be kept out of the
Church, as relentlessly as death follows its victim to the grave.
But we cannot take any higher ground than we occupy without
endangering our peace, if not our existence." The *Portfolio*
also states that "on the roll of the late Assembly were the
names of the Synods and Presbyteries which went off in the
Ross and Netherland stampede, at Cleveland. Had they all
come back with their Slaves and Slavery defences, they would
have been received with open arms. * * * * * * In the parlor,
the New-School men claim to be good Anti-Slavery men. But
they are Anti-Slavery men after the order of Saint Nicodemus.
You might listen to their preaching and their prayers for many
a long year without ever dreaming that there were four million
of Slaves in the United States, living and dying like heathens."
Statements of two facts which, taken together, are eminently
significant, are at this moment before us. Last summer, or fall,
STEPHEN BREWER, of Cortland, N. Y., for having sometimes
gone, on Sundays, to hear lectures from WENDELL PHILLIPS,
R. W. EMERSON, GEORGE WM. CURTIS, and others, was excommunicated from the Presbyterian Church, in Cortland, on a
charge of Sabbath-breaking and neglect of Christian ordinances;
and, on appeal, the Presbytery and the Synod successively confirmed the sentence. A few weeks ago, the Natchez (Miss.)
Courier disclosed the fact that the Rev. GEORGE POTTS, D. D.,
pastor of a wealthy and fashionable New-School Presbyterian
Church, in New-York City, but formerly resident in Mississippi,
foreclosed, in 1853, since he came North, a mortgage on fifty-
six Slaves and their issue, and sold the Slaves, in January, 1854,
for about $40,000. We have not yet heard that the Rev. Dr.
has lost ecclesiastical, clerical, or social standing on account of
this little business transaction.

From a report made to the General Assembly of the Cumberland Presbyterian Church, at its session in Evansville, Ia., on
the 28th of May, it appears that the late treasurer of the

Assembly, having died a defaulter, the trustees obtained judgment and execution against his estate, and, levying upon certain Slaves thereto belonging, sold them at auction for the Assembly's benefit. The money thus obtained is to go into the missionary treasury — so much of it, at least, as shall not be consumed in the litigation which we hear is likely to grow out of the proceeding. Whether "robbery for a burnt-offering" is more acceptable now, to Him whom the Cumberland Presbyterians profess to worship, than it was in the days of the old prophets, is a question which the General Assembly, perhaps, forgot to consider.

On the 29th of last September, in the Diocesan Convention of the Protestant Episcopal Church, in the Diocese of New York, JOHN JAY presented a petition from several members of the Church in that Diocese, whom he described as "men of high character and position among us, and well known for their moderate views and conservative principles, who have no wish to disturb the tranquillity of the Church." They referred to the fact, "recently made matter of public notoriety," that "the African Slave-trade hath been reöpened and is now prosecuted from the port of New York, within the jurisdiction of this Diocese;" that "the legalizing of said traffic is openly advocated, and the laws denouncing it as piracy are trampled on with impunity;" and they respectfully prayed the Convention "to take such step as should, to its wisdom, seem meet, to encourage a sound, Christian sentiment on this subject, to the intent that the city of New York may be purged of its participation in this stupendous crime." Mr. JAY moved that the petition be referred to a committee of three clergymen and three laymen, to report at the next Convention; and spoke briefly and well in support of his motion. The *Tribune* says, "the petition created quite a sensation in the Convention, and was received with a sound of suppressed laughter, and a slight attempt at hissing. When the question came to a vote, the resolution was rejected by a very decided majority, and only the sacredness of the place kept the applause from breaking forth at this result." Comely, and pleasant to behold, are dignity and decorum, and a tender reverence for sacred things!

From the *American Baptist*, an Anti-Slavery Baptist journal, published in New-York city, we learn that the American Bible

24

Union, an association, under Baptist auspices, for preparing and publishing a revised edition of the Bible, has lately put forth the Epistle to Philemon, with an elaborate commentary, aiming to prove "that Onesimus was an absconding Slave; Philemon, a Christian Slave-holder; and that Paul returned the Slave to his rightful master." Southern papers announce that, to counteract the writings of moderate men, like WAYLAND, a new work on Moral Science, by J. L. DAGG, D. D., President of Mercer University, is soon to appear, and is to be introduced into all the southern Baptist colleges; and that, so conclusive are its reasonings, it is expected to be favorably received at the North also. It "blows to the winds the doctrine of 'equality of rights,'" maintaining, "with much force, the south-side view of the Slavery question." We are told that it "is destined to be the standard in all our southern colleges, and will be used extensively at the North and West." Whether this prediction will be verified or not, we apprehend that writing such a book, using it as a text-book of moral science, or putting its lessons in practice, would be no bar to ecclesiastical fellowship with a majority of Baptists at the North; whereas, to advocate or practice communion with persons not immersed, would incur excommunication. On the Slavery question, says the *American Baptist*, "the southern Baptist papers are a unit; they are all on the side of the oppressor. Northern societies pay court to their brethren of the South, and open wide their arms to solicit their coöperation, but the South repudiates all union, even with our professedly neutral organizations." On the other hand, we sometimes meet such testimonies as the Warren (R. I.) Association bore, last fall, in the name of its thirty-eight Baptist churches, and more than seven thousand communicants, by adopting, on motion of CHARLES HOWARD MALCOM, of Newport, a resolution avowing sympathy with the oppressed, and declaring "that we will use every means within our power, civil and religious, to bring about the ultimate removal from our country of a system which, judged by the teachings of Jesus, is cruel towards men and offensive to God."

The Congregational Association of the State of New York, at its last meeting, resolved "that the holding of human beings as property is an immorality, the renunciation of which ought to be made a condition of membership in the Christian Church, and that this sin is one against which the Law of God and the Gospel of Christ ought to be proclaimed, in preaching, persistently, until the iniquity be overthrown." Whatever credit for Anti-Slavery growth is due to those who passed this resolution, the great body of the Congregational churches are far below the standard of duty, certainly by no means extravagantly high, which it sets up. Few, indeed, are the churches of that sect which practically accept it, with all its logical consequences; which treat Slave-holding as a sin, shut the Slave-holder from the privileges appertaining to church-membership, and "persistently proclaim the Law of God and the Gospel of Christ against his transgression." An allusion, now and then, in a sermon or a prayer, to Slavery as not altogether right and Christian, even the preaching of a whole sermon about it on the annual Fast, or Thanksgiving-day, goes but a little way towards that *persistent* proclamation which the resolution recognizes as a duty. Yet even this, we fear, is more than the majority are prepared to do, while many still persist in advocating or apologizing for the wrong, or holding fellowship with those who do so, and by far the greater part continue to sustain such Pro-Slavery organizations as the Tract Societies and Mission Boards. It is a sadly significant fact, moreover, that the one soundly "evangelical" Congregational church in the city of New York, whose pulpit *does* "persistently proclaim the Law of God and the Gospel of Christ against the sin" of holding men as property, suffers, from those of its own theological household, such persecution as this age permits; and finds so little favor among professors of Congregational Christianity here, that it is obliged to seek pecuniary aid in a foreign land, to keep it from dying, as it were, of sheer starvation. Meanwhile the Rev. Dr. LORD holds the presidency of Dartmouth College, and the high esteem of the New-England churches and their clergy, although he is notoriously a defender of Slavery as right and Christian, and predicts its prevalence in New England within "another eighty years;" and his son, the Rev. W. H. LORD, keeps his place as the popular and honored pastor of a Congregational church in the capital of Vermont, preaching there, as we are told he did last Fast-day, "that Slavery is not a wrong or sin;" and the General Association of Congregational Ministers of Massachusetts chooses Pro-Slavery Dr. BLAGDEN for its Mode-

rator, and sends a delegate to the New-School Presbyterian
General Assembly, which expresses its "cordial confidence in
the New-England Congregationalists," and in return is congratulated in their name, by their representative, "on its present
noble position and past record on the subject of Slavery;" and
three Rev. Doctors, BLAGDEN, South-side ADAMS, and TODD,
with other representatives of New-England Congregationalism,
are invited to Charleston, S. C., and heartily made welcome
there, as helpers in the installation of a Massachusetts clergyman over a Charleston church and congregation, with no peril
to their standing in the ministry, the Church, or the religious
society of the North on account of their fraternizing with those
who hold, in theory and practice, the blasphemous heresy which
calls Slavery divine; and Young Men's Christian Associations
at the North commission delegates to a Convention of Young
Men's Christian Associations to be gathered in New Orleans,
although those delegates must submit to the indignity of being
certificated by a magistrate, as untainted with notions dangerous to the cherished southern system; and the spirit of Hindoo
caste, embodied in the "negro pew," still holds its ground in
some of the Congregational churches of highest repute in our
great northern cities, and, among them, in that where ministers
a Rev. Dr. understood to be chief editor of the probably most
widely-circulated and influential Congregational journal in the
country, claiming withal to be the most Anti-Slavery organ of
its sect; and other tokens, more than we have space to name,
concur with these to show that this sect, as a whole, is in substantially the same condemnation as its sister sects of which we
have spoken.   Even HENRY WARD BEECHER's church, which
many have supposed to be over-zealously Anti-Slavery, continues to contribute money, and of course to give moral support,
to the American Board of Foreign Missions.   A movement
made last winter, for the discontinuance of the customary yearly
contribution to the Board, was defeated through the strenuous
exertions and great personal influence of the pastor, though it
was nobly sustained by a minority, strong in worth if not in
numbers, whose views found eloquent utterance and a masterly
vindication, from the lips of THEODORE TILTON.   His victory
in the argument was so complete that it would probably have
won the vote also, but for the personal regard of the members

of the church for their pastor. But whatever was their motive, their act was a recognition of the Board as Christian in its attitude and policy, and, in the words of Mr. BEECHER, as having "reached a ground of the most positive and substantive Anti-Slavery truth;" although the very documents quoted from, to prove this, show that the Board concedes that Slaves *may* be held without offending "against the law of Christian right;" that in possible cases its missionaries may properly employ Slave-labor; that they must act on their own judgment, "under a sense of responsibility to Christ," in regard to admitting Slave-holders into the mission churches; and that they cannot exercise discipline for the mere buying and selling of Slaves, or for the separation of parents and children by sale or purchase; not to mention other points in perfect keeping with these.

In showing how far the American Church is implicated in the Slave system, Mr. TILTON cited "an authentic table of statistics," from which it appears that ministers and members of the Methodist Church, North and South, hold 219,000 Slaves; of the Presbyterian Church, Old-School and New, 77,000; Baptists, 125,000; Reformed Baptists [not past the need of further reformation], 101,000; Episcopalians, 88,000; and all other denominations, 55,000; making 665,000 human beings held as chattels by members of self-styled Christian Churches in this country. Now, by the ecclesiastical law and usage of nearly all the sects, the holders of this multitude of Slaves are in religious fellowship with an overwhelming majority of the professed Christians of the country; or, if any of them are not, it is for wholly other reasons than their Slave-holding.

The Church Anti-Slavery Society has been at work during the year — we hope not altogether in vain — to bring "the Church" into "its true position in relation to this great problem of our land and age;" but if its success, or the aid or countenance given it by the churches, has been at all commensurate with its good intentions, the pleasant news has not yet reached us. We learn, on the other hand, from "a distinguished clergyman," who was active in organizing the Society, that "many of the New-England ministers refuse to come upon its platform, because its cardinal doctrine is that Slavery is *malum in se*." It was announced, indeed, last summer — as a cheering sign of the movement's having "fairly begun," by which "Orthodoxy in

Massachusetts is redeeming itself" — that one church of two hundred and fourteen members, in Worcester, Mass., had, after three weeks' discussion, unanimously adopted resolutions renouncing all fellowship with Slave-holders, and with all who knowingly and persistently uphold or countenance Slavery; and declaring that individuals or churches failing to yield all their influence to destroy the abomination of Slavery, must be treated as none of Christ's. But it afterward came out that, of the two hundred and fourteen members, only fifteen voted on the adoption of the resolutions; that, shortly after, a motion to suspend the monthly collections for the American Board, while it maintains a Pro-Slavery attitude, was opposed by the pastor, and rejected by a vote of 21 to 7; and though subsequently it was voted by 14 to 11, to omit the *next* monthly collection, with an understanding that the action of the Board at its then approaching meeting should determine the future course of the church, yet the pastor gave notice that all who chose might hand their contributions for the Board to the treasurer of the church, and it was boasted that the collection, which was to have been omitted, was a larger one than usual.

On the 10th and 11th of last August, a Convention, summoned by a call addressed "to Anti-Slavery Christians throughout the State" of Ohio, was held at Columbus, "to pray, deliberate, and give public expression against Slavery." It was "well attended, particularly by ministers," and from the southern as well as the northern part of the State, showing, we are told, "that the Anti-Slavery sentiment is diffused all over the State." Resolutions were adopted, that Liberty is the law of Nature and the clearly revealed will of God; that Slavery is a most momentous crime, and its turpitude rests on all who, in any way, help enslave or reënslave human beings; that government cannot legalize it; that the Fugitive-Slave Act has no essential element of law, and gives no right to reënslave, and imposes no duty to submit to reënslavement; that voluntary agency by a church member in the rendition of a Fugitive Slave deserves excommunication, and the Zanesville Baptist Church did right in excommunicating a member who, as United-States Marshal, restored a fugitive to his claimant; that the example of the Oberlin-Wellington rescuers is worthy of commendation, and calls for gratitude to God; and that Christians and Christian ministers ought to bear faithful testimony against the sin of Slavery, ecclesiastically, socially, and politically, through pulpit and religious press, and pray importunately for speedy deliverance to those in bonds. A plan of operations for the future was presented by a committee, but we do not learn whether it was adopted. It looked to the appointment of a committee of twelve, from different parts of the State, and different denominations, to employ lecturers, circulate Anti-Slavery publications, enlist the coöperation of churches and ministers, establish, if deemed expedient, "a Christian Anti-Slavery paper," and correspond with friends of the cause in other States, recommending a similar system of action there, and proposing a "Northern Christian Anti-Slavery Convention," to be held late in the autumn.

The Reformed Presbyterian [Old-School Covenanter] Synod, at its meeting in Pittsburg, last June, unanimously resolved that Slavery is " evil in itself," contrary to the divine word, and an outrage on our common humanity; that the Constitution of the United States is its stronghold, and " therefore we will continue to refuse allegiance to it, or obey its unholy requirements;" that the Fugitive-Slave Bill and the Dred-Scott Decision are such perversions of justice as ought to be violated in letter and spirit, and the ministry should direct against them the denunciations of God's word; that as "we discover no hope for the Slave in any of the political organizations of the day, we stand aloof from them, and rely on the power of truth blessed by the Spirit, in the contest with oppression;" that it is " our duty to bear explicit testimony" against ecclesiastical organizations which admit Slave-holders within their pale, and refuse to testify against this evil; that our motto is, "No union with Slave-holders, political or ecclesiastical;" that those who attempt to defend Slavery, from the Bible, are guilty of one of the worst and most dangerous forms of infidelity; and "that we will continue, as God gives us opportunity, to labor and pray for the deliverance of the captives."

THE AMERICAN BOARD.

Our last Report spoke of suggestions, at the last preceding meeting of the American Board, looking to some change whereby "the Board should be relieved from the embarrassments and perplexities" growing out of the tolerance of Slaveholding in the churches of its Indian Missions. The change has since been partly made. At the last Annual Meeting of the Board, held in Philadelphia from the 4th to the 7th of last October, the Prudential Committee reported that they had discontinued the Choctaw Mission. But their reason, plainly, was not that the Mission Church keeps Slave-holders in its communion, nor that the missionaries will not preach, nor that the Indians will not hear, an Anti-Slavery Gospel; for all these exist with equal force in relation to the Cherokee Mission, which is still retained. Besides, the language of the Report implies that Slave-holding is quite compatible with Christian character. "In closing our labors among the Choctaws," it says, "we have the satisfaction of reflecting that a work of permanent value has been accomplished in their behalf. Whatever may be said of other attempts to Christianize the aborigines of our country, there has been *no failure here.*" So, if this boast may be believed, converting men to a religion which permits them to hold and buy and sell Slaves, and to sunder families in the traffic, is "no failure of the attempt to Christianize" them.

So much of the Prudential Committee's Report as related to the Indian Missions, was referred to a Select Committee of seven, with Rev. ALBERT BARNES for Chairman. In the evening of the third day, Mr. BARNES — so widely known as having said that Slavery could not stand a year, but for the support which the Church gives it — presented a majority Report against the discontinuance of the Choctaw Mission, especially as it was proposed "solely on the ground of a difference of opinion between the missionaries and this Board in respect to the manner of preaching the Gospel, or the application of its principles to the evil of Slavery," and recommended the reference of the whole subject to a Special Committee, to report next year, and that meantime the mission receive the usual support. Hon. LINUS CHILD and another member of the Committee joined in a minority Report, speaking of the missionaries among the Choctaws as devoted and faithful men, whose labors have been -blessed of God to the temporal and spiritual welfare of the Choctaw nation, and for whom the Board entertain feelings of the highest respect, confidence, and affection; but adding that, nevertheless, "the termination of their connection will greatly relieve the Board of serious and painful embarrassments.;" and recommending, with regret for the necessity of the movement, that the Board concur in it, but present to the missionaries the usual amount of a year's expenses.

The debate on the Reports continued till after midnight. Mr. CHILD, in defending his Report, represented that the missionaries had not conformed to the principles laid down for their guidance, by the Prudential Committee and the Board, in 1848 and 1854; that they resigned in 1855, because of difference of views between them and the Board, and, when requested to withdraw their resignation, consented on condition "that the Board should withdraw all its past action on the subject of Slavery, and leave the missionaries to act in regard to it according to their enlightened judgment and the principles of the Word of God;" that "it was impossible, for a moment, to entertain this proposition;" that "in 1856 they wrote that they could not conduct the missions on the basis" prescribed in 1848; and that "their last letter, received within two or three months, stated that they adhere to their letter of 1856." He argued that to continue the mission after the missionaries have refused to "conduct it on the principles laid down by the Board in 1848," is to take "the ground that we must not carry out the principles of the Gospel in regard to all sin;" and his conclusion was, not that these missionaries, who stand in the way of so "carrying out the principles of the Gospel," should be dismissed, and better men put in their places; but that "the best which can be done for this mission is to let them seek some other connection. There is another Board all around them. The missionaries are all Old-School Presbyterians, and they can form a connection with that Board." That is, the American Board can best shun "the ground that we must not carry out the principles of the Gospel in regard to all sin," by resigning the Pro-Slavery mission to "another Board," notoriously as hostile as the missionaries themselves are to carrying out those principles against the sin of Slave-holding.

Mr. CHILD did not explain how it happened that these missionaries were still in the service of the Board, three or four years after "it was impossible, for a moment, to entertain" the conditions on which alone they consented to withdraw their resignation. Had he more carefully examined the record, he might have learned that those conditions were not quite what he has stated, and that the Board *did* tacitly accept them, signifying its assent in the very way which the missionaries proposed. In 1856 they wrote to the Prudential Committee, reciting their previously-communicated views — in substance that the Apostles sanctioned Slave-holding in the Church; that Slave-holding, of itself, is not sufficient ground to excommunicate a member or reject a candidate; nor would they discipline for either merely buying and selling Slaves, or selling children from their parents; nor would they adopt any train of measures tending in the end to abolish Slavery — and then added; "If, *with the foregoing views — which are known by the people among whom we labor* — the Prudential Committee should deem it wise to continue our support, we are willing to try to remain in their service. Accordingly, we have estimated our expenses for the ensuing year. If, on the other hand, the Committee should not think it best to retain us, we shall not expect them to grant us the estimates." The *New-York Observer*, of Dec. 2, 1858, tells the result, agreeing, also, with the Annual Report of the Board for 1856. "The Prudential Committee took the subject into consideration, and, *with this letter before them, made the usual appropriations.* The missionaries, being thus left at liberty to pursue their work in their own way, have continued to prosecute their labors with their usual success." This makes quite clear what Mr. CHILD left unexplained, and shows that the Board has taken on itself the responsibility for the missionaries' neglect to "carry out the principles of the Gospel in regard to" Slavery.

Rev. Dr. ANDERSON, senior Secretary, was for discontinuing the mission. "Great difficulties were found in carrying it on. Positive instructions have been given to the missionaries, which they have disregarded. * * * * * * Believing that the mission could get along without us, the Prudential Committee voted to discontinue it." It "could get along without us," the Rev. Dr. evidently expected, in the way just spoken of by Mr. Child, the same which Dr. Bacon hinted at less clearly the year before, that is, by passing into the hands of those who, as Dr. Bacon worded it, "represent Christianity as a warrant for Slavery, and Christ as the minister of sin." But, in talking of "positive instructions" given and disregarded, if the Secretary had in mind, as we suppose he had, "the letter of 1848," the missionaries' disregard of which is the burden of Mr. Child's complaint, he is forgetful of the record, too, beyond what one would look for in a senior secretary. For, in the Annual Report of 1849, the Prudential Committee say emphatically of that letter, "it expressed *opinions*, * * * * * not *decisions* or *instructions*. The Committee have given no *instructions* to the missionaries in relation to Slavery; they say expressly that they address their brethren '*with suggestions and arguments.*'" Of course, then, the missionaries were at liberty to dissent from these opinions, and hold these arguments unsound; and when, having deliberately done so, and told the Board "we will leave your service unless you are willing we should do so still," they are retained, and "the usual appropriations" are made for their support, year after year, where is their disregard of positive instructions? or why attempt to lay on them the whole responsibility for the Pro-Slavery character of the mission, and the "great difficulties" consequently "found in carrying it on?"

Dr. Cheever moved to amend the majority Report by adding "that in the opinion of the Board the holding of Slaves should be pronounced an immorality inconsistent with membership in any Christian church, and that it should be required that these missionary churches should immediately put away from themselves this sin, and should cease to sanction it, even in appearance." He supported the amendment with a strong and characteristic speech, earnestly opposing the surrender of the mission, and urging the expulsion of Slavery from the mission churches. His brother seconded the amendment, but it found no other support. Dr. Bacon opposed it, earnestly deprecated agitation, condemned the missionaries with severity, and wished the matter decided now. The amendment was laid on the table *unanimously;* as was also a resolution from

HENRY T. CHEEVER, instructing the Prudential Committee to carry on the Choctaw Mission, employing missionaries who will comply with the Committee's instructions. Both Reports were also laid on the table; and, more than half an hour past midnight, the Report of the Prudential Committee was approved, adopted, and ordered to be printed. So the Board ratified the discontinuance of the Choctaw Mission, leaving its uncured patients to the care of doctors who regard the flush of fever as the glow of ruddy health; and congratulating itself that, if it has not put away the sin of its complicity with Slave-holding, it is, at least, "relieved of the serious embarrassments" which have troubled it so long. But why it should be so relieved, we do not clearly see, so long as it continues in the same relation to Slave-holding in the Cherokee Mission, which it has just abandoned in the Choctaw.

On the morning of the third day of the session, Dr. CHEEVER created an intense excitement by presenting, for adoption by the Board, a memorial to Congress, setting forth that one of the principal obstructions to the progress of civilization and Christianity in Africa is the Slave-trade there, which owes its origin and prevalence chiefly to the foreign Slave-trade; that citizens of the United States are engaged in this traffic, and are combining to re-legalize it; and that the memorialists, in view of this crime and sin, and their disastrous effects on their own country, as well as upon their missions in Africa, entreat that the law against the trade be rigorously enforced, and the country be saved from the disgrace of renewing it, and from the displeasure of the Supreme Ruler.

Dr. ANDERSON said, "this subject is much in the way among some of the missions. It is, in fact, a question whether the Board should not withdraw from the African Mission, on account of the revival of the Slave-trade. [Withdrawal seems to be the Rev. Doctor's favorite plan in cases of difficulty. "Flee from the devil, if he resists you," appears to be his reading of St. James.] Something should be done, but he was not prepared to say whether the Board should memorialize Congress. If it was done, a memorial should be drawn up containing no expression objectionable to any member of the Board. [Not even to Dr. ADAMS, whose South-side View suggested the expediency of reöpening the trade in question.] He thought the best way would be to refer the whole matter to a committee, to be reported on next year." Chancellor WALWORTH called the memorial "a fire-brand," and, to get rid of it, "would have moved the previous question at once, had he gained the attention of the Board in time." Though "he abhorred the Slave-trade as much as any one, he feared if the memorial was referred to a special committee for the year, the motive would be misconstrued, and collections in the churches greatly impaired." About a dozen members, eight of whom were Rev. Doctors, having spoken on the subject, and only one "in favor of some proper action," without postponement, the memorial was referred to the Business Committee, which reported, the next morning, by preamble and resolution, the Board's "unqualified condemnation of the African Slave-trade," and "liveliest regret and alarm at the disposition manifested to revive it, especially in view of its interfering with the missionary work;" yet that, for want of "time to deliberate and determine properly upon the course to be pursued in so grave a matter, the whole subject be referred to the Prudential Committee," for such action as, in their judgment, its relation to their work demands. This Report was adopted unanimously, without discussion.

The Board reëlected its Pro-Slavery officers, including the Rev. Doctor of the South-side View, as, of course, was altogether fitting. Its last action was a unanimous vote that the Prudential Committee make arrangements, annually, for a delegation to the General Assembly of the (Pro-Slavery) Presbyterian Church.

Among the consequences of the Board's decision to give up the Choctaw Mission — not to mention the lamentations of the *New - York Observer*, and the objurgations of the *Journal of Commerce* — was a Convention of Old-School Presbyterians, called by Rev. Dr. SPRING, of New York, and held in that city, on the 7th of last March. One of the resolutions reported by Dr. SPRING, as Chairman of the Committee on Resolutions, affirmed that, on the subject of Slavery, the Presbyterian Church is, and ought to be, controlled by the example of Christ and his Apostles; that the Scriptures give no authority for regarding a Slave-holder as an outcast from Christ's kingdom; that no church ought to be regarded as unchristianized because

25

some of its members are Slave-holders, and such a principle is
subversive of the spirit of missions; and to deny the Gospel to
a Slave-holding community is a most unwise method of amelio-
rating the evils of Slavery. The discussion to which this led,
as sketched by the *New-York Evangelist*, is eminently instruc-
tive in regard to the character of that guardianship to which
the Choctaw Mission has been resigned. Rev. Dr. MURRAY, of
New Jersey, opposed the resolution. "It would produce useless
agitation. The true policy was, not to agitate the subject of
Slavery. We must act discreetly, and many from New England
and elsewhere would contribute. He had little doubt that the
$8,000 [to support the Mission] would be given by those who
had not heretofore contributed to the Presbyterian Board.
There were differences, however, on the subject of Slavery, and
it would be *impolitic* to endorse it thus without qualification.
The passage of the resolution would greatly lessen our prospects
in New England and elsewhere." DANIEL LORD, Esq., "took
the same view, although he thought Slavery, as a tutelage, was
often a benefit to the inferior race. But some in the church
would regret the adoption of this resolution, as an unqualified
endorsement of Slavery. Many of our churches contain a large
proportion of New-England men, Scotchmen, and Scotch Irish.
Let us not scatter firebrands among them." ELEAZAR LORD
"thought every man who comes into the Presbyterian Church
ought to know that we will not have discussion on this subject.
The resolution accords with the views of the Church. The
being a Slave-holder is not matter of controversy or church
recognition." Dr. SPRING said "the Presbyterian Church is
called upon to take sides in this controversy. He did not fear
the result on the churches, congregations, or General Assembly.
These were all with them." A pastor from New Jersey said
"there were strong Abolitionists in his church, who would be
offended if this resolution was passed." Dr. McELROY regarded
it as "simply a question of expediency. There was not a principle in the resolution which all did not know the Presbyterian
Church holds to. The question was whether the views should
be thrown out at this juncture. He *had bought and sold
Slaves*, and under similar circumstances would do so again.
He preached the same views from his pulpit." Dr. PLUMER
"hoped the Convention would take no Pro-Slavery or Abolition

ground. They were merely to say to those who have contributed to the American Board, but are now dissatisfied, we are in a way to receive your aid, without annoying you with further agitation." Finally, on report of a committee to whom the subject was referred, resolutions were adopted, declaring "that the Convention recognizes no standard in the missionary enterprise, but the conduct and instructions of Christ and his Apostles; that the missions of the Presbyterian Church have been conducted on this principle; that the existence of Slavery in the community, and of Slave-holders in the Church, is no ground for withdrawing the Gospel from them; that, in their conduct of the Choctaw Mission, the beloved and honored missionaries of the American Board had never departed from these principles; and that in so modestly and firmly adhering to them, at every sacrifice, they deserve our implicit confidence, and shall receive our hearty support and patronage."

THE TRACT SOCIETIES.

The last Annual Meeting of the American Tract Society was held in New-York City, on the 11th of last May. Immediately after the opening exercises, and a brief statement by the chairman of the Executive Committee, reviewing the doings of the Society since it began, thirty-four years ago, during which time no word of dissension had been heard among the members of the committee, Rev. Dr. McGEE moved that the officers of the preceding year, except the Executive Committee, be reëlected. Mr. BENEDICT, rising to move, instead, a resolution to instruct the officers as to their conduct of the Society's affairs, was interrupted by cries of "Order," and, the chair deciding him out of order, he sat down. Then Rev. Dr. PATTON took the floor, and moved to postpone Dr. McGEE's motion, in order to offer a resolution which, amid wild confusion, hisses, whistling, cries of "Order," "Sit down," and "Question," he tried to read. For some time his voice was drowned by the clamor, but at last, at the suggestion of Rev. Dr. SPRING, the turbulent *conservatives* became quiet long enough for the resolution to be read. It denounced the African Slave-trade as anti-christian and inhuman; spoke of indi-

cations that it is, or is about to be, reöpened by adventurers
from this country; declared that the only barrier to it is the
moral sense enlightened by the Gospel; and directed the
Publishing Committee to issue, during the year, a tract or
tracts adapted to arouse the religious sentiment of Evangelical
Christians against the trade. Dr. PATTON was going on to
speak upon his motion, when the president stopped him, on
the ground that the Society had no right to instruct the committee. A motion to lay the resolution on the table was carried by a very large majority, the vote eliciting "immense
applause."

To avoid the objection to Dr. PATTON's resolution, Mr.
WOLCOTT offered one, the same in substance, except that, instead of instructing the committee, it declared that the publication of the tracts proposed would "meet the warm approbation
of this Society." He attempted to speak, but the tumult was
renewed, and only fragments of sentences could be heard. Dr.
ALEXANDER thought it out of order to discuss the merits of the
resolution, on the motion to postpone another motion; Mr.
WOLCOTT, trying to explain, was hooted down; and the president sustaining Dr. ALEXANDER's objection, the motion to
postpone Dr. McGEE's motion was put and rejected by a very
large vote, "followed by great applause, with a few hisses."
Another attempt by Mr. WOLCOTT to get a hearing was rudely
clamored down, and the Society, by a vote of 331 to 23, reëlected its old officers, including Dr. South-side ADAMS, and adding
WM. C. ALEXANDER, of New Jersey, as vice president, and
CHRISTOPHER B. GASTON, of Charleston, as director.

Mr. JOHN JAY then offered a resolution, which recited the
famous fourth resolution of 1857, about the duty of fraternally
discussing the duties and evils growing out of Slavery; alluded
to the "special apology" offered in 1858, for the non-perform-
ance of that duty in the year then past; affirmed that no
sufficient reasons now appear for continuing to neglect it, while
there are weighty reasons for the prompt fulfilment of it; and
concluded by instructing the Publishing Committee to publish,
during the coming year, one or more tracts on the moral evils
and vices which Slavery is known to promote, and which are
so much deplored by Evangelical Christians. DANIEL LORD,
Esq., a Pro-Slavery lawyer of some note, retained, it is said, by

the Tract-House managers, to defend their policy, immediately took the floor against the resolution, and contended that the Society has no right to instruct its officers, its functions being only to elect them; then they are to do the work, according to their own discretion. Afraid to expose his sophistry to the ordeal of a reply, he closed with the undebatable motion — with a view, he said, to make it a test question for this time and for all time — that Mr. JAY's resolution be laid on the table; and thus, by a cowardly and dishonorable trick, quite worthy of his cause and of his argument, put a sudden end to the discussion. Rev. Dr. THOMPSON asked if he meant to cut off all debate. "In this meeting, I do," he promptly answered. "You can get enough of it in the *Independent*." Mr. JAY claimed the right to speak, but his voice was drowned by loud cries and hisses, and, amid the utmost confusion, Mr. LORD's motion was put and carried by a large majority.

When the clamor had somewhat subsided, Mr. WOLCOTT renewed his attempt to present his resolution touching the Slave-trade; and, after persevering for some time through a storm of cries and groans and hisses, succeeded in reading it and saying a few words upon it. As to the impossibility of circulating tracts, he said that the first order for a thousand copies of a tract published by the Boston Society, after this Society had refused to publish it, came from the South. Rev. R. W. CLARK supported the resolution, said the Society had published tracts on specific sins, was convinced that by adopting this resolution it would plant itself on a rock, but he trembled for its future if it would not utter its sentiments on a traffic which, if reöpened, would peril the existence of the Republic. Mr. HIRAM KETCHUM thought this was not the place to discuss these questions. He loved debate, but if abstract questions were allowed, there was no end of debate. He was not to be told he was a Pro-Slavery man either. After eulogizing some of the southern bishops, and declaring that if there was a successor to the Apostles it was Bishop MEADE, of Virginia, he ended by moving that the resolution be laid on the table. The motion was carried by a large vote. [The Washington *Republic* calls attention to the fact that the preamble to this resolution is precisely the same as of that offered in Congress, by Mr. ETHE-RIDGE, of Tennessee, two years before, and *adopted* by a majority of about two to one. The Tract Society, organized to promote "vital godliness and sound morality," *laid it on the table*, by a large majority!]

Even Dr. SPRING thought this was going rather too far in subserviency to the Slave-power. He was evidently alarmed for the effect it might produce on the public mind at the North. He "regretted that the resolution was proposed, but doubly regretted that the Society should lay it on the table. I accede," he said, "most cordially, to the vote on the question conclusively settled by my learned friend, Mr. LORD, but the gentlemen who differ from us have crowded us into a narrow place here. Will you lay upon your table a resolution simply affirming — without instructing — that it would gratify the Society should the Publishing Committee issue a tract in regard to that accursed traffic? In this nineteenth century, after the noble efforts of such men as CLARKSON and WILBERFORCE, [Ye build the tombs of the prophets!] I am sorry to see the Society hesitate to declare itself against this infernal traffic. You stand on the brink of a deep abyss, and are making shipwreck of morality and God. I think as to Slavery in the southern States, this Society ought to be silent; [Is Slavery less "infernal" than its mere incident, the Slave-trade?] but, on the naked question of approving or disapproving the African Slave-trade, we ought not to be silent." To avoid "such a dilemma," he proposed a resolution, that the Society had not laid the preceding resolution on the table from any doubt in relation to the sin of the African Slave-trade, or the great wickedness of reviving it in any form. This, he said, the Society ought to adopt, in justice to itself and the cause of Christianity. Nothing less would save them from a year of conflict and of deserved obloquy.

Mr. JAY, attempting to speak, was met with another uproar, but, persevering till silence was partially restored, was able to explain, briefly, that his resolution was no new thing, but what the Society had adopted in former years, and now the reasons for such action were ten thousand times stronger than then. He claimed, as a right, that Slavery should be discussed in a Christian and fraternal manner. Rev. Dr. VAN PELT "thought Slavery a controverted question; he was satisfied that God told Moses if the children of Israel wanted Slaves they were to go and buy them of the heathen. If it was right then, why is it not right now?" Whence we infer that the Rev. Dr. does *not* think the African Slave-trade "wicked" and "sinful" and "accursed" and "infernal." Another case of doctors disagreeing; but we must say the Dutch-named Dr. seems to us the more consistent of the two. Mr. HIRAM KETCHUM wished the other Dr. to allow an amendment to his resolution, so as to read "the individual members of the Society." He thought the *Society*, as such, had nothing to do with the subject.

Dr. BACON asked if the Society has no right to express its own opinion, where under heaven it gets the right to express his, as an individual member. "This Society," he continued, "has a tract on the evils of tobacco, yet one of the venerable brethren has, this morning, handed out a paper and asked me to take a quid. We are told the business of the Society is to circulate tracts. It circulates tracts against the use and culture of tobacco; yet of these venerable men who handed us the regular ticket to vote, to-day, how many are there on whose consciences rests the deadly sin of using tobacco! This Society may have and circulate opinions which, if universally adopted, would send desolation through the lower counties of Virginia, and along the banks of the Connecticut; but we are to have no opinion at all about a wickedness which the laws of the United States, for more than forty years, have pronounced to be a crime against human nature — piracy. Is there any member of the Executive Committee of this Society, just reëlected, on whose table sparkles the red wine? I know there is. Any whose parlors echo to the feet of the merry dancers? I know there is. Yet here we bind these burdens about dancing and tobacco and wine-drinking, and lay them on men's shoulders, when ours bear not the least part of that burden. Is it not time to have done with such foolery, and address ourselves to the weightier matters of the law." Referring to the assertion that tracts on Slavery could not be circulated at the South, he said that his son, who was in New Orleans when the South-side View of Slavery was issued by a member of this Publishing Committee, went to the bookstores there to see if it could be found. It was not there; but wherever he went he found Uncle Tom's Cabin. Dr. BACON went on to charge the Society and Executive Committee with faithlessness in regard to the

South, and said the statements of a lack of Anti-Slavery feeling there were slanders upon the best portions of the southern States. [In this part of his remarks he was almost silenced by hisses and cries of " Question," &c.] "A year ago the subject of the African Slave-trade would have been called an abstraction. A year hence it will be a political question. In a year or two more we may have ministers preaching here in New York, 'if you want niggers, go and buy them of the heathen,' that is, of the Africans." He hoped Dr. SPRING'S resolution would be carried, that even that faint testimony of the moral sense of the Society might not be obliterated. Professor CROSBY "looked upon such action as inexpedient. It would open the door for expressions of opinion upon matters which would create even more discussion. Next year they might be called upon to express their opinion upon the introduction of Slavery into the Territories." Rev. Dr. THOMPSON, to show the need of passing such a resolution, referred to the fact that when the Society published Mr. GURNEY'S book on The Love of God, in the passage, "if this love had always prevailed among professing Christians, where would have been the African Slave-trade?" it changed "African Slave-trade" to "tortures of the Inquisition." He thought the passage of this resolution would place the Society right before the community.

After some further discussion the resolution was adopted; thus putting the Society in an attitude which, in relation to a less sadly serious matter, would be truly ludicrous; and, in this, most clearly showing the folly and absurdity of trying to serve God and not offend the devil. For in one breath it has emphatically refused to approve the publication of a tract against a practice, which, in the next, it calls a sin and a *great* wickedness. In fact, it has said by resolution, in brief, what it is unwilling to have its Publishing Committee say more at large, in a tract, with demonstration of its truth, and proper practical inferences therefrom; but what, if true, renders its duty as a promoter of "vital godliness and sound morality" imperative and urgent, to counteract, with hearty zeal and persistent vigor, the attempt notoriously making to revive the traffic it has so characterized. The Society next proceeded to the regular Anniversary exercises, heard the Reports of Secretary and Treasurer, and addresses from several speakers, and adopted resolutions gratefully recognizing "God's rich blessing upon the Society's labors and publications;" "rejoicing to coöperate with the missions of our several respected Boards;" and taking encouragement, from the results of the "harmonious coöperation of Christians, of various names, in the diffusion of saving truth," to "cherish 'the unity of the spirit in the bond of peace.'" How beautifully this was done at that very meeting, its rude trampling on the rights of the minority, its clamor and hisses and despotic suppression of debate as soon as the mouthpieces of the majority had had their say, and all its turbulent and indecorous proceedings, which we have only faintly sketched, abundantly bear witness.

The Boston American Tract Society held its Annual Meeting on the 23rd of May last, and, without discussion, adopted, almost unanimously, a resolution rescinding the vote of 1825, which made it a branch of the New-York Society, and resuming "its original position as an independent national institution;" with the hope "that the two Societies may henceforth operate in their different spheres with harmony and greatly increased usefulness, in promoting the glory of our common Lord, and the salvation of souls." It indefinitely postponed, by a nearly unanimous vote, a resolution advocated by Rev. Mr. COPP, of Chelsea, and Rev. Dr. KIRK, of Boston, but decidedly opposed by Rev. Messrs. DEXTER, WOLCOTT, and others, avowing charity, forbearance, love, and Christian regard toward the New-York Society, and a hope so to act "as to avoid all just causes of strife between us, and, as far as possible, to conduct our operations in harmony and peace with theirs, as brethren and Christians, having, in the main, the same great objects in view." It adopted the resolution, laid on the table at the New-York meeting, approving the publication of tracts against the Slave-trade; then chose anew mainly the old Board of Officers, who have always favored the policy of the New-York Society; some of the more Pro-Slavery members being left out only because they formally declined a reëlection. It seems, too, that separation from their old associates does not necessarily involve the withholding of "material aid;" for the last March number of the New-York Society's monthly organ acknowledges $1,000 received into its treasury from the Boston Society, in payment for publications.

The Boston Society has published, during the past year, seven tracts bearing more or less upon the Slave question. One of these, an able vindication of the Bible from the charge of sanctioning Slavery, is a work of nearly unexceptionable excellence, maintaining substantially the doctrines, and with substantially the arguments, published by the American Anti-Slavery Society more than twenty years ago. Another touches Slavery but incidentally, condemning it, however, and implying also a condemnation of the spirit of caste in the northern Church. But the Society has set a more emphatic implication in the opposite direction, by putting upon its Executive Committee the pastor of the church in Park Street, Boston, which by its practice and by-laws has established caste in its own house of worship, and still maintains it there, without rebuke from him. The other tracts, although containing much which we can heartily commend, are all in greater or less measure flawed with errors, express or implied, of doctrine or of fact. In one is an attempt to show how a man may continue a Slave-holder, under certain circumstances, without sin. Another imputes to God the curse on Canaan, which, the Bible says, Noah uttered after he "awoke from his wine," of which "he drank and was drunken." Another assumes that the laws of Moses "temporarily tolerated" Slavery among the Hebrews; that the Slave-holders of this country enjoy a true "Gospel ministry;" and that the caste which exists in the American Church is caste "in the Kingdom of God." Another implies that those who, for "twice ten years," have "strenuously excluded" the subject of Slavery "from the prayer-meeting, the monthly concert, and the sanctuary," are the people of God; and affirms that "every mode of opposition" to Slavery, except prayer, "has been vigorously employed;" that "the moral influence of the nation has borne against it with a pressure seemingly irresistible;" and that "political measures have been tried in good faith, and with the utmost energy." Another represents the Society as dreading "equally the danger of having any child grow up in the belief that Slavery is not an enormous evil — a wrong to the Slave, and a sin against God," and "the danger of creating in their minds indiscriminate prejudices against all who hold the legal relation of owners of Slaves." That is, if we understand it rightly, the Society is *equally* anxious to teach children that Slavery is a great sin, and that men may "hold the legal relation of owners of Slaves," without being sinners.

Foreign Intelligence.

Within the year just past, some of the most active friends of the Anti-Slavery cause in Great Britain have begun a new movement, whose purpose is more fully to enlist the moral and religious influence of the British people in aid of the American Abolitionists. On the 28th of May last, a meeting held in London organized "The London Emancipation Committee," with GEORGE THOMPSON for its chairman. Among the speakers at the meeting were the Haytian Minister, the Secretary of the Haytian Legation, and one of the Magistrates of Surinam. Resolutions were unanimously adopted, announcing that among the objects of the committee will be to guard the British public against the unwarranted assumption of Anti-Slavery character by Pro-Slavery visitors; to protest against the union of the religious bodies of Great Britain with the Pro-Slavery churches of America; to collect and diffuse information as to Slavery generally, and especially as to its aspects in the United States; to assist deserving Fugitive Slaves who may visit Great Britain as representatives of their race; to coöperate with kindred Anti-Slavery Committees and Societies in the United Kingdom, and with the American Anti-Slavery Society and other foreign bodies having the same object in view; to welcome, and aid in the prosecution of their Anti-Slavery labors, all visitors accredited by, or belonging to, the American Anti-Slavery Society or its auxiliaries; and to hold, on each anniversary of the abolition of British Colonial Slavery, a public meeting to celebrate that event, and to promote the cause of negro emancipation, especially in the United States. Resolutions of sympathy with Dr. CHEEVER, and congratulating Miss REMOND upon the success of her mission in Great Britain, were also unanimously adopted. From the Glasgow *British Friend*, of the 2nd of last April, we learn that "GEORGE THOMPSON has once more thrown himself vigorously into the Anti-Slavery field; and has, for the last two months, been holding large, enthusiastic, and effective meetings both in England and Scotland," with the prospect of proceeding to Ireland, after some further labor in Edinburgh and Glasgow.

Last June an address was sent from the Baptist Union of Great Britain and Ireland to the Baptist Churches in the United States. It referred, "with lively satisfaction," to "the large measure of civil and religious liberty" enjoyed here, and to the "wide-spread revival of religion in the Union during many months past;" then glanced with "grief and indignation" at the evils of Slavery, and "with pungent regret" at the Fugitive-Slave Bill, the Dred-Scott Decision, and "the violent measures employed in Kansas to extend the hateful system;" lamented that "many who bear the honored names of Christians, and of Baptists, connive at, and plead for the maintenance of Slavery, and share alike in its cruelties and its gains;" expressed gratification that increasing numbers of the Baptist body here abstain from so doing, and protest against the evil, using their influence and recording their votes in favor of Freedom; and avowed an "earnest wish that in this important enterprise all were 'of one heart and of one soul.'" "We are waiting with much interest," it continued, "to see what influence the late revival of religion among you will exercise on behalf of the Slave. * * * * * * If it should not promote a change in the prevailing views and feelings with regard to Slavery, and to further wise and peaceful efforts to let the oppressed go free, we shall be grievously disappointed, and shall fear that we have much overrated its worth." It concluded, "We implore you, beloved brethren, to put forth your noblest energies in endeavoring to terminate a system which is the darkest stain on the banner of the Union, and the most lamentable source of division and weakness in your churches." In October last, "The First Calvinistic Baptist Church in England sent an address to the Baptist Churches in the United States, telling them "a great work devolves on you in separating from the defences of American Slavery the prestige and moral influence which they derive from connivance or open advocacy in the churches, by the members or the ministers of your communion;" affirming that "American Slavery contains, in itself, elements which can never exist but in direct hostility to God," and "is supported by means which cannot be tolerated without rebellion against the Christ of God;" and that, "instead of compromising the laws of Christ by which these sins are condemned and the perpetrators of them called to repentance or excommunication, the time and the occasion call for greater faithfulness;" and enumerating, among the results and incidents of Slavery which place its "agents, authors, and defenders more prominently forward than any other men," as proper objects of a faithful Christian discipline, "your assemblies for prayer, in which four millions of your own enslaved citizens must not be named; your conversions, which bring no compassion for the oppressed and no abhorrence of the impure; and your ministers, who, defending this barbarous crime, blaspheme the name of Jesus."

The Appeal of Anti-Slavery Methodists, in this country, to foreign Methodists, of which we spoke on a former page, was promptly published by the Leeds Young-Men's Anti-Slavery Society, as soon as it reached England; and copies were sent, with a memorial from that Society, to the several Conferences then about to assemble in that country. The "Methodist New Connection," on receiving it, immediately resolved "that a memorial be sent to the General Conference of the Methodist Episcopal Church in the United States, earnestly entreating our brethren to purify their Church by ceasing to hold communion with Slave-holders." The "Assembly of the United Methodist Free Churches," meeting at Sheffield, unanimously adopted a resolution declaring that it "rejoices in the movement for excluding Slave-holders from church-fellowship in the American Methodist Episcopal Church North, and, therefore, will gladly avail itself of the opportunity of addressing a respectful memorial, on this subject, to the General Conference of the aforesaid Church, to urge it to employ its powerful influence for the suppression of Slavery." The "Wesleyan Conference," assembled at Manchester, received the Appeal directly from this country, as well as the memorial in support of it from the Leeds Young-Men's Anti-Slavery Society, and appointed a committee to prepare a suitable address on the subject, from the English to the American Conference.

The manufacturers of Great Britain are evidently setting themselves, with serious earnestness, to the solution of a question which must have an important bearing on the interests of American Slavery — that of the practicability of obtaining elsewhere than in this country a supply of cotton for their mills. The efforts to encourage the cotton culture in Africa are reported as increasingly successful; and not only is perseverance encouraged by the increase in quantity, but the quality of the African cotton is said to be such as to give high hopes of its complete success in competition with the American. At a meeting in Liverpool, last summer, it was stated that "cotton from any part of Africa will sell in Liverpool or Manchester for two pence or three pence a pound more than the East-India product, which indicates that the quality of African cotton is at least equal to that of the American." The Cotton-Supply Association, in Manchester, has lately received from Dr. LIV- INGSTONE "samples of excellent cotton and cotton-yarn spun by the natives, well spun and very strong," produced "in the valley of the Shire," where cotton is said to be "so abundant that a vast number of cotton trees are annually burned to the ground." Among the samples was a ball of yarn weighing 16¼ ounces, which cost one penny. Rivers navigable a great portion of the year traverse the valley; "it is therefore evident," says the *Manchester Guardian*, "that a large supply of cotton may be readily obtained from this part of Africa by the adoption of an effective agency." Lord BROUGHAM, in a speech in Parliament, a few weeks ago, alluded to the "great facilities for the growth of cotton" presented by some of the British Colonies, and hoped that the government would encourage the cultivation of it in Jamaica and British Guiana; and, "above all, he trusted that a trade in cotton would be opened upon the east coast of Africa, in the districts explored by Dr. LIVINGSTONE; for, upon the high lands of that country, cotton to any amount, and of the best quality, might, with a slight encouragement, be raised."

At the Annual Meeting of the British and Foreign Anti-Slavery Society, on the 28th of last May, CHARLES BUXTON, M. P., was one of the speakers. Alluding to the state of the West Indies, he said, "In this respect the friends of emancipation had great cause for triumph. It was true those islands had suffered great calamities, though not because of emancipation, but because of the destruction of the monopoly in sugar, and because monopoly and Slavery had engendered a state of society so unsound that a collapse was sometime or other inevitable. That time had now, however, passed away; and the statistics of the Board of Trade, the reports of the governors of the colonies, and the reports of private individuals all testified that emancipation was, at last, producing its proper fruits, and that these islands were fast rising into a state of great wealth and prosperity." Rev. W. B. INGRAM, of British Guiana, said "the West-India Colonies were never so prosperous as at the present time. In British Guiana, during the twenty-one years since freedom, the colored population had acquired property and held conveyances of it from the British Government to the amount of a million sterling. Before freedom not one of them knew a letter of the alphabet; now, every adult could read while the children were receiving as good an education as were the children of the working classes in this country. A large number of young men are also being trained up for the preaching of the Gospel, and others as select teachers. The exports of British Guiana are larger than they ever were in the palmy days of Slavery. Then the sugar exported was eighteen or nineteen thousand hogsheads; while, last year, it amounted to 53,000." Rev. JOHN CLARK, of Jamaica, declared that "it would be easy to show that emancipation, so far from injuring the planters of Jamaica, had really averted the ruin of that island. For years previous to freedom the exports of sugar had been diminishing in such a ratio that, had it continued to the present year, not ten hogsheads would have been exported, and in three or four years more none at all; whereas they now export 53,000 hogsheads a year, with the prospect of a yearly increase." [A table now before us, published from the Journals of the Assembly of Jamaica, two years before the date of complete emancipation in that island, shows that, in the sixteen years immediately preceding, the exports of sugar thence had fallen off from 123,850 hogsheads in 1820, to 68,364 in 1836.] At a meeting on the first of last August, to celebrate the Anniversary of West-India Emancipation, Governor Hincks, of Barbadoes, maintained that "the emancipated population of those colonies have triumphantly vindicated their right to freedom, and the justice of the Act of Emancipation by the signal progress they have since made, morally, religiously, and politically;" and declared his belief that the planters were themselves convinced of the good results of emancipation. He had

not arrived at the convictions he entertained from his experience in Barbadoes only, but had carefully examined the subject
in the southern States of America, in Cuba, and in the other
colonies of the West Indies."

The *Edinburgh Review*, for April, of last year, in an article
on the alleged ruin of the West Indies through the idleness of
the negroes, since emancipation, showed, from official statistics,
that although during several years since 1846 the planters
suffered much, and some of them were indeed reduced to ruin,
yet so far was their distress from being due to the want of labor
and a consequent decrease of production, that at that very
period production was largely on the increase. The exports of
sugar to Great Britain, in the six years ending with 1846,
amounted to 14,629,550 cwt. In the next six years, to the end
of 1852, 17,918,362 cwt.; a gain of 3,288,812 cwt., or very
nearly 22½ per cent. In the next six, to the end of 1858,
18,443,341 cwt., a still further gain; besides which, a large
quantity had gone to the United States, Australia, and other
countries, to which a trade entirely new had sprung up, whereof
there are no published returns. Including this, the gain of the
third period over the second would probably be fully equal to
that of the second over the first. In the eight years ending
with 1846, the whole production of sugar in the British West
Indies was just about 20,000,000 cwt. In the next eight years,
24,500,000 cwt., a gain of 22½ per cent. In 1832 and 1833, the
last two years of Slavery, the British sugar colonies exported
8,471,744 cwt. of sugar. In 1856 and 1857, to Great Britain
alone, 8,736,654 cwt., besides a large export to other countries,
including the supply of that new trade above mentioned. Thus
it will be seen that, in the latter period, the export to Great
Britain alone exceeded, by more than three per cent, that to
Great Britain and all other countries, in the former period.
Such is the "ruin" which emancipation causes. Whence, then,
came the admitted distress of the planters, in the five or six
years following 1846? From the fall in the price of sugar,
caused by the withdrawal of protective duties; a cause with
which the negroes had nothing to do, and the effects of which,
therefore, it would be absurd and unjust to impute to their fault.
West-India sugar, which, in 1840, sold for 49s. per cwt., exclusive of duty, had sunk, in 1848, to 23s. 5d. In the eight years

ending with 1846, the average price was 37s. 3d. per cwt. In the next eight years, 24s. 6d. — less than two thirds as much — so that the larger crop of the latter period sold for $34,000,000 less than the smaller crop of the former period. But prices have risen again, while also, as we have seen, crops have continued to increase. In 1857 the value of sugar exported to the United Kingdom alone was more than $26,000,000; exceeding, by about $3,000,000, the average yearly value of the whole production in the period of high prices before the end of 1846; and, by more than $7,000,000, the yearly average of the eight succeeding years of low prices.

The London *Anti-Slavery Reporter*, for June last, has a letter from a superintendent of schools in the parish of Clarendon, Jamaica, having more than three hundred negro children under his care. To show his competency to judge of the subject on which he writes, he states that he had spent twelve years in conducting public schools in Scotland, and obtained his last school there by competition with three hundred candidates, "and, therefore, must know what teaching is, and what progress scholars should make." He then affirms his candid conviction that the children in one of his schools, numbering one hundred and thirty, "would contrast favorably with those of the same age in any school throughout Great Britain;" adding, "I have proved, within the last three years, that the negro children can learn every branch of education quite as speedily and accurately as the English children, and that the emancipated people can appreciate proper education for their children, and pay for it, too, as regularly and cheerfully as the English, or even the Scotch people do."

While our much esteemed friend and fellow-laborer, THEODORE PARKER, was sojourning in the Danish West Indies, last spring, for the benefit of his health, seriously impaired by his too severe exertions in the cause of humanity, one of his fellow-travellers wrote from Santa Cruz, under date of April 3, to a friend in this country: "I often think how delighted you would be with the results of emancipation as we see them all around us, and have abundant opportunity to examine them; not, as with us, some individuals or a family set free, and earning a hard subsistence, under painful circumstances, in an ungenial climate; but twenty thousand people raised at once from the

condition of cattle to that of responsible beings — protected
(and assisted if need be) by the government; and all this in
the tropical climate suited to their nature, and in the very
houses where they once lived the miserable life of a Slave.
* * * * * * The thrifty and industrious already succeed in
laying up enough to put themselves forward in the world, build
a comfortable little home in town, and bring up their children
to trades. They do not, like persons of some nations, lie flat
down upon you, if you lend them a helping hand. On the contrary, they have great pride in being independent. Of course,
it is not all *couleur de rose.* The profitable vice, for the masters'
gain, which has always been encouraged among them, carries
its poison among them yet, though they are gradually acquiring
a pride of matrimony. A noble young man here, an Episcopal
minister, is laboring most wisely, unweariedly, and much at his
own expense, for the moral and intellectual elevation of the
colored people. * * * * * * The tears would have been in
your eyes, this morning, to see his Sunday-morning school for
adults, many of whom had walked five miles, under this scorch-
ing sun, to attend. He has established a day school for children
of his parish, and I was never so pleased with any school I have
ever visited. He thinks the blacks capable of receiving as much
instruction as the whites, judging from the two years of trial in
this school. The progress has been surprising indeed."

Mrs. FRANCES D. GAGE, writing from the same place, four
days earlier, dwells with lively satisfaction on various tokens of
the happy influence of freedom upon the condition of the island;
and seems in none to find more pleasure than in the sight of
groups of children gathering to the schools, "well-dressed, neat
and clean," and not one failing, as the travellers passed, "to lift
the hand and wish us a good morning, with a bright, pleasant
smile. The school-house, large, airy, well-ventilated, capable of
accommodating two hundred children, would be an honor to
many a country place even in New England. * * * * * * We
passed three of these school-houses, well filled with children
studying or reciting their lessons. These were the children of
the field-hands. These schools are established by the Danish
government. There are nine of them on the island. Besides
the government schools there are many others, some kept up by
private endeavors, some by church influence. The teachers tell

me that the children learn quite as fast as white children. One gentleman here assures me that the children born in freedom are much brighter, smarter, and better looking than those born in Slavery, taking them *en masse ;* and no one has yet asserted that the emancipated Slaves were not as moral as before, while many admit that they are more so, and improving." Of the laborers, Mrs. GAGE says, " The law will not allow an overseer or manager to strike them; they work only ten hours per day, unless they choose; Saturdays and Sundays are their own; each man and woman is entitled to a spot of land, to till for vegetables; the laborers on an estate own all the fruit that grows upon the estate, and each laborer is paid by law for all his lawful working hours, and extra for all hours he chooses to work that are not lawful; and men and women receive the *same price* (mark that, too,) for the same labor."

On the 20th of last September Slavery was completely abolished in the Dutch East Indies, compensation being granted to the masters. A Commission awarded to each his share, and the sum was in the treasury awaiting the order of claimants; "but at Surabaya," says the New-York *Tribune*, " as we learn from a letter in *The Hong Kong Register*, many of the Slave-holders refused to receive an equivalent for their pecuniary sacrifice, preferring to possess the satisfaction of the consciousness of voluntarily restoring their servants to liberty, rather than seem to submit to the legal compulsion which compensation, in some sort, implies; many others, however, accepted the sum with the still higher and more unselfish purpose of giving it to the emancipated people whose assessed value it represented." Whether the same generous justice was practiced in any of the other colonies we are not informed.

The Secretary of the Society for the Abolition of the Slave-trade, at Rio Janeiro, in a letter published, last spring, in the London *Anti-Slavery Reporter*, says that the question of emancipation is making rapid progress in Brazil. Societies have been organized in different provinces of the empire, for the purpose of liberating Slaves. Owners of Slaves, on dying, almost always liberate those Slaves who have served them well — particularly nurses of children, who have been faithful. Female Slaves, approaching white, instead of being sold, as in this country, at a high price, for a life of shame, easily find the

means of purchasing their freedom.   Slaves who have performed any act of heroism for their masters, usually receive their
freedom as a recompense.   The thoughts and feelings of the
Brazilians, in general, differ widely from those of the North
Americans, with regard to emancipation, and they would see
with horror, among themselves, the immoral means employed in
the United States to indefinitely prolong Slavery.

We have learned within the last two or three months that a
society has been lately formed, in the Swiss canton Vaud, to
raise money for the purchase of freedom for Slaves in this
country.   Acting through a Swiss clergyman, in Madison
County, Illinois, it procured, not long ago, for about four
hundred dollars, the liberation of a colored Methodist minister
of St. Louis, Mo., who now intends to go to Liberia, and labor
there in establishing schools.

The work of emancipating the Serfs, in Russia, still goes on.
A correspondent of the London *Times* writes from St. Petersburg, on the 27th of last July, "The Serf question has advanced
so far toward a solution that retrogression is impossible.   The
emperor is honestly determined to carry out his views.   The
younger nobility afford their full support.   The Serfs themselves
have learnt they have rights as well as duties, and, though the
old Russian party may delay and obstruct, they cannot prevent
the final result."

A letter written in Berlin, December 29, 1858, gives, more
fully than we have elsewhere seen it, the basis proposed by the
Imperial Central Committee, for the labors of the several provincial committees.   It provides that Serfdom shall be abolished
forever, without compensation to the former proprietors; "for,"
it says, "a money payment in return for rights which belong to
the peasantry by nature, and should never have been taken
away from them, would form a disgraceful page, indeed, in
Russian history."   The peasant is to pass into "a state of provisional obligation," to continue twelve years, during which he
remains attached to the estate, but may leave it if the landlord
fails to find him a certain prescribed quantity of land to cultivate for himself, or if he finds a substitute to cultivate his allotment.   Every village community retains the dwelling-houses of
its members, with their farm-yards, gardens, &c., paying the
landlord a rent of three per cent a year on the value, as ap-

praised by a mixed commission of two landlords and two peasants; or may buy them outright by paying the appraised value. Two-thirds of the arable land of the estate are to be allotted, in equal shares, to the adult male peasants, unless that proportion should make each share exceed, by more than eighty per cent, the minimum allotment, or least quantity thought sufficient to support the peasantry. If two-thirds are not enough to give each the minimum allotment, as many receive that share as can, and the rest are free to go where they like. The landlord is bound to supply fire-wood for the peasants, from his forests, at a price to be fixed beforehand. For these advantages the peasants are to give the landlords, each year, at the rate of a hundred days' work of a man and fifty of a horse for the minimum allotment, and in the same proportion for all beyond that; but in fixing the money-value of this "*corvée*," as it is called, one day of free labor is to be reckoned equal to three days of *corvée*; so that the actual yearly rent of land enough to support the peasantry, is to be thirty-three and a third days' work of each adult male, aided half the time by a horse. After seven years the *corvée* is to be gradually commuted into a corn-rent. The Serfs attached not to the estate but to the person of the lord, are to serve ten years, but will receive wages, and may buy their freedom, at once, for three hundred roubles [about $170] a man, and a hundred and twenty roubles [about $68] a woman. The landlord remains chief of the village community, with a veto on its resolutions, but subject to an appeal to a mixed commission of nobles and peasants.

This we understand to be the plan referred to in our last Report, as proposing "a transition state;" while those suggested by some of the provincial committees propose complete emancipation at once. Some of the proprietors seem unwilling to wait for the action of the committees and the emperor. We learned, last winter, that HERR NICOLAI FURGINIEW, "a large proprietor in Stardub, a Russian village, has voluntarily emancipated his one hundred and eighty-one Serfs, and has given to them one-third of his land, requiring from them capitation taxes and all subsisting imposts, and declaring them at liberty to withdraw from the arrangement as soon as the negotiations between the government and the nobility shall offer them more favorable conditions."

Last spring the St. Petersburg *Gazette du Senat* announced that "most of the provincial committees have finished their plans of emancipation," and that "the emperor had placed these in the hands of a Special Commission, composed of some of the most experienced proprietaries in the empire, to be digested into one general plan which shall satisfy all the special needs of each province." Of this Commission, Count PANIN is president. From a letter written at St. Petersburg, on the 13th of March last, we gather that the deputies from the provincial committees — two from each province, according to the arrangement mentioned in our last Report — have met in the capital, with the Special Commission, and been addressed by the emperor, by way of introduction to the work before them. "You are aware, gentlemen," said he, "how much this affair interests me, and how much it affects my heart; and I am certain that it is as dear to you as it is to me. I have but one object — the happiness of my empire, and I am convinced that you have no other. I desire that the improvement of the condition of the peasants may shortly become an accomplished fact, and that this reform may be effected without violence. But that cannot be obtained without certain sacrifices on your part. My desire is to render these sacrifices as little onerous as possible to the nobility. I have caused a sketch of your labors in the capital to be prepared, and your duties are defined in it in a positive manner. Act then, in accord, animated by one feeling — the public good. At the beginning, I addressed myself to the nobility in full confidence; I now address myself to you with the same belief that you will realize my expectations. The Minister of the Interior and Count PANIN know my ideas, and can communicate them to you in detail. Your duty, gentlemen, is to second us, and I advise you to invoke the Divine protection." Then to Count PANIN; "I present to you your colleagues. I am convinced that they will set themselves seriously to work. I request of you to bring this affair to a conclusion in a prudent and serious manner, without, however, too long delaying the solution. Adieu, gentlemen; I wish you success."

The mere prospect of freedom to the bondmen already begins to work out happy results for the empire. A letter from Warsaw, on the 18th of last March, says, "landed property throughout the Russian empire has quadrupled in value since the ques-

of a character highly and justly respected wherever he was known; and unhesitatingly making whatever sacrifice of personal reputation, or sectarian connections or prepossessions, fidelity to its righteous claims demanded. He assisted at the formation of this Society, signed its Declaration of Sentiments, and from the first has been one of its managers; as well as Vice President of the Massachusetts, and President of the Worcester County, South Division, Anti-Slavery Society, auxiliary to this. In its notice of his death the *Liberator* truly said, "he was a pattern of devotedness and punctuality, ever at his post, and making a regular attendance upon all local meetings, and at every anniversary, for the furtherance of the cause of the enslaved, a part of his Abolition duties. The presence of no one will be more missed at our gatherings than his own, which was a benediction in itself. He abounded in all that makes up excellence of character in its most perfect symmetry. Gentleness, benignity, firmness of purpose, moral intrepidity, the soundest judgment, a generous sympathy, a world-wide humanity, the largest conscientiousness and reverence, admirable circumspection without feebleness or faltering in the performance of duty, radical without rashness, blending gravity with geniality, manly strength with womanly modesty, an ever-progressive spirit with an even frame of mind — these were his distinctive traits, commanding the implicit confidence and the highest respect of all who had the privilege and the pleasure of his intimate acquaintance. * * * * * * Doubtless his severest struggle was in withdrawing his sympathy and fellowship from the Society of Friends, of which he had been, for many years, a much respected member, and to which he was tenderly and strongly attached. A primitive Quaker in his spirit, worthy of Quakerism in its purest and most vital period, he was sorrowfully convinced, after a long and painful experience, that humanity had nothing to hope from the organized body, as such, which, conforming to the corrupt and time-serving spirit of the age — especially as pertaining to the Anti-Slavery movement — was clearly incapable of grappling with the prevailing sins of the times, or giving an effective testimony against popular wrong-doers." Another witness, who knew him well, bears this testimony, which we cordially accept as our own. "Wise, benevolent, liberal of hand and of soul, cheerful and serene, the straight coat and broad brim of Quakerdom never graced a purer philanthropist or a more thorough gentleman." He will be seen no more in our assemblies, but long will his venerable and benignant countenance be remembered, and his kindly and cheering influence felt by those who have been his fellow-laborers in the service of humanity.

Another of our long-tried, ever-trusty, and much-esteemed associates, SAMUEL PHILBRICK, was summoned from us on the 19th of September, in the seventy-first year of his age. Among the earliest to take part in our great enterprise, for nearly twenty years he had rendered it invaluable service as Treasurer of the Massachusetts Anti-Slavery Society, and during much of that time as member of the Financial Committee for the *Liberator*. For these offices he was most admirably fitted, alike by his rare business talent, consummate judgment in all financial matters, and most perfect order and method, and by his perfect fidelity and rigid uprightness of character. It has been well said of him, "a more just or a more clear-sighted man did not live." Eminently valuable was he as a sagacious counsellor in every exigency of the cause. With strongly-developed individuality, there was nothing enthusiastic, impulsive, or wayward in his nature. In whatever he did, he endeavored to keep "a conscience void of offence," to meet all his engagements and discharge all the duties of life in a spirit of exact rectitude. His marked characteristic was INTEGRITY. He abhorred everything that bore the semblance of dissimulation, and appreciated, at its true value, an ingenuous, straightforward course of conduct; being himself a pattern of trustworthiness, and remarkable for his frankness and plainness of speech, without respect of persons, in all his dealings.

The 26th of January last bereft us of the loved and revered presence of one of the noblest of those noble women, whose lives have so brightly illustrated the history, and so effectually aided the progress of our movement. The death of ELIZA LEE FOLLEN, coming as it did when she had half completed the seventy-third year of a life as beautiful as the fairest graces of Christian Humanity, blending in most symmetrical accord, could make it, and rich with all the fruitful uses which those graces could adorn and serve, might not have seemed to us a premature one, had it not found her still as young in soul, as

27

abounding in judicious zeal and beneficent activity, as clear and vigorous in mind, as warm in sympathy, as buoyant in hope and faith, as fresh in feeling, as serenely joyous in temperament, as genial in spirit, as amply endowed with social and domestic affections, as glad in all the innocent and refining pleasures which bless and sweeten life, as if the years had never scattered snow upon her temples, or written lines of serious meaning on the spiritual beauty of her face. So early in the field of Anti-Slavery labor that only the foremost pioneers preceded her; so diligent and faithful and wisely energetic through all the following years that it would be hard to say who has excelled her in constancy and heartiness and value of service to the cause; she has wrought the memory of her person and her deeds into the reminiscences of its past; has given it no small measure of its present strength; and, through the ripening of the fruitage from the seed she planted, will have an ample share in its certain future triumph. With her illustrious husband, to whose bright fame no eulogy of ours can add, she met with quiet courage and a steady firmness the early trials and perils of the enterprise; and taking then the highest ground of principle, and, passing through them guided by that clear, moral vision of the "single eye," which sees, as cunning worldly wisdom never does, that right is the only true expediency, they both held fast their integrity against temptations of whose variety and force souls of less compass, depth, and sensitive vitality throughout, could form no adequate conception.

For more than half of her Anti-Slavery life, Mrs. FOLLEN has been immediately connected with the conducting of the movement, as a member of the Committees of the American and Massachusetts Anti-Slavery Societies. To this service she brought her rare natural gift of organization, which was to be seen in the daily beauty of her domestic life, and the details of her refined and happy home. No one was clearer of vision as to what should be done, and as to the method of doing it. To her long experience in the cause she added an intuition into its nature and its needs, at each successive crisis of its fate, and an enthusiasm of feeling and of manner, in developing it, which made her the wisest, the discreetest, the best, and the most delightful of counsellors and of co-workers. The secret of it all lay more in the heart than in the head. It came from the singleness of her devotion to the Anti-Slavery cause. It was entire, disinterested, fearless. Those only who have rejoiced in her sympathy and her help can fully understand the loss her death brings to them, and to the cause she loved best. The principle of perfect love, not only casting out fear, but giving clearness of vision and perfectness of action, informed her whole character and shone from her whole presence. With the impulsive energies of the poetic temperament, she possessed its sympathetic and magnetic forces. No one could be in her society without feeling how magical a sway her mind exerted over his. Her powers of conversation were of the highest and rarest description. Mrs. FOLLEN was an authoress of no small reputation. She has written many books, some of which have a wide reputation, and will become a permanent portion of English literature. Her life of her husband has been pronounced, by high English critical authority, a perfect example of that most difficult kind of composition. Some of her fugitive poems are among the most beautiful in the language. But no one who judges of her powers or graces by her published works, can have any adequate idea of them. Her fluent tones, her wealth of pictured words, her fertility of imagery and illustration, her flashing wit, her earnest eloquence, the musical contagion of her laugh, are things which have died with her, or live only in the remembrance of those that knew and loved her. But these are many, and are found on both sides of the Atlantic.

A letter from MARY CARPENTER, of Bristol, England, says of her, "I myself had the privilege of knowing and loving her from personal intercourse under the same roof, after I had learnt to esteem and honor her from her works and from correspondence. She was universally esteemed and respected in England, both for her own sake and as the biographer of her noble husband. They were inseparably connected in our minds, as she desired they should be." Lady BYRON paid a poetical tribute to her memory. HARRIET MARTINEAU wrote to the *Anti-Slavery Standard,* "To all Mrs. FOLLEN's many friends in England, the news of her death was not the less sad for not being surprising. At her years, we knew we should not see her again; and I, especially, who was intimate with her a quarter of a century ago, was aware that her course must be nearly run; but her fidelity and vigor in regard to the Anti-

Slavery cause were so complete and so glowing, that the sense of your loss is as vivid as if she had been in the prime of life· The event is the more touching as it revives the sense of our former loss, in the death of her husband. The pair will hence-forth be remembered together in the immortal sense in which patriots and confessors are remembered in the history of their country and time. Their fidelity and devotedness never were and never can be exceeded, on any occasion and in any cause. They did all that it was possible for them to do. They sacrificed whatever the cause required; and they would have sacrificed all, to their very lives, if so called upon by the duty to which they had dedicated themselves. For all the rest of her long life, Mrs. FOLLEN spoke and wrought unflinchingly, unremit-tingly, and with a steadiness of purpose and composed ardor of manner which testified to the depth and soundness of her con-victions. * * * * * * She brought her eloquence to the cause, because she brought to it all her gifts; but it never became of lower quality from its abundance, or from the stimulus which instigated it. It was always worthy of the great occasion — for she felt that every occasion of pleading such a cause was great. Those who survive have sorely missed, and long will sorely miss, such fellow-workers as the FOLLENS; but it will be for-ever a cause for joy and thankfulness that such comrades were in the midst of them in the hardest days of the cause."

On the 5th of April death removed another of the early, earn-est, and ever-faithful friends of the Anti-Slavery cause, in the person of Rev. CYRUS PEIRCE, long well-known as Principal of the Normal School, at West Newton, Mass., and later as teacher of a private school in the same town. He openly committed himself in favor of our enterprise almost at its very beginning, and has never faltered in his adhesion to it since. He accepted an office in the Massachusetts Anti-Slavery Society, when to do so brought upon him derision and reproach, even if it did not risk the loss of the employment by which he earned his bread. He was the bearer to Congress of the great "Latimer Petition," presented to that body by JOHN QUINCY ADAMS. He was no public speaker, but at times appeared upon our platform when occasion seemed to call for the public bearing of his testimony. He was a man of sterling worth, exceedingly modest and retir-ing, amiable in disposition, gentle in speech and manner, but

firm and uncompromising wherever principle was involved. As
a teacher he had rare tact and eminent success, and was largely
instrumental in raising the standard of education in Massachusetts. The reverent affection of his many pupils named him
"FATHER PEIRCE," a title by which, through a general appreciation of its fitness, he had come to be more familiarly known
than by his baptismal name or ecclesiastical designation.

AGENTS AND PUBLICATIONS.

This Report has already extended to so great a length that
we forbear to enter upon a detailed statement of the Society's
operations during the year; suffice it to say here that its accustomed instrumentalities — the living voice, the printed page —
were employed during the year to the full extent of our ability
and of the means at our command. Owing to the liberal
coöperation of the Trustees of the Fund, left by the late
CHARLES F. HOVEY, for Anti-Slavery purposes, a much larger
number than usual of tracts and other publications were issued
and distributed far and wide over the land. A more particular
account of the Agency and Tract-publishing operations of the
year past may be expected in connection with the next Annual
Report.

In the earnest and increasing faith that all these and kindred
efforts, put forth to terminate the wrongs and woes of Slavery
by terminating its baneful existence, will result in a not distant
success, we close this report and condensed history of a most
momentous year.

The NATIONAL ANTI-SLAVERY STANDARD is the Society's
organ. It is published every Saturday, in the city of New York,
at No. 5, Beekman Street; and the Executive Committee urge
in its behalf a more extended circulation. The subscription
price is $2.00 per annum. OLIVER JOHNSON, Esq., is the Edi-
tor; assisted by an able corps of Associate Editors and Correspondents, both at home and abroad. Its Washington, Philadelphia, Boston, Dublin, English, and French correspondence
has all been, and will doubtless continue to be, of a highly
valuable and important character. Subscriptions, in Great

Britain and Ireland, may be sent to RICHARD D. WEBB, 176, Great-Brunswick Street, Dublin.

THE LIBERATOR, established in 1831, of which WM. LLOYD GARRISON is Editor and Proprietor, is published at No. 221, Washington Street, Boston, every Friday morning. It is the oldest Anti-Slavery journal in the country, and is conducted with the same vigor, sagacity, and uncompromising devotion to Liberty which marked its first years. Its columns are principally devoted to the Anti-Slavery cause. The subscription-price is $2.50 per annum.

Applications for any of the Society's publications, — books or tracts, — *many of which are for gratuitous distribution,* should be made to SAMUEL MAY, Jr., at the Anti-Slavery Office, in Boston, 221, Washington Street; JAMES MILLER McKIM, at the Anti-Slavery Office, in Philadelphia, 106, North Tenth Street; or to the Society's Office, in New York, 5, Beekman Street.

[Since the statement, on page 39, relating to GEORGE W. BISHOP, was printed, we learn from the *New-Haven Palladium* that he was acquitted of the charge of kidnapping, having produced in court the boy whom he was supposed to have kidnapped.]

ERRATA.

Page 29, line 19, for "brought" read "bought."
Same page, line 23, the word "country" should be in roman.

OFFICERS

OF THE

AMERICAN ANTI-SLAVERY SOCIETY,

ELECTED MAY, 1860.

PRESIDENT.

WILLIAM LLOYD GARRISON, Massachusetts.

VICE PRESIDENTS.

Peter Libbey, Maine.
Luther Melendy, New Hampshire.
John M. Hawks, ,, ,,
Jehiel C. Claflin, Vermont.
Francis Jackson, Massachusetts.
Edmund Quincy, ,,
Asa Fairbanks, Rhode Island.
James B. Whitcomb, Connecticut.
Samuel J. May, New York.
Cornelius Bramhall, ,, ,,
Amy Post, ,, ,,
Pliny Sexton, ,, ,,
Lydia Mott, ,, ,,
Henry A. Hartt, ,, ,,
Lucretia Mott, Pennsylvania.
Robert Purvis, ,,

Edward M. Davis, Pennsylvania.
Thomas Whitson, ,,
Joseph Moore, ,,
Rowland Johnson, New Jersey.
Alfred Gibbs Campbell, ,,
Thomas Garrett, Delaware.
Thomas Donaldson, Ohio.
Benjamin Bown, ,,
William Hearn, Indiana.
William Hopkins, ,,
Joseph Merritt, Michigan.
Thomas Chandler, ,,
Cyrus Fuller, ,,
Carver Tomlinson, Illinois.
Caleb Green, Minnesota.
Georgiana B. Kirby, California.

CORRESPONDING SECRETARY.

CHARLES C. BURLEIGH, Plainfield, Ct.

RECORDING SECRETARY.

WENDELL PHILLIPS, Boston.

TREASURER.

FRANCIS JACKSON, Boston.

EXECUTIVE COMMITTEE.

William Lloyd Garrison.
Francis Jackson.
Edmund Quincy.
Maria Weston Chapman.
Wendell Phillips.
Anne Warren Weston.

Sydney Howard Gay.
Samuel May, Jr.
William I. Bowditch.
Charles K. Whipple.
Henry C. Wright.
Charles Follen.

Dr. Francis Jackson, *Treas., in acc't with Am. A. S. Society, from May* 1, 1859, *to May* 1, 1860. **Cr.**

To Balance from last year	$2,452.65
" Amount received from subscriptions to Anti-Slavery Standard, donations, and sale of pamphlets	14,239.11
Total	$16,691.76

By Amount expended for publication of Anti-Slavery Standard and pamphlets, and for lecturing agents . . . . , . .	$11,320.34
" Expense Account, — for rents, office agent, and incidental expenses	1,891.54
" Balance to new account	3,479.88
Total	$16,691.76

(E. E.)

(Signed) FRANCIS·JACKSON, *Treasurer.*

New York, May 1, 1860.

APPENDIX.

TWENTY-SEVENTH ANNUAL MEETING OF THE AMERICAN ANTI-SLAVERY SOCIETY.

THE Twenty-seventh Anniversary of the AMERICAN ANTI-SLAVERY SOCIETY was held on Tuesday and Wednesday, May 8 and 9, 1860, at the Cooper Institute, in the city of New York. The meetings commenced on Tuesday morning, at 10½ o'clock.

Among those present were many of the long-tried, faithful, and uncompromising friends of the Slave, from various sections of the country.

The assembly was called to order by the President of the Society, WM. LLOYD GARRISON, who opened the exercises by reading passages of Scripture from Ezekiel and Jeremiah; at the conclusion of which he stated that an opportunity would be afforded for vocal prayer, by any friend of the cause who felt moved to do so; whereupon REV. DANIEL WORTH, late of North Carolina, came forward and offered an appropriate and earnest prayer to the God of the oppressed, that he would make the deliberations of the Society effective to the breaking of every bond, and letting the oppressed go free.

FRANCIS JACKSON, of Boston, Treasurer of the Society, then read his annual report, which will be found elsewhere.

The report was laid upon the table, to be subsequently acted upon.

Mr. GARRISON then presented the following series of resolutions for the consideration of the meeting : —

1. *Resolved*, That, in the language of HENRY CLAY, "Those who would repress all tendencies towards liberty and emancipation, must go back to the era of our liberty and independence, and muzzle the cannon which thunders its annual joyous return; they must revive the Slave-trade, with all its train of atrocities; they must blow out the moral lights around us, and extinguish that greatest torch of all, which America presents to a benighted world, pointing the way to these rights, their liberties, and their happiness; and, when they have achieved all their purposes, their work will be yet incomplete : They must penetrate the human soul, and eradicate the light of reason and the love of liberty. Then, and not till then, when universal darkness and despair prevail, can you perpetuate Slavery, and repress all sympathies, and all humane and benevolent efforts among freemen in behalf of the unhappy portion of our race doomed to bondage."

2. *Resolved*, That they who are for suppressing the Anti-Slavery agitation are really laboring for the complete supremacy and enduring sway of the Slave-power; that they who are deploring the excitement of the times arising from this question, are really lamenting that there is any manhood or moral sentiment left in the land, and arraigning the Almighty for inspiring the human mind with a detestation of robbery, injustice, and oppression.

3. *Resolved*, That to compromise with the dealers in human flesh, to accede to any of their demands, to enter into an alliance with them from which they shall derive strength and security, to acknowledge in any manner the rectitude or necessity of their course, is to participate in their guilt, to insure general demoralization, to lose the power of a virtuous example, and to betray the cause of Freedom universally.

4. *Resolved*, That this Society entirely accords with the Richmond (Va.) *Enquirer* in the sentiment, that " two opposing and conflicting forms of society cannot, among civilized men, co-exist and endure; the one must give way and cease to exist, the other become universal. If free society be unnatural, immoral, and unchristian, it must fall and give way to Slave society;" the reverse of all this must inevitably follow.

5. *Resolved*, That he who asserts that there is not an " irrepressible conflict" between Freedom and Slavery, between free institutions and Slave institutions, between the spirit which abolishes human chattelism and the spirit which perpetuates it, but that these are harmonious elements, or by compromise and forbearance can be made such in the same government, and can be brought into collision only by the efforts of fanaticism or sedition, is either idiotic, morally speaking, or a self-convicted demagogue, intent on nothing but the gratification of his own desperate ambition.

6. *Resolved*, therefore, That the party which talks of "the glorious Union" existing between the North and the South, and of the duty of maintaining it as an object of paramount importance, is smitten with judicial blindness, talks of what has never been, and in the nature of things can never be possible, is either the dupe or the ally of a stupendous imposture, which an insane and criminal experiment of three-score years has demonstrated is working the overthrow of all the safeguards of freedom, and, consequently, is a party neither to be trusted nor followed.

7. *Resolved*, That, in the words of the lamented Judge JAY, the Union is "a most grievous moral curse to the American people ; to the people of the South, by fostering, strengthening, and extending an iniquitous and baneful institution; to the millions among us of African descent, by riveting the chains of the bondman and deepening the degradation of the freeman ; to the people of the Free States, by tempting them to trample under foot the obligations of truth, justice, and humanity, for those wages of iniquity with which the Federal Government rewards apostates to liberty and righteousness."

8. *Resolved*, That the "glorious Union," ever since its formation, has signified nothing but the supremacy of a southern Slave oligarchy, who have always dictated the policy of the nation, and who claim a divine right to rule, according to their pleasure, alike the Slaves on their plantations and the people of the Free States, without remonstrance or interrogation, and as the condition of the perpetuation of the "glorious Union" aforesaid.

9. *Resolved*, That the privileges accorded to southern citizens sojourning or travelling in the North, under this Union, are these : To speak with impunity whatever they please against free institutions and free society; to advocate Slavery and the Slave traffic as worthy of universal extension, without interference, menace, or personal danger, and to an unlimited extent; to hold any meeting, or publish any journal they may choose, in which to assail the uncompromising friends of Freedom as fanatics and traitors, and to glorify the "lords of the lash" as the only true friends of their country; and, in short, to threaten, bully, and calumniate, *ad libitum*, whatever or whoever is deemed by them to be adverse, in spirit and sentiment, to "the sum of all villanies."

10. *Resolved*, That the privileges accorded to northern citizens sojourning or travelling in the South, under this Union, are these: To wear padlocks upon their lips; to forswear their manhood by bowing down to the Moloch of Slavery; to speak in behalf of the enslaved at the peril of their lives; to be tarred and feathered, if they are suspected of cherishing Anti-Slavery sentiments; to be thrust into prison, and sold as Slaves on the auction-block, if they are of African descent; to be scourged, branded, lynched, and driven out by mobocratic violence, even while in the prosecution of their legitimate business, simply because they are northern men.

11. *Resolved*, therefore, That the motto of the American Anti-Slavery Society, "No Union with Slave-holders," commends itself to the reason, conscience, and hearty adoption of every man claiming to be loyal to the Declaration of Independence; and it becomes the solemn duty of the North to carry it into immediate practice, as demanded by every instinct of self-preservation, and by all that is obligatory in the claims of justice and humanity.

OPENING REMARKS OF MR. GARRISON.

The President then addressed the audience as follows : —

LADIES AND GENTLEMEN : This is the first time that our Society has been in this large and commodious hall. I like it in all respects excepting one. There seems to be here a compromise between light and darkness [laughter] , and, for one, I would rather revel in excess of light than to be groping at all in darkness. However diverse may be your opinions in regard to all the measures of this Society, I trust I may take it for granted that there is but one opinion here respecting the inhuman, wicked, unchristian, diabolical character of American Slavery [loud applause]; and that we are resolved, as one man, to enter upon this conflict, and never to go back one jot or tittle, but to press onward and upward, until the goal of Universal Emancipation shall be reached.

I feel an "irrepressible" desire to congratulate you all upon the triumphant progress of the "irrepressible conflict" in all parts of our country [loud cheering]. In the Free States, undeniably, the conflict is going on; and may I not say that in all the Slave States it is going on, with even more vehemence and zeal than among ourselves? For, at last, even the invincible Democratic party has been reached; and, by the power which has been brought to bear upon it through the Anti-Slavery agitation, thank God, that party is no longer a unit in behalf of Slavery [applause]. It has been divided, I trust, never again to be united, by any compromise whatsoever, with the Slave-power. It seems to me to be one of the most striking proofs of the cheering progress of the movement in which we are engaged, that has yet been given to us. Only think of it ! The party which has, for so many years, cried out, "There must be no agitation on this subject," is now the most agitated of all the parties in the country ! The party which declares that there ought not to be any sectionalism, as against Slavery, has now been sundered, geographically, and on this very question ! The party which has said "Let discussion cease forever," is busily engaged in the discussion, so that, possibly, the American Anti-Slavery Society might adjourn *sine die*, after we get through with our present meeting, and leave its work to be carried on in the other direction ! [Laughter and cheers.] The party which says that Anti-Slavery must be put down in this country, is itself divided, discomfited, and, I believe, overthrown. "Oh, give thanks unto the Lord, for he is good; for his mercy endureth forever." [Rev. Mr. WORTH,— "Amen !"] "To him that overthrew Pharaoh and his host in the Red Sea, for his mercy endureth forever ! " [Loud applause.] In view, therefore, of these cheering signs of the times, I think we may all of us thank God and take courage.

The work of the American Anti-Slavery Society continues the same as from the beginning. It is the work of moral agitation. Standing, as the Society does, outside of all parties, all sects, it is compelled to criticise them all in an impartial spirit, to give to each one its due, and to bestow rebukes where rebukes are merited. We shall go on in this work, and, united by the simple bond, that the Slave is a man, and that he has, therefore, a right to his freedom now, as against all claimants,— not stopping to ask of what religious creed, or of what political party, a man may be, but only whether he is willing to recognize in the Slave a brother man, created in the same Divine image,— we hold out the hand of brotherly love and kindness and co-operation, and say; "Let us forget all other differences, and join heart and hand, until there is not a Slave left in the land to clank his chain in the hearing of God!"

If our platform has not been occupied by the clergy of the country generally, it has not been our fault. It has always been a free platform for them, as for us; and we, this day, invite them, as we have done ever since the organization of the Society, to come here, and, if they will, take the lead, and go forward and carry the banner of emancipation, until liberty shall be given to all in the land. We are here to settle no other question, excepting the right of the Slave to his freedom, excepting the sinfulness of making man the property of man; and we have always scrupulously endeavored to make our platform such that every man, whatever may be his peculiar religious opinions, should have no excuse for standing aloof therefrom. I am glad to be able to present to you, as the first speaker on this occasion, one whose orthodoxy, at least, has never yet been called in question [applause]. There are those who say that the reason they do not co-operate with this Society is that some of us hold theological opinions which are distasteful to them; we are heretics, and, of course, the Jews can have no dealings with the Samaritans [laughter]. Now, we are to listen to one who is thoroughly evangelical,— "a Puritan of the Puritans;" and yet, I ask you how has this noble man been met by the evangelical clergy of the country, as a body? How has he been treated, in this city, by his own evangelical brethren? Why, if he had been a heritic, as bad as any who has ever yet appeared on earth, he could not have received worse treatment at the hands of the orthodox body of our country. But I bless God that he has not faltered; that he has manfully stood his ground; that he has made up his mind, if need be, to die in the "imminent deadly breach;" and I am glad that he has found, at least, a faithful few to rally to his side, who are resolved to sustain him to the end. All my sympathies have been with him, because he has nobly been striving in behalf of the oppressed in our land, vindicating the character of God, the nature of man, and the claims of our suffering humanity; and my heart goes out to him, and mingles with his own, and I feel to bid him God-speed, and to wish him the most entire success, even as "a Puritan of the Puritans" [loud applause]. I now have the pleasure of introducing to you the Rev. GEORGE B. CHEEVER, of the city of New York [enthusiastic cheering]. Allow me just to add, that, in inviting our friend to speak here, to-day, we have invited him to speak what GEORGE B. CHEEVER thinks, not the American Anti-Slavery Society; not to endorse anything pertaining to this platform, or the measures or principles of the American Anti-Slavery Society, but to speak here as he knows how to speak in his own pulpit [renewed cheering].

The Society and audience were then addressed by Rev. Dr. CHEEVER, in a very able speech, a full report of which may be found in the *National Anti-Slavery Standard*, of May 12, 1860.

The meeting was next addressed by ROBERT PURVIS, Esq., of Pennsylvania; afterwards by Mrs. ELIZABETH CADY STANTON, of Seneca Falls, N. Y.; and, in conclusion, by WENDELL PHILLIPS, Esq., of Boston. All these speeches will be found fully reported, as above.

The Society then adjourned to meet at 3 o'clock, in business session.

TUESDAY AFTERNOON.

At the business meeting of the Society, held at the Cooper Institute, at 3 o'clock, P. M., the chair was taken by the President of the Society.

SAMUEL MAY, Jr., of Massachusetts, and SUSAN B. ANTHONY, of New York, were chosen Assistant Secretaries.

The question of amending the Constitution, in conformity to notice already given to the Executive Committee, was brought before the Society. The proposed amendments are as follows : —

By striking out of Article II. the following words : " While it admits that each State in which Slavery exists has, by the Constitution of the United States, the exclusive right to *legislate* in regard to its abolition in said State," and by making the word " It," which follows the words above quoted, the beginning of a sentence.

Also that the reading of the first sentence of the same article shall be, " The object of this Society is," &c.

The first amendment was favored by OLIVER JOHNSON, WENDELL PHILLIPS, WM. H. HOISINGTON, J. MILLER McKIM, J. H. STEPHENSON, EDWARD GILBERT, SUSAN B. ANTHONY, MARY GREW, and the President. Adopted, *nem. con.*

The second amendment was then unanimously agreed to.

The following persons were nominated by the Chair, and elected, a Committee to nominate officers for the ensuing year : —

J. MILLER McKIM, of Philadelphia; MARCUS SPRING, of New Jersey; THOMAS GARRETT, of Delaware; G. B. STEBBINS, of Michigan; MARIA E. WHITCOMB, of Connecticut; J. ELIZABETH JONES, of Ohio; J. H. STEPHENSON, of Massachusetts; JOSEPH POST, of New York; JOSEPH CARPENTER, of New York.

Mr. MAY read several letters addressed to the Executive Committee. — Those of Rev. M. D. CONWAY, of Cincinnati, Ohio, and Rev. JOSHUA YOUNG, of Burlington, Vt., were printed as above.

On motion, the following Committees were nominated and chosen : —

28

On Business. — WILLIAM LLOYD GARRISON, WENDELL PHILLIPS, MARY GREW, MARTHA WRIGHT, OLIVER JOHNSON, J. MILLER McKIM, JANE ELIZABETH JONES.

On Finance. — SUSAN B. ANTHONY, ROWLAND JOHNSON, JOSHUA T. EVERETT, GILES B. STEBBINS, BENJAMIN SNOW, Jr., J. H. STEPHENSON, JAMES B. RICHARDS.

Adjourned to 7½ o'clock.

TUESDAY EVENING.

The evening session was largely attended, and the meeting was called to order by the President, at 7½ o'clock. The first speaker was the Rev. ARTHUR B. BRADFORD, of Newcastle, Pa., editor of the *Church Portfolio*. His address was a masterly delineation of the unequalled sinfulness of Slavery, the frightful demoralization of the land, and the guilty complicity of the Church. It was heard with deep interest, and at various points was heartily applauded.

Rev. BERIAH GREEN, of Whitesboro', N. Y., next addressed the meeting in a speech of remarkable analytical clearness and force, reviewing the late speech of Hon. WILLIAM H. SEWARD, in the United States Senate.

Rev. J. R. W. SLOANE, of the Covenanter Church, in New York, made the closing speech. It was of the deepest feeling and power, and fitly closed the day's meeting, when three able and eloquent Orthodox ministers had appeared and spoken on the platform of the American Anti-Slavery Society, cordially welcomed by the Anti-Slavery host, although having little honor among their fellow-theologians.

The Society then adjourned, to meet on Wednesday morning, at 10 o'clock.

WEDNESDAY MORNING.

The Society re-assembled at the Cooper Institute, at 10 o'clock, the President in the chair.

The Committee appointed to nominate officers of the Society, for the ensuing year, reported. Their report was adopted, and the officers named were elected unanimously. [See list, elsewhere.]

The speakers, at this session, were GILES B. STEBBINS, of Michigan; Mrs. J. ELIZABETH JONES, of Ohio; Rev. GEORGE F. NOYES, of New-York City; SAMUEL MAY, Jr., of Massachusetts; the President (Mr. GARRISON); and Rev. Mr. BALME, of Wisconsin.

A letter of earnest sympathy, from Rev. Dr. FURNESS, of Philadelphia, was read by the President.

Adjourned to 3 o'clock, P. M.

WEDNESDAY AFTERNOON.

The Society re-assembled at the Cooper Institute, Mr. GARRISON in the chair. WILLIAM WELLS BROWN, once a Slave in Missouri, but for many years a freeman, was introduced by the President, and received with welcome applause. He testified strongly to the determination of the colored people to remain in this country, in spite of all efforts to remove them.

Rev. SAMUEL LONGFELLOW, of Brooklyn, addressed the meeting in earnest commendation of the objects, purpose, and courageous spirit of the Anti-Slavery Society, declaring the great need of its continued action, and particularly dwelling upon the inhumanity of the land as shown in all its treatment of the colored people.

A speech of deep interest was next made by Mr. GARRISON, which will be found fully reported in the *Liberator* of May 25, 1860.

SAMUEL MAY, Jr., from the Business Committee, offered the following resolution : —

Resolved, That the imprisonment of THADDEUS HYATT, by the Senate of the United States, for his conscientious refusal to appear as a witness before the Committee appointed by that body to investigate the facts pertaining to JOHN BROWN's interposition in behalf of the Slaves, at Harper's Ferry, is a usurpation of power not conferred by the Constitution, and a dangerous infraction of the liberties of the people ; and that we give Mr. HYATT assurance of our gratitude for his brave resistance to this new exhibition of the insolence of the Slave-power.

Rev. BERIAH GREEN, in some able remarks, showed where the *real infidelity* of this nation lies; viz., with those, in an especial manner, who bring the sanctions of a Divine command or permission, or who, in any way, employ the authority of the Bible, as a revelation from God, to justify, or to excuse, or in any manner support, the American Slave-holder in his robbery and oppression of the Slave.

The resolutions before the Society were then taken up and put to vote, and were adopted without a dissenting voice. And the Society adjourned, *sine die*.

WILLIAM LLOYD GARRISON, PRESIDENT.

SAMUEL MAY, Jr.,
SUSAN B. ANTHONY, } ASSISTANT SECRETARIES.

INDEX.

Cox, Marshal, excommunicated, 56.
Crangale, James, driven from Georgia, 184–186.
Cuba, 13.
Cushing, Caleb, on Slave-catching, 53.

Davis, Jefferson, on African Slave-trade, 19.
Delaware, Slave-trade in, 32.
Democrats aiding Under-ground Railroad, 49, 50.
DOMESTIC SLAVE-TRADE, 30–36.
Douglas on extent of African Slave-trade, 20.
Down's, Judge, marvelous sagacity, 169.
Doy, Dr., convicted, rescued, 7.

Elegant Epistle, 196.
Emancipation, British, good effects of, 306–309; Danish, 309–311.
Enquirer, Richmond, on choice of Speaker, 233.
Escapes of Slaves defeated, 55.
Examiner, London, on President's Message, 236.

Fee, John G., and his friends driven from Kentucky, 174–177.
Fisk, S. H., mobbed in Savannah, 169.
Florence, opinion of John Brown in, 162, 163.
Florida, disunion recommended in, 271, 272; free colored people of, proscribed, 212.
FOREIGN INTELLIGENCE, 303–315.
FOREIGN SLAVE-TRADE, 13–30.
FREE COLORED PEOPLE, 206–225; Testimonies favorable to, Boston Courier's, 224; Journal's, 224, 225; Journal's correspondent's, 217; New-Orleans Crescent's, 214; J. F. Emerson's, 224; New-York Tribune's, 223; Senator Wilson's, 223.
Free-State Party in Kentucky, 273.
French opinion of John Brown, 161, 162.
FUGITIVE SLAVES, 47–55.

Garrison, William Lloyd, tribute to in Congress, 251.
Georgia and free colored people, 212.
Giddings, J. R., at Cleveland, 72–74; before Mason's committee, 148.
Government warned of John Brown's design, 77, 78.

Harper's Ferry taken, 79; retaken, 86.
Hayti and John Brown, 163–166.
Hazlett convicted, 140; executed, funeral of, 142, 143.
Helper denounced, 226–228; with what effect, 233, 234.

Hickman, John, assaulted, 188.
Howe, Dr., before Mason's Committee, 148; protest of, 149.
Hugo, Victor, on John Brown, 160, 161.
HUNT FOR TREASON, 147–157.
Hyannis Slave Case, 51–53.
Hyatt, Thaddeus, United States Senate, 153–155.

Incidents of Domestic Slave-trade, 30, 31.
Indiana and Anthony Burns, 218.
Indian Territory, 11; parties in, 12.
Iowa, Slave Case in, 46.

Jerry and Joe, "conspirators," 138, 139.
JOHN BROWN, 75–134.
JOHN BROWN'S COMPANIONS, 134–147.
Judges shielding pirates, 28, 29.

Kagi, J. K., at Harper's Ferry, 80, 83.
KANSAS, 3–7; abolishes Slavery, 6; adopts Anti-Slavery Constitution, 3–5; asks admission to Union, 5; election in, 5; denies suffrage to colored men, 4; guards State Rights, 4; not admitted, 5; Slavery in, 7.
Kentucky on Canadian refugees, 273; free colored people, 216.
Kidnappers arrested in Lorain County, Ohio, 63.
KIDNAPPING, 36–43; with legal forms, 42, 43.

Langston, C. H., convicted, 63; speech of, 64; sentenced, 64.
Leeman, shot after surrender, 83, 84.
Lemmon Case, 262–265.
Letters of Brown's companions, 141–144.
Liberty or Death, 47, 48.
London Emancipation Committee, 303.
Louisiana, free colored people of, 214; bill touching colored convicts, 272; mob law in, 191.

McKinney, Solomon, driven from Texas, 190, 191.
McRae, J. J., on African Slave-trade, 17, 18.
Mann, Horace, statue of, proposed, 258, 259.
MANUMISSIONS, 43–47.
Maryland, Brown's men in, 77, 80, 87–89; Convention on free colored people, 207–211; Governor's Message, 270; Legislation, 211, 212; on Canadian refugees, 270.
Mason, Emanuel, and little Ben, 74, 75.
Massachusetts, Legislature of, 258–260.
Meigs County, Ohio, Slave Case in, 45, 46.